General Edit

MW01292852

Asbury Theological Seminary Series in World Christian Revitalization Studies

This volume is published in collaboration with the Center for the Study of World Christian Revitalization Movements, a research initiative of Asbury Theological Seminary. Building on the work of the previous Wesleyan/Holiness Studies Center at the Seminary, the Center provides a focus for research in the Wesleyan Holiness and other related Christian renewal movements, including Pietism and Pentecostal movements, which have had a world impact. The research seeks to develop analytical models of these movements, including their biblical and theological assessment. Using an interdisciplinary approach, the Center bridges relevant discourses in several areas in order to gain insights for effective Christian mission globally. It recognizes the need for conducting research that combines insights from the history of evangelical renewal and revival movements with anthropological and religious studies literature on revitalization movements. It also networks with similar or related research and study centers around the world, in addition to sponsoring its own research projects.

The titles which appear in this series fall under five main sub-series: Early Church Studies, Medieval and Reformation Studies, Pietist and Wesleyan Studies, and Pentecostal and Charismatic Studies.

We are pleased to present this volume as a new entry in the Series. It demonstrates congruence with the mission of the Center and serves to advance its research objectives.

J. Steven O'Malley
General Editor
The Asbury Theological Seminary Series in World Christian Revitalization Studies

Dear Stan,

I pray that God will give you fresh anointing and blessing as he guides you.

Matt Zeller

Sub-Series Foreword

Pentecostal and Charismatic Studies

Of all the renewal traditions that have engaged the theological landscape, the Pentecostal Movement has undoubtedly made the most significant impact since it emerged at the turn of the twentieth century. Starting as a revival in a small African-American congregation on Azusa Street in Los Angeles, California, the movement soon swept the world, establishing itself in more than forty countries in the first three years. One hundred years later Pentecostalism has grown to an estimated 500 million global adherents or approximately twenty-five percent of all of Christendom. In the same manner that Wesleyanism burst beyond the bounds of Methodism to embrace an interdenominational holiness movement following the American Civil War in the nineteenth century, Pentecostalism transcended denominational lines in the form of the Charismatic Movement during the second half of the twentieth century.

This sub-series is designed to explore the historical, theological and intercultural dimensions of the twin twentieth-century Restorationists traditions from a global perspective. In this work Matt Tallman writes the biography of a man who as much as anyone prepared the groundwork for the emergence of the Charismatic Movement. The story of Demos Shakarian, founder of the Full Gospel Business Men's Fellowship International (FGBMFI), has been told thousands of times and published in countless forms. However, this is the first comprehensive critical assessment of the man and his work. Tallman begins by examining the origins of Shakarian's brand of charismatic Christianity, which began with a group of Russian Molokans who interacted with his ancestors in Armenia. He then traces the Shakarian family's migration to the United States where they founded the First Armenian Pentecostal Church in Los Angeles in 1905 prior to the Azusa Street Revival. After describing Demos' early years, the author focuses on his encounter with Charles Price and his subsequent involvement in the Christian Business Men's Committee (CBMC) which provided the organizational framework when he later founded the FGBMFI. According to Tallman, 1948 proved to be a pivotal year for Shakarian. Organizing the Hollywood Bowl Full Gospel Youth Rally, he met several emerging healing evangelists including Oral Roberts who became his new mentor. The formation of the Pentecostal Fellowship of North America (PFNA), the outbreak of the New Order of the Latter Rain Revival and the establishment of the state of Israel all led to a circumstantial gestalt in his life. Convinced that God was about to do a new thing in preparation for Christ's Second Coming, Shakarian began to lay plans for the formation of the FGBMFI. And as the saying goes, the rest is history. More than any other single factor, the FGBMFI provided both a forum for and gave visibility to the emerging Charismatic Movement within the mainline denominations. Tallman tells the story with grace, objectivity and humor as he chronicles the events in the life of Demos Shakarian.

D. William Faupel
Sub-series Editor

Demos Shakarian

The Life, Legacy, and Vision of a
Full Gospel Business Man

Matthew William Tallman

The Asbury Theological Seminary Series in
World Christian Revitalization Movements in Pentecostal/Charismatic Studies,
No. 2

EMETH PRESS
www.emethpress.com

Demos Shakarian,
The Life, Legacy, and Vision of a Full Gospel Business Man

Copyright © 2010 Matthew William Tallman
Printed in the United States of America on acid-free paper

Library of Congress Cataloging-in-Publication Data

Tallman, Matthew William.
 Demos Shakarian : the life, legacy, and vision of a Full Gospel Business Man / by Matthew William Tallman.
     p. cm. -- (The Asbury Theological Seminary series in world Christian revitalization movements in Pentecostal/Charismatic studies ; no. 2)
 "This manuscript originated from a dissertation"--Pref.
 Includes bibliographical references and index.
 ISBN 978-1-60947-002-9 (alk. paper)
 1. Shakarian, Demos, 1913- 2. Full Gospel Business Men's Fellowship International--Biography. 3. Pentecostals--United States--Biography. I. Title.
 BX8762.Z8S4357 2010
 267'.24994092--dc22
 [B]   2010009283

Dedication

To my beautiful wife, Cheryl,
an encourager,
an inspiration,
a wonderful distraction, and
the most amazing person I have ever known

Contents

Foreword

It is a pleasure to introduce two of my dear friends that this book is all about. The first is Demos Shakarian, the founder of the Full Gospel Business Men's Fellowship International (FGBMFI). I first met Demos in 1955 while I was a student at Emmanuel College. He and his pilot spoke in Chapel. I still remember his startling message about the thousands of mainline church people who were receiving the baptism in the Holy Spirit. It was also amazing to see a Pentecostal who was a successful and wealthy businessman. I also remember his airplane pilot who spoke of flying 200 miles on an empty fuel tank. I was honored to meet Demos and shake his hand. Our paths were to cross many times over the following years.

A major turning point in my life was at a FGBMFI meeting in Charlotte, NC in 1970 where I was introduced to the Protestant Charismatic renewal. Here I saw a Lutheran pastor speak in tongues. It opened a new chapter in my life and led to a cover story of my life and ministry in the *FGBMFI Voice*. Many years later, I was invited by Jerry Jenson to write a short history of the FGMBFI which appeared under the title, *Under His Banner: a History of the Full Gospel Business Men's Fellowship International*. It was published by Gift Publications in Costa Mesa, California in 1992. In researching this book, I had the privilege of interviewing Demos and his wife Rose for a full sixteen hours. The transcripts of these interviews became the basis for the book. In this process, I got to know Demos and Rose on a very intimate basis. They were truly spiritual giants. My only regret was the final title of the book. I wanted to use the wonderful name Oral Roberts had suggested, *God's Ballroom Saints*, but since Rose overruled this choice, I went with *Under His Banner*, the title of the favorite song of the fellowship.

The second friend that made this book possible is Matt Tallman, one of the first graduates of the Ph.D. program in Renewal Studies at Regent University. He was in the very first class that I taught in this, the first Ph.D. program in the world on Pentecostal/Charismatic renewal. He was a very fine student indeed. But as time went on, I found him to be a brilliant researcher and writer. At my suggestion, he took on the task of writing a biography of Demos Shakarian.

Although I had published a short history of the FGBMFI, I knew that much more needed to be done on Shakarian, one of the major religious figures of the twentieth century and one of the major Pentecostal patriarchs. When I saw Tallman's meticulous outline and bibliography, I was deeply impressed. I found that he was an exhaustive researcher who made many trips to get at his primary sources. He left no stone unturned. Then I was impressed with his writing ability. This book is truly the definitive biography of Shakarian and will take its place as a major resource for future researchers and historians of religion in the twentieth century.

Vinson Synan
Dean Emeritus, Regent University School of Divinity, Virginia Beach, Virginia

Preface

This manuscript originated from a dissertation, but ultimately it began as a serious inquiry into the life of Demos Shakarian and his contribution to modern Christianity. In the 1970s, at the height of Demos Shakarian's influence, he wrote a popular inspirational autobiography which captured my attention along with millions of other readers curious about a business man who was arguably one of the most important catalysts for the Charismatic movement. The book was filled with miraculous stories and anecdotal information about Shakarian's ancestors, his life, and how he formed the Full Gospel Business Men's Fellowship International.

Given Shakarian's stature in the Charismatic movement, it is surprising that no one has previously attempted a comprehensive biography of his life and this book offers an attempt to correct that historical omission. In addition, this book is a scholarly manuscript which attempts to reach a broad audience of scholars, students, and others who might be curious or critical of Demos Shakarian and the Charismatic movement. As such a critical analysis and evaluation of Shakarian's life is offered in this book that may not satisfy those inside or outside the Charismatic movement. However, all who read this manuscript will gain a broader understanding of Demos Shakarian's life, and hopefully many will acquire a better perspective of the Charismatic movement in the context of modern Church history.

As one who considers himself a participant of Charismatic Christianity, I do not claim the illusion that I have eliminated all bias from this analysis of Shakarian's life. However, I do find it necessary to recognize the bias of my own tradition, as Hans Gadamer once suggested, in order to gain a vantage point or historical horizon from which a proper hermeneutical understanding of Demos Shakarian's life can begin to take place. While I have taken as much care as possible to avoid prejudice, presumption, historical anachronisms, or faulty analysis, any errors that may be found within this text are entirely my own.

I would like to thank a variety of people who assisted me in completing this book. Vinson Synan not only served as one of my dissertation readers, but he also gave me the initial encouragement to write about Demos Shakarian, he provided a significant number of primary resources during the research stage of this project, and he served as a wonderful resource from his first-hand knowledge of the Charismatic movement in general. My advisor, Stanley Burgess, was thorough and patient in guiding me through the process of defining and shaping exactly what it was I wanted and needed to say about the life of Demos Shakarian. David Harrell, as my third outside reader, also provided valuable insights and recommendations from his research on the healing evangelists that interacted with Shakarian and his recommendations regarding the influence of the Shepherding movement. I am also extremely grateful to my editor, Bill Faupel, for believing in this project. Other scholars who helped contribute ideas, direction, and support to this project included Cecil Robeck, David Bundy, Paul Andersen, David Moore, Robert Menzies, and especially Terry Minter and David Cole.

I also want to thank my dear friend David Gallagher for having patience, and for providing me a desk and a quiet place from which to write this study. Without the assistance of Natasha Zhurauliova, my research in Russian texts would have been sorely lacking. Thank you to my friend Barbara Derkacht for being a helpful and thorough editor. I want to thank the Shakarian family for allowing me to interview them, and especially for the Scalf-Shakarian family for being gracious hosts during my stay in Colorado. The members of the Downey Historical Society were wonderful in providing helpful background information about the city of Downey, the Shakarian family, and Reliance Dairies. Paul Sobolew provided irreplaceable resources regarding his Russian Molokan beliefs and ancestry. Stan Perumean was as gracious as his cousin Demos Shakarian in opening his church, inviting me to join his congregation for worship, and giving me a number of valuable primary source documents.

My family, and especially my lovely wife, Cheryl, deserve accolades for their patience in walking with me and living with me through this process. Thank you to the men of the Raleigh Hills FGBMFI chapter in Portland, Oregon who first introduced me to the Full Gospel Business Men's Fellowship International in 1977 and gave me my only opportunity to meet Demos Shakarian in 1979. Finally, thank you "to him who is able to do immeasurably more than all we ask or imagine."

Chapter One

Introduction

Demos Shakarian was born in Los Angeles, California on July 21, 1913 and died eighty years later in Downey, California on July 23, 1993.[1] In the Whispering Pines Lawn section of Rose Hills Memorial Park in Whittier, California lies a simple marker recording Shakarian's birth and death.[2] There is no grandiose monument, nothing at his grave site that mentions his contribution to global Christianity or modern church history, and no university or foundation named after him. Yet over a half billion Christians today have been directly or indirectly influenced by Demos Shakarian and the organization he founded. How could an unassuming Christian business man have such an impact upon Christianity in the twentieth century? Perhaps his impact upon modern Charismatic renewal was rooted in his Armenian background, reinforced by his relationship with Charles Price (1887–1947) and Oral Roberts (1918–2010), renewed through the pneumatic vision he experienced on December 27, 1952, and reflected in how he initiated and organized the Full Gospel Business Men's Fellowship International (FGBMFI – 1951–).

The only scholarly attempt to describe the impact of the FGBMFI by H. Vinson Synan (1934–) laments the lack of any serious research regarding the organization or its founder, Demos Shakarian.[3] The focus of this study will be to offer a biography of Demos Shakarian's life within the context of the organization he founded which influenced a significant portion of Christians globally. The FGBMFI helped inaugurate the Charismatic movement (1960–) which grew to encompass over five hundred million Christians worldwide.[4]

In examining Shakarian's life, the most significant questions exist within Shakarian's Armenian ancestry and his contemporary American context. First, how did the culture of Shakarian's Armenian background shape his ecclesiology and ecumenism? Second, how did those elusive and previously ignored Russian immigrants encountered by his grandfather, influence Shakarian's pneumatology? Third, how did the Armenian Pentecostal Church Shakarian was raised in shape his religious perspective? Fourth, how did the events of Shakarian's contemporary context in Southern California, and specifically the events surrounding his young adult life in the 1940s (especially 1948) shape his worldview? Fifth, how did the charismatic expressions of his pneumatological Christianity, especially prophecy, provide a spiritual impulse that guided much of Demos Shakarian's life? Sixth, how did his past and contemporary contexts form an ecclesiological, pneumatological, eschatological, ecumenical, and theological gestalt in the formation, development, and growth of the FGBMFI? Seventh, how did Shakarian, and his organization, reach across a broad segment of Christian ecclesiologies and impact a significant portion of Christianity globally? Eighth, what factors led to the denouement of Shakarian and his organization's influence in North America in the 1980s? Ninth, how has Demos Shakarian's most important legacy, the FGBMFI, continued to have a lasting influence upon Christians globally and the Charismatic movement worldwide?

The answers to these questions suggest a hermeneutical lens to assist one in understanding how Shakarian's vision helped shape Christianity globally. His Armenian background offers the context for his pneumatic emphasis, his inclusive ecclesiology, and his broad ecumenism. Perhaps the most interesting aspects of his background are his family's interaction with pneumatic Russian Molokans while in Armenia, his family's immigration to the United States and interaction with another pneumatic movement which emerged in Los Angeles in 1906 (the Azusa Street revival – 1906–1909), and his father's success as a dairyman in Southern California. Perhaps just as significant as Shakarian's Armenian ecclesiology and ecumenism was the Armenian Pentecostal Church in Los Angeles, California, the church in which Shakarian worshipped and was nurtured.

This study is organized as a critical chronological narrative describing a biographical sketch of Demos Shakarian's life. The chronology begins with Shakarian's grandfather in Karakala, Armenia, the Shakarian family's interaction with Russian pneumatics and Isaac Shakarian's immigration to the United States. The narrative continues with Isaac Shakarian's early experience in Los Angeles, his success as a dairyman, and Demos Shakarian's birth and childhood. The rest of the study analyzes Demos Shakarian's life, his relationship with the healing evangelists of the 1940s and 1950s, his family life, his business ventures, his leadership as the founder of the FGBMFI, his death, and his legacy. This narrative does not begin traditionally with his birth, but rather with the introduction of his ancestors into charismatic Christianity. This unusual starting point is important for an understanding of the context of Shakarian's life. In addition, this ancestral chronology was chosen as the introduction to the analysis of Shakarian's life because he thought it was important to begin the story of his own autobiography with this same ancestral story.

The organizational structure of this manuscript emphasizes the hermeneutical context in which Shakarian influenced modern Charismatic Christianity. Subsections such as "Armenian ecclesiology and its relationship to Demos Shakarian" in chapter two, or "The Armenian Pentecostal Church" in chapter three, consider the theological, pneumatic, and ecclesiological influences upon Shakarian's life. Other subsections, such as "Demos Shakarian as a young business man," in chapter five or "the consecration of Demos Shakarian," in chapter five evaluate Shakarian economically, theologically, and psychologically. Several subsections in chapter seven, including "the beginning of the Latter Rain movement," "the Christian eschatological impulses caused by Israeli statehood" and "the affluence of a rising middle class after WWII" allow the reader to see the further development of sociological, economic, pneumatic, theological and eschatological impulses in Shakarian's life. Subsections such as "the vision of Demos Shakarian" and "how the FGBMFI reflected Shakarian's vision" in chapter eight allow the reader to see the culmination of these influences in his life and legacy. Throughout this manuscript, chapter divisions are often purposefully made at significant turning points in Shakarian's life to assist the reader in understanding his life, his context, and his contribution to modern Christianity and the Charismatic movement.

The rise and decline of the Charismatic movement in the United States has mimicked the ascendancy and fall of the FGBMFI in North America over the same period. However, just as Charismatic Christianity has continued to dramatically increase globally, so has the organization that Demos Shakarian founded. There are over 6,000 chapters of the FGBMFI in more than 160 countries, and it still claims to be the largest Christian business men's organization in existence today.[5] Ironically, in its infancy, Demos Shakarian himself questioned the need for such an organization, but then in December of 1952, he had a vision that changed everything.[6] What was the hermeneutical lens through which he saw this divine vision? The lens was shaped and focused by his Armenian ancestry, his success and failure in business, his own pneumatic experience, his early attempts at evangelism, the influence of certain healing evangelists, the context in which he saw exponential success and receptivity for his fledgling organization, and the way he handled the public and personal challenges and successes in his life. However, to examine this hermeneutical lens further, the reader should begin where Shakarian began his own story. This is a story that began in the foothills of Mount Ararat in Karakala, Armenia.

NOTES

1. Demos Shakarian, John and Elizabeth Sherrill, *The Happiest People on Earth* (Chappaqua, NY: Steward Press, 1975), 12; "Demos Shakarian Memorial Issue," *Voice*, October 1993, 18; and information gathered from Demos Shakarian's Social Security death records at http://ssdi.rootsweb.ancestry.com (accessed September 10, 2008).

2. Rose Hills Memorial Park and Mortuary, Whittier, CA.

3. Vinson Synan, *Under His Banner* (Costa Mesa, CA: Gift Publications, 1992), 12.

4. David Barrett, George Kurian, and Todd Johnson, *World Christian Encyclopedia* (2nd ed.; New York: Oxford University Press, 2001), 1:19–21. Barrett describes this movement and its various branches of Pentecostal, Charismatic, and neo-Charismatic renewal in his comprehensive analysis of global Christianity. In 2001, when he published his atlas, he estimated that this movement represented over 523 million Christians worldwide.

However, at its current rate of growth, he estimates that by 2025, the Pentecostal/ Charismatic movement will have at least 811 million members.

5. Richard Shakarian, "An Introduction to the Full Gospel Business Men's Fellowship International," FGBMFI, http://www.fgbmfi.org, (accessed November 4, 2007).

6. Demos Shakarian, *The Happiest People* (1975), 133–134.

Chapter Two

The Foundation of Shakarian's Story

The context of Demos Shakarian's life springs from a variety of sources including Russian pneumatology, Armenian ecclesiology, and a small community in Anatolia called Karakala. Most importantly, because Shakarian begins his own autobiography with the origins of his ancestors, these origins prove an excellent starting point for understanding Demos Shakarian's life.

The Shakarians in Armenia

The origins and location of Karakala, Armenia are somewhat disputed. Whatever remained of Karakala in the nineteenth century was swept away and destroyed by the Ottoman Turks in the twentieth century during the Armenian genocide. What seems certain is that the word "karakala" means rocky area or place, and the Armenian ancestors of Demos Shakarian and other families chose to live in the Russian section of Armenia for protection from the Ottoman Turks.[1] Shakarian described Karakala as a little village "sitting solidly in the rocky foothills of Mount Ararat."[2] While this confirms the meaning of the town's name, the foothills of Mount Ararat comprise a rather large geographical area which overlaps the borders of modern Armenia and Turkey. Joyce Bivin (1934–) gives three possible locations for the Armenians of Karakala, all three being somewhere in the north central area of Anatolia in the Kars region.[3] While all three locations may have been under Russian control at some point, they were in dispute; with the decline of the Russian Romanov dynasty, the pull of the Ottoman Empire during WWI, and the peace settlement and reorganization of a modern Turkish government, all three locations are currently within the borders of Turkey. No living descendents of these Armenians remain in this region and only anecdotal evidence and a few maps with noted discrepancies offer any clues to the actual location of this small Armenian village.[4]

By Demos Shakarian's comments, and the description of his relatives, Karakala was a small farming community with a predominantly simple peasant class of Armenians and Russian immigrants.[5] Demos Shakarian described his grandfather Demos (d.b.a.1855–1906), for whom he was named, as a Presbyterian with five daughters.[6] Shakarian mentioned that "although most Armenians were Orthodox, Grandfather and many others in Karakala were Presbyterians."[7] The Shakarian family was originally Armenian Orthodox, but they converted to Presbyterianism in 1875.[8] The presence of a Presbyterian community in Orthodox Armenia could perhaps be explained by the active work in nearby Persia of the Presbyterian Church which had successfully recruited a large number of indigenous missionaries in the latter part of the nineteenth century. These missionaries went throughout Persia, Transcaucasia and Russia spreading their version of Reformed Christianity.[9] This notwithstanding, it is believed that most of the ancestral community of Karakala remained Orthodox, with an additional smattering of Protestant millenarians, Seventh Day Adventists, and even Paulicians.[10]

In his autobiography, Shakarian makes two other curious comments calling Armenians "Old Testament people, the past and the present so woven together in our minds that what went on a hundred or a thousand or two thousand years ago is as real to us as the date on the calendar."[11] The comment referring to Armenians as "Old Testament people" might be more influenced by the specific traditions of the Armenian Pentecostal Church in which he grew up, and not necessarily indicative of the larger Armenian Apostolic Church. While this point will be examined later in this study, the comment about his concept of time might also reflect a broader Asian cyclical view of time in contrast to the Western linear view of time.

Demos Shakarian's grandfather may have viewed time from a non-linear Asian perspective, but he also hoped that his wife would bear a son in a timely manner. If the Shakarians were not quite yet "Old Testament people" they were certainly from the old country where it was common in many, if not most cultures, to revere male children, and particularly the first born son. In any case, it was viewed as a disgrace or perhaps even a curse by Shakarian's ancestral neighbors that Grandfather Shakarian and his wife had not produced a male heir.[12]

Yet, on May 25, 1892, Shakarian's father Isaac (1892–1964) was born into a simple agrarian family as the first son of Demos Shakarian.[13] The occasion of his birth caused quite a stir in this remote village of Transcaucasia and was seen as the fulfillment of an earlier prophecy given by Magardich Mushegan (d.b.a.1860–d.d.a. 1940), the brother-in-law of Grandfather Shakarian.[14] Prophecy was not completely foreign to this community; utterances had been delivered as early as 1855 warning of impending doom coming upon the entire region.[15] Unfortunately, Armenia had quite a lengthy history of impending doom teetering as it did between the Persian Empire, the Roman territories, the Byzantine armies, the conquests of Islam, and, more recently, Tsarist Russia and the Ottoman Empire, while still trying to maintain its identity as the first Christian nation.[16]

Armenian Ecclesiology and its Relationship to Demos Shakarian

Three things are significant about the ancient and tragic origins of Armenian Christianity for use in assessing Armenian ecclesiology and its influence upon the Shakarians. First, there is the ancient connection between Armenian Christianity and apostolic Christianity. Most significantly, Armenians make a historical claim to being the first Christian nation, encouraging all Armenians to observe the historical continuity of Christianity. Unlike Protestant reformers who desired to restore the New Testament church and more recent Pentecostals who asserted they were reviving an ancient form of Christianity, most Armenians saw God at work throughout the history of their nation. Some of the villagers of Karakala had been converted to Presbyterian Christianity, but they were Armenians who saw their faith first ignited by the flame of Gregory the Illuminator (ca. 257–ca. 331C.E.) late in the third century.[17] It was supplemented by a long line of pneumatological enthusiasts and ecumenical innovators rather than restorationist reformers such as John Calvin (1509–1564) and John Knox (ca. 1510–1572).[18] Armenians, be they Orthodox, Presbyterian, Paulician, Pentecostal, or a Full Gospel Business Man, when questioned about their religious tradition, quickly mention their Christian heritage as the first Christian nation.

Why is this hermeneutical point important for understanding Armenian ecclesiology and specifically Shakarian ecclesiology? All Armenians can trace their Christian origins to antiquity, and unlike many of his Pentecostal peers, Demos Shakarian did not see sudden divine restoration in modern Pentecostalism but rather pneumatological and spiritual continuity that was traced throughout the history of Christianity.[19] In other words, it was possible to see God at work from antiquity in areas of the world and areas of the Church previously dismissed or overlooked by modern Pentecostals, Protestants, and Roman Catholics. In the case of Demos Shakarian, there was no question that God was at work in Armenia and Russia among members of both the Protestant Presbyterians and the Russian and Armenian Orthodox Christians. This sense of historical continuity helped shape and broaden Shakarian's ecclesiology.

The second aspect of Shakarian's ecclesiology shaped by his Armenian background was forged in the fires of Armenia's tragic history. The seventeen years of post-Soviet history (1991–2008) have been one of the few times in the past two thousand years that Armenia has maintained its status as a sovereign and predominantly Christian nation. While it may be able to claim or at least share the prestige of becoming the first Christian nation, it never shared or held the recognition or reign of Christendom instigated in a post-Constantinian Christianity that affected both Eastern and Western Christianity for over a millennium.[20] Armenian Christianity was not noted for its dominance, but rather its diplomacy. Armenian Orthodoxy survived simultaneous threats from the Persian Empire and the Roman Empire, Islamic, Byzantine, and Roman aggression, and sweltered under the oppression of Tsarist Russia. The suppression and the annihilation of

Armenian Christianity was almost complete under the reign of the Ottoman Empire, culminating in 1915 with one of the worst genocides in human history.

Shakarian's ecclesiology may have been shaped or at least informed by at least one or two other curious aspects of Armenian and Eastern ecclesiology. A unique aspect of Eastern ecclesiology lies in its emphasis upon the prophet hood of all believers. The Eastern Church believes that "through chrismation every member of the church becomes a prophet, and receives a share in the royal priesthood of Christ."[21] This empowerment and involvement of laity is carried even further by Armenian ecclesiastical structure. The Armenian Apostolic Church believes that nothing should be done "in ecclesiastical administration without the co-operation of the lay element."[22] As such, the local married priest for each parish is chosen or elected by the laity of each congregation. In addition, unlike the Roman Catholic See, who is elected exclusively by a ballot of cardinals, the Armenian Church elects their catholicos through the National Ecclesiastical Assembly which consists of both lay and clergy representatives.[23]

Nevertheless, the more pertinent question for the purposes of this research is how Armenian history may have shaped Shakarian's ecclesiology and ecumenism. While Shakarian never espoused any form of Christendom, this could have been affected by both his Armenian background and his immediate context in the United States. North American religious experience attracted a variety of groups from throughout the world and recreated some of the most variegated and schismatic segments of Christianity in church history. In contrast, Armenia's religious history is marked by a national identity and a long history of ecumenism.

Armenian Ecumenism and its Relationship to Demos Shakarian

Another characteristic of Armenian Orthodoxy, significant for its effect on Demos Shakarian and consequently on the growth and expansion of the Charismatic movement, is its ecumenical spirit.[24] The Armenian Church has "in all good faith always welcomed every proposition which has been made in the direction of unity."[25] Ormanian describes this ecumenism on the basis of a "spiritual communion between the Churches, of mutual respect for their several positions, of liberty for each within the limits of her own sphere, and of the spirit of Christian charity overruling all."[26] The Roman Catholic Church and the Greek Orthodox Church have historically not accepted Christian salvation or Christian ecclesiology outside of their own structures (of course Vatican II [1962–1965] and other recent ecumenical reforms have changed much of this). In contrast to both of these ecclesiological structures, the Armenian Orthodox Church has historically held to an attitude of *unitas in necessariis* in which only the decisions of the first three Ecumenical Councils of the Church should be held as universally accepted. As such, beyond the primary doctrines of the Trinity, the Incarnation, and the Redemption, each church should be able to follow its own dictates and still be considered part of Christendom.[27]

The Armenian Church holds only to the first three Ecumenical Councils by suggesting that the decisions made in these first three councils communicate the essence of the Christian faith and that going beyond this limit involves "unnecessary speculation and attempts to reduce the fundamental mysteries to a level of human comprehension."[28] Typically, the Eastern churches are cautious about delving too far into the mysteries of the faith and avoid a rationalistic Western theological approach. The Oriental Orthodox Churches are uniform in their acceptance of only the first three Ecumenical Councils, and interestingly, they are also uniformly engaged in ecumenism with all five of these autonomous churches being actively involved in the World Council of Churches.[29]

It is evident that Malachia Ormanian (1841–1918), as the Armenian Patriarchate of Constantinople, was several decades ahead of his time in suggesting the desire for ecumenical communion with other branches of Christianity. However, there is also strong evidence for ecumenism much earlier in Armenian Church history. Nerses Snor'hali (the Gracious – ca. 1100–1173) was actively involved in successful ecumenical dialogue with the Roman Catholic Church and also became engaged in ecumenical conversation with the Byzantine Church a century after the Schism of 1054. Although his tone was conciliatory, and he offered no polemic against Chalcedon, the Byzantine demands were too stringent for most of the Armenian bishops; thus his negotiations failed.[30] However, dialogue with both Rome and Constantinople continued under Armenian Archbishop Nerses of Lampron (1153–1198). His response to the monks of Tzoroked, who had been protesting his desire for communion with other Christians, aptly demonstrates his ecumenical nature.

> The grace of God has given me an understanding which surpasses indifferent traditions so my only concern is for fraternal charity. To my eyes, the Armenian is the same as the Latin, the Latin is like the Greek, the Greek resembles the Egyptian, and the Egyptian is no different from the Syrian...By the grace of Christ, I would destroy all barriers of separation. My affection extends to the churches of Latins, Greeks, and Syrians for in Armenia, I remain serene in the midst of them all and without ever concerning myself with their particular customs.[31]

As medieval ecumenists, Nerses Snor'hali and Nerses of Lampron were at least seven hundred years ahead of their time. While modern Armenian ecumenists such as Shahan Sarkassian (d.b.a. 1950–) and Aram I, Catholicos of Cilicia (1947–), acknowledge the contributions of their medieval predecessors,[32] they also recognize the political and geographical factors that have often forced the Armenian Church into ecumenical dialogue as an inescapable reality for its very survival.[33]

While Demos Shakarian's ancestral family was far removed from the confines of the Armenian patriarchate, they were both influenced by a historical reality that was teetering on the edge of contemporary existence and extinction. Their ancestors before them had already proven that diplomacy was their best course for survival up to that time; however, the ominous specter of genocide loomed ahead of them, conflict between Russia and the Ottoman Empire lay before them, and the prophecy of a small Russian pneumatic boy, lingered in the minds of Shakarian's ancestors all suggesting that a diasporic departure rather than diplomacy might be the best course to follow for their future survival. Nevertheless, the Shakarian family and many Armenians in the community of Karakala dismissed the rantings of these Russian charismatics who occasionally visited their community until one fateful day around the turn of the century.

Russian Origins of an Armenian Pneumatic Revival

The idea that the pneumatic revival which emerged in Karakala, Armenia originated from Russia is well documented in Demos Shakarian's autobiography.[34] However, Shakarian most likely relied on oral tradition and perhaps some secondary written sources to tell of his grandfather's conversion to a pneumatic form of Christianity in 1900 at his ancestral home of Karakala. Consequently, it is important to verify that Shakarian's grandfather did in fact encounter a Russian charismatic group at that time with other documented sources. In addition, the Shakarian story of widespread charismatic revival taking place in Russia for at least fifty years prior to the Azusa Street revival in Los Angeles should be corroborated with additional evidence.[35] Unfortunately, Shakarian does not identify who these Russian Pentecostals were and exactly where they came from. However, there are enough reliable clues in his autobiography to reasonably determine who they were and to which religious sect they belonged.

In his autobiography, Shakarian continued with the story of Russians who would regularly come and visit the Armenian community of Karakala and share their reports of an outpouring of the Holy Spirit upon hundreds of thousands in Russia.

> Grandfather did not accept right away the strange message that had been trickling over the mountains for nearly fifty years. The message was brought by the Russians. Grandfather liked the Russians all right; he was just too levelheaded to accept their tales of miracles. The Russians came in long caravans of covered wagons. They were dressed as our people were, in long, high-collared tunics tied at the waist with tasseled cords, the married men in full beards. The Armenians had no difficulty understanding them as most of our people spoke Russian too. They listened to the tales of what the Russians called "the outpouring of the Holy Spirit" upon hundreds of thousands of Russian Orthodox Christians. The Russians came as people bringing gifts: The Gifts of the Spirit, which they wanted to share."[36]

As a result of these visiting Russians, many families in Karakala began to accept their charismatic version of Christianity.[37] In a contemporary version of this story that Shakarian offered in *Voice* magazine in 1975, he estimated that over one million Russians were affected by this revival, and many of them were severely persecuted and fled to Armenia and Finland.[38] As this form of charismatic Christianity began to spread throughout the Kars region of Anatolia, one individual in Karakala, Shakarian's grandfather, was still resistant to their strange, new style of Christianity. However, as visiting Russian charismatic peasants came to Karakala, Grandfather Shakarian was given the responsibility of preparing a feast, but he decided to slaughter a cow that was considered physically blemished in their culture.[39]

The concern over a blemished cow in this story seemed rather odd, and Shakarian's concern for an unblemished sacrifice did not correspond with either Armenian Orthodox or Presbyterian doctrine. However, this was a doctrine reflected by many Russian sectarian groups that had already been living in Transcaucasia for decades. Many of these same groups infused Old Testament and New Testament traditions into their praxis, including dietary restrictions and the celebration of Jewish feasts.[40] It is not entirely clear at this point whether Shakarian's grandfather felt obligated to honor the Russian dietary restrictions out of respect or because he had already adopted some of their customs. Nevertheless, the story continued by recalling how Shakarian responded to the charismatic worship of these Russians.

> Soon the big steer was roasting on a spit over a huge bed of charcoal. That evening everyone gathered, expectant and hungry, around the long plank tables. Before the meal could begin, however, the food must be blessed. These old Russian Christians would not say any prayer – even grace over meals – until they had received what they called *the anointing*. They would wait before the Lord until, in their phrase, the Spirit fell upon them. They claimed, (a little to Grandfather's amusement), that they could literally *feel* His Presence descend. When this occurred they would raise their arms and dance with joy.[41]

In one account, Demos Shakarian described this ritual in further detail. After their period of pneumatic dancing, the Russians would hold a Bible above the head of the family, lay hands on each family member and pray for them. Then the Bible was opened and bread was placed upon the book. In this manner, the Russians blessed the food.[42] However, at this point in the story, the blessing was interrupted as an elderly prophet among the Russian charismatic visitors miraculously revealed that the beef they were eating came from a blemished cow. In addition, the elder Russian identified where Grandfather Shakarian had hidden the head of the blemished cow. The Shakarian patriarch responded by requesting if he could receive the same Spirit baptism that these Russian charismatics had already experienced.

One additional remark should be added to the story. On at least one other occasion when Shakarian told this story, he referred to both his grandfather and his great-grandfather.[43] In one account, the great-grandfather supposedly suggested that the Shakarians offer the blemished cow to the Russians and that he was the one who readily repented as the Russian patriarch pulled the head of the blemished cow out of the barn.[44] Nevertheless, in his autobiography, Demos Shakarian identified his grandfather and his grandmother as the ones who responded to the charismatic form of Christianity these Russians were offering. "Grandfather knelt and the Old Russian laid his work-gnarled hands on his head. Immediately Grandfather burst into joyous prayer in a language neither he nor anyone present could understand. The Russians called this kind of ecstatic utterance 'tongues' and regarded it as a sign that the Holy Spirit was present with the speaker. That night Grandmother, too, received this 'Baptism in the Spirit'."[45]

Looking beyond Shakarian's autobiography, one contextual fact suggesting how and why these Russian charismatics regularly visited Karakala was the predominantly agrarian economy and climate of Russia and Transcaucasia during this period. "The peasants were accustomed to hire themselves out as seasonal and harvest laborers. Because of the size of Russia, with its varying climate, the harvest does not all ripen at the same time. Since harvesting machines were not yet available, every possible work force was in demand at harvest time. This movement of workers also promoted the exchange of ideas, and opened avenues for spiritual influence too."[46] As a result ideas could quickly be exchanged over a broad expanse of the country, and those who did experience spiritual renewal could rapidly disseminate their testimony to a large audience. This may also explain the reason why the Russian immigrants occasionally visited Karakala, Armenia. Perhaps it was harvest time, so the Armenian community welcomed their assistance, and the Russian visitors saw this as an opportunity to share what they had experienced in the hopes that these Armenians could experience it also.

However, Transcaucasia was a great distance from the heart of Russia. Perhaps the reason these Russian pneumatics were in Armenia can best be explained within a political context. All of the religious sectarian groups in Russia flourished and benefited from the more liberal policies of Alexander I (1777–1825) from 1801 until 1825. In addition, the Orthodox Church itself was experiencing renewal under the influence of Seraphim of Sarov and others within the church. Unfortunately, under Nicholas I (1796–1855), the freedoms they enjoyed rapidly deteriorated and on October 20, 1830, Tsar Nicholas decreed that all religious sectarians including Dukhobors, Molokans, and Subbotniks were to be relocated to Transcaucasia.[47] "Over the next 50 years, tens of thousands of dissenters left central Russia for the southern frontier."[48] Dukhobors were relocated to Transcaucasia in entire communities while Molokans and Subbotniks were relocated individually or in small groups.[49]

Nevertheless, Molokans, Subbotniks, and Dukhobors alike, being exiled to the far extremes of the Russian Empire had found a certain measured freedom. Certainly life was harsh, there were numerous economic and social adjustments, and many of them died en route to their new homes or in the first few harsh winters in their locations. However, the result of their exile actually brought "a spiritual ferment and vibrant religious life that breathed new strength into religious movements that had been increasingly constricted in the central Russian provinces."[50] As a result, these groups were able to flourish away from the watchful eye of the tsar, sharing their faith, their miracles, their testimonies, and their charismatic experiences with their new neighbors. Apparently, one of these groups caught the attention of the Armenian community of Karakala, but who were they? Perhaps this can best be explained by first offering a brief overview of charismatic renewal in Russia, and the groups that were involved in it, particularly the groups that emerged and flourished during the nineteenth century.

Origins of Charismatic Renewal in Russia

Charismatic renewal is not a novel idea that emerged from the pages of twentieth century Christianity. It has appeared throughout the pages of church history, even if Christendom and the hierarchal structures of church ecclesiology and the strictures of church theology have often overlooked it, attempted to silence it, or simply ignored it. Vibrant charismatic Christianity did not disappear permanently after the apostolic age as some cessationists propose, or suddenly reappear as some early Pentecostals have suggested. Beginning with Montanism (ca. 155–700 C.E.), a long list of charismatic groups and individuals have dotted the pages of ancient and medieval church history including Tertullian (ca.150–ca. 220 C.E.), Perpetua and Felicitas (ca. 180–ca. 202 C.E.), Cyprian (ca.200–258 C.E.), Origen (ca.185–ca. 254 C.E.), Athanasius (ca. 296–373 C.E.), Hilary of Poiters (ca. 300–368 C.E.), Ephrem of Syria (ca. 306–373 C.E.), the Cappadocians (ca. 329–ca. 394 C.E.), Didymus the Blind (ca. 309–ca. 398 C.E.), Pseudo-Macarius (ca..385–ca. 560 C.E)., Abdisho Hazzaya (ca. 615–ca. 690), Isaac of Nineveh (ca. 620–ca. 700), the Paulicians (ca. 650–ca. 872 C.E.), Symeon the New Theologian (949–1022), Nerses Snor'hali (ca. 1100–1173), Hildegard of Bingen (1098–1179), Joachim of Fiore (ca. 1130–1202), Thomas Aquinas (ca. 1225–1274), the Cathari (ca. 1000–ca. 1325), Birgitta of Sweden (ca. 1302–1373), and Catherine of Siena (ca. 1347–1380). In the modern era, while Jansenists (1640–1801), Quakers (ca. 1650–), German Pietists (1675–ca. 1750), the prophets of Cevannes (ca. 1685–ca. 1715), Wesleyan enthusiasts and revivalists (ca. 1740–ca. 1790), Edward Irving (1792–1834), and the Awakened of Finland (1796–ca.–1900) were spreading charismatic forms of Christianity in western Europe, streams of pneumatic fervor emphasizing inner renewal and the baptism in the Holy Spirit (sometimes with frequent widespread occurrences of glossolalia) were taking place in Russia at the beginning of the nineteenth century.[51]

Certainly some of this Russian renewal may have been influenced by the spread of German Pietism and Wesleyan revival in western Europe, but most of what occurred was indigenous to Russia. This is perhaps why Demos Shakarian's grandfather was surprised to find people in 1906 Los Angeles "who worshipped as they did."[52] They had already experienced something similar to what the congregation at Azusa Street was experiencing, and the Shakarian family identified with it. In addition, because of the emphasis on the baptism in the Holy Spirit and glossolalia, this Russian renewal could be considered a form of proto-Pentecostalism that mirrored the Pentecostal revival at the beginning of the twentieth century. However, this Russian charismatic renewal began a century earlier and its origins date back to the eighteenth or possibly even the seventeenth century. In addition, it emerged from a smorgasbord of Russian indigenous charismatic groups that rivaled, if not exceeded, the variety of charismatic groups that emerged in western Europe during the modern period.

Of course, the charismatic renewals of African indigenous churches in the nineteenth century and also the rise of indigenous charismatic renewal in southern India at the same time are excellent examples of nineteenth century proto-Pentecostal revivals. However, the Russian autochthonous charismatic renewal likely predates these other indigenous examples by several decades if not more. In addition, while tsarist and communist Russia almost led to its extinction as an autochthonous movement, the exile of these nineteenth century Russian pneumatics to Transcaucasian areas such as Georgia, Azerbaijan, and in particular Armenia facilitated bringing about worldwide Charismatic renewal in the latter part of the twentieth century.

However, in order to find out exactly what occurred in Karakala and who these Russians were, it would be prudent to begin with a brief review of the history of Christianity in Russia, the origins of renewal in Russia, and also the forces and institutions that resisted this renewal. Officially, Russia became a Christian nation in 988 when Prince Vladimir of Kiev (ca. 950–1015) married a Byzantine princess and forcibly baptized the whole population of medieval Russia in the Dniepr as he introduced them to Byzantine Christianity.[53] Even though everyone was baptized, few had any understanding of this new religion. The further evangelization and development of Christianity in Russia was a slow process, sometimes hampered by raiding Mongols "exercising an alien spiritual influence upon the people."[54] These same raiding Mongol parties destroyed Kiev in 1240, and so the Russian tribes migrated northwards making Moscow the cultural and political center of Russia.

As Russian Christianity began to grow and mature, several factors led to the development of charismatic renewal and the sectarian movements that developed from that renewal. First of all, pneumatology had always been prominent in the Eastern Church and Orthodoxy had consistently emphasized the role of the Holy Spirit in the Trinitarian relationship of God. This is unlike the Western Church with its insertion of the *filioque* (589 C.E.) that often resulted in a theology that left the Holy Spirit in a subordinate role.[55] The Eastern Church had an abundance of pneumatologists and charismatic leaders, including pseudo-Macarius who sought deeper experiences with the Holy Spirit in his *Fifty Spiritual Homilies* in the late fourth century; Symeon the New Theologian who emphasized the need for a baptism of the Holy Spirit beyond conversion in his *Discourses* and his *Ethical Treatises* in the eleventh century; Gregory Palamas (1296–1359) who defended a charismatic group of Hesychast worshippers in his *Triads* in the fourteenth century; or Seraphim of Sarov, whose healing ministry touched a significant portion of the Russian Empire. In addition, Messalian (360–ca. 800) and later Paulician charismatic dualists, dating back to the fourth century, may have brought greater receptivity to these pneumatic Molokans as they spread their message throughout southern Russia and Armenia. Consequently, charismatic groups and movements found a fertile audience in the fields of Russia and Transcaucasia.

Other developments took place in the Russian Orthodox Church that were important for understanding the origins of this nineteenth century Russian renewal. A controversy initiated by two prominent Russian monks arose over how to deal with heretics. Joseph of Volokolamsk (ca. 1439–1515) started a monastery early in the sixteenth century near Moscow, supported the state church, and believed in dealing harshly with heretics (even executing them). However, Nil Sorsky (ca. 1433–1508), a contemporary of Joseph, and the abbot of a monastery in southern Russia along the Volga River, believed in the separation of church and state, promoted freedom of thought, and was against the collection of power and money within the church. In addition, these monks lived simple lives based "upon the New Testament, against which all other writings were measured."[56] While Joseph's camp prevailed, the inner piety, humility, and poverty of Nil Sorsky and his followers captured the attention of future generations of monks, priests, and lay people who developed a great deal of respect for the *startsy* or elders.[57]

Another important development occurred when a new patriarch of Russia, Nikon (1605–1681), began to institute some modest reforms, including a greater emphasis on sermons, more independence between the church and the tsar, and using original Greek texts to correct some of the copying errors of the past.[58] As a result of his reforms, a schism resulted in the Orthodox Church over small details such as whether somebody should cross himself with two or three fingers, which direction the procession should go around the altar, or "how many hallelujahs should be sung at a certain point in the liturgy."[59] Thus began a long history of persecution against those whom the Russian Orthodox Church viewed as schismatics. This long litany of persecution will perhaps help explain the sectarian nature of the Russian pneumatic group who influenced Shakarian's ancestors, and why they remained sectarian and insular long after they immigrated to the United States. These Old Believers (ca. 1666–) as they were called represented a sizeable portion of the Russian population. According to pre-revolutionary statistics, ten percent of the Russian Empire, or sixteen million people, were Old Believers although it is likely this number is very low.[60] Because of their separation from the Russian Orthodox Church, the Old Believers soon encountered serious problems relating to clergy. "As a result, they were, in reality, forced to live like Protestants."[61] In many ways, the Old Believers were the counterparts of Luther (1483–1546) and Calvin, though they took on a Russian form of reformation.[62]

Another development that took place was the sizeable German population in Russia that began to bring a form of German Pietism into many areas of the Empire. After the reign of Ivan the Terrible (1530–1584), the Germans established a small colony in Moscow.[63] German peasants continued to immigrate into Russia until World War I (WWI). It is estimated that by 1914, two million German farmers lived in Russia.[64] Under Peter the Great (1672–1725), Russia became heavily influenced by German Pietism. Peter read much of August

Francke's (1663–1727) writings and even sent a special envoy to Halle every two years. Peter's wife, Empress Catherine (1684–1727), visited the pietist schools in Halle incognito. In fact, the first Russian secondary school was a pietist foundation.[65] Catherine the Great (1729–1796) brought many of these German farmers to the Volga River as a sort of buffer between the Germans and invading Tatar peoples.[66] While this last piece of minutia may not seem significant, German Pietism may have been one of the preliminary factors leading to the development of Pentecostal renewal in western Europe and North America. Pietism also had a significant influence upon some of the indigenous renewal movements in the region of the Volga River, particularly the Molokans (ca. 1550–).[67]

Although there are other factors that could be mentioned including the development of a tsarist secular state or the relationship between the church and the state in Russia, the most significant remaining development relevant to the subject of Russian charismatic renewal was the emergence of the *startsi*, or elders, which developed into a school of spirituality. This development, among others, may help explain why Demos Shakarian recalled that there was an "outpouring of the Holy Spirit upon hundreds of thousands of Russian Orthodox Christians."[68] The Russian *starcestvo* continued the monastic tradition, but the *starets*, or elder, possessed the gift of discernment of spirits and became a spiritual father to others.[69] In the *starcestvo* tradition, there arose the conviction that a *starets* "knew both the mysteries of God…and the mysteries of human hearts."[70]

The *startsi* were present in Russia long before the nineteenth century, but Paisij Velickovski (1722–1794) inaugurated this as a school of spirituality. Other well known *startsi* were Seraphim of Sarov (1759–1833), Leonid Nagolkin (1769–1841), Makarij Ivanov (1788–1860), and Amvrosij Grenkov (1812–1891).[71] With the translation of the Philokalia into Slavic by Velickovski, there came a renewed interest in the Fathers of the Eastern Church, and within the *starcestvo* movement in particular, the readings of the Hesychastic movement became popular.[72] The Hesychast movement, whose name comes from the word peace or silence, involves the strict practice of silence and hiddenness in order to meet, discover, and know God. The prayer of Jesus, "Lord Jesus Christ, Son of God, have mercy on me a sinner" is often repeated as a form of meditation and prayer in this tradition.[73] However, the *startsi* were not only interested in reading about and discussing patristic texts; they believed in "the continuation of the 'Fathers.'" The *startsi* also widely read the mystical writings of Symeon the New Theologian and believed in the power and operation of the Holy Spirit in their lives and in the world.[74]

In many ways, the *startsi* were a reaction to a growing rationalism that had crept into Russia as a result of European enlightenment. Competing against the *startsi* was a more traditional movement in Orthodoxy that believed "because of the weakness of his faith the man of the 'present time' was no longer capable of receiving the direct revelation of the Holy Spirit."[75] However, this traditional movement diminished "the eternal, living power of the Spirit working in the Church."[76] Besides, the state's attempts at secularizing the church or attempting to control the mystical elements of the church merely increased the spiritual thirst of the people. Both Peter the Great's and Catherine the II's secularizing policies, including closing 754 of the existing 954 monasteries in Russia, merely created a political backlash and led to an increasing spiritual hunger by the end of the eighteenth century.[77]

A tradition likely related to the *startsi*, and probably as old as the *staretz* in Russia, is the tradition of the *yurod* or holy fool.[78] In Russian Orthodoxy, the strange, the bizarre, the unusual, and the inexplicable are often considered spiritual, respected, and revered. Towards the latter part of the eighteenth century, as the thirst for spiritual satisfaction began to reach unbearable proportions in Russia, a holy fool approached a young man named Prokhor Moshnin (1759–1833) and prophesied that he would become a mighty intercessor and servant of the Lord, and, consequently, this young man grew up to be one of the most famous *staretz* of Russia. This *staretz* entered Russian soil at a time when the region was ripe for Charismatic renewal, a renewal that would quickly spread far beyond the confines of Moscow or Kiev, even as far as Armenia.

Seraphim was born on July 19, 1759, in Kursk with the given name of Prokhor Moshnin and died on January 2, 1833, at the Sarov Monastery.[79] He practiced a strict form of the Hesychast tradition and spent most of his monastic life in solitude and silence. Seraphim's hagiography claims he once cried out to God on a granite rock for one thousand days and nights.[80] It was only in the last seven years of his life that the elder, the *starets*, emerged and took on a much more charismatic and evangelistic expression.

Seraphim was credited with many miracles and supernatural knowledge during this period of his life. It was acknowledged that Seraphim often understood the hearts of men through words of knowledge and discerning of spirits such as in the case of a general who came to visit him and upon leaving the *staretz's* cell, wept, stripped himself of his medals, and was heard to say, "I have crossed Europe during our campaigns and nowhere have I come across so holy a man."[81] The first miracle Seraphim performed was upon Michael Manturov (ca. 1800–ca. 1860) who had a crippling disease in his legs and had to be carried in to see the monk. Seraphim anointed the man's legs with oil, and Manturov rose up and walked.[82] In September of 1831, Nicholas Motovilov was healed of severe rheumatic pain that had left his legs paralyzed and his knees twisted and swollen. Seraphim asked him if he believed that God could heal him, and upon Motovilov's positive response, Seraphim told him to walk and even gave him a little push, but Motovilov walked on his own power.[83] Word quickly spread about Seraphim "the wonder-worker," and before long, well over one thousand people were visiting the monastery every day wanting to see Seraphim. In addition, many in the royal family visited Seraphim, and it is reported that even Alexander I came to visit him in 1825.

Seraphim left no autobiographical information, so most of what has been written about him came from the accounts of those whose lives he touched.[84] The only work directly attributed to Seraphim was the *Spiritual Instructions,* but many agree that these may have been edited by a later redactor.[85] Nevertheless, his *Spiritual Instructions* did give both some practical advice and a mystical, spiritual emphasis that reflected Seraphim's public charismatic ministry. He exhibited an emphasis upon Scripture when he stated, "The soul must be provided with the word of God...Most importantly, one must practice reading the New Testament and the Psalter...It is very useful to spend time reading the word of God in solitude and to read the whole Bible with understanding."[86] However, he sounded more like a mystic when he wrote, "He who has achieved perfect love exists in this world as though he does not exist in it, for he considers himself a stranger to what is visible, and patiently awaits the invisible."[87] He also reflected some of his emphasis upon the charismata when he stated, "When a man walks in the ways of peace, he picks up the gifts of the Spirit as it were with a spoon... When a man attains a state of peace, he can shed on others the light of an enlightened understanding."[88]

Perhaps one of the most important works about him was written as a conversation that Seraphim had with Nicholas Motovilov titled *The Aim of the Christian Life*. Nicholas wrote this account in his memoirs, probably shortly after he had the conversation with Seraphim in November, 1831. After his death, it remained in the Diveyevo Convent with his wife until shortly before her death at which time she gave the memoirs to Serge Nilus (1862–1929), who published the conversation between Seraphim and Motovilov in the *Moscow Gazette* in May, 1903.[89] Much of this conversation demonstrated Seraphim's emphasis upon the Holy Spirit and his charismatic pneumatology, especially when he began the conversation by saying that "the true aim of our Christian life consists in the acquisition of the Holy Spirit of God."[90] He also displayed his charismatic emphasis in a later statement to Nicholas. "What can be more precious than the gifts of the Holy Spirit which are sent down to us from above in the sacrament of Baptism?"[91] Seraphim represented the latest in a long list of pneumatics who emphasized Spirit baptism, but the timing of his influence was important for understanding how a Charismatic renewal that began in Russia could have dispersed and affected communities of Russians and Armenians as far away as Karakala.

In the introduction to the conversation that Nicholas had with Seraphim, he described waiting to speak to him as "thousands of people came to the great Elder,"[92] thus offering direct eyewitness testimony to the impact that Seraphim had upon Russia. Given the number of people that the *staretz* was seeing on a daily basis, it is likely that hundreds of thousands of Russians were directly impacted by his ministry and likely millions more were impacted indirectly. In 1833, when Seraphim died, Russia was at the height of a spiritual renewal. A new tsar, Nicholas I, would try to extinguish this revival, but he only succeeded in spreading it further throughout the Empire.

Nineteenth Century Russian Renewal Groups and the Shakarians

While the reason these Russian pneumatics were interacting with Demos Shakarian's ancestors in Karakala has already been established, their identity has not yet been revealed. During the nineteenth century, it is possible that as many as four hundred distinct, sectarian religious groups emerged from a milieu of Russian sociological, cultural, and political forces and flourished during the charismatic renewal that Seraphim of Sarov helped ignite.[93] These sectarian movements began towards the end of the eighteenth century as the pneumatic fervor of the Russian people reached a climactic period. Under the secularizing policies and persecution of Catherine II, who reigned from 1762–1796, much of what began in the Orthodox Church was dissected, squelched, and often forced to become sectarian. At least four primary groups emerged during this time period: the Subbotniks (ca. 1780–), the Molokans, the Dukhobors (ca. 1750–), and the Khlysty (ca. 1690–). To compare or categorize these groups according to modern twenty-first century denominations or affiliations would be difficult, but they ranged from legalistic and/or judaizing sects, to distinctly evangelical,[94] to clearly charismatic and pneumatic, with a wide variety of other sects and sub-groups which incorporated some or all of these characteristics.

The Subbotniks held to many or most of the laws of Judaism.[95] In many cases, their services and ceremonies were completely Jewish and almost impossible to distinguish from those of local Jewish groups. There is no clear evidence of glossolalia or any type of charismatic practices or experiences taking place within Subbotnik groups in Russia. Interestingly, there are three theories for the origin of the Subbotniks. Either they came about through the interaction between Jews and Orthodox Russians, or they represented another appearance of the Judaizer heresy in Russia dating back to the fifteenth century, or they were a divergent wing of the Molokans.[96] The Subbotnik groups, while having some cross-pollination with the other renewal groups, did not impact nearly the number of people in Russia that the other three groups did. There seems to be some Subbotnik influence in both the Russian and Armenian groups that Shakarian mentioned in his book as evidenced by their concern for kosher dietary restrictions.[97] In addition, consider the description that Shakarian gave of these Russian charismatics when he described them as wearing "high-collared tunics tied at the waste with tasseled cords, the married men in full beards."[98] Finally, the Armenian immigrants from Shakarian's family celebrated many of the traditional Jewish feasts, all possible indications of the influence of Subbotnik Russians who adopted much of the Old Testament.[99] However, while the Subbotnik ceremonies and beliefs may have influenced some of the other Russian sectarian groups, their lack of pneumatic expression and the diminutive size of this group would seem to exclude them from being likely candidates for the Russians who came to visit Karakala, Armenia.

The same cannot be said regarding the Molokan communities. The Molokans did sometimes follow some Old Testament practices like the Subbotniks[100] and some Molokan groups began to celebrate the Sabbath on Saturdays.[101] In fact, one of the founders of the Molokan movement, Matvai Semeonovich Dalmatov (ca. 1520–ca. 1570), was from a Subbotnik background.[102] However, the Molokans, who were generally not as ecstatic as the Khlysty or the Dukhobors, represented a reaction against formalism and ritualism. They rejected the traditions of Orthodoxy and advocated a return to the Bible as their sole authority for faith and conduct. At the end of the nineteenth century, there were as many as 1,200,000 Molokan believers in Russia.[103] Molokans rejected all the sacraments and had no need for priests; they believed that "Christianity is a spiritual matter between God and the individual,"[104] thus affirming the concept of "the priesthood of all believers."

Interestingly, Molokans derive their name, "milk drinkers" from their non-participation in the formal fasts of the Orthodox Church. While Orthodox believers abstained from milk during Lent, Molokans did not.[105] The Molokans saw no need for the sacrament of baptism; they spoke instead of the baptism of the Holy Spirit.[106] Many of their groups like the Pryguny or "jumpers" were often later confused with Pentecostals because of their ecstatic forms of worship.[107] This unique practice of jumping in worship may correspond with Demos Shakarian's description of his grandfather's experience with the Russian pneumatics who raised "their arms and danced with joy."[108]

During the time of persecution under Nicholas I, the Molokans theologically divided into two predominant groups. Many Molokan communities resembled a more scripturally oriented evangelical style of beliefs and practice, while other groups resembled a more Pentecostal or charismatic style. The Constant Molokans under Semen Uklein (ca. 1740–1809) adhered to their traditional concepts of salvation, while the Maksimists, following Maxim Rudometkin (ca.1818–1877), "held that the baptism of the Holy Spirit was essential, accepted the absolute authority of personal revelation and practiced glossolalia; they resembled today's charismatics."[109]

There were a number of other sub-groups or sects within the Molokan movement such as the *Donskyo tolka*, Evangelical Molokans (who reverted to some form of Orthodoxy), *vodnye, pryguny, postoiannye, obshchie, dukhovnye, voskresniki,* and *presniki*.[110] As mentioned earlier, some of these Molokan groups were scripturally oriented, many were proto-Pentecostal, and a few groups tended to emphasize Jewish law. However, there was also a lot of interaction with other groups, cross-pollenization between groups, and even groups that reflected all or most of these tendencies.

While the Dukhobors had much in common with the Molokans, they tended to be more ecstatic in their worship style. They also emphasized the baptism of the Holy Spirit and practiced glossolalia like many of the Molokans. A core belief of the Dukhobor "is the belief in the immanence of God and in the presence within each man of the Christ spirit."[111] They believed that in each generation "a per-

sonification of Christ would appear who would manifest the strength and characteristics of the son of God…The Christ-spirit, and leadership, was passed hered-
itarily from generation to generation within one bloodline."[112] This seemed like
an Adoptionist perspective which was also held by the Khlysty with their
Christology.[113] Perhaps because of this Adoptionist characteristic, the Dukhobors
were often confused with the Khlysty by Russian authorities and are still confused with, or not distinguished from, the Khlysty by many modern historians.
Finally, since all humans are deified according to their theology, Dukhobor did
not recognize social distinctions. In addition, they were strict pacifists.[114] Their
strict pacifism led to some severe confrontations and conflicts with the Russian
authorities from time to time. This was also true of many of the Molokan groups
in Russia, and led to a confrontation with the United States government when
some of them immigrated to Los Angeles before WWI.[115]

The Khlysty groups were probably the most visible and widespread ecstatic
movements of the nineteenth century. Their name, meaning flagellants, is a pejo-
rative term for their own name, Khristy or Christs.[116] At the beginning of the
twentieth century, there were probably 300,000 Khlysty believers of various sub-
groups in Russia.[117] The Khlysty also believed in a radical form of dualism, with
strict diets, lengthy periods of fasting, and celibacy.[118] The Khlysty rejected the
church sacraments much like the Molokans and the Dukhobors, and in their
place, accepted only two sacraments; the sacrament of suffering, which often was
self-inflicted such as lengthy periods of fasting or exposure to the elements; the
second, and far more important sacrament, was the gift of the Holy Spirit.[119] The
most bizarre Khlysty sect, the *Skoptsy*, practiced castration or the disfigurement
of sexual organs as an initiation rite.[120]

Many of the branches of Khlysty regarded themselves as part of the Orthodox
Church, "as a sort of Wesleyan movement within Orthodoxy."[121] Perhaps the size
of this movement and the fact that this group considered itself to be a part of the
Orthodox Church, allowed Shakarian's ancestors and the Russian pneumatics
who influenced them to believe that their revival was impacting hundreds of
thousands of Russian Orthodox Christians.[122] It is this characteristic attitude of
Orthodox inclusion that likely spared the Khlysty from much of the persecution
that the Molokan, Dukhobor, and Subbotnik groups encountered. Certainly all of
these groups had much in common with each other and with the Russian
Orthodox Church. Nevertheless, the secularizing policies of the government and
an Orthodox Church that was too closely enmeshed with this government caused
most of these groups to consciously separate themselves from the Orthodox
Church.[123]

A last piece of trivia may significantly help in identifying which type of group
visited Karakala, Armenia. Since the group of Russians who visited Karakala
always came in a large caravan of wagons, it seems plausible this was a large
community of Dukhobors who had been transplanted to Armenia, and perhaps
they came to help the people of Karakala during their harvest. However, this
would not explain the existence of Efim Klubnikin, the "boy prophet", and his

Molokan family arriving in Karakala (or near there, in the region of Kars) fifty years earlier, at the beginning of Nicholas' edict, as one of the first proto-Pentecostal families to cross the border into Armenia.[124] Klubnikin clearly had a connection with these Russian visitors, and perhaps his family was responsible for inviting them to come and assist his village in gathering their harvest. His presence in that region would tend to indicate the possibility that these were Molokans.

As a result of the edict of Nicholas I in 1830, this charismatic revival quickly spread to the farthest regions of the Russian Empire, which of course also impacted a little community in Armenia. However, in the midst of this potpourri of pneumatic and schismatic religion, the identity of the group of Russians who would visit Karakala, Armenia from time to time has not been mentioned. Vinson Synan identifies these Russians as Priguny Molokans. But why?[125]

The conjecture that these Russians were a Molokan sect with charismatic characteristics known as the Priguny is based on seven facts. First, since the Molokan, Dukhobor, and Subbotnik sects were the groups primarily exiled to Transcaucasia, this would likely rule out the possibility that these Russians belonged to a Khlysty sect. Second, since this was clearly a charismatic Russian community that emphasized the baptism of the Holy Spirit, it could have been either a Molokan or a Dukhobor sect, but probably not a Subbotnik sect. Third, since Molokans and Subbotniks were exiled to Transcaucasia in small groups, while entire Dukhobor communities were uprooted, it is most likely that Efim and his family were from a Molokan sect. Fourth, these Molokan Russians had some subtle Judaizing influence that is evidenced by their concern, and Grandfather's concern, about eating an "unclean" animal. While Molokans had some Subbotnik tendencies, there is no evidence that any of the Dukhobor communities had Subbotnik or Judaizing tendencies within their philosophy. Fifth, it is doubtful that the strong influence of Presbyterianism in Karakala would have tolerated any Adoptionist Christology from a Dukhobor community. Yet the theological interchange between the villagers in Karakala and these Russians seemed to be quite cordial in spite of their different worship styles. Sixth, it is likely they are Priguny, which means "jumpers" in Russian, because of the worship style Demos Shakarian described in his autobiography when he mentioned their characteristic style of dancing during their worship.[126] Finally, and most conclusively, the Armenians and the Russian Priguny Molokans of Karakala still exist intact as immigrant communities of worship in Los Angeles, California.[127]

The Molokan Revival of 1833

When Shakarian's ancestors in Karakala, Armenia, encountered these charismatic Russian Molokans for the first time, the Priguny Molokans possibly appealed to the pneumatic background of their Armenian Apostolic context (and perhaps traces of a pneumatic and dualistic Paulician or Messalian background) rather than their more recent Western rationalistic conversion to Presbyterianism.

Molokan theology as a whole derived its origins from the latter part of the seventeenth century as a form of indigenous Russian Protestantism. The sect of Priguny Molokans who encountered the community of Karakala experienced a significant pneumatic revival in 1833, which led to the rapid dissemination of this experience among hundreds of thousands of Russians and eventually to thousands more Armenians when the Molokans were exiled to Transcaucasia by the edict of Nicholas I.[128] As mentioned earlier, these and other pneumatic and schismatic groups were either seen as a threat to the Russian Orthodox Church or to the tsar or to both. Either way, they were sent far away from the Muscovite center of power to the outer regions of Transcaucasia where their pneumatic revival spread geographically far beyond their origins in central and southern Russia.

The timing of this pneumatic revival may have had several causes beyond providential explanations. Considering the regional potpourri of pneumatic groups that emerged from central and southern Russia over the past century, an outbreak could have occurred among any one of the groups, but as it came about among one of the largest sectarian groups of that period, its impact penetrated deeply into the peasant class of Russian society. In addition, it occurred concurrently with or immediately after the pneumatic and healing influence of Seraphim of Sarov, who died the same year, possibly creating a pneumatological gestalt in central and southern Russia. Other factors may have contributed to the pneumatic fervor of this Molokan renewal, including Nicholas' edict of Molokan exile, decreed in 1830, and the cholera outbreak and the Cholera Riots of 1830–1831, which may have created the political and psychological furnace in which this pneumatic revival was forged.[129]

Whatever the various explanations, David Yesseyevich (ca. 1809–ca. 1880) recorded that "in the year of 1833, there appeared an awesome phenomenon among our brethren – a powerful outpouring of the Holy Spirit, acting in miraculous fashion with many people dedicated to the will of God."[130] He also added that some Molokans rejected their pneumatic revival and slandered the Priguny before the Russian Synod, resulting in heightened persecution against the Priguny.[131] These charismatic Molokans defended themselves by pointing to Acts Chapter 2, a popular proof text for later Pentecostals and many modern Charismatics.[132]

The size, breadth, and scope of this pneumatic revival was uncertain. Demos Shakarian stated that the renewal had spread to hundreds of thousands of Russians in the Orthodox Church before it ever reached his Armenian community in Karakala.[133] Berokoff estimates the Priguny represented less than ten percent of the entire Molokan community in Russia, and the internal witness of David Yesseyevich implied this revival was largely contained within the Molokan community.[134] Although even at ten percent, this renewal impacted at least one hundred thousand Molokans, and because of the influence of Seraphim of Sarov, the pneumatic fervor initiated by this renewal may have reached a much larger numerical and ecclesiological audience, including certainly the Khlysty groups and many within the Russian Orthodox Church. What is certain is that the renewal eventually reached to the far ends of the Russian Empire and a small farming village called Karakala, Armenia.

The Pneumatic Nature of Molokan Christianity

The Molokans had a developed pneumatology that reflected a later Pentecostal emphasis on Spirit baptism and glossolalia as an expected sign of baptism. Thus, another well known early Molokan leader, David Yesseyevich, writes, "This baptism must always be within all of us who are of one mind. And every one of us thus baptized must have on himself a spiritual sign, that is, the speech of the Spirit in the new tongues of fire."[135] In addition, Yesseyevich mentioned how these Molokans believed in and practiced the charismata of 1 Corinthians 12, adding the common manifestation of the Holy Spirit in verse seven as a tenth gift of the Holy Spirit.[136] Adding a distinctly proto-Pentecostal flavor to their pneumatology, he stated that they also prayed earnestly "unto Him for the descent to us of the gift of the Holy Spirit in signs of the new tongues of fire…we ourselves are always baptized in the manner of the holy apostles and all of those who are like them, who in that time all spoke in the new tongues of fire."[137] In addition, the boy prophet, Efim Klubnikin gave a sample of his own glossolalia in *Spirit and Life* (1983).[138]

The charismatic nature of Maxim Rudometkin also left an indelible mark on Molokan pneumatology. His writings, preserved in the Molokan book *Spirit and Life* reflected both an apocalyptic and pneumatic tone. His imprisonment and persecution under Alexander II (1818–1881), in spite of the humanitarian intervention of Leo Tolstoy (1828–1910), inevitably led to his near sainthood in many Molokan circles.[139] Interestingly, *Spirit and Life* is considered a sacred text among Priguny Molokans, particularly those exiles who traveled with a band of Armenians from Karakala to Los Angeles in 1905.[140]

While the Presbyterian influences of Shakarian's ancestors may have rejected the cultic status of Maxim Rudometkin and the sacerdotal devotion to *Spirit and Life*, the Orthodox origins of Shakarian's ancestors accepted the pneumatological nature of these visiting Molokans. However, one lingering question regarding the Pentecostal distinction of glossolalia remains. Did the Molokans have a doctrine of Spirit baptism similar to modern Pentecostals, and was this doctrine transferred to Shakarian's ancestors – helping to shape his own pneumatology? In their sacred text, *Spirit and Life*, the Molokans required a sign of glossolalia to accompany Spirit baptism which is remarkably similar to modern twentieth century Pentecostalism. Thus, Maxim G. Rudometkin (d.b.a. 1818–1877), one of the Molokan prophets, stated, "This baptism must always be within all of us who are of one mind. And everyone of us thus baptized must have on himself a spiritual sign, that is, the speech of the Spirit in the new tongues of fire."[141]

It should be noted that glossolalia was not a phenomenon unique to the Molokans in the nineteenth century. Other groups including Edward Irving's church in London and the West Scotland Revival (1830), some of Charles

Finney's (1792–1875) revival meetings, Shakers (1747–), Quakers, Mormons (1833–), the Awakening of Finland, the revival meetings of Marie Woodworth-Etter (1844–1924), revivals in India (1860–1880), South Africa (1861), and Indonesia (1870), and of course the neighboring Khlysty of Russia, all recorded glossolalic expressions. However, the Priguny Molokans may be unique in the nineteenth century for actually requiring glossolalia to be the sign of Spirit baptism, even if they do not necessarily phrase it with the precise twentieth century terminology of classical Pentecostals. In fact, at least one Russian scholar speculated that a large group of Priguny Molokans who migrated to North America in the 1890s was responsible for introducing the Pentecostal movement to North America.[142] Nevertheless, even with their use of glossolalia, they would consider their own charismatic distinction as one of jumping or "Priguny" which they believe is the common manifestation of the Spirit's presence in a believer, in contrast to the modern Pentecostal distinction of glossolalia.[143]

The Relationship between the Russian Molokans and the Armenian Shakarians

When Demos Shakarian's father walked down Azusa Street with Magardich Mushegan looking for work in 1906, they discovered the Azusa Street Mission, rushed back home to Boston Street and declared, "Come on, we found a place where they worship in the church like we do."[144] "They began attending the old Azusa Street Mission…As the Americans were shouting the praises of God for the outpouring, the Armenians were able to say, 'This is that which God gave to us in Armenia many years ago.'"[145]

The Molokans and the Armenians who immigrated to Los Angeles in 1905 clearly identified with the pneumatic nature of the revival that erupted at Azusa Street in April 1906. Their encounter at Azusa Street only confirmed their understanding of the continuity of the Holy Spirit's role in the Church from its foundation to the present age. Thus, a far different pneumatological ecclesiology was forged in the minds of these Armenians as compared to early Pentecostal thinkers who were convinced of the unique pneumatological reawakening brought on by their revival, consequently excluding eighteen hundred years of church history.[146] Of course, there were influences that the Molokans gave to the Armenians dissimilar from their experiences at Azusa Street such as "holy jumping" or the strict dietary and dress requirements of the Molokans.[147] Both these similarities and differences will be more exhaustively examined in the next chapter.

While the sacred text of these nineteenth century pneumatics reveals some surprisingly twentieth century Pentecostal tendencies, their glossolalic expressions may not have been imitated by their Armenian neighbors. While Shakarian's ancestors may have been deeply affected by the spirituality of these Molokans, Shakarian mentioned, in a series of interviews, that his ancestors did not speak in tongues until they came to Azusa Street. In one interview later in his life, Shakarian stated that his church in Armenia "didn't speak so much tongues…

They didn't have tongues and interpretation until they come [sic] here. That came later."[148] Later in the same interview, Demos Shakarian admitted that his church never had glossolalia before Azusa Street.[149] However, Vinson Synan indicated that Azusa Street was where the original North American Pentecost occurred, but Shakarian countered by saying "We were original Pentecost."[150]

There does seem to be a slight difference between the pneumatology of the Molokan Christians and the Armenians they interacted with. The Priguny Molokans appear to be a lot closer to classical Pentecostalism than the Armenians they influenced; that is of course, until the Armenians came into contact with the Azusa Street Mission. There can certainly be several explanations for this discrepancy. Perhaps the Armenians in Karakala were influenced by some Russian religious sect other than the Priguny Molokans, although this seems unlikely based on the description of them given by Demos Shakarian.[151] Another explanation may be that the oral transmission of information regarding what the Armenians were like before they interacted with the Azusa Street Mission may be slightly distorted. It is also plausible that the Armenian Presbyterians, influenced by the Russian Molokans, simply rejected certain aspects of their worship and pneumatology while emphasizing other aspects. Many of the Charismatic and Neo-Charismatic Christians did this in digressing from traditional Pentecostalism. Regardless, the Armenian Christians had ecstatic worship and practiced much of the charismata, especially prophesy, even before they interacted with the Azusa Street congregation.[152]

Conclusion

Demos Shakarian's ancestors were profoundly impacted by a group of Russian pneumatics who had experienced a significant renewal of their own in 1833. This renewal spread throughout the Russian Empire either through voluntary evangelism or involuntary tsarist edicts. Most significantly for an understanding of the modern Charismatic movement and the life of Demos Shakarian, some Priguny Molokans visited Demos Shakarian's grandfather and introduced him to the pneumatic experience of Spirit baptism. While the similarities with classical Pentecostalism are significant, the distinctions in pneumatic praxis and ecclesiological understanding cannot be overemphasized in understanding Demos Shakarian's context. This context was once again profoundly shaped by the charismatic gift of prophecy. The very survival of Demos Shakarian's ancestors depended on it, and Demos Shakarian himself would repeatedly recognize the importance of this charismatic gift throughout his life

Notes

1. Harding Mushegian, interview with Matthew Tallman, San Dimas, California, January 16, 2008. See also Joyce Keosababian Bivin's article, "The Armenians of Karakala and Their Relationship with Russian Molokans: 1870–1920," unpublished article (n.d.).

2. Demos Shakarian, *The Happiest People* (1975), 14.

3. Bivin (n.d.), 2–4.

4. In Bivin's article, she does mention interviewing one descendent, a great aunt, who lived in Turkey. This woman lived in another Molokan village in the Kars region called Vorontsovka (now called Incesu) and had been converted to Islam to marry a Muslim but still had some knowledge of her Christian ancestry (33).

5. Demos Shakarian, *The Happiest People* (1975), 14; and Mushegian-Tallman interview, January 16, 2008.

6. Demos Shakarian, *The Happiest People* (1975), 14.

7. Ibid.

8. Demos Shakarian, "Moment of Truth," *Voice* October 1975, 22.

9. Hans Brandenburg, *The Meek and the Mighty: The Emergence of the Evangelical Movement in Russia* (London: Mowbrays, 1974), 61. One notable example was Yakov Delyakov, a Persian Nestorian by birth, who was sent to Russia as a missionary and did some very effective work with a number of Molokan communities.

10. Bivin (n.d.), 6; and Mushegian-Tallman interview, January 16, 2008.

11. Demos Shakarian, *The Happiest People* (1975), 14.

12. Ibid.

13. Demos Shakarian, *The Happiest People* (1975), 16. See also Demos Shakarian, "God's Dairyman," (1956), 40; and Thomas Nickel, "The Amazing Shakarian Story: Part One," *Voice*, October 1953, 3. There is some discrepancy regarding his birth since his headstone at Rose Hills Cemetery in Whittier, California, states he was born in 1882. However, the consistency of the written record, in addition to the fact that his family immigrated to Los Angeles when he was a teenage boy confirms the latter date (this last point is also confirmed by photographic evidence of Isaac Shakarian as a thirteen year-old boy, standing with eight other Armenian men who had recently immigrated to Los Angeles from Karakala, Armenia – see Jeff Janoian, *God at Our Side*, DVD, 2005). Without considering the possibility that the funeral home made an error on the headstone, it is difficult to explain the discrepancy between these two accounts of Isaac Shakarian's date of birth.

14. Demos Shakarian, *The Happiest People* (1975), 16.

15. Ibid, 14.

16. Recent scholarship has proposed a later date for the conversion of Armenia in 314 C.E. concurrent with Constantine's Edict of Toleration rather than the earlier traditional date of 301 C.E. See Leon Arpee, *A History of Armenian Christianity from the Beginning to Our Own Time* (New York: The Armenian Missionary Association, 1946), 15 for evidence of the traditional date. See Vigen Guroian, "The Ferment of Faith in Post-Soviet Armenia," *Christian Century* 109:3 (January 22, 2006): 67; or A.E. Redgate's *The Armenians*, (London: Blackwell Publishers, 1998), 116 for more recent scholarship on the later date.

17. See Demos Shakarian, *The Happiest People* (1975), 14; and Bivin (n.d.), 11.

18. A short list of these pneumatologists and ecumenists could include the Cappadocians, Hilary of Poitiers, Didymus the Blind, Pseudo-Macarius of Egypt, Isaac of Nineveh, Symeon the New Theologian, Nerses of Snor'hali, Joachim of Fiore, Gregory Palamas, the Quakers, the prophets of Cevennes, the Jansenists, the Moravians, the Molokans, the Awakened of Finland, the Shakers, and much more. For a more comprehensive list see Stanley M. Burgess' trilogy *The Holy Spirit: Ancient Christian Traditions* (Peabody, MA: Hendrickson Publishers, 1984); *The Holy Spirit: Eastern Christian Traditions* (Peabody, MA: Hendrickson Publishers, 1989); and *The Holy Spirit: Medieval*

Roman Catholic and Reformation Traditions (Peabody, MA: Hendrickson Publishers, 1997).

19. For an example of the alternate view, see Carl Brumback's *Suddenly from Heaven: A History of the Assemblies of God* (Springfield, MO: Gospel Publishing House, 1961).

20. For a brief discussion of Christendom and its effects upon Christian ecclesiology, pneumatology, theology, and ecumenism, see Lyle Dabney's "Starting with the Spirit: Why the Last Should Now be First," pages 3–27 in *Starting with the Spirit*; edited by Gordon Preece and Stephen Pickard (Hindmarsh, Australia: Australian Theological Forum, 2001).

21. Burgess, "Implications of Eastern Christian Pneumatology," in Jan A.B. Jongeneel, ed. *Experiences of the Spirit: Conference on Pentecostal and Charismatic Research in Europe at Untrecht University, 1989*, Studien zur interkultureen Geschichte des Christentums (Peter Lang: Frankfurt am Main, 1991), 26.

22. Malachia Ormanian, *The Church of Armenia* (2nd edition; London: A.B. Mowbray, 1955), 133.

23. Hratch Tchilingirian, "Armenian Apostolic Church," Armeniapedia, http://www.armeniapedia.org/index.php?title=Armenian_Apostolic_Church, (accessed April 1, 2006).

24. While Synan, Hollenweger, Harrell, and other scholars have clearly stated the significance of the Full Gospel Business Men in helping to initiate the Charismatic revival – see Walter Hollenweger, *The Pentecostals: The Charismatic Movement in the Churches* (Minneapolis: Augsberg Publishing House, 1972), 4 – no one has ever suggested the origins of the ecumenical characteristics of this organization being formed within the context of the ecumenical nature of the Armenian Orthodox Church.

25. Ormanian (1955), 45.

26. Ibid, 45–46.

27. Ibid, 99.

28. Carnegie Samuel Calian, "The Armenian Church and Ecumenism," *Christian Century* 81 (August 12, 1964): 1008.

29. Barsamian, Khajag Barsamian, "The Oriental Orthodox Churches," *Ecumenism* 77 (March, 1985): 29.

30. Charles A. Frazee, "The Christian Church in Cilician Armenia: Its Relations with Rome and Constantinople to 1198," *Church History* 45:2 (June 1976): 175–176.

31. Ibid, 183–184.

32. Aram I has even authored a book on Nerses Snor'hali titled *Nerses the Gracious as Theologian and Ecumenist* (Beirut, Lebanon: 1974). Unfortunately, this book has not yet been translated into English. However, Stanley Burgess gives a brief summary of Snor'hali's contributions to ecumenism and pneumatology in *The Holy Spirit: Eastern Christian Traditions* (1989), 131–136.

33. Shahan Sarkissian, "Ecumenism in the Armenian Catholicosate of Cilicia," *Ministerial Formation* 91 (October, 2000): 7.

34. See Demos Shakarian, *The Happiest People* (1975), 14–15.

35. Demos Shakarian, *The Happiest People* (1975), 14. See also Demos Shakarian, "The Amazing Shakarian Story," *Voice*, November 1953, 6–7; and December 1953, 8–10.

36. Demos Shakarian, *The Happiest People* (1975), 14–15.

37. Ibid, 15.

38. Demos Shakarian, "Moment of Truth," *Voice*, October 1975, 24. It is possible that the Russians who fled to Finland may have had some influence or interaction with the Awakened Renewal that occurred in Finland in 1798, but it is also possible that the pneu-

matological enthusiasts from Finland may have spread their brand of charismatic Christianity to Russia.

39. Demos Shakarian, *The Happiest People* (1975), 15–16.

40. See Breyfogle, "Heretics and Colonizers," (1998), 20. Also see Bivin, "The Armenians of Karakala," (n.d.), 12, 16.

41. Demos Shakarian, *The Happiest People* (1975), 16.

42. Demos Shakarian, "Moment of Truth," *Voice*, October 1975, 23.

43. Demos Shakarian, "Moment of Truth," *Voice*, October 1975, 23.

44. Ibid.

45. Demos Shakarian, *The Happiest People* (1975), 18–19.

46. Brandenburg, *The Meek and the Mighty* (1974), 83.

47. Breyfogle, "Heretics and Colonizers," (1998), 1.

48. Breyfogle, "Heretics and Colonizers," (1998), 2. These dissenters primarily objected to the hierarchical control of the Russian Orthodox church and the tsar both of which restricted their religious practices and desired to move these sectarians as far away as possible from the seat of religious and political power in Moscow. The conflict between these two groups is seen as just one of many historical examples of the tension between prophecy and order and is discussed most cogently in Jeffrey Burton Russell's groundbreaking volume titled *A History of Medieval Christianity: Prophecy and Order* (Arlington Heigths, IL: AHM Publishing Company, 1968).

49. Breyfogle, "Heretics and Colonizers," (1998), 84.

50. Ibid, 14.

51. For a more thorough treatment of these groups and individuals see Stanley M. Burgess' trilogy The Holy Spirit: Ancient Christian Traditions (1984); The Holy Spirit: Eastern Christian Traditions (1989); The Holy Spirit: Medieval Roman Catholic and Reformation Traditions (1997); and Gary McGee's Initial Evidence: Historical and Biblical Perspectives on the Pentecostal Doctrine of Spirit Baptism (Peabody, MA: Hendrickson Publishers, 1991).

52. Demos Shakarian, *The Happiest People* (1975), 24.

53. Brandenburg, *The Meek and the Mighty* (1974), 4.

54. Ibid.

55. Admittedly, there is some debate regarding this assumption. See Lyle Dabney, "Starting with the Spirit," or Kallistos' *The Orthodox Way* (Crestwood, NY: St. Vladimir's Seminary Press, 1995) for a discussion of the *filioque* from this perspective. See Raneiro Cantalamessa's *Come Creator Spirit: Meditations on the Veni Creator*, trans. by Dennis and Marlene Barrett (Collegeville, MN: Liturgical Press, 2003) for an opposing Western perspective from a leading Charismatic Catholic scholar.

56. Brandenburg, *The Meek and the Mighty* (1974), *8*.

57. Ibid, 8–9.

58. Ibid, 11.

59. Ibid.

60. Lyudmila Vorontsova and Sergei Filatov, "Paradoxes of the Old Believer Movement," *RSS* 28 (2000): 53.

61. Ibid, 55.

62. Ibid.

63. Brandenburg, *The Meek and the Mighty* (1974), 14.

64. Ibid, 19.

65. Ibid, 15. Adolph Harnack and his family of theologians descended from these German pietists in St. Petersburg. (Ibid, 30).

66. Ibid, 20.

67. There is certainly much debate regarding the origins of the Molokans. Some would argue that the Molokans began even before the Old Believers in the mid sixteenth century with Matvei Semenov Bashkin and Fedosius Kosei. The Russian government did not identify the sect as Molokans or "milk drinkers" in Russian until 1765 (*Spirit and Life* [1983] 22–23). The Molokan sect which is discussed in this chapter traditionally regards Matvei Semeonovich Dalmatov as the founder of the Molokan movement (*Spirit and Life* [1983], 23).

68. Demos Shakarian, *The Happiest People* (1975), 15.

69. Tomás Spidlik, "The Theological Renewal of the Russian Startsi," *Communio* 15 (1998): 62.

70. Ibid, 75.

71. Ibid, 62.

72. Ibid, 62–63.

73. Igumen Symeon, "The Search for God in the Hesychast Tradition," *RPDS* 73, trans. Sister Seraphina (1998): 31–33.

74. Spidlik, "Theological Renewal," (1998): 65.

75. Ibid, 67.

76. Ibid.

77. Valentine Zander, *St. Seraphim of Sarov*, trans. Sister Gabriel Anne (Crestwood, New York: St. Vladimir's Seminary Press, 1975), xiii.

78. William C. Fletcher, *Soviet Charismatics: The Pentecostals in the USSR* (New York: Peter Lang, 1985), 25.

79. A.F. Dobbie-Bateman, "The Life and Spiritual Instructions of Saint Seraphim of Sarov," in *The Spiritual Instructions of Saint Seraphim of Sarov: A Spirit-Baptizer in the Eastern Christian Tradition*, ed. Da Avabhasa (Clearlake, California: The Dawn Horse Press, 1991), 59.

80. Zander, *St. Seraphim* (1975), 19.

81. Ibid, 34.

82. Archimandrite Lazarus Moore, *St. Seraphim of Sarov: A Spiritual Biography* (Blanco, Texas: New Sarov Press, 1994), 375.

83. Ibid, 389–391

84. Zander, *St. Seraphim* (1974), 7.The lack of autobiographical information may be due to Peter the Great's decree that no monks were allowed to have ink in their cells.

85. Donald Stanford Webley, "An Introduction to Saint Seraphim of Sarov and the Great Process of Spiritual Transmission, in the Light of the Wisdom-Teaching of Da Avabhasa (The 'Bright')," in *The Spiritual Instructions of Saint Seraphim of Sarov: A Spirit-Baptizer in the Eastern Christian Tradition*, ed. Da Avabhasa (Clearlake, California: The Dawn Horse Press, 1991), 29.

86. Constantine Cavarnos and Mary-Barbara Zeldin, *St. Seraphim of Sarov*, vol. 5 of *Modern Orthodox Saints* (Belmont, Massachusetts: The Institute for Byzantine and Modern Greek Studies, Inc., 1980), 130.

87. Ibid, 124.

88. Ibid, 132.

89. Ibid, 150.

90. Moore, *St. Seraphim of Sarov* (1994), 169.

91. Ibid, 189.

92. St. Herman of Alaska Brotherhood, *St. Seraphim of Sarov*, vol. 1 of *Little Russian Philokalia* (New Valaam Monastery, Alaska: St. Herman Press, 1991), 82.

93. F. Fedorenko, *Setky, ikh vera i dela* [The sects, their faith and works] (Moscow: Publishing House for Political Literature, 1965), 3, 11, and 21.

94. Many modern observers would categorize some of the groups as being evangelical because of their emphasis upon Scripture and their exclusion of religious traditions in the Orthodox Church that were not specifically mentioned or supported by Scripture.

95. Nicholas Breyfogle, "Heretics and Colonizers: Religious Dissent and Russian Colonization of Transcaucasia 1830–1890" (Ph.D. diss., The University of Pennsylvania, 1998), 20.

96. Breyfogle, "Heretics and Colonizers," (1998), 20.

97. See Demos Shakarian, *The Happiest People* (1975), 14, 17.

98. Ibid, 15.

99. Stan Perumean, interview by Matthew Tallman, La Habra Heights, CA, March 26, 2006; and Paul Sobolew, interview by Matthew Tallman, La Habra Heights, CA, March 26, 2006; and in Los Angeles, CA, January 15, 2008. See also Demos Shakarian's comments in *The Happiest People* (1975), 14 about his ancestors being "Old Testament people".

100. Breyfogle, "Heretics and Colonizers," (1998), 20.

101. Ibid.

102. Paul Samarin, "The Teachings of the Molokan Religion," *The Molokan Review* 1:2 (1941): 5.

103. Fletcher, *Soviet Charismatics* (1985), 21.

104. Ibid.

105. Ibid, 22.

106. Roman Lunkin and Anton Prokof'yev, "Molokans and Dukhobors: Living Sources of Russian Protestantism," *RSS* 28 (2000): 86.

107. Fletcher, *Soviet Charismatics* (1985), 22–23.

108. Demos Shakarian, *The Happiest People* (1975), 18.

109. Lunkin, "Molokans and Dukhobors," (2000): 88.

110. Breyfogle, "Heretics and Colonizers," (1998), 19. Breyfogle here uses the term Evangelical Molokans to describe a certain group of Molokans with an emphatic use of Scripture in their theology and praxis.

111. Breyfogle, "Heretics and Colonizers," (1998), 18.

112. Ibid.

113. Fletcher, *Soviet Charismatics* (1985), 12.

114. Breyfogle, "Heretics and Colonizers," (1998), 18.

115. See John Berokoff, *Molokans in America* (1987), 63–76. He records in detail a group of Molokans in Los Angeles who were imprisoned for a period of time until their religious group was recognized as a pacifist organization during WWI.

116. Fletcher, *Soviet Charismatics* (1985), 11.

117. Ibid.

118. Ibid, 12–13.

119. Ibid, 14.

120. Ibid, 20.

121. Ibid.

122. Demos Shakarian, *The Happiest People* (1975), 15.

123. Breyfogle, "Heretics and Colonizers," (1998), 16.

124. Demos Shakarian, *The Happiest People* (1975), 19. It also should be mentioned that Efim Klubnikin is a highly revered prophet in the Priguny Molokan group that immigrated to Los Angeles, and he was buried in East Los Angeles in 1915. His prophecies are

preserved in the Priguny Molokan text, *Spirit and Life — Book of the Sun: Divine Discourses of the Preceptors and the Martyrs for the Word of God, the Faith of Jesus, and the Holy Spirit, of the Religion of the Spiritual Christian Molokan-Jumpers,* translated by John Volkov from the 1928 2nd Russian edition, edited by Daniel Shubin (Los Angeles, CA: Privately printed, 1983).

125. Synan, *Under His Banner* (1992), 19–20.

126. Demos Shakarian, *The Happiest People* (1975), 18.

127. Stan Perumean, interview by Matthew Tallman, March 26, 2006, La Habra Heights, California; and Paul Sobolew, interview by Matthew Tallman, March 26, 2006, La Habra Heights, California.

128. John K. Berokoff, ed. and trans., "Selections of Works of David Yesseyivitch," in *Selections from the Book of Spirit and Life Including the Book of Prayers and Songs by Maxin G .Rudametkin* (Whittier, California: Stockton Trade Press, 1966), 23.

129. On page 678 of *Spirit and Life* (1983), Klubnikin gave a prophetic exhortation calling the Molokans to prayer and fasting because a cholera epidemic was imminent. Political and psychological forces behind pneumatic renewal are not without precedent in church history. The Montanist renewal and even many of the monastic movements of the medieval period could be considered a theological and political protest against the moral laxity and Christian hierarchy of that period. Many of the Protestant reformers and modern Protestant historians felt the early church was birthed and flourished in this political tension with Rome but floundered when this tension was lost after Constantine's Edict of Toleration. Jeffrey Burton Russell gives an excellent account of the tension between political and pneumatic or prophetic forces in his book, *A History of Medieval Christianity: Prophecy and Order* (Arlington Heigths, IL: AHM Publishing Company, 1968). It is likely this tension participated in the milieu which brought about the conditions for a Molokan revival.

130. David Yesseyevich, "Book of Zion," Article 1 in *Selections from Spirit and Life* (1966), 80.

131. Ibid, 80–81.

132. Ibid, 80.

133. Demos Shakarian, *The Happiest People* (1975), 15.

134. See Berokoff, *Molokans in America* (1987), 17; and David Yesseyevich, *Selections from Spirit and Life* (1966), 80.

135. David Yesseyevich, *Selections from Spirit and Life* (1966), 75.

136. Berokoff, *Selections from Spirit and Life* (1966), 61.

137. Ibid, 66–67.

138. Efim Klubnikin, Article 43:9 in *Spirit and Life* (1983), 669.

139. A few more devout followers of Maxim Rudometkin in the Molokan community actually have elevated this prophet to Messianic status. (Paul Sobolew-Tallman interview, January 15, 2008).

140. Paul Sobolew-Tallman interview, March 26, 2006. Different Molokan communities have various collections of *Spirit and Life*, which include some books and exclude others, but the copy made available for this study is the one most widely circulated among the Priguny Molokans of Los Angeles who are associated with the First Armenian Pentecostal Church. This edition, in particular, offers the prophecies of Efim Klubnikin, the boy prophet, who warned the Russian and Armenian Molokans of the Kars region to flee Armenia.

141. John K. Berokoff, ed. and trans., *Selections from the Book of Spirit and Life Including the Book of Prayers and Songs by Maxin G. Rudametkin* (1966), 75.

142. Nikolai Vasil'evich Kol'tsov, *Kto takie piatidesiatniki* [Who are the Pentecostals] (Moscow: Znanie Press, 1965), 5.

143. Paul Sobolew-Tallman interview, January 15, 2008.

144. Synan-Shakarian interview, October 5, 1987, 4.

145. Thomas Nickel, "The Amazing Shakarian Story," *Voice*, November 1953, 6.

146. Burgess, "Implications of Eastern Pneumatology for Western Pentecostal Doctrine and Practice," in Jan A.B. Jongeneel, ed., *Experiences of the Spirit: Conference on Pentecostal and Charismatic Research in Europe at Untrecht University, 1989*, Studien zur interkultureen Geschichte des Christentums (Peter Lang: Frankfurt am Main, 1991), 23. Some early Pentecostal historiographers tended to view church history from a restorationist viewpoint in an attempt to validate their similarities with primitive Christianity. Others such as Carl Brumback in *Suddenly...from Heaven; A History of the Assemblies of God* (Springfield, MO: Gospel Publishing House, 1961) tended to invalidate or ignore the pneumatic revivals that preceded modern classical Pentecostalism but only compared their Pentecostal perspective with primitive New Testament Christianity.

147. Consider this interesting quote from the *Los Angeles Times* on October 9, 1906, page 17 comparing the Priguny Molokans to the Azusa Street worshippers. "Before the meeting closed the picturesque 'Priguni' outrivaled the wildest orgies of the Azusa Street revelers."

148. Demos Shakarian-Synan interview, October 5, 1987, 5.

149. Ibid, 9.

150. Ibid, 3.

151. One additional fact that may seal the correlation between Shakarian and these Priguny Molokans is the fact that Efim Klubnikin's prophecy mentioned in Shakarian's autobiography was also included in the sacred Priguny text, *Spirit and Life* (1983).

152. Synan-Shakarian interview, October 5, 1987, 5.

Chapter Three

From Armenia to the United States

As Shakarian's predecessors became immersed in Russian pneumatological and charismatic experiences, they became familiar with the oracles of a boy prophet, Efim Gerasimovitch Klubnikin (1842–1915), who, in 1900, was an elder in the Russian Molokan community. At the beginning of the twentieth century, he told the Molokan communities in the Kars region that it was time to leave Transcaucasia. As a result, several thousand Molokans heeded his advice and immigrated to the United States, most of them eventually settling in Los Angeles, California. Among these Molokan believers were some Armenian families from Karakala, including Demos Shakarian's father and grandfather, and their extended families. Several hundred thousand Russians and Armenians, who either ignored or never heard of Efim's prophecies, perished at the beginning of WWI as the Ottoman Empire began its genocide. This chapter focuses on the prophecies of Efim Klubnikin, the Armenian and Russian Molokan families that immigrated to the United States, and what the majority of them encountered when they settled in Southern California. In particular, this section will examine the plight of the Shakarian family.

From Armenia to the United States

Sometime between 1853 and 1855 an eleven-year old Russian Molokan boy's prophecy engraved the importance of his pneumatic manifestation on the hearts and minds of Armenian and Russian Molokans alike. Efim Klubnikin was born in Nikitina, in the province of Eravan, Armenia on December 17, 1842. His family had moved from the Russian province of Tambov two years before he was born, encouraged by the earlier edict of Nicholas I in 1830.[1] Later, after the Russo – Turkish War of 1877–1888, his family moved to the region of Kars, Armenia near Karakala.[2] His family's interaction with their Armenian neighbors likely softened the relationship between the two groups. But it was the economic benefits of trade and labor between the local Armenians and the relocated Molokans, who helped them with the seasonal harvests that proved naturally beneficial. The fact that the Armenians, long held under the dominion of tsarist Russia, could speak the same language as the Molokans was fortunate.

The nature of Efim's prophecy seems apocalyptic in nature, warning of impending doom on the region if they should not heed his oracle. The type or occurrence of prophecy, in times of economic, political, or sociological crisis, is not unusual. Prophecy could arguably be considered one of the most common charismata exhibited throughout church history. Apocalyptic prophecy, such as that delivered by Klubnikin, could be considered a popular style of oracle given by individuals as temporally distant as Perpetua of Carthage or Hildegard of Bingen, or as near as Seraphim of Sarov when he warned of impending doom upon Russia if they did not draw near to God.[3] As already mentioned, much of what was written in the Molokan text, *Spirit and Truth* was riddled with apocalyptic style and content. [4]

However, Shakarian's autobiography makes three curious comments about the prophecy that Efim delivered. First of all, Shakarian mentioned that Klubnikin was illiterate when he wrote this prophecy in the middle of the nineteenth century. This added to the supernatural and divine import of his prophetic message.[5] The message was written over a period of a week while young Efim prayed and fasted.[6] Shakarian also mentioned a second prophecy that Efim delivered about the future that was sealed by Efim and the community. It was believed that if it was opened by anyone other than a later prophet, it would bring death upon the reader.[7] The mortal nature of this prophecy may seem curious, but not without precedent in the history of prophecy, and strengthened the sacred nature of prophecy. Finally, Shakarian mentioned the Molokans and charismatic Armenians, who heeded Efim's prophetic warning, were jeered as they fled.[8] An earlier version of this story, not softened by the cultural sensitivities of the latter part of the twentieth century, declared that "the mockers and scoffers and unbelieving Christians were destroyed."[9] While modern readers might view this interpretation harshly, it does represent how seriously and sacredly this prophecy was held by the Armenian and Russian refugees who fled from Transcaucasia. After all, this prophecy not only saved their lives, it supposedly encouraged them to travel to the United States, where they prospered in Southern California.[10]

In 1900, Klubnikin felt the fulfillment of his childhood prophecy was imminent. Apparently, he based this conclusion on various signs ranging from a prayer vigil to an atmospheric phenomenon, but increasing political and religious persecution may have also been a factor.[11] Klubnikin went throughout the Erevan and Kars regions communicating the import of his message, but his message was received with less resistance in Kars, so he apparently concentrated more of his time warning the various villages of that region.[12] Demos Shakarian recalls that Klubnikin arrived in Karakala shortly after the turn of the century and warned Shakarian's grandfather the time had come to leave the region and travel across the ocean.[13] According to the chronology of the events Shakarian recounted, Klubnikin would have announced this warning to the inhabitants of Karakala in 1901 or 1902.[14] In 1900, the Molokan communities in the region of Erevan, fearing political reprisals for their strict pacifism, sent a petition to the tsar requesting permission to leave the country.[15] When their petition was rejected, they still sent several Molokans from the region to Canada to determine if that country was suitable for their religious communities.[16]

Shortly after this sponsored group left for Canada, a younger group of Molokans left for Canada in April of 1900 at their own expense. After spending nine months in Canada, they were advised, by a Russian they met in Winnipeg, to travel to Los Angeles. There they found employment working for the Pacific Electric Railroad Company for wages between $1.75 and $2.00 per day.[17] After working in Los Angeles for one year, Aleksy Agalstaff (d.b.a. 1860–d.d.a. 1930) returned to Russia in early 1902; his three nephews followed him back to Russia in 1903.[18]

The Molokan community was divided on how to respond to Klubnikin's prophecy and the growing threat of involuntary military service. Apparently the earlier prophecies of Maxim Rudometkin, promising a place of refuge at Mount Ararat, seemed to conflict with Klubnikin's promise of refuge across the ocean.[19] However, when the Agalstaff brothers arrived with positive reports of employment, a warm climate, and a prosperous land in Southern California, the elders of ten Molokan villages, including an Armenian elder from Karakala named Ardzuman Ohanessian (1868–1932), met in the village of Novo-Mihailovka in early 1904 to discuss their options.[20] After much discussion and three days of fasting one of the Russian elders took a banner from the wall of the meeting room and tucked it under a bench. Another Russian prophet slid the banner further under the bench, completely concealing the object from the other elders. After some consternation and discussion, the Armenian elder interpreted the act of this prophet to mean that they must leave quickly and in secret.[21]

On May 1, 1904, the first group of Russian Molokans left for the United States taking a steamship to Odessa; a train to Brennen, Germany; another steamship to New York City and finally another train across the United States to Los Angeles.[22] For the next eight years hundreds of Molokans arrived each year, peaking in 1907, and ending in 1912.[23] Quite a number of Armenian families also departed from Karakala during this time including the Shakarians on June 10, 1905.[24] Geraldine Shakarian Scalf recalls that eleven Armenian Molokan families left Karakala during that time period, including her grandfather and her great-grandfather.[25] However, Joyce Bivin (1934–) claims that at least thirteen Armenian Molokan families left Karakala during that time period.[26] Most of them left in haste, many abandoned their properties, a few, like the Shakarians, sold their farms at a bargain price, and some left with only a traditional wood-burning brass samovar on their backs.[27]

In the interim, just one decade after the Shakarian family left Armenia, Ottoman Turks slaughtered thousands, and perhaps even more died on a forced death march across Transcaucasia to concentration camps in what is now modern Syria. In total, it is estimated that more than 1.5 million Armenians died in this genocide; yet modern Turkey still denies complicity. Efim's prophetic word saved many lives in Karakala, but to what extent his prophecy was spread beyond the region of Kars is uncertain. At least one Armenian member of the FGBMFI in Southern California states his descendants never heard of this prophecy before they came to America, but his ancestors lived hundreds of miles apart from Shakarian's ancestors.[28] Nevertheless, many Armenians did not need a prophetic word to see the writing on the wall. From 1891 to 1898, 12,500 Armenians went to North America and 20,000 of them went to Russia in the short span between 1892 and 1893. From 1895 to 1896, persecution against the Armenians became much more severe; consequently, between 1899 and 1914, a much larger group of 51,950 emigrated from Armenia to the United States.[29]

According to Shakarian's autobiography, the remaining descendants of Karakala all perished in the ensuing genocide.[30] Unfortunately, the tales of Christians being burned alive in churches were too common to be fictional, but the world largely ignored the death of almost one million Armenians as they perished in a wave of systematic deportation that began in May of 1915.[31] What remains of Karakala today is uncertain. Even the exact location of Karakala is unclear after the confusion surrounding the genocide.[32] What remains certain to the survivors of Karakala is that a prophecy saved their lives. Thus the charismatic nature of the Molokan Christians was transferred to the Armenians and their descendants as the prophecy was retold countless times, beginning when the Shakarian family sailed to America and eventually arrived in Los Angeles in 1905…just in time for another pneumatic revival of no small consequence.

Russians and Armenians in 1905 Los Angeles

Efim Klubnikin, the young illiterate boy prophet, wrote out a series of instructions, warnings, and drew maps that "at some unspecified time in the future… every Christian in Karakala would be in danger."[33] On one of his maps, Klubnikin drew what appeared to be the Atlantic Ocean and the East Coast of the United States. "But the refugees were not to settle down there, the young prophet continued. They were to continue traveling until they reached the west coast of the new land. There, the boy wrote, 'God would bless them and prosper them, and cause their seed to be a blessing to the nations.'"[34] Shortly after the turn of the twentieth century, Efim announced that the words of the prophecy were about to be fulfilled and the people must flee to America or perish.[35] In 1915, the Armenian genocide began and every inhabitant of Karakala perished.[36] Except of course, for the families who earlier heeded the warning of Efim.

> Grandfather Demos was among these who had fled. After his experience with the Russian patriarch, Grandfather no longer discounted the validity of prophecy. In 1905 he sold the farm which had been in the family for generations, accepting whatever bit of money he could get for it…The family reached New York safely but, mindful of the prophecy, did not settle there. In accordance with the written instructions they kept traveling across the vast bewildering new land, until they reached Los Angeles. There, to their delight, they found a small but growing Armenian sector where several friends from Karakala were already living.[37]

The families from Karakala who fled Armenia in 1905 traveled across Europe to Marseilles, France and from there they boarded a ship to New York City.[38] However, according to various family members and the Ellis Island website, there is no record of any Shakarians entering Ellis Island in 1905 or even in the decade before or after this time period.[39] Perhaps the records were lost or the spelling was changed, but the family quickly headed west and finally arrived in Los Angeles in the same year.[40]

At the beginning of the twentieth century, Los Angeles was a rapidly growing metropolitan area in Southern California. Significant economic and sociological shifts were beginning to bring rapid population growth to Southern California. Los Angeles was founded as a Spanish colonial pueblo in 1781; consequently, when it became a territory of the United States after the Mexican-American War (1846–1848), it still retained a predominant Hispanic population in 1905. However, immigrants from Asia, Latin America, and Europe were rapidly filling the tenements and neighborhoods of Los Angeles and the surrounding areas.

The two largest concentrations of Armenian immigrants in Southern California lived in East Los Angeles near downtown and in Fresno, north of Los Angeles. The first Armenians to immigrate to Southern California succeeded in agriculture. With tensions escalating in Anatolia, rapid emigration from Armenia to Los Angeles resulted in the second largest Armenian diasporic community in the world.[41] When Shakarian's ancestors arrived in North America, there were already at least 25,000 Armenians living in the United States, the majority of them emigrating to various communities in Southern California.[42] The majority of these Armenian immigrants were Orthodox. A smaller percentage of Armenians, influenced by the Russian Molokans, established several small Armenian Pentecostal congregations in Southern California.[43] There were approximately four thousand Molokans living in the United States at that time, the majority of them living as neighbors with the Los Angeles Armenians.[44]

The completion of the Southern Pacific Railroad in 1876 and the discovery of oil in 1892 helped secure the economic future of Los Angeles, even though the nation was still recovering from the recession of 1890 that continued into the twentieth century. Jobs were still scarce in 1905, especially for newly arrived immigrants. The senior Demos Shakarian apparently found some intermittent work in downtown Los Angeles, but eventually found more permanent work helping to build a railroad in Nevada. It was there he tragically met his death, due to pneumonia, in the summer of 1906.[45] The senior Shakarian's premature death meant severe financial hardship for his immigrant family with six daughters and only one fourteen year old son. But Isaac Shakarian was an industrious teenager, who managed to sell newspapers, fresh produce, and finally, fresh milk from his first of many dairy cows. It was this last business venture that proved fortuitous in a burgeoning agricultural mecca and an even faster growing dairy industry. While the Shakarian family eventually prospered financially, they did not neglect their spiritual needs. Upon their arrival in California, they immediately became part of a charismatic Armenian church in Los Angeles.

The Armenian Pentecostal Church

From April 25 through April 29, 2006, thousands of Christians from around the world descended on Los Angeles to celebrate the centennial of the Azusa Street revival which has either directly or indirectly touched the lives of over 500 million Christians from all ecclesiastical branches. However, another church centennial celebration had taken place in Los Angeles on October 30, 2005, just six months earlier. Unnoticed and unrecognized by most of these Christian groups, it was attended by approximately one hundred celebrants. Yet the founding of this church, either directly or indirectly had as much impact on the later Charismatic revival as the Azusa Street Mission had on the Pentecostal movement.

Demos Shakarian, the founder of the FGBMFI, was born into this Armenian Pentecostal community and baptized in the Holy Spirit at the age of thirteen in their church on Gless Street in Los Angeles. Later, Demos Shakarian married Rose Gabrielian (1917–1996) on August 6, 1933 in that same church.[46] Ultimately, it was the pneumatic emphasis, the ecclesiastical structure, and the ecumenism of this small, seemingly insignificant congregation and the broader influence of the Church of Armenia that helped shape the hermeneutical lens through which Shakarian later founded his business men's organization.

While hundreds of books, articles, and essays have been written about the Armenian Apostolic Church for over a millennium, the First Armenian Pentecostal Church has not had a single article or book published about it in its brief one hundred year history.[47] Nevertheless, because of the significance of one of its members, Demos Shakarian, it has been briefly mentioned in two books: Shakarian's autobiography and Vinson Synan's *Under His Banner* (1992).

The Armenian Pentecostal Church in Los Angeles was established in 1905 by Armenian immigrants fleeing Ottoman persecution. They moved to Los Angeles and first met in the house of Demos Shakarian, Senior at 919 Boston Street near modern downtown Los Angeles.[48] However, they first identified themselves as *Hai Hokevore Yeghesti*, or the Armenian Spiritual Church, because of the influence of their Russian Molokan neighbors while still in Karakala.[49] Their first pastor or presiding elder was Magardich Perumean, and within a short time the church was moved to a more permanent location on Gless Street. In 1942, the church moved to Goodrich Boulevard where Ohannas Katanian (d.b.a. 1886–1952) became the presiding elder in 1948 after the death of Perumean. In 1952, Isaac Shakarian (Demos Shakarian's father) became the pastor and served until his death in 1964. David Mushakian (1916–1989) served as presiding pastor from 1964 until his death in 1989. Harding Mushegian (1921–) served as the interim pastor from 1989 until 1993.The church moved to its current location in La Habra Heights, California in 1983, where Stan Perumean (1939–2007), the cousin of Demos Shakarian and grandson of Magardich Perumean, served as the pastor from 1993 until he passed away from bone cancer in the summer of 2007.[50] Art Lalian (d.b.a. 1945–) is the current pastor of the congregation in La Habra Heights.

While its history in America is the most documented aspect of the Armenian Pentecostal Church, its origins in Armenia cannot be ignored. In Karakala, Armenia, many in the community had become Protestant as a result of early Protestant missionary endeavors in the mid to latter part of the nineteenth century. The Shakarian family itself became Presbyterian in 1875.[51] However, this Protestant phase of Christianity in Karakala was overshadowed by its greater Armenian Christian identity and its encounter with the pneumatic experiences and worship practices of Russian Molokans who came to Transcaucasia beginning in the early 1830s.[52] While they were still in Armenia, the Shakarians and some other Armenian families became part of the pneumatic Molokan Brotherhood affiliated with dozens of Russian Pryguny Molokan congregations in the Kars and Erevan regions of Anatolia. The Armenian families eventually formed an indigenous Armenian charismatic congregation in Karakala called the Spiritual Christians and affiliated with the Molokan Brotherhood.[53] After arriving in Los Angeles, they renamed their church the First Armenian Pentecostal Church shortly after the Azusa Street revival, thus identifying themselves with the burgeoning Pentecostal movement.

Until recently, the First Armenian Pentecostal Church maintained much of its traditional Armenian worship, language and Russian manner of dress. The Armenian congregation adopted the Russian Molokan manner of dress, which included white peasant shirts and long beards for the men and *kosinka* or head coverings for the women.[54] Both Armenian and Russian congregations had the women and men enter the church building through different doors and the presiding elder of the congregation seated at a rectangular table with a white tablecloth.[55] On this rectangular table was a Bible, a song book, a prayer book, and a copy of *Spirit and Life*.[56]

After the church moved to La Habra Heights, it lost much of its distinct Armenian Molokan religious culture. The noticeable Russian peasant attire was only slightly evident after the move to La Habra Heights in 1983, and is currently no longer worn.[57] Until 1985, the men and women of the congregation entered the building through different doorways.[58] Today, men and women enter the building from the same entrance. The congregation also changed its name from First Armenian Pentecostal Church to Hillside Pentecostal Church to offer a more inclusive invitation to its non-Armenian neighbors. Now most visitors would not immediately recognize this congregation's Armenian heritage. Unless someone happened to visit on one of the significant feast days in the church's tradition, an observer would not notice anything unique about the congregational observances, style of worship, style of dress, or language.[59]

Currently, the podium or lectern is stationed off-center on the left hand front side of church, a reminder of the building's previous Lutheran worshippers.[60] However, the Lutheran reverence towards the Eucharist did not transfer to these Armenians, who partake in communion only once a year.[61] While the congregation today largely consists of descendants from Karakala, Armenia, including many of Demos Shakarian's relatives, the church is open and welcoming to anyone.[62] Currently, the worship at Hillside Pentecostal Church is consistent with many traditional Pentecostal church practices such as some congregation members lifting their hands toward heaven, the occasional charismata expressed during worship services, and the yearning for a new and fresh Pentecost to occur in their congregation. Average attendance at the church on Sunday mornings approaches one hundred participants.[63] Often there is a prayer for healing at the end of the service, reflective of both their ancient charismatic heritage and their more current Pentecostal influence. Many of the sermons proclaim holiness themes that may be influenced as much by modern holiness groups in Los Angeles as older holiness groups including the Russian Subbotniks and Molokans.

While Hillside Pentecostal Church has changed significantly since its inception in Los Angeles in 1905, it retained some of its early Armenian culture and heritage. Until twenty years ago, all the services including the hymns were in Armenian. An Armenian hymnbook is still available in the pews.[64] Occasionally, the church opens its worship service by singing an Armenian hymn. However, the one unique tradition they have consistently honored throughout their century of existence is the celebration of the five major feast days included in the church calendar.[65] The church honors several of the most important Jewish feast days mentioned in the Pentateuch, a legacy of the influence passed onto them by their Russian Molokan neighbors.[66] While this little church still offers unique glimpses into its Armenian origins from a century earlier, another revival, this one in California, influenced the Armenian church's beliefs and practices almost from the beginning of its American introduction.

Russians and Armenians at Azusa Street

Toward the end of Shakarian's account of his grandfather, he wrote,

> Grandfather and his brother-in-law, Magardich Mushegan...were walking down San Pedro Street in Los Angeles, looking for work in the livery stables. As they passed a side road called Azusa Street they stopped short. Along with the smell of horses and harness leather came the unmistakable sounds of people praising God in tongues...The door was flung open. There were embraces, hands lifted to God in thanksgiving, singing, and praising the Lord, and Grandfather and Magardich returned to Boston Street with the news that Pentecost had come even to this distant land across the sea.[67]

Grandfather Shakarian was able to offer a first hand account of his visit to Azusa Street and declared the remarkable similarities between his own experiences in Armenia and what was emerging in Los Angeles. As Demos Shakarian's grandfather and Magardich Mushegan (d.b.a. 1870–d.d.a. 1940) left Azusa Street, they rushed back home to Boston Street and declared, "Come on, we found a place where they worship in the church like we do."[68] "They began attending the old Azusa Street Mission...As the Americans were shouting the praises of God for the outpouring, the Armenians were able to say, 'This is that which God gave to us in Armenia many years ago.'"[69]

Other sources verify that there were Armenians present at the Azusa Street Mission as the Pentecostal revival began to spread. R.J. Scott (d.b.a. 1870–d.d.a. 1930) recorded in *The Apostolic Faith* newspaper that during a time when he attended an Azusa Street meeting, a young lady began to sing a familiar Indian song that no one had taught her and then she,

> changed into another unknown tongue, which afterwards proved to be the Armenian language. After speaking for a few moments in this tongue, she drew my attention by signs, as her English was gone, to an Armenian man near by who was greatly interested in what she was saying. He replied, "I no speak your tongue, but that lady speak my tongue and talk to me about Jesus." The perspiration broke out upon the man like beads, and he commenced to tremble; and this was the means of his conversion.[70]

Another citation from that same newspaper recorded that "Russians and Armenians in Los Angeles are seeking the baptism. The Armenians have a Pentecostal cottage meeting on Victor Street, between 4th and 5th. Some have been baptized with the Holy Ghost."[71] It does not appear that this was the same congregation that the Shakarian family attended since their house church was on Boston Street but it does demonstrate that the events at Azusa Street were spreading rapidly into the Armenian sector of Los Angeles.[72]

Another interesting source is from the *Los Angeles Times* which compared a group of Priguny Russian immigrants in Los Angeles to the Azusa Street Mission after observing a worship service among the Priguny and stating that "before the meeting closed the picturesque 'Priguni' outrivaled the wildest orgies of the Azusa Street revelers."[73] Interestingly, Lilian Solokoff (1899–1974) indicated there were 3,300 Russians living in Los Angeles in 1905, 3,100 of whom were Molokan Christians.[74] The article further described the services as "unbridled, and with nothing to check its madness, religious fanaticism has broken loose in the Russian colony, and is running wild among the simple Caucasians...in which about two hundred of 'Priguni' (Russian 'Holy Jumpers') are engaged."[75]

The *Los Angeles Times* article further described the service by stating how "women and men danced themselves into exhaustion, rolled upon the floor in agonies of supplication, or stood with hands upraised to heaven."[76] While there is no mention of glossolalia as in the original article on Azusa Street in the *Los Angeles Times*, there were similar descriptions of their worship as "fanatical rites" and asserted that at their worship at Azusa Street "pandemonium breaks loose, and the bounds of reason are passed by those who are 'filled with the spirit'".[77] In addition, another early description of the Azusa Street revival in the *Los Angeles Times* described the worshippers as "holy jumpers" who "rolled and jumped about, screeching at the top of their voices,"[78] While it is true the *Los Angeles Times* mistakenly compared the Azusa Street revival with other groups such as "labor-union anarchists...Socialists"[79] and "murderers"[80] in an obvious attempt to disparage the revival, there seemed to be no attempt to discredit either the Russian Molokans or the Azusa Street congregation by associating them with one another.

These other sources indicated that there was an Armenian and a Russian presence at the Azusa Street Mission. These individuals were greatly influenced by this Pentecostal renewal and they began to spread the Pentecostal message within their respective ethnic communities. Even Demos Shakarian admits that after his grandfather and Magardich Mushegan came back to the Armenian community with the report of Azusa Street, "they all started going there."[81] There is no doubt that the Azusa Street Mission had a remarkable influence on the Armenian Pentecostal Church. Demos Shakarian stated that his church received much of their classical Pentecostal influence from Azusa Street.[82] However, he still insisted there were already charismatic and Pentecostal or pre-Pentecostal influences which had come from Armenia and Russia instilled in the church they started on Boston Street. Therefore, they could honestly say "they worship... [at Azusa Street]...like we do."[83] In fact, the Armenian Pentecostal Church they started in Los Angeles was merely a continuation of a church that had simply transferred "from the old country"[84]

The Pneumatology, Ecclesiology, and Ecumenism of the Armenian Pentecostal Church

Exactly what this church retained "from the old country" is significant in shaping the hermeneutical lens of Demos Shakarian. The influence of the Russian Molokan Brotherhood and the ecstatic worship of the Priguny Molokans have already been discussed at some length in Chapter Two. However, to this point, exploring the influence of Armenian Christianity upon Demos Shakarian and the Armenian Pentecostal Church has not been addressed adequately.

Armenian Christianity historically belongs to the larger Eastern branch of Christianity, and as such, has historically been among the most pneumatological segments of Christianity. Recent Pentecostal scholars have argued that this is theologically due to their balanced trinitarianism and their historical rejection of the filioque clause.[85] However, it is just as likely due to their historical mysticism, emphasizing an experiential union with God, most eloquently stated by the Cappadocian fathers and more recently stressed by Symeon the New Theologian in his exhortation to be baptized in the Holy Spirit.[86]

In Armenian theology, the *Catechism* of Gregory the Illuminator establishes both Armenian trinitarianism and pneumatology from the very inception of established Christianity in Armenia. The concept of a "consubstantial hypostasis of the Trinity" establishes a fervent trinitarianism in the Armenian Church long before the filioque clause minimized the role of the Spirit in the Western church.[87] In addition, the pneumatological emphasis of the *Catechism* is reflected in its frequent mention of the Spirit's empowerment, charismata, and glossolalia.[88] Grigor Narekatsi (951–1003 C.E.) and Nerses Snor'hali also offer excellent examples of medieval Armenian pneumatology.[89] In reading Snor'hali's exhortation to be renewed in the Spirit by seeking "baptism anew, as well as gifts of grace and Pentecostal Fire,"[90] the modern reader wonders if he has been reading from *The Pentecostal Evangel,* while Nerses himself may have been reading from Symeon's *Discourses.* In other words, the pneumatic nature of Armenian Christianity was already part of the Shakarian family even before they encountered the Russian Molokans in the nineteenth century.

Chapter Two discussed the egalitarian nature of Armenian Christianity and the Eastern concept concerning the prophethood of all believers. However, how Armenian ecclesiology may have influenced the First Armenian Pentecostal Church that Shakarian's grandfather helped establish in Los Angeles has not been examined.[91] Currently, in the congregation at La Habra Heights, the church administration is overseen by a board of elders who are all laymen. While this is not unusual in many Protestant ecclesiastical structures, the pastor of this particular Armenian Pentecostal church has not received a salary in the history of the church. When asked why this was, Pastor Perumean responded by saying, "that is the tradition of our church."[92] It can just as easily be surmised, or at least hypothesized, that this tradition has been handed down from their ancestor's background in an Armenian Orthodox culture immersed in a lay-led ecclesiastical structure. To reinforce this hypothesis, it should be mentioned that no Armenian Orthodox married priest receives a salary from his local parish; however, he may occasionally receive voluntary gifts from his flock.[93]

Significantly, Demos Shakarian modeled that philosophy as he led the FGBMFI for over forty years without ever receiving a salary from them.[94] As a result, the FGBMFI was led and driven by business men, not by pastors or professional ministers. In fact, ministers were not even allowed to become chapter presidents or executive members of the FGBMFI.[95] Thus, visitors to the FGBMFI meetings did not need to feel threatened by the ecclesiastical hierarchy of other denominations.

Just as the ecumenism of Armenian Christianity was often shaped by the geopolitical forces that surrounded its history, the Armenian Diaspora from Karakala that came to Los Angeles and formed a congregation faced some similar choices.[96] They could have isolated themselves from the variety of Christian congregations around them in order to preserve their culture, their distinctive beliefs, and their heritage. Interestingly, that is exactly what the Russian Priguny Molokans who traveled with them to Los Angeles chose to do.[97] These Armenian Pentecostal Christians could have immersed themselves into the variegated Christian groups in surrounding Los Angeles and abandoned their own cultural and doxological distinctives, and to a small extent they did, simply by calling themselves Pentecostal. However, their own identification with Pentecostalism is merely the recognition that what happened at Azusa Street and what happened among their own Armenian ancestors decades earlier in Karakala was brought about by the same Spirit of God. Instead of immersing themselves or isolating themselves, they chose a path similar to their Armenian Apostolic brethren. They considered themselves as autonomous, but equal members of the greater body of

Christ.[98] As such, Demos Shakarian was raised in a church which was not part of a denomination but rather an independent Pentecostal church. Demos Shakarian himself admitted that "if I had been involved in an organization, I couldn't have done what I did, Full Gospel Business Men."[99] In addition, the FGBMFI could not have made the impact it did across all ecclesiastical boundaries without the ecumenical understanding of its founder, an understanding forged through centuries of dialogue from Nerses until now.

Isaac Shakarian in Los Angeles

Isaac Shakarian found a job selling newspapers in downtown Los Angeles shortly after his family arrived in the city. Jobs like this to help supplement the family income were common for older boys in the Armenian and Russian Molokan communities. Isaac Shakarian added at least ten dollars every month to the household coffers.[100] One story Demos Shakarian recollected emphasized his father's integrity. Isaac was mistakenly given a five dollar gold coin instead of a five cent piece as payment for selling a newspaper to a business man in downtown Los Angeles.[101] Realizing the error, Isaac boarded one of the new electric trolleys in Los Angeles to pursue the man and returned the gold coin without any compensation or apparent gratitude from the gentleman in question. Occasionally, as on April 19, 1906, the day after the tragic San Francisco earthquake, the *Los Angeles Times* provided a feature edition that enabled Isaac Shakarian to sell more newspapers than usual. That day he garnered the significant sum of sixty dollars; while the boy's income was helpful, Isaac's father, Demos, still provided the primary household income with his weekly postal money orders sent from his railroad job in Nevada.[102] However, the economic impact of his father's early demise forced Isaac to find income beyond what he could earn selling newspapers in Los Angeles.

After the tragic death of Grandfather Demos in 1906, Isaac Shakarian was left to support his younger sister and mother by himself.[103] He started doing some intermittent jobs, but he eventually went to work in a harness factory and was able to supply the family with a monthly income of fifteen dollars.[104] The work confined Isaac Shakarian to the factory and may have prevented him from celebrating some of the feast days or other religious observances that the Armenians and Russian Molokans observed. John Berokoff suggests that many of the Russian Molokan men, who worked in various factories or other jobs in Los Angeles, chose to quit their jobs rather than miss the religious feast days, funerals, and other religious observances of the Molokan Brotherhood.[105] There is no record of Isaac Shakarian making such a choice as he stayed employed at the harness factory for three years.

Nevertheless, with the *Hai Hokevore Yeghesti* still meeting in the Shakarian home at 919 Boston Street in Los Angeles in 1906, Demos Shakarian's father, Isaac, was assured frequent, and possibly daily, interaction and exposure to the Armenian Molokan community.[106] The congregational move to Gless Street in the same year may have removed some of this regular religious influence on Isaac Shakarian. Nevertheless, the Armenian Spiritual Church and the Russian Molokan Brotherhood retained a significant amount of influence upon its constituents and remained a close community to preserve its cultural and religious identity.[107]

After working in the factory for two years, Isaac Shakarian began to develop a chronic cough likely produced from the dust that collected in the harness factory building.[108] Demos Shakarian recalled that his father's cough grew worse and was eventually diagnosed as tuberculosis.[109] Isaac's mother tried to help financially and offered laundry service to a family in Hollenbeck Park.[110] This act was not unusual since other Armenian Molokan and Russian Molokan wives had been doing laundry service to provide steady income when Molokan men were unemployed or underemployed.[111] However, due to the cultural restraints of Isaac Shakarian's Armenian background, Isaac insisted on being the sole bread winner for the family.[112]

With the family's economic survival in question, and Isaac Shakarian's health rapidly deteriorating, the future looked bleak for the Shakarian household. Even though Isaac had now been made a foreman at the harness factory, he made a decision that would prove fortuitous. Partly for health reasons and partly because of another prophetic word, he determined to leave his meager salary in the harness factory and start a small produce business.[113] In 1910, at the age of nineteen, he took some of the money he had been saving for his younger sister's dowry and purchased a two-year old horse that he named Jack and a flatbed wagon which he used to haul fresh produce.[114]

The produce business that Isaac Shakarian established quickly flourished and he began considering the possibility of buying land and raising dairy cattle. He also began deliberating the possibility of marriage and considered a young fifteen year old Armenian girl named Zaroohi Yessayian as a potential spouse.[115] However, the custom of these Armenian Molokans, adopted from their Russian counterparts, would not allow the two of them to speak to each other until the two families had agreed upon marriage.[116] The marriage was arranged between Zaroohi's parents and an elder at the Armenian Pentecostal Church since Isaac's father was deceased.[117]

Demos Shakarian does not give a description of his father's wedding, but John Berokoff gives a description of a typical Molokan wedding in Los Angeles in 1912 which was likely similar, if not identical, to the cultural and religious dictates of the Shakarian-Yessayian wedding that same year.[118] The wedding involved a lengthy procession from the groom's house on Boston Street to the bride's house on Gless Street where part of the ceremony was performed. Then a long processional march brought the wedding party back to the groom's house where the rest of the ceremony was completed.[119] After the wedding ceremony, the bride and groom typically enjoyed a wedding meal with their close friends while a larger contingent of family, relatives, and church members gathered in a separate tent or building to eat a similar meal.[120]

In 1912, shortly after the Shakarian wedding, Isaac purchased three dairy cows and acquired fourteen acres of property in Downey, California on South Cerritos Avenue.[121] Together, Isaac and Zaroohi began to build a small, rustic home using one by twelve wooden planks.[122] Within a decade, Isaac Shakarian began to multiply his small herd of dairy cattle into a burgeoning dairy business that would eventually rival or exceed some of the largest dairy herds in the world.

Conclusion

The words of a prophet, Efim Klubnikin, brought the Shakarian family and quite a number of other Russian and Armenian Molokan families from the Kars region of Armenia to Los Angeles in 1905. There the Shakarian family encountered some loss and hardship, but they entered a city full of opportunity. In addition, while the Shakarian family struggled to survive with economic and physical hardships, they found solace in the newly formed pneumatic Armenian Molokan community. In April 1906, this same community identified with and flourished in the midst of a religious revival ten city blocks away. Demos Shakarian grew up in the midst of this religious community and in the shadow of a pneumatic renewal. The Armenian Pentecostal Church adopted much of the distinctive North American Pentecostal characteristics, while retaining many of the religious practices brought from Armenia. This background served Demos Shakarian well in helping to lead a Charismatic movement that emphasized ecumenism, a lay ecclesiastical organization, and charismatic praxis, and pneumatology.

Demos Shakarian's father helped provide financial security for his family and he instilled a strong work ethic in his son. In the midst of financial and physical crisis, Isaac Shakarian worked for three years in a harness factory to the detriment of his own health and retained steady employment, perhaps sacrificing some of the obligations he had towards the religious community to which he belonged. It is possible this was simply an economic choice that overruled his religious convictions, since he felt obligated to support his mother and sister, but perhaps he did not share the dichotomous beliefs of his Molokan brothers, who opted for the celebration of religious festivals over steady employment, or the choice of secular citizens of Los Angeles who ignored or overlooked any religious obligations for the sake of economic gain. It is possible Isaac Shakarian chose to honor all of these obligations by providing for his family and supporting the efforts of his religious community. As such, business and religion were not compartmentalized into two categories. They were likely integrated into the ethos that Isaac Shakarian passed onto another generation.

As Isaac and Zaroohi commenced building their wood plank home in Downey, California, they also started building a small dairy business. Soon they would begin a new family. Before long, Zaroohi became pregnant with their first child. Before they completed their simple house, Zaroohi gave birth to their first born son who they named Demos Shakarian after his grandfather.[123]

Notes

1. Berokoff, *Molokans in America* (1987), 15.

2. Berokoff, *Molokans in America* (1987), 16; also see the prophecy that Efim Klubnikin gave about moving to Kars in *Spirit and Life* (1983), Article 4:1, 637.

3. The best source for Seraphim's apocalyptic prophecy is given in Moore's biography on the Russian saint and prophet. Other sources for prophecy, and specifically apocalyptic prophecy, can be found in David Aune's seminal work *Prophecy in Early Christianity and the Ancient Mediterranean World* (Grand Rapids, MI: William B. Eerdmans Publishing Company, 1983). Other sources could include Cecil M. Robeck's *Prophecy in Carthage: Perpetua, Tertullian, and Cyprian* (Cleveland, OH: Pilgrim Press, 1992) in which Robeck gives an excellent explanation of early apocalyptic prophecy and prophetic visions delivered in third century North Africa. An excellent anthology of the primary sources for these apocalyptic visions and prophecies are given in Shawn Madigan's, ed., *Mystics, Visionaries, and Prophets: A Historical Anthology of Women's Spiritual Writings* (Minneapolis: Fortress Press, 1998).

4. For examples, see some of Klubnikin's apocalyptic prophecies in *Spirit and Life* (1983), 674–678; or a small portion of Maxim Rudometkin's prophecies in *Spirit and Life* (1983), 504–515.

5. Demos Shakarian, *The Happiest People* (1975), 19–20. The written record does not describe whether Klubnikin merely transcribed divine words or whether he was supernaturally given the ability to write out the prophecies. However, it is not clear whether there were any eyewitnesses to his written oracles, or if any of his original scrolls remain in existence, except for a secret scroll which remains in the hands of his ancestors in Los Angeles and has never been opened (see Demos Shakarian, *The Happiest People* [1975], 33; and the Tallman-Sobolew interview, January 15, 2008 in Los Angeles, California).

6. Efim Klubnikin, *Spirit and Life* (1983), Article 1:4, 636. As already mentioned, Russian society, and Molokan religion in particular, was well acquainted with the pneumatic nature of this type of prophetic oracle. As such, it was not unusual for some Russian communities, especially one which had already experienced a significant pneumatic revival to heed a prophetic warning, especially one written by an illiterate boy.

7. Demos Shakarian, *The Happiest People* (1975), 20. This prophecy, a sealed scroll, is still held in a safety deposit box somewhere in Southern California and is safeguarded by the descendants of Efim Klubnikin.

8. Ibid, 21.

9. Nickel, "The Amazing Shakarian Story," *Voice*, October 1953, 12.

10. The book *Spirit and Life* (1983), actually does not mention specifically where they would settle. However Efim prophesied, "Those that believe in this will go on a journey to a far land, while the unbelievers will remain in place. When these scenes are completed, then our people will go on a long journey over the great and deep waters...People from all countries will go there...There will be a great war; all kings will shed blood like rivers. Two steamships will leave to cross the impassable ocean." *Spirit and Life* Article 5:6–12, 638–639. The Molokan community later interpreted this prophecy as referring to their Diaspora as they crossed the Atlantic Ocean. In one of Shakarian's earliest written recollections of this story, he does mention that the prophecy only mentions they were to flee "to a land across the ocean" but additional charts and pictures they received from Klubnikin allowed them to conclude that he was referring to the United States (Thomas R. Nickel, "The Amazing Shakarian Story," *Voice* October 1953, 3). In addition, while the historical record of Klubnikin's written prophecies claims to have been written in 1855,

the actual collection of his prophecies collected in *Book of the Sun* was compiled and translated into English in 1983 from a Russian revised edition written in 1928. The original Russian collection of Molokan prophecies, which includes the prophecies of David Yesseyevich, Lukian Sokolov, Maxim Rudometkin, and Efim Klubnikin, were first published in 1915 from handwritten manuscripts of the founding prophets of the Molokan Brotherhood. However, as additional material became available to the Los Angeles Russian Diaspora, in particular, considerable supplemental material regarding the prophecies and diagrams of Efim Klubnikin, a revised edition was deemed necessary and produced in 1928 (see *Spirit and Life* [1983], 3–5).

11. Berokoff, *Molokans in America* (1987), 16–18. The Molokans were strict pacifists and the Russian government had given them a reprieve from military duty from 1840 until 1890 with an additional ten year extension, but in 1900, the tsar was going to require their young men to serve in compulsory military service.

12. Ibid, 19.

13. Demos Shakarian, *The Happiest People* (1975), 19–21.

14. Ibid, 19–20.

15. Shubin, ed., *Spirit and Life* (1983), 749.

16. Berokoff, *Molokans in America* (1987), 18–19.

17. Berokoff, *Molokans in America* (1987), 21; Bivin, "The Armenians of Karakala," (n.d.), 25; and Manya Rudometkin Kobzeff, "Flight from Russia," *Besednyik* 4.4 (December, 1991): 6.

18. Berokoff, *Molokans in America* (1987), 22.

19. See Maxim Rudometkin's prophecy in *Spirit and Life* (1983), Book 14, Article 30, 631.

20. Berokoff, *Molokans in America* (1987), 23 and Bivin, "The Armenians of Karakala," (n.d.), 26.

21. Kobzeff, "Flight from Russia," (December, 1991): 11.

22. Berokoff, *Molokans in America* (1987), 23.

23. Ibid, 24 and 30.

24. Demos Shakarian, *The Happiest People* (1975), 22; see also Demos Shakarian, "God's Dairyman," in *God's Formula for Success and Prosperity* (Tulsa, OK: Oral Roberts, 1956), 42,

25. Geraldine Scalf-Tallman interview, January 12, 2008.

26. Bivin, "The Armenians of Karakala," (n.d.), 9.

27. Demos Shakarian, *The Happiest People* (1975), 22; and Berokoff, *Molokans in America* (1987), 24–30.

28. Mark Chakarian, interview by Matthew Tallman, Garden Grove, CA, January 8, 2005. John Berokoff mentions that there was a conference held in the Kars region of Armenia in 1904 to decide what to do about Efim's urgent prophecy. They had already sent a few Molokans ahead to the United States and Canada, and the Agalstoff brothers had returned to Kars, reporting of a prosperous opportunity in Southern California, where they secured work laying track for the Pacific Electric Railroad Company. Representatives from nine Russian Molokan communities and one representative from the Armenian Molokan community of Karakala, Ardzuman Ohanessian, were present at this meeting, and they decided to move to Los Angeles through various means from 1905–1912 (Berokoff, *Molokans in America* [1987], 20–24).

29. A.E. Redgate, *The Armenians* (Malden, Massachusetts: Blackwell Publishers, 1998), 270–271.

30. Demos Shakarian, *The Happiest People* (1975), 21–22.

31. To this day, the Turkish government largely ignores the facts of this genocide, instead claiming the atrocities against Armenians as a work of fiction. It has also created tension in American-Turkish relations as recently as November 2007, when the United States Congress proposed a resolution condemning the genocide. In addition, the European Union has presented Turkey's acknowledgment of this genocide as a requirement for entry into the Union, but this obstacle is still in deliberation. For a more thorough treatment of the history of the genocide, and the current but mystifying obstacles for internationally recognizing this tragedy, consult Peter Balakian's *The Burning Tigris: The Armenian Genocide and America's Response* (New York: Harper Collins, 2003).

32. Joyce Keosababian Bivin's unpublished article, "The Armenians of Karakala and Their Relationship with Russian Molokans: 1870–1920," (n.d.) probably offers the best research available on the fate of Karakala by suggesting that it was in the Kars region, but probably vanished in the aftermath of the genocide.

33. Demos Shakarian, *The Happiest People on Earth* (1975), 20.

34. Demos Shakarian, *The Happiest People on Earth* (1975), 20. Actually, the words that Klubnikin used in his prophecy are translated as "There is much land there, and there are people. And it is the land of the living." (*Spirit and Truth* Article, [1983], 5:14, 639). In addition, the diagram that Klubnikin drew vaguely resembles the East Coast of the United States. Interestingly, there is a diagram on the preceding page that also has a figurehead resembling the statue of liberty, but neither these diagrams, nor the written prophesies of Klubnikin ever mentioned the United States. (See "The Plans of E.G. Klubnikin," in *Spirit and Life*, [1983], 696–697). The Molokans that followed him to America only interpreted them that way after they came to the United States.

35. Shakarian, *The Happiest People* (1975), 21.

36. Ibid.

37. Ibid, 22.

38. Darlene Janoian, interview by Matthew Tallman, La Habra Heights, CA, January 13, 2008. Geraldine Shakarian Scalf, in the author's interview with her on January 12, 2008, recalls that her grandfather and father recalled that eleven other families left with the Shakarians from Karakala in 1905.

39. In every interview the author has had with Shakarian family members, they recall that the family went through Ellis Island in 1905, but even family members have tried to track down their immigration records at Ellis Island without success. One alternative suggestion made by Harding Mushegian in an interview with him on January 14, 2008, was that they came through Mexico. He recalls that his mother tried to go through Ellis Island but they were returned to France where they boarded another ship to Mexico and came illegally across the Mexican border. John Berokoff's account of the various groups of Molokans that came to Los Angeles confirms this possibility including a few other possibilities of sailing to Panama, and then taking a steam ship up to the West Coast of the United States. (Berokoff, *Molokans in America*, [1987], 23–31).

40. At least thirty different spelling variations were attempted by the author in trying to find any Shakarians who emigrated from Armenia from 1900 to 1910, but no matches were found.

41. Redgate, *The Armenians* (1998), 271; see also Nicole Vartanian, "A Fruitful Legacy," n.p., cited December 29, 2007, online http://www.armeniapedia.org/index/diaspora/usa.

42. Redgate, *The Armenians* (1998), 270–271.

43. Berokoff, *Molokans in America* (1987), 13.

44. Ibid, 67.

45. No exact date for his death has been recorded. The tombstone of Grandfather Shakarian in the old Molokan cemetery only records the fact that he died but leaves no date. In the early part of Russian and Armenian Molokan history in Los Angeles, the community did not bother registering births or deaths with the county (see Berokoff, *Molokans in America* [1987], 45–50). While Shakarian's autobiography seems to imply that his grandfather expired as a result of a heat stroke (see Demos Shakarian, *The Happiest People* [1975], 25), in an oral interview with Vinson Synan, Shakarian stated that his grandfather died of pneumonia (Demos Shakarian-Synan interview, October 5, 1987, 2).

46. Demos Shakarian, *The Happiest People* (1975), 31–47; and Demos Shakarian, "God's Dairyman," (1956), 43–46.

47. For a current overview of Armenian history see, A.E. Redgate, *The Armenians* (Malden, MA: Blackwell Publishers, 1998). Some primary sources available on the Armenian Apostolic Church include Moushegh Mardirossian, *The Armenian Church: Celebrating Seventeen Hundred Years* (Los Angeles, CA: Western Prelacy of the Armenian Apostolic Church of America, 2000); and Malachia Ormanian, *The Church of Armenia*, 2nd edition (London: A.B. Mowbray, 1955); also see Shahan Sarkissian, "Ecumenism in the Armenian Catholicosate of Cilicia," *Ministerial Formation* (October, 2000): 7–9; and for a brief summary of the Armenian church see Stanley M. Burgess, *The Holy Spirit: Eastern Christian Traditions* (Peabody, MA: Hendrickson Publishers, 1989) 111–136.

48. Thomas Nickel, "The True Azusa Street Story," *Voice* July 1956, 5.

49. Bivin, "The Armenians of Karakala," (n.d.), 13.

50. This information was gathered from a DVD produced by the church for its centennial celebration, *God at Our Side: 100 Years*, DVD, produced by Jeff Jonoian and Mark Perumean, La Habra Heights, California: First Armenian Pentecostal Church, 2005. In addition, a phone interview with Stan Perumean's widow on November 11, 2007, offered additional information.

51. Synan, *Under His* Banner (1992), 20; see also Demos Shakarian, *The Happiest People* (1975), 14.

52. Nicholas Breyfogle, "Heretics and Colonizers: Religious Dissent and Russian Colonization of Transcaucasia," Ph.D. diss., The University of Pennsylvania, 1998, 1.

53. Berokoff, *Molokans in America* (1987), 23; and Bivin, "The Armenians of Karakala," (n.d.), 8–10.

54. Bivin, "The Armenians of Karakala," (n.d.), 16; and Berokoff, *Molokans in America* (1987), 7.

55. Bivin, "The Armenians of Karakala," (n.d.), 14; and Stan Perumean-Tallman interview, March 26, 2006.

56. Bivin, "The Armenians of Karakala," (n.d.) 14. The copy of *Spirit and Life* was removed from the Armenian Pentecostal Church at some point after immigrating to Los Angeles.

57. See Jeff Janoian, *God at our Side*, DVD (2005); and Bivin, "The Armenians of Karakala," (n.d.), 13.

58. Stan Perumean-Tallman interview, March 26, 2006.

59. Under the leadership of the current pastor, Art Lalian, the congregation has made a conscious effort to sing at least one Armenian hymn in weekly worship services. A remaining reflection of their Russian Molokan influence includes the celebration of certain Jewish holidays including Passover, Pentecost, the Feast of Trumpets, the Day of Atonement, and the Feast of Tabernacles (see Bivin, "The Armenians of Karakala," [n.d.], 12).

60. Stan Perumean-Tallman interview, March 26, 2006.

61. Ibid.

62. This is a unique contrast that they did not inherit from their Russian Molokan neighbors who generally have remained isolated, and most of their congregations in Los Angeles are closed to outsiders to this day.

63. Stan Perumean-Tallman interview, March 26, 2006.

64. Ibid.

65. As mentioned earlier, these five feast days included Passover, Pentecost, the Feast of Trumpets, the Day of Atonement, and the Feast of Tabernacles (see Bivin, "The Armenians of Karakala," [n.d.], 12). However, the Russian Molokan and Armenian congregations interpret the meaning of these feasts from a Christian context in contrast to Jewish religious beliefs (see Berokoff, *Molokans in America* [1987], 207–208).

66. Stan Perumean-Tallman interview, March 26, 2006. Recently, under the leadership of their new pastor, Art Lalian, they have regularly opened their worship services with an Armenian hymn.

67. Shakarian, *The Happiest People on Earth* (1975), 24.

68. Demos Shakarian-Synan interview, October 5, 1987, 4.

69. Thomas Nickel, "The Amazing Shakarian Story: Part Two," *Voice*, November 1953, 6.

70. Fred T. Corum, *Like as of Fire*, a reprint of *The Apostolic Faith* from September 1906 to May 1908, (Wilmington, Massachusetts: Fred T. Corum, 1981), February–March 1907, 7.

71. Corum, *Like as of* Fire (1983), April, 1907, 2.

72. Actually, at some point shortly after the Armenian Molokans arrived in Los Angeles, they quickly divided into at least three separate Armenian Pentecostal Churches including the one on Victor Street, one on Pecan Street, and the one that met at the Shakarian house on Boston Street. However, these were all started as house churches that expanded as their numbers grew. (Interview with Harding Mushegian, January 14, 2008; also see Bivin, "The Armenians of Karakala [n.d.], 26).

73. "Death Dance of 'Priguni,'" *Los Angeles Times*, October 9, 1906, 17.

74. Lillian Solokoff, "The Russians in Los Angeles," *Studies in Sociology* (March 1918): 1.

75. Ibid.

76. "Death Dance," *Los Angeles Times*, October 9, 1906, 17.

77. "Weird Babel of Tongues," *Los Angeles Times*, April 18, 1906, III.

78. "Rolling and Diving Fanatics 'Confess,'" *Los Angeles Times*, June 23, 1906, 17.

79. "Police Asked to Raid Reds," *Los Angeles Times*, August 6, 1906, III.

80. "Find Hut but No Cook," *Los Angeles Times*, September 5, 1906, II3.

81. Demos Shakarian-Synan interview, October 5, 1987, 9.

82. Ibid, 9.

83. Ibid, 4.

84. Ibid, 9.

85. See for example, Edmund J. Rybarczyk's *Beyond Salvation: Eastern Orthodoxy and Classical Pentecostalism on Becoming like Christ,* (London: Paternoster, 2004), 5; or Burgess, *The Holy Spirit: Eastern Christian Traditions* (1989), 1–2.

86. C.J DeCatanzaro., ed., Symeon *the New Theologian: The Discourses* (New York: Paulist Press, 1980), 312–313, 342. Since these were Byzantine scholars, it is uncertain that Armenian pneumatology was directly influenced by their writings; however, as mentioned earlier, Seraphim of Sarov was influenced by Symeon the New Theologian and his

charismatic ministry may have had some impact upon Russian Molokan praxis and theology (and consequently, had some later influence upon Armenian pneumatology, at least the Armenians of Karakala).

87. Robert W. Thomson, ed., *The Teaching of Saint Gregory: An Early Armenian Catechism,* translation and commentary by Robert W. Thomson (Cambridge, Massachusetts: Harvard University Press, 1970), paragraph 420.

88. Thomson, *Saint Gregory* (1970), paragraphs 614, 629, 632, 640, 661, 663, 674, 675, 681, 682, 683, 685, and 694 are samples but certainly not a comprehensive list of early Armenian pneumatology.

89. See Stanley M. Burgess, *The Holy Spirit: Eastern Christian Traditions* (Peabody, Massachusetts: Hendrickson Publishers, 1989), 126–136.

90. Jane S. Wingate, ed., *Jesus the Son, Only-Begotten of the Father: A Prayer by Nerses the Grace-Filled, Armenian Catholicos* (New York: Delphic Press, 1947), 50, quoted in Stan Burgess' *The Holy Spirit: Eastern Christian Traditions* (1989), 133.

91. See Burgess, "The Implications of Eastern Christian Pneumatology," (1991), 26; and Malachia Ormanian, *The Church of Armenia* (1955), 133.

92. Stan Perumean-Tallman interview, March 26, 2006.

93. Ormanian, *The Church of Armenia* (1955), 131.

94. Demos Shakarian-Synan interview, October 5, 1987, 5.

95. Vinson Synan, *Under His Banner* (1992), 47. Ironically, it was Oral Roberts who made this suggestion, actually encouraging the organization not to allow ministers even as members.

96. As mentioned in Chapter Two, for a further discussion of the historical ecumenism of Armenian Christian and the geo-political forces that may have shaped that ecumenism see Charles A. Frazee, "The Christian Church in Cilician Armenia," *Church History* (June, 1976): 166–184; or Carnegie Calian, "The Armenian Church and Ecumenism," *Christian Century* (August 1964): 1007–1008.

97. Paul Sobolew-Tallman interview, March 26, 2006, La Habra Heights, California. According to the author's conversation with Sobolew, many of the Priguny Molokans still choose to isolate themselves from other Christian groups culturally and linguistically, and do not welcome outsiders into their services or regard other Christian groups as part of their concept of Christianity.

98. Stan Perumean-Tallman interview, March 26, 2006. They still are considered an independent church without any formal ties to any larger ecclesiastical council or denomination.

99. Demos Shakarian-Synan interview, October 5, 1987, 5.

100. Demos Shakarian, *The Happiest People* (1975), 25; and Berokoff, *Molokans in America* (1987), 36.

101. Demos Shakarian, *The Happiest People* (1975), 25.

102. Demos Shakarian, *The Happiest People* (1975), 25; also Ed Ainsworth, "A Lot of Faith: A Lot of Cows," *Los Angeles Times,* May 8, 1960, 119.

103. Darlene Janoian, interview with Matthew Tallman, La Habra Heights, CA, January 13, 2008. *The Happiest People* (1975), records that Isaac was supporting all six of his sisters (25), but in fact, at the time that Demos Shakarian, Sr. died, the five oldest sisters were already married and being supported by their own families.

104. Demos Shakarian, *The Happiest People* (1975), 26. There is some discrepancy as to when he started working at the harness factory. Shakarian's autobiography implies that he might have gone to work at the factory when he was fourteen (Shakarian, *The Happiest People* [1975], 25–26), but other accounts state that he started working there at the age of

sixteen (Demos Shakarian, "God's Dairyman," [1956], 43; and Thomas Nickel, "The Amazing Shakarian Story: Part Two," *Voice*, November 1953, 6).

105. Berokoff, *Molokans in America* (1987), 7.

106. Bivin, "The Armenians of Karakala" (n.d.), 26 suggests that the Armenian congregation moved to Gless Street sometime during 1906; also see Jeff Janoian, *God at Our Side*, DVD (2005).

107. See Berokoff, *Molokans in America* (1987), 32–36. In Demos Shakarian, *The Happiest People* (1975), 27, Shakarian described the construction of the church on Gless Street as a simple thirty by sixty foot wood framed structure with backless benches and the traditional rectangular table in the front of the room where the residing elder would be seated.

108. Demos Shakarian, *The Happiest People* (1975), 26.

109. Demos Shakarian-Synan interview, October 5, 1987, 2–3.

110. Demos Shakarian, *The Happiest People* (1975), 26.

111. Berokoff, *Molokans in America* (1987), 36.

112. Demos Shakarian, *The Happiest People* (1975), 25–27.

113. Ibid, 27–29.

114. Demos Shakarian, "God's Dairyman," (1956), 43; and Demos Shakarian, *The Happiest People* (1975), 28.

115. Demos Shakarian, *The Happiest People* (1975), 29.

116. Demos Shakarian, *The Happiest People* (1975), 29; also see Berokoff, *Molokans in America* (1987), 45–46; and Bivin, "The Armenians of Karakala," (n.d.), 18. Both Berokoff and Bivin mention that the Armenian Molokan and Russian Molokan communities did not issue marriage licenses or even allow marriage licenses in their weddings until at least ten years after they arrived in Los Angeles (Berokoff [1987], 45–46).

117. Demos Shakarian, *The Happiest People* (1975), 29; and Bivin, "The Armenians of Karakala," (n.d.), 18.

118. Berokoff, *Molokans in America* (1987), 46.

119. This information is surmised from Berokoff's description of a Molokan wedding in 1912 (Berokoff, *Molokans in America* [1987], 46) and the limited information about the wedding that Demos Shakarian gives (Shakarian, *The Happiest People* [1975], 29). Interestingly, because of the size of these wedding processions, in 1915, due to increased traffic and safety concerns, the Molokan community and the city of Los Angeles restricted the size of future wedding processionals to the bride and groom's family.

120. Berokoff, *Molokans in America* (1987), 46.

121. Demos Shakarian, *The Happiest People* (1975), 29. Actually, the account in his autobiography mentioned that he only purchased ten acres originally, while earlier accounts in *Voice* state he acquired twenty acres. See Thomas Nickel, "The Amazing Shakarian Story: Part Two," November 1953, 6. In 1930, the local water company recorded that Isaac Shakarian owned two separate lots in Downey, one was 13.89 acres at 1260 South Cerritos Avenue and another property was a seven acre lot which was four blocks further South on Cerritos Avenue ("Map of Arroyo Ditch and Water Company at Downey and Vicinity," Los Angeles, CA, 1930). However, the Downey City Directory in 1914 listed no Shakarians, but they did list Magardich Perumean as a farmer in Downey ("Downey City Directory – 1914–1915," [Watts, CA: V.P. Franklin, 1915], 108).

122. Demos Shakarian, *The Happiest People* (1975), 29; and Demos Shakarian-Synan interview, October 5, 1987, 3.

123. Demos Shakarian, *The Happiest People* (1975), 30; and Thomas Nickel, "The Amazing Shakarian Story: Part Two," November 1953, 6.

Karakala, Armenia ~ circa 1890

Shakarian Family Circa 1906 ~
Isaac Shakarian is the One Standing in the Middle

The Grave Marker of the Russian Molokan Prophet, Efim Klubnikin

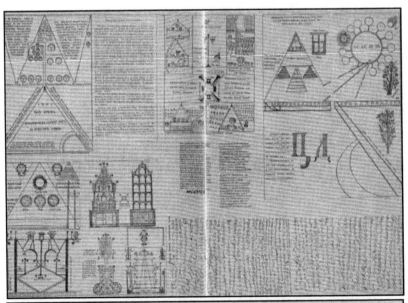

Writings and Symbols of the Russian Prophet, Efim Klubnikin

Chapter Four

Demos Shakarian's Birth and Beginnings (1913–1926)

Demos Shakarian's story begins with his ancestors, but his own life had humble beginnings in Los Angeles and Downey, California. While he was born into poverty, his family soon experienced prosperity in business. Shakarian gained experience in the family business at an early age. Growing up on a dairy farm shaped his future acuity, adeptness, and skill in the dairy business, but other experiences in his childhood defined his future legacy in business and in Christianity.

The Birth of Demos Shakarian

On July 21, 1913, Isaac and Zaroohi Shakarian's first child, Demos Shakarian, was born at 9:25 in the morning.[1] No specific detail was given about the manner or location of Shakarian's birth, but at least one source mentioned that Isaac had already moved to Downey in 1912.[2] A conflicting source mentioned Shakarian was born in a house at 528 South Gless Street, which may have been a rented house or the home of Isaac Shakarian's in-laws, the Yesseyians.[3] Demos Shakarian's birth certificate confirms that Isaac listed the Gless Street home as his residence when Shakarian was born.[4]

In the early twentieth century, Los Angeles Russian and Armenian Molokans often delivered their children at home. Doctors were shunned and *babkas*, or Russian midwives, were used to assist in the delivery of babies. Only later, in the 1920s, were the Russian midwives required by order of the city health authorities to hold licenses to practice their services in Los Angeles.[5] The Los Angeles health department also encouraged the *babkas* to learn to write, so they could sign the birth certificates. However, rather than go through a lengthy educational process, the midwives eventually gave up the practice of midwifery, so second generation Armenian and Russian Molokans began to use the services of obstetricians.[6] Isaac Shakarian deviated from this practice of using midwives earlier than many Molokan households as Nellie S. Hayes was the attending physician at his son's birth.[7]

After Demos Shakarian was born, the Shakarian household prospered financially and grew in numbers, as five younger sisters, Ruth (1915–), Lucy (1916–1940), Grace (1918–), Roxanne (1921–2007), and Florence (1923–1965), were born, and the three cows and fourteen acres Isaac bought in 1913 multiplied into five hundred cows and two hundred acres by 1923.[8] With more mouths to feed, Isaac Shakarian eventually diversified into hauling milk to the bottling plant, raising hogs, and packing meat. Nevertheless, the core business of the Shakarian Empire proved to be the Reliance Dairies which eventually grew to be the largest dairy business in North America with over five thousand head of cattle.[9] After Demos Shakarian was weaned as a young infant, the first skill he learned was to milk a cow.[10]

The Funeral of Efim Klubnikin

Another early childhood memory of Demos Shakarian was the weekly trip on Sunday to the Gless Street Armenian Pentecostal Church in Los Angeles. Isaac had trained his son Demos Shakarian to harness the family horse to the carriage that would carry the Shakarian family on the three hour journey from Downey to Los Angeles. Demos Shakarian was so young he had to stand on an orange crate to harness Jack, the family horse, and the family made an all day affair of the six hour round trip carriage ride. The service and the midday meal lasted an additional five hours.[11]

Another early childhood memory Shakarian had of his time spent at the Gless Street Church was a picture of the men in the church worshipping God with "their long black beards pointed straight out."[12] The Russian Molokan Church established a custom in which their married men grew long beards, and this tradition was transferred to the Armenian Molokan Church.[13] However, this tradition was not universally transferred to the Armenian Church and over time, the Armenian Church abandoned the practice of wearing beards for religious reasons altogether.[14]

The most memorable event in the Russian and Armenian Molokan community during Shakarian's early childhood was the funeral of Efim Klubnikin. Klubnikin had ultimately heeded his own prophecy and immigrated to Los Angeles with the thousands of Russian and Armenian Molokans who fled Transcaucasia at the beginning of the twentieth century. He also helped re-establish the Molokan religious community in Los Angeles as one of the presiding elders along with Nikolai Agalstoff (d.b.a. 1870–d.d.a. 1930), Philip Shubin (d.b.a. 1865–d.d.a. 1935), and Magardich Perumean, who represented the Armenian Molokan community.[15]

On August 5, 1915, Efim Klubnikin died in Los Angeles at the age of seventy three. His grave is marked by the largest headstone in the old Molokan cemetery at Easter Road and Second Street in Los Angeles.[16] In the Molokan community, the deceased body was typically bathed by family immediately after death and clothing selected by the immediate family was placed on the body.[17] Typically six volunteers from the community were assigned the task of digging the grave, and on the day of the funeral, the body was placed in the middle of the street on a carpet for a brief ceremony and then the body was placed in the casket and transported to the burial plot on a funeral street car.[18]

Isaac Shakarian described Klubnikin's ceremony as the largest funeral ever seen in the Boyle Heights section of Los Angeles as members of the Russian Molokan, Russian Orthodox, Armenian Molokan, and Armenian Orthodox communities gathered to honor the death of a prophet.[19] While a motor-driven hearse replaced the electric street car for funeral transportation by the early 1920s, in 1915, the large entourage of mourners followed Klubnikin's family to the end of the street car line where a series of pallbearers were enlisted to relay the casket a significant distance further to the cemetery on Second Street.[20] At the end of the funeral procession, Klubnikin's body was buried in a plot only thirty feet from the grave of Shakarian's grandfather.[21]

Two years after Klubnikin's death in the spring and summer of 1917, Isaac Shakarian began to organize and sponsor evangelistic crusades in Southern California.[22] He also joined the Kiwanis Club and reached out beyond his insulated Molokan community.[23] He eventually became the president of the Kiwanis Club in 1940 and the Downey Chamber of Commerce in 1938.[24] In doing so, Isaac established a precedent his son would eventually follow. The Armenian Pentecostal Church had already slightly deviated from their Russian Molokan brothers by allowing some of their married men to shave their beards and by not placing the sacred Molokan text *Spirit and Life* on the rectangular table in the center of their worship services. Now Isaac Shakarian was venturing further beyond the Molokan world to include the larger world of his business dealings. His business and his spiritual life were merging.

Demos Shakarian's Childhood

Although Isaac Shakarian quickly prospered financially, to say that Demos Shakarian was born into wealth would be far from the truth. The rustic nature of the Shakarian childhood home was reinforced by Zaroohi's sense of humor as she told her son why she enjoyed cleaning the floors in the house. Apparently, the twelve inch floorboards were far enough apart "that the scrub water simply ran through the cracks."[25]

Demos Shakarian described the property his father purchased as twenty acres full of "cornfields, eucalyptus trees, and pasture land in the heart of Downey."[26] By the time Demos Shakarian became a teenager, Isaac had replaced the old wood plank house with a two story white stucco Spanish style house with a red tile roof, at 1260 South Cerritos Avenue in Downey.[27] By 1926, Isaac Shakarian's herd had grown to one thousand head of cattle.[28]

Today it is hard to imagine having two hundred acres of farmland in the heart of Downey, California, which had a population of over 110,000 and a population density of 8,450 people per square mile according to a census in 2000.[29] However, the population did not exceed ten thousand until the 1940 census, and the city did not become incorporated in the County of Los Angeles until December 4, 1956.[30] Downey was established by and named after a former governor of California, John G. Downey, who purchased ninety six acres in the area and created the Downey Land Association in 1873.[31] At the beginning of the twentieth century, the city had already established itself as a commercial and agricultural hub with the completion of a Southern Pacific Railroad depot and a Sunkist packing plant.[32] In addition, downtown Downey already contained banks, mercantile shops, and a department store by 1900.[33] By the time Demos Shakarian was born, the community had already organized a citrus cooperative, the Downey Board of Trade (later named the Downey Chamber of Commerce), and a fledgling oil and aviation industry began to emerge after World War I.

As a young boy, Demos Shakarian went to elementary school at Alameda Grammar School. Elbert W. Ward (1887–1971) was the principal during Shakarian's tenure at the school. Some of his instructors included Katherine Woessner (1887–1966) and Elsie Vrooman (1896–1967).[34] The other elementary school North of Shakarian's home was Downey Grammar School. While the wooden auditorium of Downey Grammar School temporarily served as what would become Downey Union High School, the auditorium burned down shortly before Shakarian was born.[35] A far more significant fire occurred while Shakarian was attending Alameda Grammar School on April 21, 1922. A gas tanker refueling the main gas station at the corner of Downey and New Street caught fire and exploded. In attempting to extinguish the fire, nine people were killed and twenty others were disfigured.[36] No Shakarians were killed or injured in the disaster. However, another disaster nearly destroyed the burgeoning Shakarian dairy business as an epidemic of *aphtae epizooticae* (hoof and mouth disease) spread to the dairies in Downey in 1922. Fortunately for Isaac Shakarian, his herd was largely spared while the herd at the neighboring Los Angeles County Farm was completely destroyed.[37]

Demos Shakarian's Early Pneumatic Experiences

One year after the tragic fire, Demos Shakarian was injured as he was playing or working on his father's farm though Shakarian did not recall exactly how he was injured. Nevertheless, at the age of ten, Shakarian broke his nose, eventually causing blockage in his nasal passage and ear canal which led to some hearing loss.[38] Demos Shakarian went to the hospital and received surgery several times over the next few years to release the pressure in his sinuses and open up his ear canals, but each time the blockage reoccurred and his hearing got successively worse. During this time, Shakarian found solace weeding the corn fields where "the long dim aisles seemed to me like a green cathedral, the great veined leaves arching overhead. There I would lift my hands in the air the way the men did at church."[39]

During this time, Demos Shakarian also described himself as a loner since he had difficulty hearing other people thus affecting his conversation skills.[40] Shakarian also found refuge in the Armenian Pentecostal Church he grew up in. During the worship services, Shakarian enjoyed observing the men sporting long beards and the charismatic practice of jumping, a trait peculiar to Molokan worship.[41] The long horse drawn rides to the church ended in 1925, when Isaac Shakarian retired Jack, the horse with which he had begun his produce business. The horse was replaced by a long black Studebaker touring car.[42]

In 1926, spiritual expectations were elevated at the Armenian Pentecostal Church on Gless Street. Demos Shakarian's uncle, George Stepanian, had given a prophetic utterance declaring that a worried daughter's mother would arrive safely to Los Angeles in three days.[43] Often, as in this case, the prophetic utterance was a simple oral declaration, but the Armenian Pentecostal Church also practiced a form of prophecy in which a Bible was opened randomly and the verse or verses read by an elder, leader, or prophet were considered a prophetic utterance that should be obeyed.[44] Nevertheless, in 1926, when the mother arrived safely three days later, the congregation, including Demos Shakarian, was reminded of the importance of prophecy and how prophetic utterances had defined and delivered these Armenian Molokans and their ancestors.

On the following Sunday Demos Shakarian had his own experience with Spirit baptism. For four hours on that Sunday evening, Shakarian was unable to speak in English, Armenian, or Spanish, his three familiar languages.[45] In this experience, he said he also felt the presence of God wrap around him like a mantle. He often had similar experiences when he prayed to God in the corn fields behind his house, running through the fields and screaming at the top of his voice, praising God.[46]

Nevertheless, this experience was unique. In his initial glossolalic experience, Demos Shakarian claimed he spoke in tongues constantly for four hours and during that period of time he was unable to give anything but a glossolalic response to bystanders who observed his experience.[47] He defined this experience as separate from his own water baptism. In fact, his own Armenian church tradition perhaps influenced both by the Russian Molokan Brotherhood and by his ancestor's Armenian Orthodox origins, practiced sprinkling and infant baptism.[48] Demos Shakarian was sprinkled as an infant but he was also immersed as an adult by the Armenian Pentecostal Church in the early 1940s and in 1961 in the Jordan River by an early charismatic Presbyterian evangelist, Reverend James Brown (1912–1987).[49]

After the prophetic fulfillment of the previous week and Shakarian's introduction to Spirit baptism, Demos Shakarian had two other experiences on that same Sunday night which would continue to define and inform his charismatic Christian hermeneutic. The first occurred later that night as Demos Shakarian continued in prayer on his bed, enjoying his newfound Pentecostal experience. As Shakarian remained in prayer, he felt unable to move, and he heard what he believed was God's voice asking him, "Demos, will you ever doubt my power?"[50]

Three times Shakarian was asked this question, and three times he responded by saying, "Lord, I will never doubt your power."[51] As Demos Shakarian would later reflect upon this experience, he was often reminded to rely on God's power and not his own strength. "In trials and testings I have been able to remember that, when I was completely helpless, flat on my back on the floor in my bedroom, God called upon me to trust him completely, and I assured him that I would."[52]

After witnessing the Armenian church's tradition of prophecy, experiencing Spirit baptism, and being reminded of God's power, Shakarian had a healing experience early the next morning when his ear canal opened, restoring his hearing.[53] He described the experience in detail in his autobiography. He told how he could now hear birds singing outside of his bedroom window, dishes clinking downstairs as breakfast was prepared, and his footsteps ringing as he walked downstairs to announce his healing experience to his parents.[54] As recorded in the autobiography, Shakarian recovered ninety percent of his hearing, so he did have partial hearing loss for the rest of his life. In searching for an explanation for the remaining ten percent of his impaired hearing, Shakarian stated, "I don't know and I don't worry about it."[55] However, Demos Shakarian's daughter and son-in-law suggested this partial hearing loss may have caused him to be more attentive and appear more personable when talking to people[56]

Conclusion

Demos Shakarian was born into poverty, but later his father Isaac prospered in business, and Shakarian began to experience the benefits of that prosperity as he entered his teenage years. By 1926, he lived in a new house and his family drove a new car. Isaac Shakarian even had a large double tennis court built on the property behind the Shakarian house.[57] Financially and in business, things were dramatically improving for the Shakarian family. Certainly some of this prosperity can be attributed to the community Isaac Shakarian settled in, the nearby railroad depot, the emerging mercantile business in downtown Downey, and the burgeoning agricultural economy of the surrounding area. In the midst of this environment, Demos Shakarian was introduced to the dairy business at an early age, learning to milk cows about the same time he learned to walk.[58]

Of course, other factors in Shakarian's childhood would help shape and define his life, his hermeneutic, and his legacy. After the death of the prophet, Efim Klubnikin, in 1915, the emergence of new prophets guided the Armenian Pentecostal Church and the Shakarian family. However, beyond Shakarian's introduction to the dairy business and the death of Efim Klubnikin, the most significant series of events that occurred were on two concurrent Sundays in 1926, when Demos Shakarian began to participate in the experiential, pneumatic tradition of his ancestors. On the first Sunday, a prophecy was delivered and fulfilled later that week. On the next Sunday, Shakarian experienced Spirit baptism, healing, and divine power. Spirit baptism, prophecy, divine power, and divine healing were all crucial experiences which molded and shaped the pneumatology and experiential nature of Shakarian's Christian hermeneutic. They would define much of his life and shape the direction of his lasting spiritual legacy.

As Demos Shakarian became involved in the family business, his ancestors and the experiential nature of his church would help define his spiritual hermeneutic. As he entered his teenage years, these same four experiences of prophecy, Spirit baptism, healing, and God's supernatural power would weave through the spiritual and secular events in his life. Like his ancestors, Shakarian was guided by prophecy and what he saw as the hand of providence upon his life. Demos Shakarian believed his prophetic and charismatic experiences would guide him, and he interpreted his prosperity as a sign of God's blessing However, not everything would prosper in his life as he hoped or planned for, and soon he would understand the extent of his own experience and the importance of reliance upon God's power in the midst of "trials and testings"[59]

Notes

1. Demos Shakarian, *The Happiest People* (1975), 30; Demos Shakarian, "God's Dairyman," (1956), 43; and Los Angeles County Bureau of Records, Birth Certificate for Demos Shakarian, Los Angeles County, California, filed July 22, 1913.

2. In Demos Shakarian's account in "God's Dairyman," (1956), 43, Shakarian implied that his father had already moved to Downey before Shakarian was born and lived in the house before it was completed. However, the earliest available records of any Armenian Molokans listed as living in Downey at that time only record Shakarian's cousin, Magardich Perumean as living and working in Downey as a farmer ("Downey City Directory – 1914–1915," 108).

3. Shakarian-Synan interview, February 2, 1988, 1. Shakarian stated he was born in an old house on Gless Street.

4. Los Angeles County, Birth Certificate for Demos Shakarian, County of Los Angeles, California, filed July 22, 1913.

5. Berokoff, *Molokans in America* (1987), 45.

6. Ibid.

7. Los Angeles County, Birth Certificate for Demos Shakarian, July 22, 1913.

8. Demos Shakarian, *The Happiest People* (1975), 33.

9. Demos Shakarian-Synan interview, October 5, 1987, 3.

10. Demos Shakarian, *The Happiest People* (1975), 31

11. Ibid.

12. Ibid.

13. Demos Shakarian, *The Happiest People* (1975), 31.

14. Berokoff, *Molokans in America* (1987), 7 and 35; and Bivin, "The Armenians of Karakala," (n.d.), 16.

15. A photo recorded in the DVD, "God at Our Side," (2005) by Jeff Janoian, taken shortly after the Armenian Molokans arrived in Los Angeles in 1905, pictures a young thirteen year old Isaac Shakarian standing with eight older Armenian Molokan men, only one of whom (Magardich Perumean) has a beard.

16. Berokoff, *Molokans in America* (1987), 52.

17. This information was ascertained by a visit to the cemetery on January 16, 2008 and an interview with the caretaker of the cemetery, Paul Sobolew, on the same date; see also Berokoff, *Molokans in America* (1987), 48.

18. Berokoff, *Molokans in America* (1987), 47.

19. Berokoff, *Molokans in America* (1987), 47; see also Bivin, "The Armenians of Karakala," (n.d.), 18–19.

20. Demos Shakarian, *The Happiest People* (1975), 33.

21. Berokoff, *Molokans in America* (1987), 49.

22. This information was acquired by the author's visit to the gravesite on July 16, 2008 and an interview with the cemetery caretaker, Paul Sobolew, on the same date.

23. Demos Shakarian, "God's Dairyman," (1956), 51; and Thomas Nickel, "The Amazing Shakarian Story: Part Three," December 1953, 8.

24. Demos Shakarian, "A Prophecy Fulfilled," *Vision* July/August 1981, 18.

25. Jerry Jensen, "Isaac Shakarian: Son of Promise," *Voice* January 1965, 7 and 16.

26. Demos Shakarian, *The Happiest People* (1975), 29; and Demos Shakarian-Synan interview, October 5, 1987, 3.

27. Demos Shakarian, *The Happiest People* (1975), 29; Demos Shakarian, "God's Dairyman," (1956), 43; Thomas Nickel, "The Amazing Shakarian Story: Part Two," November 1953, 6; and Demos Shakarian-Synan interview, October 5, 1987, 3.

28. Los Angeles County, Certificate of Marriage for Demos and Rose Shakarian, Los Angeles County, California, filed August 11, 1933.

29. Demos Shakarian, *The Happiest People* (1975), 34; also see Thomas Nickel, "The Amazing Shakarian Story: Part Two," November 1953, 2.

30. "Demographics," Downey, California, http://www.downeyca.org (accessed August 1, 2008).

31. Ibid.

32. Ibid.

33. Demographics," Downey, California, http://www.downeyca.org (accessed August 1, 2008); see also John Adams, "Downtown Downey Grew after Railroad," *The Downey Eagle*, December 6, 1996; and Adams, "Downey as it was in the Last Century," *The Downey Eagle*, September 3, 1993.

34. Ibid.

35. John Adams, "Names that Survive from School Archives," *The Downey Eagle*, March 3, 1995; and Charles Russell Quinn, *History of Downey* (Downey, CA: Elena Quinn, 1973), 155.

36. Adams, "The Growth of our Fine School System," *The Downey Eagle*, February 24, 1995.

37. Adams, "Inferno Proved Need for Fire Department," *The Downey Eagle*, December 5, 1997; and Quinn, *History of Downey* (1973), 131–132.

38. Quinn, *History of Downey* (1973), 133.

39. Demos Shakarian, *The Happiest People* (1975), 34; Thomas Nickel, "The Amazing Shakarian Story: Part Two," November 1953, 7; and Demos Shakarian, "God's Dairyman," (1956), 44–45.

40. Demos Shakarian, *The Happiest People* (1975), 34.

41. Ibid, 34.

42. Demos Shakarian, *The Happiest People* (1975), 27 and 31; see also Bivin, "The Armenians of Karakala," (n.d.), 16.

43. Demos Shakarian, *The Happiest People* (1975), 35.

44. Ibid.

45. Demos Shakarian-Synan interview, Downey, CA, October 5, 1987, 5–6. For an example of the scripturally dictated form of prophecy, see the prophecy scripturally dictated to Isaac Shakarian in *The Happiest People* (1975), 27–28 by Aram Mushegan which Isaac Shakarian interpreted by leaving the harness factory, starting his vegetable business, and eventually purchasing property for his dairy business.

46. Demos Shakarian, *The Happiest People* (1975), 35–36; Demos Shakarian, "God's Dairyman,"(1956), 44–45; and Thomas Nickel, "The Amazing Shakarian Story: Part Two," November 1953, 7.

47. Demos Shakarian, *Come Let Us Exalt Him* (Costa Mesa, CA: Full Gospel Business Men's Fellowship International, 1992), 45; and Demos Shakarian, *The Happiest People* (1975), 35–36.

48. Demos Shakarian, "God's Dairyman," (1987), 44–45; and Demos Shakarian, *The Happiest People* (1975), 35–36.

49. Sydney Jackson, "The Molokans: A Study of a Religious Minority," thesis, George Fox University, 1962, 94.

50. Demos Shakarian-Synan interview, Downey, CA, February 2, 1988, 3; also see Jeff Janoian, *God at our Side*, DVD, 2005. In the oral interview, Shakarian believed that the practice of infant baptism in his church was derived from their Armenian Orthodox tradition. Shakarian does not mention being baptized by full immersion by his church but rather says he was sprinkled as an infant. However, the DVD has photographs of Shakarian and his wife Rose being baptized in full immersion sometime shortly after the church moved to Goodrich Street in 1942. In addition, quite a few other long standing members of the church were baptized at this time, so it is possible the church gave up the practice of sprinkling and infant baptism in or before 1942.

51. Demos Shakarian, "God's Dairyman," (1956), 45; Demos Shakarian, *The Happiest People* (1975), 36–37; and Thomas Nickel, "The Amazing Shakarian Story: Part Two," November 1953, 7.

52. Demos Shakarian, "God's Dairyman," (1956), 45; and Demos Shakarian, *The Happiest People* (1975), 36–37.

53. Demos Shakarian, "God's Dairyman," (1956), 45.

54. Demos Shakarian, *The Happiest People* (1975), 37.

55. Demos Shakarian, *The Happiest People* (1975), 37. While Demos Shakarian's account of this story in "God's Dairyman," (1956), 44–45 makes reference to a healing incident, the account makes no specific reference regarding the restoration of his hearing. In addition, Thomas Nickel's account in "The Amazing Shakarian Story: Part Two," November 1953, 7 makes no reference to a healing experience when he experienced Spirit baptism.

56. Demos Shakarian, *The Happiest People* (1975), 37.

57. Gene and Geraldine Scalf-Tallman interview, Colorado Springs, CO, January 8, 2008.

58. Demos Shakarian, *The Happiest People* (1975), 44.

59. Ibid, 31.

60. Demos Shakarian, "God's Dairyman," (1956), 45.

Chapter Five

His Early Years (1926–1940)

After Demos Shakarian's charismatic experience of healing and Spirit baptism, his life seemed filled with the ordinary concerns of a growing teenager such as building automobiles from spare parts and later as a young adult concerned about making a living for his new family. His was an ordinary story of a young man trying to make his way in the world and discern how he might fit into some divine plan. As Demos Shakarian would soon find out, life was not always simple and this divine plan was filled with "trials and testings".[1]

Demos Shakarian's Teenage Years

Shakarian's teenage years were filled with innovation, exploration, and entrepreneurial experiments as he began to decide what he would do with his life. At one point, Shakarian thought he might try to learn playing the violin, but his family was grateful when this pursuit was abandoned, and the violin was handed down to his younger sister Florence.[2] After giving up on his musical career, Shakarian was much more successful at building a car out of parts he collected from his Uncle Raphael Janoian's junkyard.[3] He also used his mechanical skills regularly to repair tractors and other machinery for Isaac Shakarian's growing dairy farm.[4] Demos Shakarian's grammar school and high school education was delayed by two years because of his earlier hearing loss.[5] He should have graduated from high school in the spring of 1930, but instead he was completing his sophomore year at Downey Union High School.[6] The fact that he was attending a high school at all was another Armenian departure from the traditions of their Russian Molokan brothers. Russian Molokan teenagers typically left school at the permissible age of fourteen to work in the family business.[7] In fact, Demos Shakarian continued his formal education by studying at the University of California's agricultural school in Davis, California.[8]

At the same time Demos Shakarian was receiving a formal education, he was eager to get into the business world. Isaac Shakarian chose to give his son a valuable business education by giving him a nest egg of two thousand dollars.[9] With enough capital to start a business, Shakarian asked his friend and cousin from the Armenian Church, Dan Mushegan (d.b.a. 1914–d.d.a. 1950), to become his business partner in his entrepreneurial enterprise. Together, they purchased a small herd of thirty dairy cows which quickly grew to sixty.[10] In spite of Musegan's club feet and Shakarian's hearing loss, the pair proved quite adept at business as they quickly made more money than most of their teachers at Downey Union High School.[11]

Dan and Demos, as they were called in the community, also decided to make their contribution to the burgeoning aeronautics industry in Downey. They attempted to build an aircraft from the chassis of a Model T Ford.[12] The aviation industry in Downey was first established by E.M. Smith (1895–1992), but Willard Rockwell (1888–1989) also made his contribution as the industry became more established.[13] At the same time, a variety of aeronautical entrepreneurs in Downey, including Demos Shakarian and Dan Mushegan, tried their hand at constructing experimental aircraft, and many of them met in a cow pasture called Aardis Field in nearby Clearwater, California, and gathered the cattle behind a fenced area so they could test their aviation and engineering skills.[14]

Unfortunately, the great depression began to take its toll on the recreation and the economy of Southern California, and soon Demos Shakarian and Dan Mushegan were losing money with their dairy herd. They lost everything in their business venture except the initial capital of two thousand dollars Isaac Shakarian had given his son.[15] As a result Mushegan and Shakarian quit the dairy business, and Shakarian experimented with the beef cattle industry. He made some profit for awhile, and then Shakarian began to specialize in the baby beef market, but once again, he lost everything except his father's initial capital investment of two thousand dollars.[16]

However, while Shakarian struggled in his early business ventures, his father Isaac Shakarian continued to thrive in the dairy industry and other businesses he initiated. Even as the depression began to take its toll on Southern California, Isaac Shakarian purchased a second dairy farm, built silos, and installed automatic milking machines.[17] Isaac also diversified into hauling milk to the bottling plant, raising hogs, and packing meat.[18] Isaac sought additional capital and found additional business partners as he established the Great Western Milk Transport Company with four hundred milk tankers to help transport their dairy products throughout California.[19] Isaac Shakarian also acquired garbage contracts in San Pedro, California, and used much of the garbage to provide food for ten thousand hogs he raised and sold. He also helped establish a meat packing company called the Great Western Packing Company which slaughtered seven to eight hundred cattle daily.[20] The packing house was one of only two businesses in Downey that kept a significant number of people employed during the height of the Depression; the other major business was an asbestos company started by E. M. Smith (1904–1976).[21] The rest of the community sustained themselves through the various farms, several dairies (one of them being the Shakarian Dairy), and ranches that established Downey as an agricultural center even before the beginning of the twentieth century.[22]

Even though Isaac Shakarian encountered success and growth in the dairy business, he also faced financial, labor, and business challenges during the years of the Depression. A milk price war threatened to undercut Shakarian's profits and the Los Angeles Milk Industry Board, representing Shakarian and other dairy producers in the region, was commissioned to help regulate pricing.[23] In early January 1934, labor unrest forced Shakarian and other milk producers in the Los Angeles area to seek dairy employees from other areas of California as two hundred striking employees congregated outside of Shakarian's Reliance Dairy Number One in Norwalk, California.[24] The Los Angeles County Sheriff's Department sent ten deputies to keep the protests peaceful, but two weeks later, violence erupted at the Norwalk Reliance Dairy when two of Shakarian's employees were fired upon three separate times by an unknown assailant in an automobile.[25] The price wars and the unrest eventually subsided, and Shakarian gained a new business partner, George A. Cameron (1903–1990), as his dairies continued to expand.[26]

The prosperity in the Shakarian household soon brought politicians, business men, and community leaders to Cerritos Avenue for weekly dinner parties. Zaroohi Shakarian was able to demonstrate her hospitality and Demos Shakarian boasted that her presentation of Armenian foods became famous throughout California.[27] However, what impressed Shakarian the most was his mother's gracious hospitality toward anyone who happened to visit the Shakarian household: the rich and the poor, the powerful and the disenfranchised.[28]

Demos Shakarian was busy as a teenager being introduced to the realities of business, but he also experimented with the religious praxis of his pneumatic Christianity as he maintained a commitment to the Armenian Pentecostal Church. He sometimes speculated about whether he would be a prophet like Efim Klubnikin or be involved in some other specialized area of ministry in his church.[29] When he was seventeen years old, his younger six year old sister, Florence, shattered her right elbow in an accident on the Shakarian Farm and the injury did not heal properly. One Sunday at the Armenian Church, he prayed for Florence, and she stated she felt heat flow through her arm as Shakarian prayed for her.[30] Several weeks later, when the cast came off, the doctor was reportedly amazed that the elbow had healed properly.[31]

At this point in his teenage years, Shakarian wondered if God might want him to be a faith healer instead of a prophet.[32] After all, the Russian Molokan community had their *lekar* or elders who would regularly pray for the sick.[33] The popularity of Aimee Semple McPherson (1890–1944) and other healing evangelists in Southern California were already well established by the time Demos Shakarian had his own healing experience and introduction to Spirit baptism.[34] Nevertheless, upon later reflection, Shakarian felt this gift of healing was a charismatic gift available for all Christians but not something to which he would devote his life.[35]

Demos Shakarian and the entire Shakarian family also faced challenges which caused them to question their healing praxis and theology. In 1927, Shakarian's sister Lucille was involved in a school bus accident which crushed her chest.[36] While she survived the accident, medicine and prayer failed to bring full recovery from the accident, and later in her teenage years, she began to develop further complications from the accident which affected her breathing.[37] In addition, Isaac and Zaroohi also had two children later in life, William in 1929 and Arthur in 1930, both of whom died in infancy just months after being born.[38]

Shakarian regularly attended the Armenian Pentecostal Church throughout his teenage years and interacted with the members of the church often. One member in particular, Sirakan Gabrielian, captured Shakarian's attention with his stories of business, marriage, and Gabrielian's own conversion to Pentecostal Christianity. Sirakan and his family were originally from an Armenian Orthodox background when they immigrated to Los Angeles, but he lived on Union Pacific Avenue near the Armenian Pentecostal Church and eventually became indoctrinated to Pentecostal Christianity.[39] Shortly after his conversion, a gang of Orthodox Christians attempted to bury him alive highlighting an underlying tension between these two Armenian religious groups in Los Angeles.[40]

It is possible this incident left Shakarian with some questions regarding the ecumenical nature of his Armenian ancestry. Some of the statements Shakarian made in his autobiography may reveal a prejudicial view he had toward the Armenian Orthodox community in Los Angeles, a view that may have been reinforced later in Shakarian's life.[41] In 1961, he visited an Armenian Orthodox church in Bethlehem. As he entered the church, he found people playing cards and smoking cigarettes, two taboos that violated his Pentecostal background. He later commented "they were so near to the Savior's birthplace, and so far from God."[42] This example does leave some questions regarding his developing ecumenism, but it may simply reflect Shakarian's recognition of the tension between these two religious communities in Los Angeles he observed growing up. The fact that Shakarian reflected upon Sirakan's stories decades later may have also been influenced by his keen interest in gaining the favor of Sirakan Gabrielian (d.b.a. 1894–d.d.a. 1960), his future father-in-law.

The Wedding of Demos and Rose Shakarian

Demos Shakarian had observed the oldest daughter of Sirakan and Tiroon (d.b.a. 1902–d.d.a. 1985) from a distance at church and whenever the family business took him near her house at 4311 Union Pacific Avenue in Los Angeles.[43] Armenian custom prohibited an unmarried man and woman from talking to each other. Following the dictates of his tradition, in June of 1932, Demos Shakarian asked his parents if he could marry Rose Gabrielian.[44] Isaac and Zaroohi approved of Shakarian's choice since she was a Christian and Armenian.[45] According to their custom, the marriage was arranged between the two families, but in Armenian tradition, a third party, in this case Raphael Janoian, went to the Gabrielian family to make the formal marriage request on behalf of the Shakarian family.[46]

On July 20, 1932, the two families had a formal meeting to discuss the details of the marriage proposal.[47] The patriarchs agreed on the details of the marriage, and Rose Gabrielian agreed to the proposal. More tradition followed as the two families gathered at the Gabrielian home for five nights of celebration.[48] On one evening of celebration, Rose played the piano, demonstrating a talent she would exhibit throughout her adult life.[49] On another evening, Demos Shakarian gave Rose a customary gift to symbolize their new relationship; in this case, he gave Rose a wristwatch selected by Isaac and Zaroohi which was set with diamonds.[50] On the fourth night, Shakarian violated tradition by requesting that he talk with Rose privately before their formal engagement.[51] Tiroon Gabrielian arranged two straight back chairs in the center of a room and left the room to allow Demos and Rose to talk privately for a few moments. Sirakan Gabrielian insisted only Armenian be spoken in his house, so with his best attempt, Demos Shakarian nervously tried to tell Rose how beautiful she was but only managed to say, "Rose, I know that God wants us together."[52] Rose tearfully responded by saying, "Demos, all my life I prayed that the man I married would say those words to me first of all."[53]

Both families agreed the wedding should be delayed for a year until Rose reached the age of sixteen.[54] Besides, the families still had extensive ceremonies and plans to prepare. The Shakarians, Gabrielians, and elders of the church discussed the location of the wedding and decided the Shakarians should host the wedding at their house since the Gless Street Church was too small to accommodate the number of intended guests. They also anticipated that their Armenian Orthodox friends and family would feel more comfortable in a neutral setting.[55] The engagement ring was selected with a large contingent of family in tow at a wholesale diamond house. It is interesting to note that the mother of the famous aviator, Amelia Earhart, sold the diamond ring to them.[56] A large, formal engagement dinner was prepared at a store owned by the Gabrielian family in August 1932, with three hundred people in attendance.[57]

After Rose Gabrielian and Demos Shakarian were formally engaged, Shakarian was allowed to see Rose at the Gabrielian house as often as he liked. He usually came bearing some of his mother's Armenian pastries such as *shakar lokoom* or *paklava*.[58] The groom's family traditionally purchased the bride's wardrobe, so Rose Gabrielian, Zaroohi Shakarian, and Demos Shakarian's sisters went shopping frequently during the year-long engagement. Rose Shakarian's favorite purchase during those shopping excursions was a dark maroon dress.[59]

Finally, on August 6, 1933, at the age of twenty, Demos Shakarian married Rose Gabrielian, who was sixteen years old.[60] On the morning of August 6th, the extended Shakarian family drove to East Los Angeles to begin the wedding ceremony at the bride's home and enjoyed a five course lunch. The bride's and the groom's extended family then started a twenty-five car caravan to Downey where the ceremony was officiated by Magardich Perumean on the tennis court behind the Shakarian house.[61] Perumean performed the service in the Armenian language, but he wore no priestly garments or robes while performing the ceremony.[62] George Stephanian (d.b.a. 1910–d.d.a. 1974) stood beside Shakarian as best man and as a witness who signed the certificate of marriage.[63] Five hundred guests attended the festivities at the Shakarian home and enjoyed *shishkebabs* and traditional date and almond wedding pilaf until the weary bride and groom retired some time after eleven o'clock.[64]

Demos Shakarian as a Young Business Man

Demos Shakarian moved his new bride Rose into the Shakarian household at 1260 South Cerritos Avenue in Downey, California after they were married, and within six months Rose was pregnant with their first child.[65] Richard Shakarian was born in October 1934, and Demos and Rose Shakarian promptly made preparations to build a new home next door to Isaac and Zaroohi at 1228 South Cerritos Avenue.[66] Shakarian made preparations to expand some of the Shakarian business ventures when he officially became a partner in the Reliance Dairies at the age of twenty with George Cameron and Isaac Shakarian.[67] For much of this early period, at least from 1938 through 1940, Demos Shakarian was paid a salary of one hundred fifty dollars per month.[68] Isaac gave his son the responsibility of designing and building Reliance Dairy Number Three. The Shakarians already had one of the largest dairy herds in California with approximately one thousand dairy cows, but Isaac dreamed of creating the largest dairy herd in the world. With Demos Shakarian's assistance, together they set a goal of increasing their herd to three thousand head of cattle.[69] Utilizing the latest technology which Demos Shakarian had garnered from his studies at the University of California, he purchased forty acres and began the construction of corrals, silos, a modern barn, and a creamery.[70] Demos Shakarian also developed a technique of rotating calving booths that almost eliminated premature death among the dairy calves, a technique that was innovative and effective for an emerging modern dairy industry.[71]

Demos Shakarian also assisted Isaac in the other Shakarian business ventures. Great Western Milk Transport had already grown from three hundred to four hundred diesel trucks with Demos Shakarian's assistance. They hoped to increase their transportation fleet to five hundred trucks in the next few years.[72] Demos and Isaac Shakarian also decided to maximize the profitability and effectiveness of their diesel fleet by hauling silage, hogs, and beef cattle for their growing pork and beef businesses.[73] In addition, Demos Shakarian integrated faith with business by praying for divine guidance when selecting bulls at auctions or praying for sick cattle even though he also relied upon the assistance of veterinarians for treating his livestock.[74]

In 1936, Demos Shakarian expanded into a new industry by starting a fertilizer plant.[75] Many of the industries the Shakarian family delved into were related to their staple dairy business or helped solve problems such as the transportation of milk product to buyers through the inauguration of the Great Western Milk Transport Company. A similar situation existed with the problem of cow manure, and Demos Shakarian saw an opportunity which would hopefully maximize the profits of the Shakarian family. Other dairy farmers in neighboring communities would eventually follow much of the Shakarian business model after WWII, but the uncertain economic constraints of the Great Depression forced Shakarian to close the fertilizer plant only five brief years after he started it.[76]

Nevertheless, the Shakarian Corporation remained increasingly profitable during the Great Depression and Isaac and Demos Shakarian considered moving their families to a more affluent section of northern Downey, California. In 1936, property was purchased and developed on Lexington-Gallatin Road. Eventually both Isaac and Demos Shakarian moved their families from South Cerritos Avenue to a new location next door to each other once again at 241 and 215 North Lexington Gallatin Road. In 1947, their addresses and street name would be changed respectively to 8431 and 8413 Lexington Road.[77]

The multiple businesses and industries Shakarian's family had ventured into often left him working sixteen hour days. Now, with the additional work load of running a fertilizer plant, Shakarian occasionally worked through the night.[78] Also, Demos Shakarian still managed to stay involved in the community as a member of the Lion's Club and the Kiwanis Club.[79] Shakarian's frenetic schedule assisted with the prosperity of the Shakarian family, but it also caused Demos and Rose Shakarian to question their priorities and so they began to inquire what other purpose God might have for their lives.

The Consecration of Demos Shakarian

The consecration of Demos Shakarian was likely sparked by a prophecy and birthed in the midst of a tragedy. The term consecration, in the case of Demos Shakarian, was used to describe Shakarian's point of spiritual discovery at which he began to understand himself as set apart for some special divine purpose. Some Christian Methodist and Holiness traditions might define Shakarian's discovery as an experience of sanctification and this is possible since Shakarian compared his own tradition to the holiness traditions of some North American Christian denominations.[80] However, Demos Shakarian simply defined this point in his life as a "reconsecration."[81] Demos Shakarian would have several periods of consecration in his life, most of them defined not in theological terms but rather in terms of charismatic and life experience.

Before this point of consecration, Demos Shakarian described himself as preoccupied with the affairs of the Shakarian business.[82] However, the Shakarian family had not neglected the church in which they grew up. Isaac Shakarian became an elder in the Armenian Pentecostal Church on Gless Street.[83] Church attendance, youth ministry at his local Armenian Pentecostal Church, and ministry participation in a local Youth for Christ chapter were also prominent in Demos Shakarian's young adult life.[84]

Healing and glossolalia continued to be important charismata in the early life of Demos Shakarian, but prophecy remained preeminent in shaping the direction of his life and later influence. However, two prophecies in late 1937, one from a local friend, Milton Hansen, and another from a local pastor told Shakarian that he was a "chosen vessel" who would "visit high government officials in many parts of the world."[85] Milton Hansen was not an ordained minister but a house painter, and yet, in Shakarian's ecclesiological understanding, this did not exclude Hansen's series of visits or Hansen's frequent prophecies from influencing Demos and Rose Shakarian.

While Shakarian heeded the prophetic utterances of Milton Hansen, three other things overshadowed the Shakarian household in 1938. One was the impending birth of Demos Shakarian's daughter Geraldine Shakarian (1938–). Another was the poor economic performance of the fertilizer plant Demos Shakarian had started only two years earlier.[86] The final circumstance, which concerned the entire extended Shakarian family, was the declining health of Lucille Shakarian.

Gerry was born in October 1938, and soon 1228 Cerritos Avenue was filled with joyful expectations.[87] Unfortunately, the good news of Geraldine Shakarian's birth was muted by the rapidly declining health of Lucy Shakarian in 1939. She had never fully recovered from her accident in 1927, and her pulmonary function had steadily declined for the past decade. She had graduated from Downey High School and dreamed of being a school teacher while attending Whittier College.[88] She never accomplished that goal but died on January 19, 1940, at the age of twenty-three.[89]

Conclusion

The teenage and young adult years of Demos Shakarian were filled with ingenuity, innovation, experimentation, and prosperity. While Demos Shakarian faltered in his business experiments at times, overall, the Shakarian family and Isaac Shakarian in particular were successful in the midst of the Great Depression. As Demos Shakarian entered adulthood, he also entered the responsibilities of marriage and child rearing. His social responsibilities faced economic realities as his own economic progress fluctuated over the next several years. However, self-reliance would soon give way to divine reliance as Shakarian considered himself a failure at business because he was "trying without God".[90]

Demos Shakarian described his point of "reconsecration" occurring six years after he married Rose Gabrielian.[91] The prophecies of Milton Hansen caused Shakarian to contemplate some special divine purpose for his life, and the Shakarian family already had established the importance of prophecy in their lives. The birth of Geraldine Shakarian likely brought some reorganization of priorities in the life of Demos and Rose Shakarian. The declining health of Demos Shakarian's sister Lucy brought this sense of reconsecration in Demos Shakarian's life to a circumstantial gestalt. Demos Shakarian's decision to consecrate his life was sealed with the death of Lucille Shakarian in 1940. God had brought Demos and Rose Shakarian through a period of "trial and testing," and now they felt ready to serve God with a newfound intensity as they entered a new decade and a new phase in their life together.

Notes

1. Demos Shakarian, "God's Dairyman," (1956), 45; and Thomas Nickel, "The Amazing Shakarian Story: Part Three," December 1953, 8.

2. Demos Shakarian, *The Happiest People* (1975), 44.

3. Ibid, 42.

4. Ibid, 44.

5. Ibid, 39.

6. Ibid.

7. Berokoff, *Molokans in America* (1987), 36.

8. Ed Ainsworth, "A Lot of Faith: A Lot of Cows," *Los Angeles Times*, May 8, 1960, 119.

9. Demos Shakarian, "God's Dairyman," (1956), 45.

10. Demos Shakarian, "God's Dairyman," (1956), 45–46; and Demos Shakarian, *The Happiest People* (1975), 39.

11. Demos Shakarian, "God's Dairyman," (1956), 46; Demos Shakarian, *The Happiest People* (1975), 39; and Harding Mushegian, interview by Matthew Tallman, San Dimas, CA, January 14, 2008.

12. Paul Janoian, interview by Matthew Tallman, La Habra Heights, CA, January 13, 2008.

13. "History of Downey," Downey, California, http://www.downeyca.org (accessed August 7, 2008); and Quinn, *History of Downey* (1973),

14. John Adams, "Some Odd Aircraft were Once Built Here," *The Downey Eagle*, November 5, 1993.

15. Demos Shakarian, "God's Dairyman," (1956), 46; and Thomas Nickel, "The Amazing Shakarian Story: Part Three," *Voice*, December 1953, 8.

16. Demos Shakarian, "God's Dairyman," (1956), 46; and Thomas Nickel, "The Amazing Shakarian Story: Part Three," December 1953, 8.

17. Demos Shakarian, *The Happiest People* (1975), 39; and "Ball Property Sold," *The Downey Live Wire*, January 16, 1936, 1.

18. Demos Shakarian, *The Happiest People* (1975), 39; and Demos Shakarian-Synan interview, October 5, 1987, 3.

19. Demos Shakarian-Synan interview, October 5, 1987, 3.

20. Demos Shakarian-Synan interview, October 5, 1987, 3; and Demos Shakarian, *The Happiest People* (1975), 39.

21. John Adams, "Great Depression made Residents Pull Together," *The Downey Eagle*, November 19, 1993.

22. John Adams, "Great Depression made Residents Pull Together," *The Downey Eagle*, November 19, 1993; Quinn, *History of Downey* (1973), 133; and "History of Downey," Downey, California, http://www.downeyca.org (accessed August 7, 2008).

23. "Guns Roar in Milk Strike," *Los Angeles Times*, January 23, 1934, 1 and 3.

24. "Milk Strike Stirs Rift," *Los Angeles Times*, January 7, 1934, 1.

25. "Guns Roar in Milk Strike," *Los Angeles Times*, January 23, 1934, 1.

26. "Six Hundred Dairy Cows Sold at Downey Auction," *Los Angeles Times*, May 26, 1943, 13; and Demos Shakarian-Synan interview, October 5, 1987, 3.

27. Demos Shakarian, *The Happiest People* (1975), 39.

28. Demos Shakarian, *The Happiest People* (1975), 39–40. Shakarian notes that homeless people were frequently served a hot meal at the Shakarian household during his teenage years due to the financial effects of the Great Depression.

29. Demos Shakarian, *The Happiest People* (1975), 37–38.

30. Ibid, 39.

31. Ibid.

32. Ibid.

33. Berokoff, *Molokans in America* (1987), 45.

34. For an excellent biography of McPherson see Edith Blumhofer's account, *Aimee Semple McPherson: Everybody's Sister* (Grand Rapids, Michigan: William Eerdmans Publishing Company, 1993).

35. Demos Shakarian, *The Happiest People* (1975), 38–39.

36. Demos Shakarian, *The Happiest People* (1975), 49, and also from information gathered at Rose Hills Memorial Park in Whittier, California.

37. Demos Shakarian, *The Happiest People* (1975), 49.

38. Paul Sobolew-Tallman interview, January 15, 2008, Los Angeles, CA and from information gathered at the Old Molokan Cemetery in Los Angeles. In a later phone interview with Geraldine Shakarian Scalf, she seemed unaware of the two infant children (Geri Scalf was born eight years after these two infants died), but the caretaker of the cemetery, Paul Sobolew assured the author that these were the infant children of Isaac and Zaroohi Shakarian.

39. Demos Shakarian, *The Happiest People* (1975), 40–41.

40. Ibid.

41. For examples of these experiences or perceptions see Shakarian, *The Happiest People* (1975), 33, 40–41, and 44.

42. Demos Shakarian, "Wherever You Are," *Voice* December 1984, 3.

43. Demos Shakarian, *The Happiest People* (1975), 40; and Los Angeles County Bureau of Records, Certificate of Marriage for Demos and Rose Shakarian, Los Angeles County, CA, filed August 11, 1933.

44. Ibid, 40–41.

45. Demos Shakarian, *The Happiest People* (1975), 42.

46. Ibid, 42; and Bivin, "The Armenians of Karakala," (n.d.), 18.

47. Demos Shakarian, *The Happiest People* (1975), 42; and Demos Shakarian, "Together," *Voice* February 1981, 15.

48. Demos Shakarian, *The Happiest People* (1975), 44; and Demos Shakarian, "Together," *Voice* February 1981, 15.

49. Demos Shakarian, *The Happiest People* (1975), 44.

50. Ibid.

51. Demos Shakarian, *The Happiest People* (1975), 45; and Demos Shakarian, "Together," February 1981, 15.

52. Demos Shakarian, "Together," February 1981, 15; and Demos Shakarian, *The Happiest People* (1975), 45.

53. Demos Shakarian, *The Happiest People* (1975), 45; and Demos Shakarian, "Together," February 1981, 15.

54. Demos Shakarian, *The Happiest People* (1975), 44–45.

55. Demos Shakarian, *The Happiest People* (1975), 44. Many of the Russian Molokan weddings were held at the groom's home for similar reasons (Berokoff, *Molokans in America* [1987], 46).

56. Demos Shakarian, *The Happiest People* (1975), 45–46. The family of Amelia Earhart lived in the Downey area at that time and Amelia Earhart learned to fly in nearby Southland, California ("History of Downey," Downey, California,   http://www.downeyca.org [accessed August 7, 2008]; and John Adams, "Amelia learned to fly in nearby Southland," *The Downey Eagle*, March 25, 1994).

57. Demos Shakarian, *The Happiest People* (1975), 46.

58. Ibid.

59. Ibid. Apparently, only married women were allowed to wear dark colors in the Armenian community.

60. Demos Shakarian, *The Happiest People* (1975), 46; and Demos Shakarian, "God's Dairyman," (1956), 46.

61. Demos Shakarian, *The Happiest People* (1975), 46. This tradition of starting the ceremony at the bride's home and "bringing the bride home" as Demos Shakarian stated in his autobiography, was also widely practiced in the Russian Molokan wedding ceremonies.(see Berokoff, *Molokans in America* [1987], 46–47).

62. Demos Shakarian, *The Happiest People* (1975), 46; see also Bivin, "The Armenians of Karakala," (n.d.), 13, 15, 16 and 17. Shakarian's wedding displays a fusion of customs the Armenian Molokan community adopted and rejected, with some married elders, such as Perumean, wearing the long beards, a custom adopted from their Russian Molokan brothers. The rejection of priestly robes was also influenced by the Molokans, but the insistence on reading the Armenian text instead of the Russian text recognized their own unique heritage as Armenians. Nicol Ohanessian was responsible for composing many of the early Armenian psalms and melodies of the Armenian Pentecostal Church (Bivin, "The Armenians of Karakala, [n.d.], 15).

63. Los Angeles County, Certificate of Marriage for Demos and Rose Shakarian, filed August 11, 1933.

64. Demos Shakarian, *The Happiest People* (1975), 46–47.

65. Demos Shakarian, *The Happiest People* (1975), 49; and Los Angeles County, Certificate of Marriage for Demos and Rose Shakarian, filed August 11, 1933. It was customary in their tradition for the bride and groom to live with the groom's family for the first few years of their marriage.

66. Demos Shakarian, "God's Dairyman," (1956), 43; Thomas Nickel, "The Amazing Shakarian Story," October 1953, 2; Demos Shakarian, *The Happiest People* (1975), 49; *Telephone Directory – Downey, Norwalk, Artesia, Bellflower* (Downey, CA: Consolidated Telephone Company, 1940), 40; and Los Angeles County, Certificate of Marriage for Demos and Rose Shakarian, filed August 11, 1933. South Cerritos Avenue was later renamed Clark Street.

67. Demos Shakarian-Synan interview, October 5, 1987, 3; Demos Shakarian, "God's Dairyman," (1956), 46; and "Six Hundred Dairy Cows Sold," May 26, 1943, 13.

68. Demos Shakarian, *Life Lifters* (1984), 2:42.

69. Shakarian-Synan interview, October 5, 1987, 3; and Demos Shakarian, *The Happiest People* (1975), 50.

70. Demos Shakarian, *The Happiest People* (1975), 50; "Ball Property Sold," *The Downey Live Wire*, January 16, 1936, 1; and Ed Ainsworth, "A Lot of Faith," May 8, 1960, 119.

71. Gene Scalf-Tallman interview, January 8, 2008; also see Ed Ainsworth, "A Lot of Faith: A Lot of Cows," May 8, 1960, 119. This process became much more refined when they purchased land in Merced, California, for a separate calving facility.

72. Demos Shakarian-Synan interview, October 5, 1987, 3; and Demos Shakarian, *The Happiest People* (1975), 50.

73. Demos Shakarian, *The Happiest People* (1975), 49–50; and Demos Shakarian-Synan interview, October 5, 1987, 3

74. Demos Shakarian, *The Happiest People* (1975), 50–51; and Ed Ainsworth, "A Lot of Faith," May 8, 1960, 119.

75. Demos Shakarian, *The Happiest People* (1960), 50; and Demos Shakarian-Synan interview, October 5, 1987, 17.

76. "Dairy Valley Becomes a City for Cows," Cerritos, California, http://www.ci.cerritos.ca.us/library/history (accessed August 11, 2008); and Demos Shakarian, *The Happiest People* (1975), 63–64.

77. 1940 (*Telephone Directory – Downey, Norwalk, Artesia, Bellflower* [Downey, CA: Consolidated Telephone Company, 1940], 24; and 1940 (*Telephone Directory – Downey, Norwalk, Artesia, Bellflower* [Downey, CA: Consolidated Telephone Company, 1947], 28. There is some discrepancy regarding Shakarian's move to 8413 Lexington Road in Downey, California and approximately when it occurred. The earliest publications of *Voice* magazine listed his address on Lexington Road (*Voice*, March, 1953, 2), and other sources indicate Shakarian still lived in his old residence on Cerritos Avenue in 1940 (*Telephone Directory – Downey, Norwalk, Artesia, Bellflower* [Downey, CA: Consolidated Telephone Company, 1940], 24) but that he had moved to Lexington Road by 1947 1940 (*Telephone Directory – Downey, Norwalk, Artesia, Bellflower* [Downey, CA: Consolidated Telephone Company, 1947], 28. However, the property was developed in 1936, but he may have owned both homes for several years and eventually used the old residence on Cerritos Avenue as the headquarters for Reliance Dairies. Further information on Demos Shakarian's home at 8413 Lexington Road can be found at the Los Angeles County Tax Assessor's web site, http://maps.assessor.lacounty.gov/mapping/viewer.asp (accessed August 12, 2009).

78. Demos Shakarian, *The Happiest People* (1975), 50.

79. Demos Shakarian, "A Prophecy Fulfilled," *Vision* July/August 1982, 18; and Demos Shakarian, *The Happiest People* (1975), 57.

80. Demos Shakarian-Synan interview, October 5, 1987, 8.

81. Demos Shakarian, "God's Dairyman," (1956), 46; and Thomas Nickel, "The Amazing Shakarian Story: Part Three," *Voice*, December 1953, 8.

82. Demos Shakarian, "Coming Together," *Voice*, February 1982, 17; Demos Shakarian, "A Prophecy Fulfilled," *Voice*, July/August 1982, 18; and Demos Shakarian, *The Happiest People*, (1975), 50.

83. *God at Our Side*, DVD, 2005, produced by Jeff Jonoian and Mark Perumean.

84. See Demos Shakarian, *The Vision*, DVD (Costa Mesa, CA: FGBMFI, n.d.); and also Demos Shakarian, *The Happiest People* (1975), 50.

85. Demos Shakarian *The Happiest People* (1975), 51–52.

86. Demos Shakarian, *The Happiest People* (1975), 63–64.

87. Demos Shakarian, *The Happiest People* (1975), 52; and Geraldine Scalf-Tallman interview, January 8, 2008.

88. Demos Shakarian, *The Happiest People* (1975), 52.

89. "Deaths," *Los Angeles Times*, January 21, 1940, 18; and from information gathered at Rose Hills Memorial Park in Whittier, California. In his autobiography, Demos Shakarian mentions that Lucy Shakarian died in the spring of 1939 at age twenty-two (Demos Shakarian, *The Happiest People* (1975), 52) but her headstone states she died in

January 1940 at the age of twenty-three. In addition, her social security death records confirm her demise on January 21, 1940.

90. Demos Shakarian, "God's Dairyman," (1956), 46; and Thomas Nickel, "The Amazing Shakarian Story: Part Three," December 1953, 8.

91. Demos Shakarian, "God's Dairyman," (1956), 46.

Chapter Six

Demos Shakarian the Evangelist (1940–1947)

At the age of twenty-six, after the death of Demos Shakarian's sister, Lucille, Rose and Demos Shakarian dedicated their lives to God. They decided to go into business with God and for God, and they "looked around for something to do for him."[1] With renewed vigor, they ventured into new areas of business, facing both challenges and success in the dairy industry and other related fields. Demos and Rose Shakarian also ventured into new areas of ministry, experimenting with lay evangelism at Lincoln Park in Los Angeles and organizing tent revivals with guest evangelists for the next twelve years.

New Business Opportunities

In 1940, the fertilizer plant Demos Shakarian started four years earlier was rapidly losing money. Ultimately, Shakarian had to close the plant one year later, but this failure did not deter him from venturing into other areas related to the dairy industry. In 1940, Isaac and Demos Shakarian began a grain milling operation to provide feed for their dairy. The milling endeavor seemed to make sense because they could lower their expenses at the dairy by providing feed directly to the herd from their new grain business rather than buying grain from local milling operators.[2] In addition, the Shakarian's added a special formula of molasses and other ingredients to the grain which became popular with other dairy operations, and thus they began the Reliance Milling Company in 1940.[3] The Shakarians began the operation by purchasing an existing milling operation consisting of three sixty foot grain elevators, conveniently located next to the Southern Pacific Railroad tracks on South Pioneer Boulevard in Norwalk, California.[4] With the use of a vacuum system, Demos Shakarian devised a means to transport grain from box cars to silos, dramatically reducing handling costs.[5]

In September 1940, Demos Shakarian created another subsidiary to the expanding Shakarian dairy business with an innovative drive-in dairy.[6] The Shakarians had a grand opening at the newest Reliance Dairy and in doing so, with this new business, created a seamless industry from the cattle trough to the kitchen table. Shakarian planned to recreate the success of his initial retail outlet, and ultimately the drive-in dairies became one of the most enduring Shakarian business ventures.[7]

As the businesses in the Shakarian family began to multiply, the three cows Isaac Shakarian started with in 1912 grew to three thousand head of cattle in 1943.[8] The Shakarian dairy business had continued to grow during the Depression, but war time demands for milk allowed for significant growth during WWII as a large portion of the milk was diverted to San Diego for military needs.[9] The Shakarian's also secured exclusive rights to sell their dairy products at various retail outlets, including Ralph's groceries, consequently generating additional sales.[10]

In fact, California fared better than most of the western states during the Depression, but with its military enterprises during the War and its rapidly growing aerospace, mining, petroleum, and agricultural sectors during and after WWII, California alone soon became the sixth largest economy in the world.[11] In addition, the modern mechanisms of agriculture, most efficiently implemented in California, would serve the Shakarian family well in a burgeoning dairy industry. At the height of WWII, Isaac and Demos Shakarian claimed to have the largest privately owned dairy herd in the world.[12]

However, the Shakarians still faced economic challenges in the 1940s. The American Federation of Laborers Milkers Union had become deadlocked with the Milk Producers Labor Council in negotiating wages for the dairy milkers in Southern California in 1942. In eighteen months, the monthly wages of milkers had increased forty percent, and in March 1942, the union was insisting on increasing that wage another forty percent to $224.16, a monthly wage $75 greater than what Demos Shakarian had been paid for his own salary from 1938 until 1940.[13] In addition, since most of the dairymen the Shakarians normally employed were either working in military factories or fighting in WWII, the labor shortage created higher demand for wages.[14]

Higher labor costs and labor shortages were not the only problem the Shakarians faced. A cattle feed shortage reduced the productivity of most dairies in Southern California.[15] With labor and feed shortages, Isaac Shakarian estimated he was losing $8.35 per cow every month.[16] The federal Office of Pricing Administration would not allow dairies to increase their prices, so Isaac threatened to liquidate his dairy herd unless he was allowed to increase his prices. Five months later, on May 25, 1943, Isaac Shakarian demonstrated that this was not an idle threat when he and his son sold six hundred of their dairy cows at an auction in Downey.[17]

Nevertheless, the Shakarians weathered labor shortages, feed shortages, and pricing restrictions as the War came to an end. After WWII, the Shakarian herd eventually increased to over five thousand head of cattle.[18] With business thriving and the family prospering, Rose and Demos Shakarian made plans to either build a new house or expand their current residence. Rose wanted a larger kitchen, and Demos Shakarian needed an additional room in the house from which to work. In addition, they had been regularly entertaining and housing guest evangelists often for weeks at a time. In order to accommodate these frequent guests, Demos Shakarian asked Richard or Geraldine to sleep on the sofa.[19]

Demos Shakarian's Early Evangelistic Efforts

Before Demos Shakarian invited his first guest evangelist, he took initial steps beyond his familiar business and dairy environment to the unfamiliar world of lay evangelism. Beginning on June 2, 1940, he planned and led, with limited success, weekly Sunday afternoon outreaches across the street from Lincoln Park in Los Angeles.[20] These meetings lasted all summer, dwindling in the fall of 1940. Initially, Demos Shakarian was terrified at the prospects of attempting this endeavor and fearful that one of his business associates or one of his friends from the local Kiwanis or Lions Club might recognize him; however, with Rose's encouragement, and a few backup singers from the Armenian Church, Shakarian overcame his fear. Ironically, several of Demos Shakarian's business associates did recognize him, and many of them surprised Shakarian by responding with tears of repentance and testimonies which attracted more onlookers to attend the weekly Sunday afternoon meetings at Lincoln Park.[21] Shakarian discovered that his fear was grounded in his own pride and dignity and largely based on his concern over what his fellow business associates might think about his evangelistic experiment. While he found this fear to be largely unwarranted, Demos Shakarian also discovered that he was much better at handing off the microphone to other business men who were eager to share their testimony than speaking into the microphone himself.[22]

The next summer Shakarian and his wife helped coordinate a much larger outreach on property recently purchased by the First Armenian Pentecostal Church at the corner of Goodrich Boulevard and Carolina Place in East Los Angeles.[23] Whether or not the urgency of those meetings was spurred on by much larger global events in Europe and Asia at the beginning of WWII, people and churches responded. Beginning in July 1941, Shakarian set up a tent and held meetings every night for six weeks, coordinating with churches, overseeing offerings, expenses, and accounting. As many as three hundred people were in attendance every night.[24] His younger second cousin, Harry Mushegan (1918–), gave the sermons every night and many conversions were recorded.[25] However, just as significant, was the cooperation of five different Pentecostal churches in this venture.

While the early formation of Shakarian's greater vision was likely encouraged by this ecumenical cooperation, it was also shaken by the initial reluctance of his own church.[26] As Shakarian himself suggested, the pneumatic fervency of his own church, in addition to the orthopathy of most early Pentecostalism, had been replaced by a dull orthodoxy and insular attitude.[27] Indeed, Demos Shakarian experienced his own hesitancy when he first ventured into evangelism at Lincoln Park. While Shakarian was eager to sponsor other evangelists, such as his cousin Harry Mushegan, he was hesitant to experiment further with his own evangelistic efforts. On several occasions, he told Rose that he did not enjoy his first experience with lay evangelism in Lincoln Park "where we were so well known."[28] Nevertheless, Shakarian believed that God would bless him and prosper his business for his obedience to this divine evangelistic mandate.[29]

For the next seven years, Demos Shakarian continued to sponsor various evangelists at smaller venues throughout Southern California. Most of these events were scheduled on vacant lots where a tent was erected and some limited advertising was done. Some of the early evangelists he sponsored were Robert Fiero (1916–1985), William Freeman (1913–1976), and Billy Adams (1921–1990).[30]

Another evangelist Demos Shakarian contacted in 1944 was Kelso Glover (1884–1965). Shakarian heard Glover speak on the Angelus Temple radio broadcast on Sunday evening April 9, regarding the resurrection of Christ and His healing power.[31] Demos and Isaac Shakarian heard Kelso speak about God's ability to heal any disease, and this caught their attention since their dairy herd at Reliance Dairy Number Three was experiencing an epidemic of bovine tuberculosis. Demos, Isaac, and Richard Shakarian had all been praying for the cattle since the first cow had tested positive for tuberculosis, but now three hundred of the one thousand cattle at Dairy Number Three were possibly infected. The county health department was sending out officers later that week to give a final tuberculosis test which would determine if the entire herd needed to be destroyed.[32]

Demos Shakarian called Kelso Glover the next morning and Glover came before noon to the Shakarian dairy. For three hours, Glover and Shakarian went to each corral and Glover would pray, "The cattle on a thousand hills are Yours! In Your Name Lord, we take authority over every tuberculosis germ attacking your creatures."[33] When the county health officials came to test the herd one month later, over one thousand cows were tested and no cow tested positive, not even the cattle that had previously tested positive for tuberculosis.[34]

Florence Shakarian's Miraculous Story

On another occasion, Demos Shakarian sought the help of an evangelist for a family crisis. Demos Shakarian's sister, Florence (1923–1966), had recently graduated from high school, and she was driving to Whittier College to begin her study program. In an early morning fog in late September 1941, she failed to see a stop sign and collided with an asphalt truck.[35] Her left hip and pelvis were crushed from the collision, and she was thrown from her car onto the highway. The collision caused hot asphalt to spill onto the road, and Florence received third degree burns on most of her back.[36]

Shakarian received news of the accident and rushed to the hospital. Shakarian visited the hospital frequently over the next five days, and his prayers seemed to temporarily relieve her pain, but she was not healed and remained in excruciating pain when he would leave.[37] Shakarian remembered how he once prayed for Florence's elbow when she was seven years old, and she was healed. Now Demos

Shakarian's faith in God and his own healing experiences were being challenged. Desperate for anything or anyone that could help her, Shakarian visited the healing services of Charles S. Price (1887–1947).

On September 21, 1941, Price had begun nightly revival meetings in a tent at the 3700 block on East Slausan Avenue in nearby Maywood, California. Shakarian begged Price to come and pray for Florence.[38] Price had just concluded a lengthy healing service that Monday evening in Maywood, but he agreed to come with Shakarian to Downey Hospital. Demos Shakarian drove Price to the hospital and they arrived before midnight. Charles Price touched Florence's forehead and prayed for her. For a period of time Florence moaned and swayed, the heavy traction apparatus that held her shattered hip immobile moving with her. Finally, she looked at her brother and whispered, "Jesus healed me."[39] Florence Shakarian remained in the hospital for one month as the burns on her back healed, but the morning following the visit of Charles Price, Dr. Haygood at Downey Hospital asked Shakarian to come to the hospital. Upon Shakarian's arrival, Haygood showed him an X-ray of Florence's left hip taken that morning which showed a normal, healthy pelvis and hip.[40]

Demos Shakarian and the Christian Business Men's Committee

Several months after Florence Shakarian's dramatic healing, Demos Shakarian decided to form a chapter of the Christian Business Men's Committee (1930–) and served as the founder and president of the Downey, California, chapter for several years beginning in 1942.[41] Every Saturday morning, thirty to forty men gathered at the Odd Fellows Hall in Downey to cook their own breakfast. They shared what God was doing in their lives, discussed Scripture, encouraged and prayed for each other. Shakarian observed, "These men were Methodists, Baptists, Presbyterians, Catholics, and Pentecostals, and although we worshiped in different ways, I found that we all loved Jesus."[42]

However, Shakarian felt something was missing in these meetings at the Odd Fellows Hall. They did not have the same pneumatic vitality that Demos Shakarian experienced at his own Armenian Pentecostal Church. The Christian Business Men's Committee (CBMC) was not Pentecostal and Demos Shakarian felt that the CBMC was diluting the spiritual fervor of Pentecostal men like himself who were attending these weekly breakfasts; however, he believed that most of the other business men would be unwilling to go to a Pentecostal church.[43] Eventually, Shakarian resigned from his post as president of the CBMC's Downey chapter, but his involvement in this organization served as a model and reminder of the importance for founding his own Christian business men's organization.

Both Isaac and Demos Shakarian became involved in the greater business community in the region as their dairy business continued to grow. Isaac Shakarian began serving as vice president on the board of the forty-eighth district of the California Agricultural Association in 1942, a position he served in for the rest of his life.[44] Demos Shakarian followed suit a few years later, and he was elected as vice chairman of the Los Angeles County Farm Bureau in 1944.[45] Their involvement in the business and religious community betrayed the sectarian isolation of their Molokan neighbors, but Demos Shakarian desired to share the pneumatic nature of his Molokan inheritance beyond the confines of his Armenian Pentecostal Church.

Further consecration: The Birth and Death of Carolyn Shakarian

On November 1, 1944, Rose Shakarian gave birth to their third child, Carolyn Shakarian.[46] Zaroohi Shakarian sewed small pink dresses for her granddaughter months before the delivery, somehow knowing Demos Shakarian's third child would be a girl. After all, "as far back as records went, there had never been more than one son in each generation of Shakarians."[47] Demos Shakarian's mother had recently been diagnosed with inoperable cancer and Carolyn's birth provided comfort and relief to Zaroohi as Rose brought the child next door to Isaac Shakarian's house for frequent visits.

Unfortunately, only grief came to Demos and Rose Shakarian as Carolyn developed pneumonia in both lungs from a flu virus she caught in early March 1945. Even though Charles Price prayed for the child, she did not improve. Carolyn was admitted to the hospital on March 21 and died one day later, not even five months old.[48] The extended Shakarian family, church, and friends came to mourn with Demos and Rose Shakarian, but the loss of such a young child was particularly difficult for Rose.

Occasionally, friends such as Charles Price would drop by and comfort the family, but Rose often teared up at the sight of another newborn infant. Business went on at the Shakarian farm as WWII came to an end, but somehow plans Demos and Rose Shakarian had made for a new home no longer seemed important, so they stayed at 8413 Lexington Road in Downey for the remainder of their lives.[49] One day after Richard and Geraldine had gone to school, Rose and Demos Shakarian began their usual morning prayer at the dinette table. Suddenly, without a word, they both walked across the room and knelt on the dark red Oriental rug the Gabrielian family had given them for their tenth anniversary in 1943. With tears in their eyes, they expressed their grief and consecrated their lives once again to serve God in every area of their lives.[50]

Charles Price and Demos Shakarian

Charles Price was a Methodist minister introduced to Pentecostalism at an Aimee Semple McPherson revival meeting in San Jose, California in 1920.[51] He had an international ministry but spent much of his time in the Pacific Northwest where his revival meetings helped found such early significant Pentecostal churches as

Lighthouse Temple in Eugene, Oregon.[52] There are few biographical details about the activities and events surrounding Charles Price, even from his own autobiography. He failed to mention any of his encounters or meetings with Demos Shakarian in his autobiography; in addition, Price mentioned nothing of the healing miracle that occurred when he prayed for the healing of Demos Shakarian's sister Florence.[53]

Shakarian mentioned that he and Price met on a weekly basis in the 1940s, and Charles Price is mentioned approximately fifty times in the first half of Shakarian's autobiography.[54] Price developed a mentoring relationship with Shakarian, and Demos Shakarian later recalled how much of an influence Charles Price had on his life. Whether out of friendship, generosity, or simply out of obligation for Price's weekly meetings, Shakarian gave Price two Holstein milk cows.[55]

In several of the regular mentoring sessions that Price had with Shakarian, the evangelist challenged Demos Shakarian to meet the needs of business men. Once, through the prophetic charismata that had already defined and directed so much of the life of Shakarian and his ancestors, Price spoke of a coming revival that would not be led by preachers or evangelists. But according to Price, "this is going to happen spontaneously – all over the world – to ordinary men and women – people in shops and offices and factories."[56]

Demos Shakarian greatly admired Price's speaking ability and his ministry, declaring him to be "the greatest speaker I ever heard in my life."[57] On one occasion, excited by the results of some of Price's recent crusades, Shakarian told Price, "It must feel wonderful to be riding the crest of the wave." Price replied by saying, "You never ride the crest in God's work. There is always another billow rolling in higher than the one before. If a man rests on his oars he is apt to be swamped."[58]Although Charles Price was clearly a spiritual mentor to Shakarian, the mentor failed to see the fruits of his protégé, as he died in 1947, four years before the FGBMFI began meeting in Clifton's Cafeteria.[59]

A Youth Rally at Shrine Auditorium

Demos Shakarian heeded the words of his mentor, Charles Price, and decided not to "rest on his oars." He continued to sponsor evangelistic meetings in Los Angeles, and became well known as an excellent organizer for evangelistic events in the Pentecostal community. In the summer of 1942, he sponsored another series of meetings, and he organized another six week series of tent meetings in Orange County in the summer of 1943. He also tried to organize a second series of meetings in the summer of 1943 with Charles Price as the featured evangelist, but at the last minute, Charles Price became ill, and the meetings had to be cancelled.[60] Shakarian, likely because of his business acumen, quickly discovered that he was much more adept at managing, organizing, and budgeting crusades than he was speaking at them.

Others recognized this talent, and Shakarian was asked to be the finance chairman for an interdenominational youth rally sponsored by local Pentecostal churches in 1947 and held at the Los Angeles Shrine Auditorium.[61] The committee organizing the event felt they needed to raise three hundred dollars for advertising and the rental of the auditorium, but Shakarian knew from prior experience that they needed to raise more. He challenged the committee to raise three thousand dollars, an amount that seemed incomprehensible, if not impossible to the committee.

In order to raise funds for this event, Demos Shakarian asked each member of the ten pastor committee to give him the names of ten business men from their respective churches. Shakarian invited these business men and their spouses to a free chicken dinner at the famous Knott's Berry Farm.[62] It was here that Shakarian received a further glimpse of what his future calling to business men would be like, as one business man after another got up to share a testimony. Fred Friedmeyer, Dell Arganbright, and Bryan Smith each wrote out checks for $500. Other business men followed suit as the sum of $6,200 was raised to meet the financial obligations for the upcoming rally.[63]

The rally was an enormous success with a capacity crowd of over six thousand people in attendance and an overflow crowd of people outside who listened to the impromptu preaching of a young evangelist named R.W. Culpepper (1921–).[64] Culpepper's preaching sparked an enthusiastic response both inside and outside the auditorium, and this became Shakarian's largest organized rally so far. The offering that night covered any remaining expenses and an additional five thousand dollars was raised. The committee suggested these additional funds should be saved for a future rally which would later be known as the Full Gospel Youth Rally at the Hollywood Bowl Amphitheater.[65]

After the euphoria of the Shrine Auditorium Youth Rally, the Shakarian family went back to the business of feeding cattle, milking cows, and delivering milk to thousands of families in Southern California. However, two events brought joy and respite to the hard work of these dairy farmers. The wedding of Demos Shakarian's sister, Florence Shakarian, and the birth of Shakarian's second son, Stephen, on July 12, 1947, brought hope and encouragement to a family beleaguered by tragedy and restored by hope.[66] Those two events also brought joy to a dying mother who planned Florence's wedding and held Steve Shakarian (1947–2003) in her arms before Zaroohi Shakarian died in November 1947 from inoperable cancer.[67]

Conclusion

Demos and Isaac Shakarian began the decade of the 1940s as successful business men who faced new challenges and new endeavors into milling, dairy drive-ins, expanded dairies, and innovative technological advances, some of them created by Demos Shakarian's fertile mind. They had a few set backs and challenges with the prospect of food shortages, rationing, bovine tuberculosis, labor shortages, and union demands, but most of these challenges were handled with prayer, persistence, and hard work.

The 1940s also began with a sense of deeper consecration for the Shakarians and a vow to serve God in some fashion after the death of Shakarian's sister, Lucille. The 1940s were also filled with charismatic experiences such as Florence Shakarian's healing, the prophecies of Charles Price, and the mentoring relationship Shakarian forged with Price from 1941 until Price's death in 1947. This period of Demos Shakarian's life ended with the death of his mother, Zaroohi, in November 1947. This stage in Demos Shakarian's life began with a death and ended with another death, but it was the tragic death of Shakarian's daughter Carolyn in 1944, along with the charismatic experiences and mentoring relationship of Charles Price, which directed Demos Shakarian to take a more focused approach towards Christian ministry.

Rose and Demos Shakarian decided to serve in the arena of evangelism, and their experiment at Lincoln Park taught them some valuable lessons about themselves and about their future ministry. Demos Shakarian's experience with the Christian Business Men's Committee provided a model for his future ministry and legacy, and the evangelistic endeavors during this segment of Shakarian's life culminated with a youth rally at the Shrine Auditorium.

However, these experiences were only the beginning of what would come. The winds of spiritual change were about to blast with the pneumatic forces of the Latter Rain revival, the ecumenical influences of the World Council of Churches (WCC), and the Pentecostal Fellowship of North America (PFNA), the eschatological momentum that emerged with the formation of Israeli statehood, and the soteriological energy that came from the healing evangelists of the 1940s and 1950s. In 1948, these forces either directly or indirectly reached a crescendo in the life of Demos Shakarian.

Notes

1. Demos Shakarian, "God's Dairyman," (1956), 46.

2. Demos Shakarian, *The Happiest People* (1975), 59; and Thomas Nickel, "The Amazing Shakarian Story: Part Three," *Voice*, December 1953, 8.

3. Demos Shakarian, *The Shakarian Story*, 3rd ed., edited by Jerry Jensen (Irvine, CA: FGBMFI, 1999), 25–27; and Shakarian-Synan interview, October 5, 1987, 5.

4. "Norwalk Grain Concern Sold for $500, 000," *Los Angeles Times*, December 5, 1948, A24.

5. Demos Shakarian, *The Happiest People* (1975), 59.

6. Ibid, 58.

7. Gene Scalf-Tallman interview, January 8, 2008.

8. Demos Shakarian, *The Happiest People* (1975), 50.

9. "Diary Herd Liquidation Threatened," *Los Angeles Times*, January 21, 1943, 1.

10. Display Ad, *Los Angeles Times*, January 13, 1940, 4; and interview with Brian Bittke, former vice-president of marketing for Ralph's Groceries by Matthew Tallman, Portland, OR, September 2, 2008.

11. Earl Pomeroy, *The Pacific Slope: A History of California, Oregon, Washington, Idaho, Utah, and Nevada*, (Las Vegas, NV: University of Nevada Press, 2003), 296. Currently, due to the rapid economic growth in several Asian nations, specifically in China, California has the seventh largest economy in the world.

12. Shakarian-Synan interview, October 5, 1987, 3; Demos Shakarian, *The Happiest People* (1975), 49–50; and Ed Ainsworth, "A Lot of Faith," May 8, 1960, 119.

13. Display Ad, *Los Angeles Times*, February 22, 1942, 13.

14. Demos Shakarian, *The Happiest People* (1975), 78.

15. "Dairy Herd Liquidation Threatened," *Los Angeles Times*, January 22, 1943, 1; and Demos Shakarian *The Happiest People* (1975), 75.

16. "Dairy Herd Liquidation," *Los Angeles Times*, January 22, 1943, 1.

17. "Six Hundred Dairy Cows Sold at Downey Auction," *Los Angeles Times*, May 26, 1943, 13.

18. Demos Shakarian-Synan interview, October 5, 1987, 3.

19. Demos Shakarian, *The Happiest People* (1975), 85.

20. Ibid, 53–57.

21. Demos Shakarian, *The Happiest People*, (1975), 55–57.

22. Ibid, 56–57.

23. Ibid, 61.

24. Demos Shakarian, "God's Dairyman," (1956), 47.

25. Demos Shakarian, *The Happiest People*, (1975), 63; and Harding Mushegian-Tallman interview, January 14, 2008.

26. See, for example, Shakarian, *The Happiest People*, (1975), 57–58, and especially, 61–62.

27. Ibid, 62. Orthopathy refers to emotional and experiential elements of Christian faith. For a broader definition and examples of orthopathy in Pentecostalism see Steven Land's *Pentecostal Spirituality: A Passion for the Kingdom* (Sheffield, England: Sheffield Academic Press, 1993).

28. Demos Shakarian, "The Cows Accepted It," *Voice* September 1975, 13.

29. Ibid.

30. Display Ad 11 – No Title, *Los Angeles Times* September 17, 1949, A2; also "Old Fashioned Revival Tent Series to Begin" *Los Angeles Times* September 3, 1949, A3.

31. "Sunday Sermons," *Los Angeles Times*, April 8, 1944, A2; Demos Shakarian, *The Happiest People* (1975), 77–78; and Demos Shakarian, "The Cows Accepted It," *Voice* September 1975, 14.

32. Demos Shakarian, "The Cows Accepted It," *Voice*, September 1975, 14; and Demos Shakarian, *The Happiest People* (1975), 78–79.

33. Demos Shakarian, "The Cows Accepted It," *Voice*, September 1975, 14; and Demos Shakarian, *The Happiest People* (1975), 78.

34. Ibid.

35. Demos Shakarian, *The Happiest People* (1975), 64.

36. Demos Shakarian, "God's Dairyman," (1956), 47–48; and Demos Shakarian, *The Happiest People* (1975), 65–66.

37. Ibid.

38. "Sunday Sermon Announcements," *Los Angeles Times*, September 20, 1941, A–3. In his autobiography *The Happiest People* (1975), 64, Shakarian states this accident occurred on a Tuesday morning in late September. According to the public record of Price's revival meetings the accident would have occurred on Tuesday morning,

September 16, 1941, but it is entirely possible that the meetings were held over for an extra week or two, thus placing the date of the accident on September 23 or September 30.

39. Demos Shakarian, "God's Dairyman," (1956), 48; and Demos Shakarian, *The Happiest People* (1975), 70.

40. Demos Shakarian, *The Happiest People* (1975), 70–71; and Demos Shakarian, "God's Dairyman," (1956), 48.

41. Demos Shakarian, "A Prophecy Fulfilled," *Voice*, July 1982, 18; and Demos Shakarian, *Life Lifters* (1984), 3:7.

42. Ibid.

43. Demos Shakarian, "A Prophecy Fulfilled," *Voice*, July 1982, 19–20.

44. Jerry Jensen, "Tributes to Isaac Shakarian," *Voice* January 1965, 16; "Agriculture Members for County Reappointed," *Los Angeles Times*, October 23, 1946, 6; and "Lillywhite Named to Eighth Term," *Los Angeles Times*, March 15, 1948, A11.

45. "Farm Bureau Elects Dairy Chairman," *Los Angeles Times*, February 7, 1944, A2.

46. From information gathered at Rose Hills Memorial Park in Whittier, California; and from Demos Shakarian, *The Happiest People* (1975), 80–82.

47. Demos Shakarian, *The Happiest People* (1975), 80.

48. Demos Shakarian, "Together," *Voice*, February 1981, 17; and Demos Shakarian, *The Happiest People* (1975), 84.

49. Demos Shakarian, *The Happiest People* (1975), 84; *Telephone Directory – Downey, Norwalk, Artesia, Bellflower* [Downey, CA: Consolidated Telephone Company, 1947], 28; and Thomas Nickel, "The Amazing Shakarian Story," *Voice*, October 1953, 2. The address was renamed from 215 North Lexington-Gallatin Road to 8413 Lexington Road between 1947 and 1948. However, the house was remodeled and expanded to its current size of five bedrooms, three bathrooms, and 3,089 square feet in 1957 (Los Angeles County Tax Assessor's web site, http://maps.assessor.lacounty.gov/mapping/viewer.asp [accessed August 12, 2009]).

50. Demos Shakarian, "Together," *Voice*, February 1981, 17; and Demos Shakarian, *The Happiest People* (1975), 86.

51. Charles S. Price, *And Signs Followed: The Story of Charles S. Price*, rev. ed. (Plainfield, New Jersey: Logos International, 1972), 45–49.

52. Charles S. Price, *And Signs Followed* (1972), 59.

53. Demos Shakarian, *The Happiest People* (1975), 70–71.

54. Demos Shakarian-Synan interview, October 5, 1987, 32; and Demos Shakarian, *The Happiest People* (1975), 74, 82.

55. Demos Shakarian-Synan interview, October 5, 1987, 32.

56. Demos Shakarian, "A Prophecy Fulfilled," *Voice*, July–August 1982, 19; and Demos Shakarian, *The Happiest People* (1975), 83.

57. Demos Shakarian-Synan interview, October 5, 1987, 30.

58. Demos Shakarian, "FGBMFI: Twenty Years of Charisma," *Voice* January 1973, 2.

59. Demos Shakarian, *The Happiest People* (1975), 83.

60. Ibid, 73–77.

61. Demos Shakarian, *The Vision*, DVD, (Costa Mesa, CA: FGBMFI, n.d.); Demos Shakarian, "A Prophecy Fulfilled," *Vision*, July/August 1982, 18; and Demos Shakarian, *The Shakarian Story* (1999), 31.

62. Shakarian-Synan interview, October 5, 1987, 26; Demos Shakarian, "A Prophecy Fulfilled," *Vision*, July/August 1982, 18; and Demos Shakarian, *The Shakarian Story* (1999), 31.

63. Demos Shakarian, *The Happiest People* (1975), 89; Demos Shakarian, *The Shakarian Story* (1999), 31; and Demos Shakarian, *The Vision*, DVD (n.d.). *The Happiest People* (1975) relates this fundraising story to the Hollywood Bowl Rally which occurred later in 1948, but all other sources tie the story to the earlier youth rally at the Shrine Auditorium.

64. Demos Shakarian, *The Shakarian Story* (1999), 31–32; Demos Shakarian, *The Vision*, DVD (n.d.); and "Shrine Auditorium and Expo Center General Facts," the Al Maliakah Shriners, http://www.shrineauditorium.com/shriners.html (accessed August 21, 2008).

65. Demos Shakarian, *The Shakarian Story* (1999), 32.

66. Demos Shakarian, *The Happiest People* (1975), 96–97.

67. Demos Shakarian, *The Happiest People* (1975), 97; and from information gathered at the Rose Hill Cemetery, Whittier, California.

Chapter Seven

Demos Shakarian in 1948—
Among the Happiest People on Earth

After the death of their daughter Carolyn in 1944, Demos and Rose Shakarian made a deeper commitment to serve Christ. Shakarian's friendship with Charles Price, his involvement in the CBMC, and his ongoing support and sponsorship of various evangelistic tent meetings expressed his consecration. The death of Demos Shakarian's mother in 1947 only confirmed his resolution. In 1948, Shakarian's commitment to serve Christ through the sponsorship of various evangelists, rallies, and meetings reached a feverish pace.

The Shakarians in 1948

One of the most significant issues dominating the minds of Isaac and Demos Shakarian in 1948 was the price of grain. The commodities market for oats, barley, corn, and other grain products was placed at a restricted ceiling during and after WWII, but now, with ongoing post-war economic growth, Shakarian reasoned the price ceiling set by the Chicago Commodities Exchange Market would be lifted soon. Consequently, Shakarian purchased a significant amount of grain at a contracted price anticipating that this ceiling would be lifted.[1]

Isaac Shakarian expressed some doubts about his son's speculative grain purchase, but Demos Shakarian seemed confident concerning the profit they would receive. At this time, the Reliance Milling Company, along with Shakarian's other dairy business responsibilities seemed to occupy more of his time. In addition, Demos Shakarian also organized a busy ministry schedule in the summer and fall of 1948, organizing a number of tent revival meetings and planning his largest evangelistic event so far at the Hollywood Bowl.[2]

The evangelistic schedule in 1948 was Shakarian's most ambitious so far. He organized a six-week evangelistic tent revival with the mysterious "Bob Smith", the Hollywood Bowl evangelistic rally in September 1948, and the Fresno evangelistic campaign for five weeks in October and November 1948 at the Fresno Memorial Auditorium with some of Shakarian's most enduring and popular evangelists of that era, including William Branham, Kelso Glover, A.C. Valdez, and Billy Adams.[3] In the midst of this hectic evangelistic schedule Demos Shakarian's son Richard captured the pneumatic and evangelistic fervor of his father when he also experienced a Spirit baptism at the age of thirteen in 1948.[4] Richard insisted on being admitted to an evangelistic training school in the summer of 1948 called the Soul Clinic in Los Angeles, directed by Fred Jordan.[5] After this training, Richard proceeded to introduce three hundred young people to a Christian salvation experience, initiate three hundred Youth for Christ chapters in California, and address the Washington, D.C. congressional prayer meeting, all within the next two years.[6]

Almost immediately after the Hollywood Bowl Youth Rally, Shakarian temporarily moved his family to a rented house on G Street only five blocks from the Fresno Memorial Auditorium. They moved to Fresno in early October 1948, one week in advance of the meetings, in order to plan and prepare for the evangelistic campaign.[7] In the midst of the five week Fresno campaign in October and November 1948, three things happened which distracted Demos Shakarian and almost caused him to cancel, or at least abandon his oversight of the Fresno meetings. First, during the temporary move to Fresno, Rose Shakarian misplaced the diamond wristwatch her husband had given her as a traditional gift during the process leading up to their engagement in 1932.[8] As the family went searching around the house for the missing watch, they realized Stephen, only one year old, had developed a fever which spiked to over 104 degrees.[9] Finally, the price of grain had been dropping for the past several weeks due to a record harvest in the fall of 1948, and Maurice Brunache, the Shakarian bookkeeper, called Demos Shakarian on Friday afternoon, October 8, mentioning that the Reliance Milling Company had lost $50,000 in one week due to the price decline and the speculative purchase Demos Shakarian had made nine months earlier.[10]

In the meetings in Fresno, Rose Shakarian played the organ for the worship services and Demos Shakarian organized the meetings, contacted the guest speakers, and served as master of ceremonies during the services. Since both Rose and Demos Shakarian were in the services, and Stephen Shakarian had a fever, they decided to hire a practical nurse (Mrs. Newman), who had previously cared for each child when he or she came home with Rose after birth.[11] As the meetings began, Stephen's fever remained elevated, and the grain prices continued to drain the Shakarian bank account. As a result, Demos Shakarian believed that Satan was trying to thwart their evangelistic efforts in Fresno.[12]

As the Fresno campaign continued, the worship leader, Billy Adams, asked those attending the meetings to pray for Stephen Shakarian, and eventually, his fever subsided. In addition, through an unusual set of circumstances involving a chameleon Richard Shakarian had purchased at the Fresno County Fair in October, Rose's diamond watch was found.[13] However, grain prices were still well below the contractual price Demos Shakarian had paid when he purchased feed nine months earlier, and he began to pray for someone to buy the Shakarian mill. On Wednesday, November 3, during the fourth week of the Fresno meetings, Adolph Weinberg (1901–1986) called Isaac Shakarian, declaring an interest in purchasing the Reliance Milling Company.[14]

Isaac Shakarian asked his son to drive down to Downey immediately to close the sale of the mill, but Demos Shakarian stayed at the meetings in Fresno for the final two weeks. Shakarian believed God was testing his obedience, and as he stayed in Fresno, capacity crowds continued to fill the auditorium. On the final night, as Kelso Glover spoke, Demos Shakarian witnessed the healing miracle of Oca Tatham's (1911–2001) injured eye, and he gained a new sense of energy and motivation to pursue what he perceived was a divine agenda.[15]

During the week of November 14th, Demos Shakarian concluded the financial details of the Fresno meetings and moved his family back to Downey where Adolph Weinberg continued to call, seemingly exacerbated and confused by Demos Shakarian's reasons for delaying the sale. Finally, on Monday, November 22, Isaac Shakarian, Demos Shakarian, and Adolph Weinberg met to negotiate a price. At first they could not agree on a price, but one day later they negotiated a price of slightly over $500,000, and the sale of the Reliance Milling Company was publicly announced on December 4, 1948.[16]

As 1948 concluded, the Shakarian family took a well deserved rest in Downey. On Christmas Eve, Demos and Rose Shakarian and their three children walked over to Isaac's house to exchange gifts. Rose played the organ as the extended family sang Christmas carols, and Demos Shakarian told the Christmas story of the nativity.[17] As the family ate Armenian pilaf and *shakar lokoom*, Demos Shakarian reflected upon the year, abandoned any future plans as a grain speculator, and concluded God was preparing him for something more than being a dairyman.[18]

The Beginning of the Latter Rain movement

In 1948, there may have been a variety of factors which motivated Demos Shakarian to devote an increasing amount of time to evangelistic work. The feverish tone which he took towards organizing various evangelistic speakers and tent revivals in 1948 may have been locally caused by Stephen Shakarian's illness, the deaths of Zaroohi and Carolyn Shakarian in the recent past, or the failure of the Reliance Milling Company. In addition, there were also larger events which may have motivated Shakarian, some of which he was directly aware, others he may have considered later, and still others of which he may have been oblivious.

One important religious movement which Demos Shakarian was influenced by was the Latter Rain movement (1948). The movement traces its origins from the meetings of William Branham in the fall of 1947 in Vancouver, British Columbia. Those meetings had a deep impact on some visiting teachers from Sharon Bible School in North Battleford, Saskatchewan. These teachers carried back reports of the William Branham campaign, helping to initiate a revival in February 1948 in their little school and orphanage. From this humble starting point, a charismatic renewal spread throughout North America over the next few months.[19]

The growth of this movement was something of which both William Branham and Demos Shakarian were aware when Branham came to speak at the Fresno Memorial Auditorium in late October 1948.[20] Other individuals would appear in both the formation of the Latter Rain movement and the FGBMFI, including David DuPlessis,[21] A.A. Allen, William Freeman, Jack Coe, and T.L. Osborn.[22] Perhaps the only other documented connection between Demos Shakarian and a prominent leader of the early Latter Rain movement was when Shakarian invited Carleton Spenser (1914–) to be a part of the second annual international FGBMFI in Washington, D.C. in 1953.[23] A.W. Rasmussen was also an active participant of both movements, but it is not known if he had any direct contact with Demos Shakarian.[24]

The Latter Rain movement should also be placed within the context of the larger healing crusades and evangelical awakenings that were occurring simultaneously in North America and other parts of the world after WWII. While David Harrell (1930–) places the Latter Rain within the context of the healing evangelists and their crusades that were rapidly becoming popular after WWII,[25] and Richard Riss places the Latter Rain within a larger evangelical awakening simultaneously occurring in North America,[26] the movement had its own unique ecstatic emphasis. In particular, the emphasis upon prophecy and healing in this movement may have struck a chord in the heart of Demos Shakarian.[27] In addition, the perception in this movement that the older Pentecostal denominations had become formalized and spiritually hardened resonated with the ecclesiological and pneumatological hermeneutic of Shakarian.[28] The rejection of the Latter Rain movement by the larger Pentecostal bodies paralleled the rejection of Shakarian's earliest attempts at evangelism even by his own Armenian Pentecostal Church.[29] In the midst of this rejection, a vision was birthed in the heart and mind of Demos Shakarian, albeit one that was slightly different from that of the leaders of the Latter Rain movement.

The Ecumenical Influences of the PFNA and the WCC

Ecumenical influences also appeared in 1948 which only later influenced Shakarian directly, but which may have also indirectly motivated him in 1948. Almost simultaneously, the most significant ecumenical efforts and organizations that fostered Christian unity emerged out of the morass and milieu of a post-WWII Christianity that no longer espoused or even reflected Christendom.[30] Churches both inside and outside of the traditional Pentecostalism that Shakarian had grown up in were beginning to see the need for global dialogue and cooperation in an increasingly sectarian and diverse world. A growing sense of ecumenical cooperation began with the formation of organizations like the Pentecostal Fellowship of North America (PFNA) and the World Council of Churches (WCC) which both started in 1948.

The World Council of Churches was officially organized in 1948, but its origins date much earlier to nineteenth century student and lay movements, the global missionary conference of 1910 in Edinburgh, and the Orthodox Synod of Constantinople in 1920. This suggested the need felt for an ecumenical organization, much like the League of Nations, in order to bring conversation and cooperation between all the governing bodies of global Christianity.[31] While the official inauguration of this organization was delayed by the onset of WWII, it is interesting to note that the WCC was finally organized in 1948 in Chicago, Illinois, in an era of global cooperation both inside and outside Christianity at the end of WWII.

The Pentecostal Fellowship of North America organized in the same year (1948), in Des Moines, Iowa, spurred on by a Pentecostal World Convention in 1947. In many ways it was created as a counterpart to the already existent National Association of Evangelicals (NAE – 1942–). Many of its primary members joined the NAE at this time in a wave of ecumenical support.[32] Contrary to this ecumenical growth was the exclusion of minorities in the PFNA, significantly women and African-Americans.[33] Nevertheless, 1948 represented an ecumenical gestalt both within and outside Pentecostalism which helped shape the context of Shakarian's hermeneutic.

It should be mentioned that earlier Pentecostal pioneers had begun to preach about the need for ecumenical cooperation. Alexander Boddy (1854–1930) was an early ecumenist who, as a charismatic Anglican, sponsored the Sunderland Conferences in 1908 and remained as a prophetic voice of unity outside traditional Pentecostal horizons. Donald Gee (1891–1966) remained a staunch advocate of ecumenical cooperation throughout his ministerial career. Of course, Demos Shakarian's early mentor, Charles Price, was also an ecumenical prophet whose appeals for cooperation and a grander vision of Christianity became exceedingly urgent as he approached his death in 1947.[34] However, with the deaths of Price, Smith Wigglesworth (1859–1947), Aimee Semple McPherson (1890–1944), and other significant Pentecostal leaders shortly after WWII, some Pentecostals began to wonder if the age of Pentecostalism was over. Others began to predict and prophesy a new order, a latter rain, in which a pneumatological and ecumenical order would redefine and reshape modern Christianity.[35]

The Christian Eschatological Impulses Caused by Israeli Statehood

While the ecumenism of Shakarian and the organization he founded were influenced by the emergence of these organizations in 1948, the urgency with which Shakarian pursued his evangelistic efforts were likely prompted by his eschatology and the events of 1948 that brought the parousia to the forefront of most Evangelical and Pentecostal groups.[36] The formation of Israel as a state was seen as a primary sign, if not the primary harbinger, leading toward the imminent return of Christ.

Millenarian groups have emerged and evolved throughout Christianity including the eschatological impetus of the Montanists (second to eighth century C.E.), the apocalyptic visions of Joachim of Fiore (c.1135–1202), and the radical reformers of the sixteenth century. Eschatological influences first appeared on the radar of modern church history after Napoleon exiled the Holy See in 1798 as French armies took command over large portions of Europe.[37] Almost immediately, wild and prolific eschatological speculations were generated throughout much of Europe and North America leading to a variety of millenarian groups. But the urgency of these groups paled in comparison to the eschatological explosion that occurred with the formation of Israeli statehood in 1948 which was seen as the fulfillment of biblical prophecy, predominantly by a wide variety of Evangelical and Pentecostal groups.

While Israeli statehood brought hopeful expectations of Christ's imminent return, the loss of America's nuclear monopoly and the specter of the hammer and sickle generated a variety of predictions about Armageddon and the Great Tribulation. In general, many Evangelical and Pentecostal publications began to warn of the imminent danger of communism.[38] In particular, Shakarian's *Voice* began to proclaim that Russian ascent to global power represented the biblical Armageddon and Israel's statehood would eventually foresee the parousia.[39] Of course these eschatological events were only magnified with the advent of the Korean War in 1950, and in the midst of this apocalyptic milieu, Shakarian began to see an urgent need to reach the ordinary laymen and business men of his world.

The Affluence of a Rising Middle Class after WWII

As Shakarian's hermeneutic became influenced by the events of 1948, the affluence of a rising middle class helped shape the focus of his vision. With the exception of the Great Depression, the U.S. economy had been growing significantly larger in relation to the global economy for several decades.[40] In fact, the period from 1948 until 1960 witnessed one of the largest economic booms in the history of the United States.[41] The Shakarian family did well after WWII as the dairy industry in California followed this upward economic trend.

The rapid accumulation of wealth among Pentecostals during this time period slowly began to change the theological perspectives of many Christians from an ecstatic persuasion to more formalized expressions of doxology. Although there is some debate regarding a generalized classification of Pentecostals as coming universally from the poor disenfranchised classes of society, this was certainly a common perception among many Pentecostals, and this perception was only reinforced by the Great Depression. Robert Mapes Anderson (1929–) offers a sociological explanation for how Pentecostalism emerged out of the lowest stratum of North American society, while the more nuanced approach of Grant Wacker challenges the mechanistic explanation of Anderson and others.[42]

The only sociological study of the FGBMFI, although done from a limited geographical perspective, offers an interesting twist on the social deprivation theory, perhaps first suggested by Richard Niebuhr (1894–1962), regarding pneumatic Christianity.[43] Cecil Bradfield (1907–1989) admits that traditional economic deprivation theories offer an inadequate or skewed explanation for the emergence of the modern Charismatic movement while still holding to this theory for an explanation of its earlier Pentecostal predecessor.[44] Using Charles Glock's (1919–) deprivation theory of religious groups,[45] Bradfield expands traditional sect-theory to include ethical, psychic, and organismic deprivation.[46] In addition, Bradfield rather convincingly proves that members of the FGBMFI tended to be involved in professional or managerial occupations at a much higher rate than the average United States population. In addition, they were wealthier and better educated than the local Virginia population upon which Bradfield's study was based.[47]

While Bradfield's expansion of sociological theory offers some intriguing material to consider for the emergence of the modern Charismatic phenomenon, it does not offer an accurate portrayal or an adequate explanation for Demos Shakarian himself.[48] Demos Shakarian was born into what some would categorize as a traditional, impoverished Pentecostal family. As such, both Bradfield and especially Anderson would offer social economic deprivation theory to explain his pneumatic origins. However, by the time Shakarian experienced Spirit baptism, his family had already experienced its first taste of affluence with one thousand head of cattle.[49] Just four years later, at the age of seventeen, Shakarian himself had already started his own dairy herd and acquired a level of wealth that most adults of that period had not achieved.[50]

In the era of affluence and economic growth after WWII, early Pentecostalism had to reinvent itself and reformulate some of its theological presuppositions as a growing portion of its population began to enter the middle class. Soon sermons regarding the evils of wealth were replaced with lectures on the importance of prosperity and blessing. Instead of teaching that wealth was a sin, some teachers and preachers began to teach that poverty was a sin. As a matter of course, some of these same teachers and preachers got on the FGBMFI speaking circuit and were embraced by a certain constituency in the organization. Even Demos Shakarian himself offered his advice on financial prosperity.[51] However, the "health and wealth gospel" never became an exclusive theological concern of the FGBMFI. When understanding his own prosperity and the affluence of his Armenian Christian neighbors, Shakarian merely saw his sociological status as a result of the fulfillment of prophecy. God blessed Shakarian and his family because they had heeded the warning of Efim Klubnikin to flee Armenia and had obeyed his utterance to proceed to the West Coast of this new land where they would prosper and be blessed.[52]

The Emergence of Healing Evangelists

The earlier experiences of healing in Demos Shakarian's life, beginning with the recovery of his hearing at the age of thirteen, confirmed his belief in charismatic healing. Shakarian's friendship with Charles Price and the healing experience of Demos Shakarian's sister Florence in 1941, continued to foster Shakarian's healing praxis and belief. After the death of Charles Price in 1947, other evangelists would quickly fill the void left by Price.

Kelso Glover, as already mentioned in the previous chapter, had become acquainted with Demos Shakarian and his cows in 1944.[53] Glover was also a popular guest speaker at Angelus Temple throughout the 1940s.[54] In 1948, Glover became one of Shakarian's featured evangelists and his final speaker at the Fresno Memorial Auditorium meetings in early November.[55] While Glover was a popular regional evangelist on the West Coast, he never received the national attention of some more prominent evangelists.

A.C. Valdez (1896–1988) was also a featured evangelist at the Fresno Memorial Auditorium in 1948, and early in the history of the FGBMFI, he became a popular speaker at conventions.[56] Later Valdez gained recognition by starting a new denomination and with the assistance of Gordon Lindsay (1906–1973); he also published a newsletter titled the *Evangelistic Times*.[57] In addition, he pastored a local congregation at Milwaukie Evangelistic Temple and held frequent overseas campaigns, some sponsored or promoted by the FGBMFI.

R.W. Culpepper (1921–) was another young evangelist that Demos Shakarian interacted with in 1947 and 1948. Culpepper first spoke for Shakarian at the Shrine Youth Rally in 1947, but he was also featured in early FGBMFI conventions and helped sponsor a series of Full Gospel rallies with Demos Shakarian in 1953.[58] In addition, he worked with Gordon Lindsay, went on several missionary tours, and eventually co-pastored Milwaukie Evangelistic Temple with A.C. Valdez beginning in 1970.[59]

One other evangelist Demos Shakarian worked with in 1948 was Harold Herman (1902–1999). Herman came to Christ shortly after his experiences in WWII as a staff photographer for General Douglas MacArthur; consequently, he felt a call to go on the mission field and serve in areas of the world devastated by the war.[60] Before he went overseas, one of his first ministry experiences involved being the press agent for promoting the Hollywood Bowl Full Gospel Youth Rally that Demos Shakarian was organizing.[61] Shakarian later used his relationship with Herman to help coordinate some of the early international outreaches, rallies, and the advent of new chapters, specifically in Germany.[62]

In 1948, William Branham (1909–1965) had already achieved significant recognition, and Demos Shakarian utilized Branham's popularity in his marquee ad featuring him at the Fresno Memorial Coliseum.[63] Branham was a rather controversial figure connected with the FGBMFI in its infancy. He was the keynote speaker at several of the early FGBMFI international conventions as well as being involved in the formation of several early chapters of the organization, but his influence as a healing evangelist extended far beyond the FGBMFI's meetings.[64] Branham was considered one of the most popular and charismatic ministers among the healing evangelists of the 1950s, and yet, his theology was considered heterodox by some and unique by many.[65] Ultimately, though Branham fell into disrepute over some doctrinal issues shortly before his death. In addition, after his death, some of Branham's followers elevated him to messianic status.[66] Nevertheless, Demos Shakarian admired Branham throughout his ministry and considered his spirit of service "an inspiration."[67]

In 1948, Demos Shakarian worked with several significant healing evangelists whose influence extended far beyond the confines of Southern California and the decade of the 1940s. In addition, Billy Graham (1918–) and Oral Roberts (1918–) entered the evangelistic arena in 1948 and left quite an indelible mark on the North American religious scene for the latter half of the twentieth century. Demos Shakarian did not meet either of them in 1948, but in 1949, Shakarian assisted Billy Graham in his first Los Angeles crusade, and Graham eventually became a featured contributor to the FGBMFI magazine titled *Voice*.[68] In 1951, Demos Shakarian finally met Oral Roberts, and Roberts ultimately became the spiritual mentor Shakarian sought after the death of Charles Price.[69]

Separation from the Molokan Brotherhood in 1948

At some point in Demos Shakarian's teenage years, he considered the possibility of becoming a healer similar to the Russian *lekar* in the Molokan church or the healing evangelists such as Aimee Semple McPherson he had listened to on the radio.[70] His association with healing evangelists in the 1940s may have satisfied that desire as he saw his role fulfilled in organizing and facilitating tent revivals and healing meetings. Shakarian also contemplated the possibility of becoming a prophet similar to Efim Klubnikin, but this teenage dream never materialized.[71]

While Shakarian's pneumatic background and the origins of his ancestor's exodus from Armenia caused him to revere prophecy, he himself could not be sociologically categorized as a charismatic prophet or mystagogue.[72] Indeed, Demos Shakarian never considered himself destined to be a prophet.[73] Judging by the popularity of Efim Klubnikin, the thousands of Molokans in attendance at his funeral in East Los Angeles in 1915, and the pneumatic and apocalyptic nature of his prophecies still preserved in the sacred Molokan text *Spirit and Life*, Efim could more readily be categorized as a charismatic prophet.

Nevertheless, prophecy played a large part in the lives of these Armenians and Russian Molokans of Karakala as they heeded the warning of their charismatic prophet Efim. Sociologically, however, the Armenian pneumatics and their Russian peers chose very different paths. Some of the Russian Molokan community of Los Angeles continues to be as pneumatic, sectarian, and isolated as it was a century ago, likely reinforcing some of the important characteristics of the religious deprivation theory. While many in the Armenian community remained sectarian until 1948, Demos Shakarian thoroughly assimilated himself into Southern Californian society and was a member of the Lion's Club and the Kiwanis.[74]

The sectarian isolationism of the Molokan community that tends to exist in many Russian Molokan groups in Los Angeles to this day is distinctly different from the current openness of the First Armenian Pentecostal Church in La Habra

Heights, California. Before the death of Magardich Perumean, the founding pastor of the Armenian Church, the Armenian congregation was considered part of the "Molokan Brotherhood" by their Russian counterparts, but with the change of pastors in the Armenian Church came cultural changes that were considered too westernized and spiritually unacceptable to the larger Russian Molokan community.

The fact that Shakarian sponsored and associated with evangelists outside of the Molokan Brotherhood was tolerated by the Armenian Pentecostal Church but was a taboo in most of the Russian Molokan churches. The fact that an elder in the Armenian Church, Isaac Shakarian and his son Demos, supported healing evangelists who ate pork became unacceptable to many in the Russian Molokan community. Consequently, the Armenian Church was separated from the Russian Molokan Brotherhood in 1948 after the death of Perumean.[75] While Shakarian had already rejected the sectarian isolationism of the Molokan Brotherhood, this event in 1948 only secured his more open and ecumenical outlook.

The Hollywood Bowl

In September 1948, Shakarian advertised his openness and his ecumenical outlook by cooperating with eight hundred other churches in Southern California to promote and participate in the Full Gospel Youth Rally on September 27.[76] After the initial success of the Shrine Auditorium Youth Rally, Shakarian was asked to assist with the Full Gospel Youth Rally to be held at the Hollywood Bowl Amphitheater. As preparations for the youth rally were being made, Harold Herman made all of the press and advertising arrangements; Ray Hughes (1924–), a young twenty-four year old evangelist recently back from a speaking tour in the Caribbean, was selected as the guest speaker; Eileen Huffman, a twenty-three year old soprano, was chosen as the soloist; a three-hundred voice choir and a one-hundred member symphonic orchestra rehearsed; and an estimated eight hundred churches planned on attending this historic event.[77] The event on September 27, 1948, exceeded their expectations when more than 22,500 people filled the amphitheater.[78]

The meeting gave Demos Shakarian regional and national recognition as he later proceeded to organize a rally in Fresno, California, in October 1948, and additional meetings in the Los Angeles area in 1949, with speakers such as William Freeman, Kelso Glover, and Robert Fiero.[79] Beginning in 1949, Shakarian was also advertised as the chairman of these meetings. In the euphoria of those crusades, Shakarian found himself a popular person sought out by churches, evangelists, and Christian institutions. However, he also made an important discovery at the Hollywood Bowl, as thousands of people lit candles to conclude the evening service on September 27. He shared this discovery with a group of pastors helping to organize the rally in Fresno. He ascertained his role as a Christian was not to be a healer, a prophet or a mystagogue, but rather to be a facilitator, helper, and organizer. Now he concluded that fulfilling this role would make him "the happiest person in the world."[80]

Conclusion

The way in which Shakarian began to reach out to his community after 1948 cannot only be defined by his pneumatic origins but also by the resurgence of pneumatic revival at the time and by his association with the popular healing evangelists who appeared on the scene. The fact that he reached out to his community in spite of his own church's objections could perhaps be compared to the rejection of the Latter Rain movement by much of Pentecostalism's hierarchy. The fact that he began to relate to other Pentecostal churches and eventually with church members from almost every conceivable ecclesiastical background could be explained by his own historical Armenian ecumenism and the emerging ecumenism of his time. The urgency with which Shakarian reached out could be explained best by the eschatological events of 1948, or at least as they were interpreted by most Pentecostals of that time period. How he chose to emerge from the isolation of his Armenian and Russian Molokan neighbors may be explained by the sociologic and economic shifts that were taking place in his own life and in the larger arena of Southern California.

Perhaps this shift in Shakarian's own life could also be explained by the amiable ecumenism of his Armenian ancestry. This amiableness would serve him well. As Shakarian began to contemplate his role as a facilitator, helper, and organizer, he also considered the prophetic words of his mentor Charles Price. Shakarian wondered if his only contribution to Christianity was to sponsor evangelists, or would Shakarian, as Price prophesied, take part in some great future revival that would involve ordinary lay people?[81] After the death of Charles Price, another mentor named Oral Roberts took the place of Charles Price and over a cup of coffee helped Demos Shakarian clarify exactly what this vision and Shakarian's calling would look like.

Notes

1. Demos Shakarian, *The Shakarian Story* (1999), 25 and Demos Shakarian, *The Happiest People* (1975), 99.

2. Demos Shakarian, *The Shakarian Story* (1999), 32; Demos Shakarian, "God's Dairyman," (1956), 49–50; and Demos Shakarian, *The Happiest People* (1975), 90. There seem to be some chronological errors in Shakarian's story regarding chapter six and seven of *The Happiest People* (1975), 87–115. He suggested that the sale of the Reliance Milling Company took place one year after the Hollywood Bowl Full Gospel Youth Rally mentioned in chapter six. Shakarian also implied that the Hollywood Bowl Rally took place in 1947 shortly before the death of Zaroohi Shakarian; however, the Hollywood Bowl Rally took place on September 27, 1948 ("Soloist Named for Youth Rally at Bowl," *Los Angeles Time* September 18, 1948, A3), and the sale of the Reliance Milling Company was

announced later that same year on December 4, 1948 ("Norwalk Grain Concerns Sold for $500, 000," *Los Angeles Times* December 5, 1948, A24).

3. Demos Shakarian, *The Shakarian Story* (1999), 25–26, and 32; Demos Shakarian, "God's Dairyman," (1956), 51–52; Demos Shakarian, *The Happiest People* (1975), 87, 89, 90–97, 100–102 and 113–115; and "Display Ad", *Los Angeles Times*, October 23, 1948, A3. The mysterious "Bob Smith" remained anonymous in *The Happiest People* (1975), 91–96, presumably because Demos Shakarian did not want to discredit or dishonor the ministry of an evangelist whose fundraising techniques were certainly dishonest or manipulative (see Demos Shakarian, *The Happiest People* [1975], 94–96). Interviews with his two surviving children did not reveal the identity of this evangelist. One possible identity for the unknown evangelist may be William Freeman because he had cancer in his leg and an aborted relationship with the FGBMFI, which might help explain the false leg Demos Shakarian gives in his description of "Bob Smith" (see Demos Shakarian, *The Happiest People* [1975], 91; and David Harrell, *All Things are Possible* [1975], 75). Another evangelist who may have fit the criteria described by Demos Shakarian is A. A. Allen for his notorious fundraising techniques (see Demos Shakarian, *The Happiest People* [1975], 92–96; and David Harrell, *All Things are Possible* [1975], 66–74). The chronology of the six-week tent revival with "Bob Smith" is also uncertain, since Shakarian completed the Hollywood Bowl Youth Rally in late September 1948 and almost immediately proceeded with the beginning of the five-week Fresno campaign. However, Shakarian recalls that he sponsored the six week "Bob Smith" tent revival after the Hollywood Bowl and before the Fresno meetings (Demos Shakarian, *The Happiest People*, [1975], 91 and 100).

4. Demos Shakarian, "God's Dairyman," (1956), 52.

5. See display ad on the "Soul Clinic", *Los Angeles Times*, June 30, 1951, A3.

6. Demos Shakarian, "God's Dairyman," (1956), 52; and Richard Shakarian-Tallman interview, January 16, 2008, Irvine, CA.

7. Demos Shakarian, *The Shakarian Story* (1999), 25 and Demos Shakarian, *The Happiest People* (1975), 102.

8. Demos Shakarian, *The Happiest People* (1975), 104 and Demos Shakarian, *The Shakarian Story* (1999), 26.

9. Demos Shakarian, *The Happiest People* (1975), 104 and Demos Shakarian, *The Shakarian Story* (1999), 26.

10. "Food Prices Will Drop If—," *Los Angeles Times*, October 8, 1948, A4; Demos Shakarian, *The Happiest People* (1975), 105; and Demos Shakarian, *The Shakarian Story* (1999), 25–26.

11. Demos Shakarian, *The Happiest People* (1975), 102; and Demos Shakarian, *The Shakarian Story* (1999), 26.

12. Demos Shakarian, *The Happiest People* (1975), 107.

13. Demos Shakarian, *The Shakarian Story* (1999), 27; and Demos Shakarian, *The Happiest People* (1975), 109–110.

14. Demos Shakarian, *The Shakarian Story* (1999), 27; and Demos Shakarian, *The Happiest People* (1975), 111.

15. Demos Shakarian, *The Happiest People* (1975), 114; and Demos Shakarian, *The Shakarian Story* (1999), 27. In addition, Oca Tatham belonged to the family depicted in John Steinbeck's *Grapes of Wrath* (1939).

16. Demos Shakarian, *The Happiest People* (1975), 114–115; and "Norwalk Grain Concerns," *Los Angeles Times*, December 5, 1948.

17. Demos Shakarian, "Christmas," *Voice* December 1980, 13; and Brenda Shakarian-Tallman interview, Irvine, CA, January 16, 2008.

18. Demos Shakarian, *The Happiest People* (1975), 115; and Demos Shakarian, *The Shakarian Story* (1999), 27.

19. Richard Riss, *Latter Rain: The Latter Rain Movement of 1948 and the Mid-Twentieth Century Evangelical Awakening* (Mississauga, Ontario: Honeycomb Visual Productions, 1987), 4.

20. "Display Ad", *Los Angeles Times*, October 23, 1948, A3.

21. Riss, *Latter Rain* (1987), 40. In this citation, DuPlessis helped lead a revival at Lee College shortly after the Latter Rain movement started. While David DuPlessis may not have been directly involved in the Latter Rain movement, positive references toward the revival that started in North Battleford were being made by the president of Lee College during this revival.

22. Ibid, 51.

23. Ibid, 140.

24. Bernie Rosenthal, interview with Matthew Tallman, Colorado Springs, CO, January 9, 2008. There are likely numerous other connections between the two movements but these are the only two prominent connections of which the author is aware.

25. David Edwin Harrell Jr., *All Things are Possible* (1975), 19–20.

26. Riss, *Latter Rain* (1987), 11.

27. See for example, Riss, *Latter Rain* (1987), 117. Here Riss mentions the practice of directive prophecy, a common manifestation in FGBMFI meetings but something rejected by the Assemblies of God and other traditional Pentecostal denominations in reaction to the Latter Rain movement. Also look at page 81 in Riss' book for another example of the distinctive emphasis of prophecy in this movement.

28. See Riss, *Latter Rain* (1987), 54; and Demos Shakarian, *The Happiest People* (1975), 62.

29. Shakarian, *The Happiest People* (1975), 62.

30. Much has been written in scholarly circles recently regarding the post-Christendom state of current Christianity - one in which Christianity is no longer the dominant political or sociological force that it was in the medieval or reformation era. For the best discussion of this subject pertaining to the current Charismatic renewal, see D. Lyle Dabney's "Starting with the Spirit," an essay in Stephen Pickard and Gordon Preece, eds., *Starting with the Spirit: The Task of Theology Today II* (Hindmarsh, Australia: Australian Theological Forum Press 2002).

31. World Council of Churches, "World Council of Churches History," W.C.C., http://www.oikoumene.org/en/who-are-we/background/history.html, (accessed January 2, 2008).

32. Frank Macchia, "From Azusa to Memphis: Evaluating the Racial Reconciliation Dialogue Among Pentecostals," *Pneuma* 17:2 (Fall 1995): 204.

33. While Shakarian's organization regularly featured African-Americans and Hispanics in its magazine, among its speakers, and among its members, especially internationally, women were largely absent from any leadership or notoriety in the movement. Some exceptions might include Kathryn Kuhlman, who was a regular guest speaker in the 1970s, but until recently, women were excluded from membership in all FGBMFI chapters, and even the chapters who do allow women as members or chapter presidents make these allowances contrary to the by-laws of the organization.

34. See Price's conversations with Demos Shakarian in *The Happiest People* (1975), 74–75 and 82–83.

35. Harrell, *All Things are Possible* (1975), 20.

36. Parousia is a theological term derived from a Greek word meaning "arrival" which refers to the Christian belief in the return or second coming of Christ.

37. See Ernest Sandeen, *The Roots of Fundamentalism: British and American Millenarianism, 1800–1930* (Chicago: University of Chicago Press, 1970) for a discussion of these millenarian origins.

38. Riss, *Latter Rain* (1987), 14–15.

39. See William Stoneman, "Armageddon," *Voice*, December 1956, 26–27; Thomas R. Nickel, "About Israel," *Voice*, November 1958, 13–16; and especially Richard Nixon's address to the FGBMFI at their second annual international convention in 1953, "Minds, Hearts, and Souls of Men," *Voice*, September 1954, 4–7, 11–15.

40. Milton Friedman and Anna Jacobson Schwartz, *Monetary History of the United States, 1867–1960,* (Princeton, NJ: Princeton University Press, 1963), 14.

41. Friedman, *Monetary History* (1963), 592.

42. See Robert Anderson's *Vision of the Disinherited* (1992); and Grant Wacker's *Heaven Below* (2001) for comparative views on this analysis of early Pentecostalism.

43. See Richard Niebuhr, "The Churches of the Disinherited," *The Social Sources of Denominationalism* (ed. By Richard Niebuhr; New York: Henry Holt and Company, 1929): 198–215.

44. Cecil Bradfield, *Neo-Pentecostalism: A Sociological Assessment* (Washington, DC: University Press of America, 1979), 1.

45. See Charles Y. Glock's, "On the Role of Deprivation in the Origin and Evolution of Religious Groups," in *Religion in Sociological Perspective* (ed. Charles Y. Glock; Belmont CA: Wadsworth Publishing Company, 1973).

46. Bradfield, *Neo-Pentecostalism* (1979), 37.

47. Ibid, 21, 25, and 26.

48. For a further study on the sociological assessment of the Charismatic movement, see Margaret Poloma's *The Charismatic Movement: Is There a New Pentecost?* (Boston, MA: Twayne Publishers, 1982). Also her work *The Assemblies of God at the Crossroads: Charisma and Institutional Dilemmas* (Knoxville, TN: University of Tennessee Press, 1989); and her most recent study, *Main Street Mystics: The Toronto Blessing and Reviving Pentecostalism* (Walnut Creek, CA: Alta Mira Press, 2003) offer the most thorough sociological research on the Charismatic movement to date. Her work is much broader and more nuanced, but Bradfield offers the only study that has focused specifically on the FGBMFI.

49. Demos Shakarian, *The Happiest People* (1975), 33–34.

50. Ibid, 39.

51. See Demos Shakarian, *A New Wave of Revival: In Your Finances* (Costa Mesa, CA: Full Gospel Business Men's Fellowship International, 1992).

52. Demos Shakarian, *The Happiest People* (1975), 53.

53. Demos Shakarian, "The Cows Accepted It," *Voice*, September 1975, 14 and Demos Shakarian, *The Happiest People* (1975), 78–79.

54. "Display Ads," *Los Angeles Times*, May 22, 1943, A2; April 8, 1944, A2; February 24, 1945, A2; October 6, 1945, A2; September 26, 1946, A2; and January 18, 1947, A2 are only a few ads that appeared in the *Los Angeles Times* featuring Glover at Angelus Temple.

55. Demos Shakarian, *The Shakarian Story* (1999), 27; and Demos Shakarian, *The Happiest People* (1975), 112–114.

56. Thomas Nickel, "A.C. Valdez," September, 1953 6–7, 10–11; and May 1956, 20–21.

57. Harrell, *All Things are Possible* (1975), 177.

58. Thomas Nickel, "Holy Ghost Rallies," *Voice*, February 1953, 14; March 1953, 14; May–June 1953, 15; and July–August 1953, 14–15.

59. Harrell, *All Things are Possible* (1975), 176–177.

60. Harold Herman, *From Ashes to Gold* (Springfield, Missouri: Gospel Publishing House, 1995), 15–17.

61. Mildred Herman-Tallman interview, January 6, 2005; and Demos Shakarian, *The Happiest People* (1975), 90.

62. Thomas Nickel, ed., "Full Gospel Chapters Started in Germany," *Voice*, September 1956, 11.

63. "Display Ad," *Los Angeles Times*, October 23, 1948, A3.

64. Demos Shakarian, "In Memoriam," *Voice*, January/February 1966, 29.

65. See William Branham, "God's Cure for an Opossum," *Voice*. September 1955, 3–11. Branham was from the Oneness branch of Pentecostalism, and some within FGBMFI and other Pentecostal and emerging Charismatic groups disagreed with his doctrinal stances (Harrell, *All Things are Possible* [1975], 153).

66. Synan, *Century of the Holy Spirit* (2001), 326; and Harrell, *All Things are Possible* (1975), 165.

67. Demos Shakarian, "In Memoriam," *Voice*, January/February 1966, 29.

68. Demos Shakarian-Synan interview, October 5, 1987, 10–11; Billy Graham, *Voice* December 1956, 8–9; June 1957, 28–29; "Judgment Day," May 1958, 14–15; "God's Will," July 1958, 14–18; and "On the Holy Spirit," September 1961, 31.

69. Oral Roberts-Synan interview, October 10, 1991, Tulsa, OK, 1; Shakarian-Synan interview, October 5, 1987, 11–13; and Demos Shakarian, *The Shakarian Story* (1999), 27.

70. Demos Shakarian, *The Happiest People* (1975), 38–39.

71. Ibid, 37.

72. Refer to Max Weber's *The Sociology of Religion*, trans. Ephraim Fischoff (Boston, MA: Beacon Press, 1963) 52–54 for a further discussion on the sociological and historical definition of a prophet.

73. Demos Shakarian, *The Happiest People* (1975), 37.

74. Ibid, 57.

75. Paul Sobolew-Tallman interview, January 16, 2008.

76. Demos Shakarian, "God's Dairyman," (1956), 47–49; and Demos Shakarian, *The Happiest People* (1975), 87–90.

77. "Soloist Named for Youth Rally at Bowl," *Los Angeles Time* September 18, 1948, A3.

78. Demos Shakarian, *The Happiest People* (1975), 90.

79. "Revival Tent Meeting," *Los Angeles Times* September 17, 1949, A2; and Demos Shakarian, *The Happiest People* (1975), 100–102.

80. Demos Shakarian, *The Happiest People* (1975), 101.

81. Demos Shakarian, *The Happiest People* (1975), 83; and Demos Shakarian, "God's Dairyman," (1956), 50–51.

Demos Shakarian as a Young Man (circa 1933)

Demos and Rose Shakarian
as an Engaged Couple

Demos and Rose Shakarian's Wedding Photo

*A Young Demos
Riding with his Father on the Shakarian Ranch*

*Isaac Shakarian Holding his Granddaughter Geri with
His Grandson Richard Standing in front of Him.*

*Rose Shakarian Standing with her
Daughter Geri*

Rose Shakarian as a Young Woman
(circa 1935)

Isaac and Demos Shakarian in front of the Reliance Dairy Headquarters prior to WWII

Armenian Pentecostal Church Building in 1941

Demos Shakarian with his
Father and Son

Reliance Dairy Farm headquarters - circa 1940

An Early Tent Revival that Demos Shakarian Sponsored

Shakarian Celebrating at the Opening of One of his Drive-in Dairies.

Demos and Rose Shakarian in 1949

Isaac and Demos Shakarian ~ circa 1948

Oral Roberts, Isaac Shakarian, and Isaac's sister Sarah Janoian

Rose Shakarian's Baptism

Chapter Eight

The Emergence of a
Full Gospel Business Man (1949–1958)

After the hectic pace Shakarian held in 1948, the impulses that launched him into a leadership role among North American Pentecostal Christians drove him further towards a prophetic promise that Milton Hanson and Charles Price had delivered in 1938 and 1944 respectively. Shakarian began to realize his role as a Christian organizer, leader, and facilitator, and he began serving in that role vigorously. Nevertheless, he found that his role would go far beyond his current experience in coordinating the crusades of popular healing evangelists after WWII.

The Shakarian Family Business
Matures at Forty Years

The Hollywood Bowl outreach and the Fresno meetings in the fall of 1948 gave Demos Shakarian national recognition as a coordinator of tent revivals and evangelistic events. The next summer, in 1949, Shakarian organized another set of meetings in the Los Angeles area and he invited several evangelists to speak at the services including William Freeman, Kelso Glover, and Robert Fiero.[1] These were not idle times for Demos and Rose Shakarian. In retrospect, Rose sometimes lamented that every time they had two or three thousand dollars saved in the bank, "Demos would smell sawdust, and we knew it was time for a revival meeting."[2]

Isaac Shakarian also decided his social life would no longer remain idle. When Isaac's mourning period was over after the death of his wife Zaroohi in 1947, he decided to remarry in August 1950.[3] However, in this case, he broke tradition and married a woman who was not Armenian.[4] In addition, Edna Shakarian ((1916–1994) was twenty-four years younger than Isaac Shakarian.[5] Both the Russian and Armenian Molokan communities practiced endogamy in the early period of their immigration to Los Angeles; however, as the Armenian community became more acclimated to Californian society, this practice eventually was abandoned. All of Demos Shakarian's children would soon follow suit by marrying spouses who were not Armenian.

Demos Shakarian continued to partner with his father Isaac in overseeing the expanding dairy business of the Shakarian Corporation. In addition, with rapid population growth and increasing urban encroachment on their dairy fields, they both ventured into real estate. It is possible that a dispute with the State Highway Division became an epiphany which motivated them to consider a profitable future in real estate. The highway division had announced they were building a freeway on Shakarian dairy property; as a result, a narrow strip of land at the corner of Firestone Boulevard and Pioneer Avenue, less than an acre in size, was condemned for the construction of the Santa Ana Freeway.[6] The Shakarians were offered $15,600 by the State Highway Division, but the Shakarian appraisers claimed the land was worth $24,000. In a legal dispute, the Shakarians were only awarded $13,000 by a California Superior Court judge in early February 1951.[7]

With encroaching suburban sprawl, freeway construction, the threat of imminent domain, and the opportunity of significant profit in real estate, Demos Shakarian wasted no time in venturing into a variety of property investments. Even before the court proceedings in early 1951, Shakarian had purchased a twenty acre site in Norwalk, California, for the purpose of developing a shopping center. In the spring of 1951, Shakarian invited ten thousand business leaders, many of them representing the tenants of the new Norwalk Center, and famous actors and actresses, including a popular Hispanic actor of that period named Leo Carillo (1880–1961) to attend the grand opening of the Greater Norwalk Shopping Center.[8] However, a few friends of Shakarian encouraged him to hear a new evangelist speaking at a church in North Long Beach pastored by Tommy Reed. Shakarian decided to abandon his obligations at the grand opening, and go hear the evangelist, Tommy Hicks (1909–1973), who stirred Shakarian's heart as they talked and embraced after the service.[9]

Shortly after this, Isaac and Demos Shakarian received a phone call from Bob DeWeese, associate evangelist and assistant to Oral Roberts, asking for help with an evangelistic crusade they were planning in Oakland, California. They had received permission to use property owned by the Golden State Milk Company, but at the last minute, the milk company decided to cancel their agreement. DeWeese called Isaac Shakarian asking if he could use his business influence and contacts to convince the company to change its mind. Shakarian's influence proved valuable and the tent revival went on as scheduled.[10]

Soon Demos Shakarian was "smelling sawdust" again, and the summer and fall of 1951 would become his most ambitious evangelistic campaign to date. With the pace Shakarian kept in business and evangelism, many business men wondered how he could be successful in the arena of the secular and the sacred. Demos Shakarian responded primarily by suggesting Isaac and he were partners in business which enabled Shakarian to free himself to spend more time coordinating evangelistic activities.[11]

Nevertheless, Isaac Shakarian also felt a desire to serve as both a minister and a milker. The ecclesiology of their church and their Armenian background never allowed the Shakarians to see secular work and sacred ministry as an either/or decision but as part of a seamless, holistic way in which they lived their lives. Consequently, in 1952, Isaac Shakarian became the third pastor of the Armenian Pentecostal Church.[12] Soon Isaac and Demos Shakarian enlisted the help of other Shakarians in overseeing the sprawling businesses and investments of the Shakarian Corporation. Ruth Shakarian Babajian became vice president of operations; Richard was asked to supervise the Reliance Dairies; and Florence Shakarian helped as an office administrator.[13] Eventually, Shakarian would also ask Gene Scalf (1932–) to oversee his real estate investments after Gene married Demos Shakarian's daughter Geraldine on January 24, 1959.[14]

In 1953, Demos Shakarian increased his advertising budget, focusing on the expansion of his drive-in dairy at the corner of Imperial and Woodruff in Downey, California. Beginning October 18, 1953, Shakarian ran a series of eight consecutive weekly ads featuring milk at a savings to his drive-in customers of sixteen cents per gallon.[15] The employees were dressed in white, and milk was served to vehicles from an open booth while Richard Shakarian oversaw the management of the drive-through store.[16] The drive-in business continued to grow, and a new drive through location was opened on October 30, 1955, at the corner of Orr and Day Road in Norwalk, California.[17]

By the end of 1954, Isaac and Demos Shakarian had one thousand dairy cows, one thousand five hundred automobiles stopping at their drive-in dairy daily, two shopping centers, and other real estate interests.[18] As the Shakarian Corporation expanded, dairy property was sold for commercial real estate ventures, the size of the Shakarian dairy herd was reduced, and the profits of the dairy herd diminished. With a streamlined dairy business, Shakarian saw an opportunity for increasing the profit and the butter fat content of their milk by purchasing Pabst Leader Crusader, for $4,000 from Fred Pabst (1869–1958), a brewery magnate and owner of Pabst-Knutson Farm in Oconomoc, Wisconsin.[19] Pabst Leader was the son of a gold medal sire, Wisconsin Leader, and Shakarian believed the bull would boost milk production eight percent. Along with a locally purchased sire from the Los Angeles area, Pabst Leader Crusader replaced the eighteen other bulls which had formerly served the Reliance herd.[20] The $4,000 investment in the Pabst bull proved fortuitous as Leader Crusader sired over 5,000 daughters in the next fifteen years, producing an average annual increase of 107 pounds of butter fat per cow.[21] In dairy terms, Shakarian's purchase was often seen as providential or miraculous, and Demos Shakarian was not afraid to let his friends in the dairy industry know about it.[22]

The Shakarians were also savvy in their real estate dealings. Real estate values had already increased significantly after WWII. During the war, military demand diverted the construction needs of a growing California populace, but with the availability of GI grants and loans and an unrelenting population increase, the value of real estate in Southern California had increased exponentially within a decade after the end of WWII.[23] In late 1954, Isaac Shakarian applied to rezone twenty eight acres of his property holdings for industrial use.[24] By August 1955, Isaac and Demos Shakarian sold seven and one half acres of the rezoned property for $50,000 to the Sutorbilt Corporation.[25] Other property holdings and purchases would continue to accumulate over the next two decades.

The Shakarian family also grew and multiplied during the 1950s. Richard Shakarian married a young woman he met at Southern California Bible College (now Vanguard University) named Evangeline Klingsheim on August 6, 1955, and "Vangie" and Richard announced the birth of their first child, Denice Ann, on October 9, 1956.[26] Consequently, Demos Shakarian added a new title to his name. He was an entrepreneur, a dairyman, an evangelistic coordinator, and now a grandfather.

Tommy Hicks

As mentioned earlier, Demos Shakarian and Tommy Hicks first met when Shakarian abandoned the grand opening of his new Norwalk Shopping Center to attend one of Hicks' meetings at a church in North Long Beach early in 1951.[27] Shakarian was so impressed with Hicks, he immediately prepared to sponsor Hicks in a six week tent revival beginning July 1, 1951.[28] Hicks played a crucial role in the early formation of the FGBMFI; when Demos Shakarian had his vision of the global impact of the organization, Tommy Hicks had a simultaneous vision that God was leading him to go to Argentina and preach the gospel.[29] In addition, while Hicks was not the first or most influential speaker for the newly formed FGBMFI, he may have been the most effective in the early history of the organization, starting new chapters wherever his tent revivals took place. After Shakarian received his vision on December 27, 1952, Hicks helped to start new chapters in the early years in Reading, Pennsylvania; Springfield, Illinois; Sioux Falls, South Dakota; and Washington, D.C.[30]

After Hicks and Shakarian received their simultaneous visions, Hicks went to Argentina and started meetings that resulted in the largest Christian crusade meetings up to that time in history.[31] In addition, the success of his meetings was quickly reported in early issues of *Voice* magazine.[32] As many as 400,000 people attended a single meeting and Hicks presented a Bible and copy of *Voice* magazine to President Juan Peron (1895–1974) during the crusade.[33] His successful crusade in Argentina led to other international opportunities for Hicks in Russia, Switzerland, Finland, and once again in Argentina.[34]

Oral Roberts and Demos Shakarian

In July 1951, Shakarian's meetings became more frequent and successful as he organized rallies every night for Tommy Hicks, setting up a tent at the corner of

Atlantic and Artesia Boulevards in North Long Beach.[35] This tent revival was followed shortly by one of the largest crusades in the history of Los Angeles, organized by Shakarian and led by Oral Roberts. The tent meetings were held at the same location as Hicks' earlier outreach but utilized the largest gospel tent available at that time. With a seating capacity of 10,000, there were overflow crowds for seventeen consecutive nights.[36] From the time that Shakarian started preaching on top of a soap box in 1940 in Lincoln Park until the end of the Roberts' campaign in 1951, Shakarian claimed that his meetings attracted over a million people and many thousands were converted to Christianity even before he ever started the FGBMFI.[37]

In 1951, Oral Roberts became the mentor who helped Demos Shakarian begin his ministry to Christian business men. Shakarian's organization gets much of the credit for launching the charismatic movement; however, David Harrell attributes much more credit to Oral Roberts for his role in initiating the neo-Pentecostal renewal and for his role in starting the FGBMFI.[38] According to Harrell, "it was the vision of Shakarian and the backing of Oral Roberts that launched one of the most powerful parachurch organizations in modern history."[39] Most other scholars writing on the Charismatic movement fail to mention the connection between Demos Shakarian and Oral Roberts.[40]

Clergymen were not allowed to become officers of the FGBMFI, and as such, Oral Roberts was never part of the formal organizational structure of the FGBMFI. [41] Nevertheless, Roberts' influence upon the burgeoning movement of Christian business men was considerable. At Roberts' recommendation, Miner Arganbright (1887–1984) along with Lee Braxton (1905–1982) and George Gardner (1898–1967) became the first vice-presidents of the FGBMFI.[42] George Gardner was one of Roberts' closest personal friends[43] and Lee Braxton became one of Oral Roberts' integral partners influencing and eventually directing Roberts' radio ministry and becoming chairman of the board of regents for Oral Roberts University.[44]

Oral Roberts' relationship with Demos Shakarian did not start with his invitation to be the first speaker of a FGBMFI meeting at Clifton's Cafeteria in 1951.[45] Shakarian chaired the campaign to organize Roberts' evangelistic campaign in Los Angeles in September and October 1951.[46] However, the vision of Christian business men continued to dominate Shakarian's thoughts, and he shared it with Oral Roberts during his evangelistic campaign in October 1951. Roberts encouraged Shakarian and asked if there was anything he could do to help promote his vision. Shakarian immediately invited Roberts to be the speaker at their first meeting at Clifton's Cafeteria in downtown Los Angeles.[47] Roberts' support of the new fledgling ministry continued as Shakarian followed Roberts in his next few evangelistic campaigns in Fresno and Phoenix.[48] Roberts' close relationship with Shakarian continued long after the inception of the FGBMFI. Shakarian sponsored Roberts' next major crusade in Los Angeles in 1953. [49] In 1954, Demos Shakarian became a trustee of the Oral Roberts Evangelistic Association.[50] Roberts was invited to speak at every annual international convention and major event the FGBMFI sponsored from its inception. Oral obliged the extended invitation by speaking at the first ten annual international conventions and many other annual FGBMFI conventions in the following years including the 22nd annual convention in Anaheim, California,[51] the dedication ceremony of the new FGBMFI headquarters in 1980,[52] and the 1991 annual convention in Orlando, Florida.[53]

The Beginnings of the Full Gospel Business Men

As Demos Shakarian sat down for pie and coffee one night with his new mentor, Oral Roberts, at the Ambassador Hotel Restaurant in Los Angeles, the words of his old mentor, Charles Price, filled Shakarian's mind.[54] He began to share those thoughts with Roberts, and the words resonated for both Roberts and Shakarian. For Demos Shakarian, his previous experience with the Christian Business Men's Committee and his upbringing in the Armenian Pentecostal Church led by laymen framed the concept that Shakarian shared with Oral Roberts. In addition, Shakarian's experience organizing numerous crusades with the help of other business men, and his recollection of the testimonies of business men given at a chicken dinner at Knott's Berry Farm only augmented his thoughts as he shared his vision with Oral Roberts. The words of Charles Price and the contemporary encouragement of Oral Roberts created a spiritual crescendo in Demos Shakarian's heart that required immediate action.

When Oral Roberts asked if there was anything he could do to help Demos Shakarian put this vision into action, Shakarian immediately seized the opportunity and invited Oral to be the first guest speaker. Shakarian mentioned that several of his Christian business associates occasionally met at Clifton's Cafeteria for a meal, so Roberts encouraged Shakarian to meet there since it was familiar to Shakarian's peers and business associates.[55] Thus, Clifton's Cafeteria on Broadway and Seventh in downtown Los Angeles was chosen as the location.[56] Roberts was holding crusades through Sunday night, October 14, 1951, so a plan evolved to promote Shakarian's first meeting.[57] On Friday night, October 12, Bob DeWeese, Oral Roberts' associate evangelist and outreach coordinator introduced Demos Shakarian to an overflow crowd of 12,500 at the Roberts' tent crusade off of the Santa Anna Freeway. Demos Shakarian passionately invited the thousands of business men to a breakfast the next morning with Oral Roberts as the guest speaker.[58] Shakarian had also been on the phone all week to every business friend and associate he knew, asking them to join him for the Saturday morning meeting.[59]

Demos and Rose Shakarian arrived at Clifton's Cafeteria early that Saturday morning, October 13, 1951, with Oral Roberts accompanying them. The interior of Clifton's Cafeteria looks much the same today as it did in the fall of 1951: the second-story banquet room where Shakarian held his first meeting has gold leaf wallpaper in the entryway, with dark art deco interior and bright red wallpaper on the walls. The exterior climate that surrounds this cafeteria is currently composed of a mixture of small businesses and a lively Hispanic street market, and the Spanish speaking FGBMFI's chapter that meets in Clifton's Cafeteria currently represents the contemporary business culture in that community.[60] However, in 1951, Clifton's Cafeteria was in the hub of downtown Los Angeles commerce and was still a predominantly English speaking business community.

Expectations were high. They were hoping for a crowd of 300 to 400 business men eagerly waiting to hear the now famous healing evangelist and Shakarian share this new concept of a Christian lay organization.[61] With a crowd exceeding 12,000 people the preceding night, the eighteen business men who joined Demos, Oral, and Rose that morning seemed less than auspicious.[62] While Shakarian was obviously discouraged by the poor attendance, his own tenacity had helped him overcome obstacles before.[63] After all, his own father had started out with only three dairy cows and Shakarian had begun with only thirty cattle, but together they had built one of the largest dairy businesses in the world. Shakarian stood up and shared his concept of a laymen's organization in which there were "no organs. No stained glass. Nothing that men could pigeonhole as 'religious.' Just one man telling another about Jesus."[64] As the men began to look at their watches, it was clear the men were less than impressed by Shakarian's words…that is until Oral Roberts stood up to speak. While his short sermon was inspiring, it was Roberts' prayer at the end of the meeting that electrified the room as the evangelist prayed, "that we see a little group of people in a cafeteria, but that you see a thousand chapters."[65]

With this humble beginning, the first chapter of the Full Gospel Business Men began. For the next year, Clifton's Cafeteria remained the only official chapter of the FGBMFI. Shakarian did all he could to promote this concept at the weekly meetings in downtown Los Angeles and throughout the southwestern United States. Shakarian accompanied Roberts in his next evangelistic campaigns in Fresno and Phoenix and in turn, Roberts helped promote the new organization.[66]

The crusade in Fresno, California began in early November 1951. Once again, Shakarian announced another meeting on Saturday morning, November 17, for men at a local Fresno restaurant. This gathering seemed more promising with 150 men in attendance. Roberts urged the men to legally incorporate and also encouraged Shakarian to solicit the cooperation of Lee Braxton.[67] Immediately after that gathering, the group held their first official business meeting, and Demos Shakarian was voted in as president of the newly named Full Gospel Business Men's Fellowship of America, along with three vice-presidents, Lee Braxton, George Gardner, and Miner Arganbright, and secretary-treasurer Earl Draper (1896–1972).[68]

Shakarian also spent a significant sum of money sponsoring weekly radio broadcasts of the meetings from Clifton's Cafeteria and enticing new members to join the regular meetings in Los Angeles on Saturday mornings.[69] Still the meetings at the cafeteria only managed to attract forty or fifty attendees, in spite of the occasional big name speaker who would come and attend the breakfasts. If lagging growth was not enough, rejection and discouragement quickly followed.

First, there were the suspicions of local ministers who questioned whether this organization would draw away business men with their finances from local Pentecostal fellowships in Southern California. Shakarian could not understand these accusations since he had regularly mentioned two defining principles of the organization in their weekly meetings in Los Angeles. "First, stay in your own church. If your church knows the power of the Spirit, go back determined to serve Him harder than ever. If not, go back as a missionary. And second, don't leave one penny in the offering basket that belongs somewhere else. This is not where your tithe is due."[70]

The first principle became a defining ethos of both the FGBMFI and the Charismatic movement. Interestingly, the second principle may have been somewhat unfamiliar to Shakarian since his own church did not teach the principle of tithing but simply encouraged every member to give to the church as God enabled him.[71] However, Shakarian's frequent interaction with members and clergy of a large assortment of Pentecostal churches would certainly have made him aware of this principle, especially when some of the local pastors used the pulpit to discourage their members from attending his weekly breakfasts.[72]

Even when the FGBMFI eventually erupted into an international organization, the response from their Pentecostal brethren and denominational leaders was one of either criticism, cautious congratulations, or silence. Some Pentecostal leaders were openly critical about the Charismatic movement, but strangely silent about the FGBMFI. The *Pentecostal Evangel* did not publish one article or editorial about the FGBMFI until 1998.[73] Certainly, there were a few Pentecostal leaders who were cautiously optimistic about the organization in its infancy. Important Pentecostal leaders such as British Pentecostal scholar, Donald Gee,[74] and United States General Superintendent of the Assemblies of God, Ralph Riggs (1895–1971),[75] gave complementary and congratulatory remarks to the FGBMFI in its early formation. However, it is likely that this approval was given because the Full Gospel Business Men were Pentecostal business men in the beginning.[76] The approval may have been cautious because of the suspicion that Pentecostal leaders had toward lay leadership or toward a competing denomination or group that would potentially draw away their members.[77]

When David DuPlessis (1905–1987) was invited as a guest speaker in that first year of the fellowship, he brought hope to Shakarian when he declared, "You're really on to something here…Each man a missionary to the people he works with every day!"[78] While David DuPlessis was not a healing evangelist, his contribution to the formation of the FGBMFI was both significant and unique. Initially, as general secretary of the Apostolic Faith Mission in South Africa, and later as Secretary for the Pentecostal World Conference in 1952 in London, DuPlessis was recognized as a leader in global Pentecostalism.[79] However, from 1936 DuPlessis' own urgent ecclesiological mandate was sparked by the prophetic word of Smith Wigglesworth[80] much like Shakarian's vision was shaped a few years later by the prophetic words of Milton Hansen and Charles Price.[81] Interestingly, David DuPlessis never mentions Shakarian in his autobiography, but Shakarian does mention DuPlessis and his impact early in the formation of the FGBMFI.[82]

After the meeting at Clifton's Cafeteria in 1952, DuPlessis invited Shakarian to come to the Pentecostal World Conference in London hoping that the conference would sponsor this struggling organization. After their first intercontinental flight, Rose and Demos Shakarian met David DuPlessis at the conference in July 1952. Ultimately, the conference members dismissed Shakarian's idea, apparently because Demos Shakarian was not a member of the clergy.[83] In addition, DuPlessis resigned from his post as secretary of the conference.[84] Just as the Pentecostal hierarchy of 1948 rejected the Latter Rain movement, they now dismissed this lay organization.[85]

If the suspicion of Shakarian's Pentecostal peers was not enough, the discouragement by his own wife was devastating. She said "we're just feeding people breakfast, Demos…We did a lot better with the tent meetings. We were reaching thousands every summer instead of a few dozen at best this way."[86] One cannot blame Rose for her pragmatism. After all, the idea that Shakarian had been toying with for months had left them exhausted physically, spiritually, and financially. The movement did not show any signs of future growth. Demos Shakarian was a visionary and entrepreneur, but Rose's practical realism always brought a sense of balance to him; consequently, Shakarian could not ignore her words.[87]

Nevertheless, he persevered with his idea of a Christian business men's fellowship. Admittedly, Shakarian's own self-evaluation highlighted his determination and persistence.[88] In the fall of 1952, he and Paul Fischer (1878–1972), an attorney from Santa Ana, California, drew up the organization's articles of incorporation. They held an incorporation meeting in the upper room of Clifton's Cafeteria. All of the officers of the new organization were present except for Lee Braxton. In addition, a printer named Thomas R. Nickel (1900–1993) joined the organizational meeting.[89] During this meeting, the scope of their mission was broadened, and the legal name of the organization was officially finalized as the Full Gospel Business Men's Fellowship International.[90]

However, while the name of the organization broadened their vision, all Shakarian could see was the fledgling group at Clifton's Cafeteria growing smaller. Finally, one of Shakarian's closest friends and business associates, Miner Arganbright, gave a frank assessment of where he thought the organization was heading. On Saturday morning, December 20, 1952, only fifteen people showed up at Clifton's Cafeteria, and Miner informed Shakarian that he thought "the whole idea of the Fellowship is a dud. Frankly I wouldn't give you five cents for the whole outfit."[91] As he drove home from the meeting, Shakarian could no longer ignore Miner's statement or his wife's advice. After all, he had given this venture his best effort. Now he was busily growing his dairy, developing and filling vacancies at a commercial real estate site in Norwalk,[92] and helping to open a new Goodwill Store serving the Downey and Norwalk areas.[93]

Shakarian now contemplated abandoning his experiment. It was not working as well as the tent revivals he had organized earlier. Perhaps part of his desire in going to the Pentecostal World Conference was to find a potential "buyer" to whom he could sell this now failing "business" much like he had sold his floundering mill a few years earlier.[94] Unfortunately, there were no "buyers" and he had to simply abandon this venture just like he had been forced to close his fertilizer plant in 1941.[95] On the way home from that disappointing meeting at Clifton's Cafeteria, Shakarian decided that the following Saturday would be the final meeting of the FGBMFI. But during the week he could not stop thinking about this dream that had only taken form one year earlier.[96] The night before he was ready to give up, everything changed. Ultimately, it was not his own tenaciousness or even the words of another prophet or healing evangelist that changed Shakarian's mind. Instead Shakarian received a prophetic vision that he perceived came directly to him from God. This vision changed the course of his own life, the direction of a burgeoning Christian men's organization, and eventually global Christianity today.

The Vision of Demos Shakarian

On Friday night, December 26, 1952, the Shakarians had a special house guest, Tommy Hicks. Shakarian had sponsored a six-week tent revival for Tommy eighteen months earlier in Los Angeles.[97] However, both men were troubled since Shakarian was facing a floundering ministry and Hicks was facing a floundering marriage after his wife left him.[98] Both men knelt in prayer late that night in separate rooms, and both men had almost simultaneous prophetic visions. In Tommy Hicks' vision, he perceived a great revival coming to Argentina. Consequently, he went to Argentina one year later and led an evangelistic crusade with spectacular results that were reported prominently in early editions of *Voice* magazine.[99]

On the evening of December 26, 1952, Demos Shakarian was praying on a rug in his living room when he had an experience similar to the Spirit baptism he received at the age of thirteen. Shakarian exercised glossolalia and experienced an overwhelming sense of God's presence. Just as when he was a young man, Shakarian sensed God talking to him, saying, "Demos, will you ever doubt my power?"[100] In the first experience, in 1926, Shakarian discerned that God was saying to him, "Demos, power is the birthright of every Christian. Accept power, Demos."[101] However, in this instance, an internal power struggle was going on in Demos Shakarian's heart. Shakarian began to realize that it was not his own power but rather divine power that would accomplish what had been stirring in Shakarian's heart for quite some time.

Christian mystics and pneumatics throughout church history have recorded similar internal power struggles or inner turmoil. Examples of this internal spiritual struggle are found in Augustine's *Confessions* (ca. 397) Thomas a Kempis' *The Imitation of Christ* (ca. 1418) or John of the Cross' *The Long, Dark Night of the Soul* (1585). For Shakarian, the power struggle did not last long. Almost immediately Shakarian perceived the reason for his own struggle and failure in growing the organization he had founded a year earlier.

As he continued in prayer, his wife Rose entered the room and began to play the organ. At this point, Shakarian's vision began. He saw the roof of his house disappear, and he found himself peering into a bright, daylight sky in the middle of the night. As he proceeded to observe this phenomenon, Rose offered glosso-lalia and the interpretation of that spiritual language in true charismatic fashion as she proclaimed prophetically but encouragingly, "My son, I knew you before you were born. I have guided you every step of the way. Now I am going to show you the purpose of your life."[102] The vision continued as Shakarian saw millions of people from every continent and every ethnicity dead and lifeless. Again Rose spoke prophetically, "My son, what you see next is going to happen very soon."[103] Then a picture came to Shakarian similar to that seen by the prophet Ezekiel (Ezekiel 37:1–14) as these lifeless souls were resurrected. However, in true charismatic or pneumatic fashion, he saw these millions of people now lifting their hands in worship to God, and in true Armenian ecclesiological and ecumeni-cal fashion, he saw these same people linked together in a community of love and adoration.[104]

What happened next is legendary in Full Gospel Business Men's circles. Demos and Rose Shakarian realized that it was time to go to the meeting at Clifton's Cafeteria. They were greeted by Miner Arganbright and Thomas Nickel. Miner, who only a week earlier, would not have given "five cents for the organi-zation," now gave a check for one thousand dollars and a humble apology explaining that he had heard God tell him the night before "This work is to go around the world and you're to donate the first money."[105] The other person who greeted them was Thomas Nickel, who explained that he had heard a divine com-mand also, ordering him to drive 400 miles and donate his printing press and his time to help the fledgling organization start a magazine.[106] Just like Shakarian and his ancestors, Nickel and Arganbright took prophecy seriously. They did not delay, but obeyed what they perceived God was saying to them.

As Demos Shakarian recalled, the meeting that Saturday morning in Clifton's Cafeteria was small, but that did not matter. For Shakarian, the organization was no longer his vision; it was God's vision, as he perceived it, confirmed by the prophetic words given to Rose, his friend Miner Arganbright, and his new editor, Thomas R. Nickel. As such, just like the prophetic word that was given to his ancestors over fifty years earlier, Shakarian could not ignore what he had seen and heard. Now Demos Shakarian had a divine mandate that could no longer be delayed. As Shakarian recalled later, "The first year we couldn't talk men into coming; now we couldn't keep them away.[107]

Demos Shakarian now pursued his vision at a frenetic pace. Whatever remain-ing fear of flight he or his family may have had was quickly dismissed as Shakarian frequently flew in C.C. Ford's small Cessna propeller plane, promoting new chapters in various parts of the United States.[108] The new ministry demands brought into question how much time Demos Shakarian could spend at Reliance Dairies. He relied heavily upon the experience of his father Isaac and the energy of his son Richard to supplement his absence as Isaac told his son "Demos, you go and I'll take care of the business."[109]

Demos Shakarian's vision has been described in numerous places including his autobiography with some variations.[110] Initially, it was recorded in the first edition of *Voice* magazine in February 1953 as occurring on May 2, 1952, but the December 30, 1952, date of Arganbright's check demonstrates the likelihood that the later December 27, 1952, date recorded in *The Happiest People on Earth* (1975) is correct.[111] This story, along with the story of the Shakarian family coming from Armenia to California, are sacred stories told and retold again in the history of FGBMFI's meetings and a variety of publications.[112] The rug that Shakarian prayed on when he received this vision in 1952 was eventually enshrined on the wall of the FGBMFI headquarters in Costa Mesa in 1980.[113]

How This Vision Was Reflected in Demos Shakarian's Life

While the vision brought a divine mandate to Demos Shakarian, his life before and after this pneumatic experience exemplified the concern he had for the salvation of human beings. The fact that this was an ecstatic vision preceded and followed by glossolalia and prophecy was not an unusual experience, but rather something he was familiar with from his own Armenian Pentecostal background. He did not take lightly the prophetic nature of this vision and the charismatic utterances that preceded and proceeded from this experience. After all, an earlier prophetic word had already saved his ancestors from physical destruction, and now these charismatic experiences were promising to save millions more from spiritual destruction.

This vision, while it seemed to change the course of Shakarian's life, and certainly resuscitated a nearly dead organization, had already been lived out in Shakarian's life countless times. He had preached from a makeshift pulpit across from Lincoln Park; he initiated a tent revival in East Los Angeles on his church's property; he organized revival meetings in the Shrine Auditorium; he oversaw a major evangelistic event in the Hollywood Bowl; and he facilitated numerous crusades for itinerant healing evangelists in the years leading up to this vision. Most typical American Christians in his situation would have abandoned their secular jobs and gone into full time ministry, but Shakarian did not see life in such dualistic terms. His Armenian background looked at life more holistically. His church never saw any distinction between the sacred and the secular as exemplified by their tradition of never hiring a professional minister during their century-long existence.[114]

By the same token, Shakarian prayed as readily for his sick cows at his dairy as he did for his sick sister in church.[115] He would as seamlessly pray for God's discernment and direction in the purchase of a prize bull as he would for discernment in who should testify at his early men's meetings.[116] To those who knew him best, his immediate family and close friends, he was the same in public as he was in private.[117] In reflections, they recalled that he was the most genuine person they ever knew. He never put on a religious hat at church and a business hat at the dairy or a completely different hat at home, but he always exhorted the men he mentored to always wear one hat in life.[118] In Demos Shakarian's case that was a Stetson hat that he prominently wore on his dairy farm and frequently wore at FGBMFI conventions and chapter meetings.

Just as Shakarian looked at life seamlessly, he also saw how human beings needed to be linked together as a community. An individual life that was divided and dualistic was as foreign to Shakarian as a divided community of believers. His own Armenian ecclesiology and ecumenism, passed down from generation to generation, could not accept the sectarianism of his Russian neighbors or his Pentecostal peers. This served him well as the FGBMFI spread far beyond any ecclesiological boundaries that were acceptable by Pentecostal standards in that era.

In addition, the community he saw in his vision was a community of love.[119] Demos Shakarian embodied this vision through his amiable and gentle nature as well as his personable way of relating with people. He had the rare ability to become best friends with a complete stranger, talk with someone and make them feel like they were the only person in a room of a thousand people, or even remember names and conversations he had with people when he met with them years later.[120] Perhaps he was so attentive and such a good listener because of the partial hearing loss he sustained during his childhood.[121] These social skills would serve him well in the future when, as Milton Hansen had prophesied many years earlier, he would meet with presidents, kings, and heads of state.[122] In addition, when meeting business men, politicians, and even dictators, he was not judgmental. Even though he was raised in a very conservative holiness background in his Armenian church, Demos Shakarian loved people. Any lifestyle choices which disagreed with Shakarian's holiness background, he left to the pneumatological work of the Holy Spirit.[123]

Perhaps one of the most important aspects of his life in relation to the vision he received was in understanding the role he would play in this mass spiritual revival. Years before he received this vision, while organizing a Christian rally in Fresno, California, he revealed his role as a facilitator in front of a large group of pastors. Shakarian told this gathering of Pentecostal clergy that discovering your gift and using it would make you among "the happiest people on earth."[124] As such, over time, he discovered that his role in this coming revival was not to be a pastor, a prophet, a healer, or an evangelist, but rather a facilitator, an organizer, and a helper.[125]

As the director of a burgeoning Christian men's organization that soon became the largest of its kind in the world, he was not eager to accept the limelight. He was flexible rather than structured, and as a pneumatic, charismatic Christian, he was open to whomever God would use.[126] Most importantly, he was convinced that God could use anybody, not just the clergy. Demos Shakarian's own Armenian ecclesiology saw no boundaries or barriers regarding who God could use, but this was reinforced even more when Shakarian prayed for a man who experienced a dramatic healing at the World Pentecostal Conference in Jerusalem in 1961.[127] Shakarian was convinced more than ever that ordinary lay-men, not just healing evangelists, could be used powerfully, and he wanted to make that opportunity possible for other business men.[128]

As a visionary, Shakarian often was two steps ahead of most people, and by the time his co-workers, peers, or Christian friends caught up with him, he was already on to the next project. As such, like many visionaries who succeed at what they do, Shakarian had an uncanny ability to surround himself with capable people who could help him complete various projects or evangelistic programs.[129] However, like most visionaries, Shakarian sometimes lacked focus. When it came to evangelistic rallies or crusades, it often took an encouraging or prophetic word from others to enable Shakarian to prioritize his vision. Although he clearly per-ceived this vision late Friday evening, December 26, 1952, it took the prophetic words of Milton Hansen and Charles Price long before he had this vision to real-ize the urgency of the vision, and the prophetic word of Mordecai Ham (1877–1961) one year after the vision to remind him once again that this vision was much bigger than Demos Shakarian.[130] He was going to need the help of an army of business men.

How the FGBMFI Reflected Shakarian's Vision

Rapidly, large numbers of business men began to enlist as members in the FGBMFI. The first to spread the vision and enlist members were the healing evangelists that Demos Shakarian had sponsored and supported. Tommy Hicks was first when he excitedly called up Shakarian and informed him that he had just formed group number two in Sioux Falls, South Dakota.[131] As Hicks and other evangelists connected with the FGBMFI gained an international following, they also initiated new chapters of the FGBMFI wherever they went.[132] Thus, this fledgling organization rapidly became an international ministry in 1955 and 1956, within a few short years after its inception.

Oral Roberts and William Branham also helped with the spread of new chap-ters by promoting FGBMFI in their crusades and soon chapters sprang up in Pittsburgh, Pennsylvania; Tacoma, Washington; Oakland, California; and another chapter that Tommy Hicks helped start at his crusade in Washington, D.C.[133] Jack Coe (1918–1956), along with Oral Roberts, William Branham, and Tommy Hicks, was considered one of the most popular evangelists in early FGBMFI his-tory.[134] Coe's overall popularity as a healing evangelist was only exceeded by that of Oral Roberts.[135] Like Branham, Coe's ministry was not without controversy, but unlike Branham, this was mostly due to his style of ministry. He was bold and brash, thriving on controversy; once he even sent over envoys to measure Oral Roberts' tent, so he could purchase a slightly bigger tent and have the bragging rights for owning the largest tent in the world.[136] Even though this presumably drew the ire of Roberts, Coe and Roberts were pictured together at several

FGBMFI rallies after this skirmish.[137] Evidently Coe's relationship with Shakarian was much more cordial; he invited Shakarian to be a guest speaker at the grand opening of his independent church in Dallas in 1954.[138] However, the Assemblies of God could not overlook Coe's brash style or his independent ways. In 1953, they expelled him from the denomination.[139]

Another popular figure in the early history of the FGBMFI was Raymond T. Richey (1893–1968). He was a healing revivalist before WWII and one of the few popular evangelists who regained his popularity after the war.[140] During the depression, he left the evangelistic field to pastor a church in Houston, Texas.[141] However, after the war, he resumed a full time evangelistic career and quickly found a receptive audience among FGBMFI rallies and chapters.[142] He was the featured speaker when the FGBMFI opened their first office in downtown Los Angeles on July 11, 1953.[143]

Nevertheless, Oral Roberts remained the most influential healing evangelist, friend, and mentor of Demos Shakarian. As Demos Shakarian described his idea of a Christian business men's organization to Oral Roberts in 1951, Shakarian felt that every word in the name of the FGBMFI was necessary in describing this organization.[144] It was a *full gospel* organization reflecting the Pentecostal sentiments of Demos Shakarian and the Pentecostal evangelists and lay people that surrounded him early in the formation of the movement. The doctrinal statements on the back of early *Voice* magazines proposed "divine healing through faith" and "baptism in the Holy Ghost accompanied by the initial physical sign of speaking in other tongues." This statement promoted the Pentecostal distinctive of glossolalia and a long standing tradition of faith healing in Pentecostalism then being featured by the rising tide of healing evangelists that helped spread the FGBMFI.[145] Statements on the Trinity and the infallibility of Scripture reflected both the doctrinal stance of the new Pentecostal Fellowship of North America and the partnership that many Pentecostal denominations were making by joining the National Association of Evangelicals. A statement on "sanctification by the blood of Christ, personal holiness of heart and life, and separation from the world" reflected both the holiness sentiments of Demos Shakarian and much of Pentecostalism.[146]

The FGBMFI was also a *business man's* organization led by laymen. Among his many endeavors, Demos Shakarian was a dairyman and a real estate developer. Lee Braxton of Whiteville, North Carolina, vice-president of the FGBMFI, was a banker, automobile dealer, and president of numerous corporations.[147] George Gardner of Binghamton, New York, and vice-president of the FGBMFI, was also a successful automobile dealer and the past president of the New York State Automobile Dealers Association.[148] Miner Arganbright of La Crescenta, California, and vice-president of the FGBMFI, was a building contractor and close friend of Demos Shakarian.[149] To these founding members of the FGBMFI can be included a long list of business men in the formative years of the organization including Tom Ashcraft (1909–1987), Thomas R. Nickel, Paul Fischer, and Henry Krause (1887–1972).

Of course, pastors and especially healing evangelists played a significant part in expanding the organization in its early years, and they continued to be featured as prominent speakers at FGBMFI crusades and conventions throughout its history. In addition, they were allowed to be members of the organization, but they were not allowed to hold official positions in the FGBMFI or direct the organization's activities.[150] The organization did define "business man" liberally, allowing men of any occupation, including laborers and employees, to be involved in the organization. Nevertheless, the FGBMFI prominently featured successful entrepreneurs and executives at conventions and in *Voice* magazine. As such, white collar workers and wealthier business men made up a higher percentage of the organization than the representative sociological population.[151] This emphasis on business men was consistent with the prophetic word that Charles Price gave to Demos Shakarian about a layman's Christian revival. Shakarian gave Oral Roberts a similar description regarding the effectiveness of a layman's spiritual revolution.[152]

The name of the organization also implied that it was a men's organization, and women were excluded from official membership but encouraged to participate in meetings and conventions.[153] In the past ten to fifteen years, some chapters have allowed women as members and even as chapter presidents,[154] but the 1950s were more conservative times. This conservative position was reinforced shortly after WWII, when millions of men came back from Europe expecting to regain the jobs they left behind, jobs that had been filled mostly by women during the war. This massive sociological shift repeated what had already occurred in WWI. In addition, this trend was thrust forward by a much slower but no less significant shift from an agrarian to an industrial economy. Nevertheless, these factors left an underlying tension that would eventually erupt in the 1960s with the women's liberation movement. With that eruption emerged political organizations like the National Organization of Women (1966–) and even Christian women's organizations like Women's Aglow (1967–) that paralleled and complemented those whom the FGBMFI had initially excluded.

While the FGBMFI reflected this conservative sociological shift, it should be mentioned that Demos Shakarian's emphasis on men was out of concern for a perceived and real lack of spiritual participation and ecclesiological commitment by men in North America. A conversation that Shakarian had with Charles Price in the summer of 1944 reflected this concern.[155] In addition, Shakarian did not emphasize or teach about male authority in the church but rather focused on the importance of agreement in marriages and in ministry, a teaching that he modeled in his own life.[156]

The FGBMFI was also a *fellowship* that insisted on remaining fluid and relational, not structured or impersonal. Early Pentecostal organizations such as the Assemblies of God, organized in 1914, also maintained an insistence on being a fellowship rather than a denominational institution. Nevertheless, the charismatic origins and the prophetic nature of the Assemblies of God, as with other movements and denominations throughout church history, gave way to ritualized and hierarchal structure, resulting in the organization becoming a more formal denomination.[157] This tension between the charismatic and the routine polarities of Christianity is something that has existed at various periods in church history. More often than not, the prophetic nature of Christianity has given way to the power structures of order in Christendom; consequently, the modern observer sometimes fails to see the continuity of this tension or the existence of previous prophetic or charismatic groups.[158]

Because of Shakarian's Armenian ethnicity and his background that was rooted in the Armenian Pentecostal Church, he was more apt to see this continuity, and the organization he founded in 1951 has always emphasized the prophetic and charismatic side of this tension. Consequently, the FGBMFI never became a denomination despite the suspicions and accusations to the contrary by its detractors. Shakarian's own amiable and personable nature resisted structures and organizations and preferred the relational aspects of business and ministry. In addition, the independent nature of the Armenian Pentecostal Church he grew up in resisted denominationalism. Shakarian constantly and consistently denounced any suggestion that the FGBMFI would become a denomination.[159]

The fellowship was *international* in spite of the fact that it was originally named the Full Gospel Business Men's Fellowship of America.[160] Perhaps the original name for the organization came out of Shakarian's limited context in Southern California. After all, he had not traveled internationally until 1952, and within the Armenian community, there was a fear of air travel that he had to overcome.[161] Nevertheless, the pneumatic vision Shakarian experienced in the waning days of 1952 emphasized a global renewal which included men from every continent. Chapters started up in various locations throughout the United States. Some chapters, such as the new chapter in Atlanta, Georgia, and the new chapter in Manhattan, New York, exceeded 1,000 men before the end of the decade.[162] However, the first few years after this vision, the word "international" did not seem to make sense. Eventually, a chapter was started in Johannesburg, South Africa in 1955.[163] In 1956, chapters began in Hong Kong,[164] London,[165] and Calcutta.[166] Soon Shakarian's vision became a reality as chapters began to spread throughout the globe.

The Early Ecumenism of Demos Shakarian and the FGBMFI

As mentioned previously, in 1952, the World Pentecostal Conference dismissed Shakarian's proposal for sponsoring a Pentecostal Christian business men's organization,[167] and DuPlessis resigned his position as secretary at the end of the London conference.[168] In the midst of rejection, both men had profound experiences that significantly altered the course of their ministries. DuPlessis went to the International Missionary Council of the World Council of Churches in Germany in 1952, and ecumenical opportunities began to open for him that eventually earned him the name "Mr. Pentecost."[169] A few months later, after a series of discouraging FGBMFI meetings in Clifton's Cafeteria, Shakarian had his vision which allowed him to see the future global impact of this organization. The next Full Gospel meeting at Clifton's Cafeteria turned out to be fortuitous, and the organization began to grow exponentially for the next several decades.[170]

Whether or not the rejection by their Pentecostal brethren launched both of them into a broader and more ecumenical scope of ministry, it is clear that new opportunities were made available to them.[171] In addition, this theme of rejection and suspicion continued to encourage the FGBMFI to become more ecumenical. Pentecostal churches in Los Angeles became suspicious of what Shakarian was trying to do, but his response was to encourage his members to remain faithful to their churches. If their churches were Spirit-filled, he encouraged them to continue serving in those churches, and even if their churches were not, he encouraged them to go back as missionaries.[172]

Interestingly, at the same time that Shakarian experienced rejection from his Pentecostal brethren, he received some aid from a Catholic Christian in Italy who helped assist with the plight of Full Gospel Christians in Italy. This assistance was prominently mentioned in an article in *Voice* in January 1954.[173] This early positive experience with a Catholic Christian likely broadened the scope and understanding of ecumenism in the FGBMFI. Thomas Nickel commented next year in *Voice*, "I have nothing but the utmost love for Catholics."[174] In 1955, Nickel was asked by the FGBMFI board of directors to replace the doctrinal statement on the back cover of *Voice* with the prominent phrase, "Our Banner is Love."[175]

As president of the board of directors, Demos Shakarian, with the board's approval, made unity a priority over doctrine in the early stages of the FGBMFI. Doctrine was not ignored; acceptance of the doctrinal statements of the organization was a requirement for membership. Nevertheless, Shakarian and the board felt an urgency to prominently advertise the virtues of Christian love and unity. Shakarian had the opportunity to reject Catholicism, and other Christian ecclesiologies as the FGBMFI began. Just as the organization began, one individual wanted to use Shakarian's influence and the platform of the FGBMFI to crusade against Roman Catholics, but Shakarian refused his offer.[176] The Armenian context of Shakarian's hermeneutical lens had already broadened his ecumenical horizons before Demos Shakarian's movement began.

The Early Growth of
Demos Shakarian's Organization

The difference between the FGBMFI before and after Demos Shakarian's vision was spectacular. Before the vision, the men gathering weekly in Clifton's Cafeteria, were a small group of men ranging from fifteen to fifty people. Demos Shakarian was discouraged, exhausted, disillusioned, and ready to abandon the organization he founded. Less than a year after the vision, they held their first national convention at the Clark Hotel in downtown Los Angeles with nine chapters in existence and more than 600 men in attendance.[177] Shakarian's enthusiasm for the organization after his vision in 1952 was also increased by the prophetic utterances of Mordecai Ham (1877–1961) at the Price Hotel in Houston, Texas in 1954. Mordecai Ham, also an early spiritual mentor to Billy Graham, spent three days meeting with Shakarian and confirming the earlier prophecies of Charles Price.[178]

In June of 1954, the FGBMFI became even more ambitious, holding their second national convention at the Shoreham Hotel in Washington, D.C., with then Vice-President Richard Millhouse Nixon (1913–1994) as a guest speaker.[179] A group of wealthy business men was certainly a tempting target for a politician, even if they were ecstatic practitioners, and Richard Nixon was no stranger to Pentecostalism. While growing up in Southern California, Nixon had occasionally attended services at Angelus Temple and had heard Aimee Semple McPherson.[180] However, these were strange new experiences and euphoric times for Pentecostals, who were not accustomed to receiving such prominent recognition.

Initially, evangelism and growth in the FGBMFI took place in the wake of the healing crusades of Tommy Hicks, Oral Roberts, T.L. Osborn (1923–), William Branham, Harold Herman, and others.[181] However, as a lay ministry led by lay people, FGBMFI members likely were not satisfied with simply assisting on the sidelines. Soon they began to organize their own evangelistic campaigns, beginning with their "Squadrons" of evangelistic lay teams that initially went to Mexico.[182] However, Demos Shakarian, being the creative visionary that he was, was not satisfied with just one or two methods of evangelism. He experimented with a variety of methods and surrounded himself with like-minded, innovative business men.[183]

One initial form of evangelism that became extremely popular after Demos Shakarian's vision was the distribution of *Voice* magazine. The providential timing of Thomas Nickel's appearance at that momentous breakfast meeting on December 27, 1952, was seen as a divine mandate by Demos Shakarian as he and leaders of the FGBMFI gathered to pray over the first edition.[184] Soon many business men let the magazine and its popular testimonies do the talking for them, and many would order boxes of *Voice* magazine to be distributed at various places in their community.[185] For nearly three decades, it was difficult to find a men's public bathroom, especially one on the West Coast, without a copy of *Voice* magazine in every stall. Other forms of evangelism began to occur as the FGBMFI continued to gain numbers, influence, and finances.

Much of the growth of the FGBMFI was due to the self-sacrificing nature of many of its business men, who temporarily left jobs and traveled extensively spreading chapters wherever they went. Demos Shakarian exemplified that sacrifice by never receiving a salary from the organization. In fact, for the first thirty years of the organization's existence, he was never reimbursed for any travel expenses and only in the last decade of his life did he receive any compensation for expenditures and some health insurance coverage from the FGBMFI.[186] He also spent the majority of his time traveling and speaking on behalf of the FGBM-

FI at conventions and chapter meetings. Shakarian estimated that he spent $50,000 to $100,000 annually in unreimbursed travel expenses for the FGBMFI, and he made property investments to fund these added expenses.[187] The amount of time he spent for the ministry organization created some temporal challenges for the businesses that he chaired; consequently, he asked his son-in-law, Gene Scalf, to oversee most of the day-to-day responsibilities for the real estate empire he built and Richard Shakarian took on a greater responsibility at the dairy as general sales and marketing manager.[188]

Other business men followed Shakarian's example of sacrifice and they began to multiply chapters nationally and internationally. One example internationally was Nana Kwesi Amoakohene II, who invested a small fortune of time and money in establishing chapters throughout Ghana.[189] Another example is Earl Prickett; after becoming initially involved in the FGBMFI; he spent the next several years spending most of his money, time, and resources to help establish over 100 chapters in the eastern United States.[190]

Since its inception, perhaps the most successful and widespread form of evangelism for the FGBMFI has been the testimonies of ordinary business men given at conventions and chapter meetings. Shakarian modeled this form of evangelism in his life. Even though he realized early in his adult life that he was not a preacher, Shakarian was the consummate storyteller who loved to share his own testimony and frequently encouraged other business men to do likewise.[191] He actually had a mild speech impediment (stuttering) which probably made him self-conscious, but when he stood up to give a story rather than a sermon, Shakarian's speech never faltered.[192]

Nkusi Josiah, former FGBMFI director of Rwanda, suggested testimony brought both a cross-cultural and instantaneous connection with local business men.[193] Demos Shakarian offered an excellent example of this while speaking to 200 farmers and business men at a new FGBMFI chapter in Lancaster, Pennsylvania.[194] Shakarian failed to connect with the audience until he spilled milk on his boots and began to offer a testimony about his own experience with milking cows. The audience responded with laughter and listeners became members as one man told Shakarian, "We realized then that you really were a farmer, just like us."[195] Asamoah-Gyadu suggested oral theological discourse and the use of testimony has always been a primary tool in the growth and evangelism of the FGBMFI and core parts of their worship.[196] On a broader scale, Walter Hollenweger (1927–) emphasized that oral theology was a primary reason for the rapid growth of the neo-Pentecostal movement in the two-thirds world.[197]

By the end of 1955, the FGBMFI had already organized three international conventions, added four full time office staff, and moved their office headquarters to Monterrey Park, California.[198] In addition, Thomas Nickel moved the publication of *Voice* magazine from Watsonville to Monterrey Park to consolidate the operations of the FGBMFI at one location.[199] The original chapter of the FGBMFI had an average attendance of 1,000 participants by the middle of 1955.[200] In the midst of this rapid growth, Shakarian continued to travel extensively on behalf of the FGBMFI. On longer trips, he made use of C.C. Ford's plane, but often Rose and Demos Shakarian would drive hundreds of miles, speak at a chapter meeting or church, arrive back home at three hours after midnight and wake up early in the morning to work on the farm.[201] Most often, Rose travelled with Demos Shakarian, but on trips when Rose was unable to join her husband, he would call Rose every night he was apart from her.[202]

The Emergence of New Opportunities

As Shakarian watched his organization grow, he also noticed the population growing around his dairy farm in Downey. From his early childhood until 1958, Shakarian saw the population of California grow at least five hundred per cent from under three million to over fifteen million people.[203] By itself, Los Angeles County had reached a population of over six million inhabitants by the end of the 1950s.[204] As tract housing began to cover Southern California after WWII, and Shakarian saw the city around Downey and Norwalk encroaching upon his dairy farms, he purchased a much larger dairy farm in Delano, and a 500 acre calving ranch in Modesto at bargain prices, simultaneously selling his dairy properties in Southern California at premium prices. With the extra money he also invested in real estate just as the California real estate boom began to accelerate exponentially.[205]

While Shakarian poised himself for economic real estate profits, his ecumenical approach with the FGBMFI positioned his organization to realize an opportunity that would help him fulfill the prophetic utterances of his previous mentor, Charles Price. In 1956, Shakarian helped organize the fiftieth anniversary of the Azusa Street Revival in Los Angeles (1906–1909). Evangelists such as William Branham and Tommy Hicks spoke at the rallies and meetings held at Angelus Temple and the Biltmore Bowl from September 16 until September 23, and Shakarian's new organization led the evening rally on September 22, 1956, with a list of Christian laymen including Enoch Christoffersen (1903–1990), Cliff Ford (d.b.a. 1910–d.d.a. 1990), and William Roll (1923–2002).[206] Seed money raised from the Hollywood Bowl in 1948, which Shakarian helped organize, sponsored the speakers and secured locations for the historical Pentecostal celebration in Los Angeles.[207]

At this Pentecostal celebration, Shakarian reminded his Pentecostal peers that "biblical Christianity is ecumenical rather than divisive."[208] Shakarian already began to see the divisions of denominationalism disappear at the fourth annual FGBMFI international convention in Minneapolis, Minnesota, just three months before the Azusa Street celebration. David DuPlessis spoke at the convention, and a significant number of Lutherans experienced Spirit baptism.[209] In early 1957, Harold Herman verified that this experience was not a localized event when he reported that Lutherans in Germany were also experiencing Spirit baptism.[210] After the fifth annual FGBMFI international convention in Chicago, Illinois, DuPlessis could barely contain his excitement. "The love of God, the unity of the

Holy Spirit, simply submerged all barriers of race and creed...Glorious testimonies of Pentecostal blessings came from the mouths of Lutherans, Methodists, Presbyterians, Mennonites, Baptists, and many other Protestant churches."[211]

Immediately after the convention, Demos Shakarian stated, "My work is with all denominations, and I pay my own expenses."[212] The tone of Shakarian's remarks betrayed both his ecumenical stance and a defensive posture although he did not specify who his critics were. Nevertheless, Shakarian's work was inclusive; in October 1957, *Voice* magazine featured a prominent article on a Lutheran minister who had received an experience of Spirit baptism.[213]

After the ecumenical euphoria of the Chicago convention, Shakarian decided to go on a nationwide tour in the spring of 1958, visiting existing chapters of FGBMFI and helping establish new chapters. Using the Spanish he learned from Hispanic workers on his dairy farm, Shakarian delivered his first sermon in Spanish to a newly opened Spanish speaking FGBMFI chapter in New York City.[214] During his tour, Shakarian also spoke to students at Lee College in Cleveland, Tennessee.[215] While he was on the East Coast, he also spent time with Earl Prickett (1914–1990), chairman of the sixth annual FGBMFI international convention, preparing for the meetings in Philadelphia, Pennsylvania in July 1958. Revealing his sense of humor, Shakarian mentioned calling Prickett late one night, disguising his voice and pretending to be a suicidal drunk. Prickett took the opportunity to counsel this supposed stranger, praying with him to receive Christian salvation until Shakarian could no longer contain his laughter.[216]

As Earl Prickett organized the convention in July 1958, he negotiated a rate of six dollars per night at local hotels for FGBMFI members attending the meetings. Oral Roberts spoke at his sixth consecutive international convention. Shakarian also invited a new speaker, James Brown (1912–1987), a Presbyterian professor of theology at Lincoln Seminary in Philadelphia, Pennsylvania.[217] Brown would be the first of many speakers at FGBMFI conventions who would represent the wide ecclesiological swath of influence the organization had as a neo-Pentecostal movement began to appear in a wide variety of Christian denominations.

Conclusion

At the end of 1958, Demos Shakarian and the FGBMFI were already extending their pneumatological experience far beyond the confines of Pentecostal ecclesiological boundaries and promoting ministers and leaders who would become early progenitors and leaders in the Charismatic movement. Shakarian did not know exactly how the details of "a great layman's revival" would take place, but he was sure he would be a part of it, and during this period, Shakarian began to understand what role he would take in this emerging movement.[218] Nevertheless, just as he began to understand his role, he almost abandoned his position of Christian leadership, facing dismal results and frustration for his efforts.

The vision he experienced at three hours and thirty minutes past midnight early on the morning of December 27, 1952, offered Shakarian confirmation that he should continue leading the FGBMFI. Reflecting upon that vision ten years later, Shakarian said, "That was the breakthrough and from that night on everything changed completely."[219] It is worth repeating that long before Shakarian ever witnessed this particular vision, he was already a visionary and an innovator who saw potential needs and created opportunities – often long before most people would have. As a young teenager, he was inventive and creative, even attempting to build an airplane out of a Model T Ford with his friend and cousin, Dan Mushegan.[220] He was a savvy business man as well as an innovative dairy farmer. When he faced rising mortality rates among the young calves, he invented a new design for calving booths to reduce disease and eliminate death among young dairy cows. He also saw the need and the opportunity for a Christian business man's organization long before he had this pneumatic vision in 1952 or founded the FGBMFI in 1951.[221]

He saw economic real estate and dairy opportunities during this period that advanced his fortune while the pneumatological vision he experienced advanced his organization. As the Shakarian Corporation prospered and the FGBMFI expanded, he interpreted these events as divine blessings. As the FGBMFI began to expand beyond the confines of its Pentecostal boundaries, his own interpretation would be confirmed by the birth of a new Christian movement.

Notes

1. "Revival Tent Meeting," *Los Angeles Times* September 17, 1949, A2; and Demos Shakarian, *The Happiest People* (1975), 100–102.

2. Demos Shakarian-Synan interview, October 5, 1987, 17.

3. Edna Shakarian, "Go Over Jordan," *Voice*, January 1950, 10.

4. See Demos Shakarian, *The Happiest People* (1975), 42; Bivin, "The Armenians of Karakala," (n.d.), 12; and John Berokoff, *Molokans in America* (1987), 38–39. Marriage outside of the Armenian Pentecostal community was discouraged when Demos Shakarian wed Rose Gabrielian in 1933. Both the Russian and Armenian Molokan communities practiced endogamy, but the Armenian Molokan community discontinued the practice at some point before they appointed Isaac Shakarian as the pastor of the Armenian Pentecostal Church in 1952.

5. This information was gathered from Social Security death records for Edna Shakarian and Isaac Shakarian at http://ssdi.rootsweb.ancestry.com (accessed September 10, 2008).

6. "$13,000 Awarded for Land Strip," *Los Angeles Times*, February 8, 1951, 5.

7. Ibid.

8. Demos Shakarian, *Divine Life* (1991); 43–45; and "Norwalk Center has New Store," *Los Angeles Times*, May 11, 1952, F5.

9. Demos Shakarian, *Divine Life* (1991), 44–45.

10. Demos Shakarian-Synan interview, October 5, 1987, 11–12; and Oral Roberts-Shakarian interview, October 10, 1991, 1.

11. Demos Shakarian, "God's Dairyman," (1956), 51; and Demos Shakarian, *The Shakarian Story* (1999), 33.

12. Jeff Janoian, *God at Our Side*, DVD (2005).

13. Demos Shakarian, *The Shakarian Story* (1999), 33; and *Laskey's 1961 Official Blue Book Criss Cross City Directory* (Anaheim, CA: Laskey Brothers and Company, 1961), 138.

14. Gene Scalf-Tallman interview, January 9, 2008; and *Voice*, March 1959, 2.

15. "Display ads", *Los Angeles Times*, October 18, G9; October 25, G11; November 1, H13; November 8, G11; November 15, H7; November 22, 14; November 29, 13; and December 6, 1953, H9.

16. Gene Bedley, former employee of Reliance drive-in dairy, phone interview with Matthew Tallman, August 29, 2008.

17. Display Ad, *Los Angeles Times*, October 30, 1955, J5.

18. Demos Shakarian, "God's Dairyman," (1956), 51.

19. Downey Dairy Farm Buys $4000 Prize Bull," *Los Angeles Times*, July 18, 1954, F4; and Ed Ainsworth, "A Lot of Faith," *Los Angeles Times*, May 8, 1960, I19.

20. "Downey Dairy Farm Buys $4000 Prize Bull," *Los Angeles Times*, July 18, 1954, F4; and Demos Shakarian, *The Happiest People* (1975), 147–149. In *The Happiest People* (1975), Shakarian claims he bought the bull for $5000, but the *Los Angeles Times* source is much earlier, written almost immediately after the sale.

21. Demos Shakarian, *The Happiest People* (1975), 148–149; and Ed Ainsworth, "A Lot of Faith," *Los Angeles Times*, May 8, 1960, I19.

22. Ibid.

23. John W. Caughey, *California: A Remarkable State's Life History* (Englewood Cliffs, NJ: Prentice-Hall, Incorporated, 1970), 522–527.

24. "Industry Zoning Urged for 28 Acres in Norwalk," *Los Angeles Times*, January 2, 1955, K3.

25. "Sales, Leases Top $900, 000," *Los Angeles Times*, August 7, 1955, F6.

26. "Denice Ann Shakarian Arrives October 9th," *Voice*, November 1956, 30; and Richard Shakarian, "A Life-Long Commitment to Jesus, *Voice*, October 1993, 5–6.

27. Demos Shakarian, *Divine Life* (1991), 44–45.

28. "Display Ad," *Los Angeles Times* June 30, 1951, A3. Also see the six display ads in the *Los Angeles Times* running from June 30 until August 4, 1951 advertising Tommy Hicks' tent crusades.

29. Demos Shakarian, *The Happiest People* (1975), 134.

30. Thomas R. Nickel, ed., "Chapter at Reading, Pennsylvania," *Voice*, January 1954, 8; Nickel, "Springfield, Illinois has Chapter," *Voice*, November 1953, 9; and Nickel, "God's Mighty Power Manifested at our First Annual Convention," *Voice*, September 1953, 9–10.

31. Vinson Synan, *The Century of the Holy Spirit: 100 Years of Pentecostal and Charismatic Renewal* (Nashville: Thomas Nelson Publishers, 2001), 16. Tommy Hicks' meetings in Argentina became so popular that he had to rent out the largest soccer stadium in Argentina. (See Thomas R. Nickel, "The Greatest Revival in All History," *Voice*, February–March 1955, 4–7).

32. Thomas R. Nickel, ed., "The Historic Argentina Revival," *Voice*, February 1955, 4–5; and "The Greatest Revival in all History" *Voice*, May 1955, 4–7.

33. Thomas R. Nickel, ed., "The Greatest Revival in all History," *Voice*, May 1955, 5.

34. Synan, *Under His Banner* (1992), 72.

35. "Old Fashioned Union Camp Meeting with Tommy Hicks," *Los Angeles Times* June 30, 1951, A3. Hicks ran display ads on July 14 and July 28 with a special display ad advertising an extension of the revival meetings for one more week on August 4.

36. "City Wide Evangelistic Campaign," *Los Angeles Times* September 26, 1951, 10.

37. Demos Shakarian-Synan interview, February 2, 1988, 17.

38. David Edwin Harrell, Jr., *Oral Robert: An American Life* (Bloomington, Indiana: Indiana University Press, 1985), vii. Harrell's biography of Oral Roberts painstakingly analyzes every aspect of his life including his relationship with the FGBMFI.

39. Harrell, *Oral Roberts* (1985), 153.

40. Hollenweger and Quebedeaux mention no connection; Poloma fails to even mention Oral Roberts in her book, *The Charismatic Movement: Is There a New Pentecost?* (Boston, MA: Twayne Publishers, 1982).

41. Full Gospel Business Men's Fellowship International, "Constitution and By-Laws, Articles of Incorporation of the Full Gospel Business Men's Fellowship International, Revised to March, 1977," Costa Mesa, CA, 1977, 6; and Harrell, *All Things are Possible* (1975), 147. Harrell suggests that ministers were not even allowed to be members of the FGBMFI. While Oral Roberts suggested this to Shakarian (Oral Roberts-Synan interview, October 10, 1991, 6), ultimately, Shakarian allowed ministers to become members, but they were not allowed to become officers of the organization.

42. Demos Shakarian, "How Our Fellowship Came into Being," *Voice*, February 1953, 4.

43. Harrell, *Oral Roberts* (1985), 154.

44. Harrell, *Oral Roberts* (1985), 115–116, 212–213.

45. Demos Shakarian, "How Our Fellowship Came into Being," *Voice*, February 1953, 4.

46. Demos Shakarian, "How Our Fellowship Came into Being," *Voice*, February 1953, 4. See also Harrell, *Oral Roberts* (1985), 153.

47. Demos Shakarian, *The Happiest People* (1975), 118.

48. Demos Shakarian, "How Our Fellowship Came into Being," *Voice*, February 1953, 4.

49. Display Ad 11 – No Title, *Los Angeles Times* September 25, 1953, 16.

50. Oral Roberts-Synan interview, October 10, 1991, 13.

51. Russell Chandler, "Gospel Fellowship Draws Charismatics," *Los Angeles Times* July 5, 1975, A27.

52. John Dart, "Full Gospel Fellowship Will Dedicate Building" *Los Angeles Times* January 26, 1980, B2.

53. Synan, *Under His Banner* (1992), 161.

54. Oral Roberts-Synan interview, October 10, 1991, 1.

55. Oral Roberts, interview by Vinson Synan, Tulsa, OK, October 10, 1991, 1.

56. Ibid.

57. "Oral Roberts in Los Angeles," *Los Angeles Times* October 6, 1951, A3.

58. Oral Robert's interview by Vinson Synan, Tulsa, OK, October 10, 1991, 1–2.

59. Demos Shakarian, *The Happiest People* (1975), 119.

60. Ron Weinbender-Tallman interview, January 10, 2005. There are also plans to renew an English speaking chapter at Clifton's Cafeteria. See John Carrette, "Fire Team Outreach in Los Angeles," FGBMFI, http://www.fgbmfi.org/events, (accessed January 10, 2008).

61. Demos Shakarian, *The Happiest People* (1975), 119.

62. Demos Shakarian, "How our Fellowship Came into Being," *Voice*, February 1953, 4. A photograph of that first meeting in this article showed twenty-seven people in attendance, but the written record only mentions twenty-one people at the first meeting. Is it possible that the sobering attendance caused Shakarian to underestimate the actual count, or that Clifton employees or additional business men sauntered in later after the meeting had already begun?

63. Geraldine Shakarian Scalf, interview by Matthew Tallman, Colorado Springs, CO, January 9, 2008. His daughter suggested Shakarian's own tenacity as one of his primary characteristics in this interview. Shakarian's own personality profile confirms this trait (Personality profile, submitted to Management By Strengths, Incorporated (Olathe, KS), September 20, 1989.

64. Demos Shakarian, *The Happiest People* (1975), 120.

65. Ibid.

66. Demos Shakarian, "How our Fellowship Came into Being," *Voice*, February 1953, 4.

67. Oral Roberts-Synan interview, October 10, 1991, 6–7.

68. "Full Gospel Business Men of America Start New National Association," *Healing Waters*, January 1952, 12.

69. Demos Shakarian, *The Happiest People* (1975), 122.

70. Ibid, 121.

71. Geraldine Scalf-Tallman interview, January 9, 2008.

72. Demos Shakarian, *The Happiest People* (1975), 121.

73. See Hal Donaldson, "1951–Present: Full Gospel Businessmen's Fellowship International," *Pentecostal Evangel*, May 31, 1998, 25.

74. Donald Gee, "From the Editor's Mail" *Voice*, April 1955, 20.

75. Ralph Riggs, "From the Editor's Mail" *Voice*, February–March 1954, 12.

76. As the Charismatic movement started, more and more FGBMFI members came from non-Pentecostal backgrounds. It is estimated that by 1972, eighty percent of the organization's members came from non-Pentecostal backgrounds. See Steve Durasoff, *Bright Wind of the Spirit* (1972), 151.

77. Harrell mentions the initial interest that Ralph Riggs showed toward the FGBMFI "could not remain entirely an admiring one." Harell, *All Things are Possible* (1975), 147.

78. Demos Shakarian, *The Happiest People* (1975), 122.

79. David DuPlessis, *A Man Called Mr. Pentecost* (Plainfield, New Jersey: Logos International, 1977), 91, and 170.

80. DuPlessis, *Mr. Pentecost* (1977), 12.

81. Demos Shakarian, *The Happiest People* (1975), 51 and 83.

82. See Demos Shakarian, *The Happiest People* (1975), 122–124. However, DuPlessis does mention meeting with Demos Shakarian several times and being invited to speak at several early FGBMFI meetings in his own journal preserved in his archival collection at Fuller Theological Seminary Library in Pasadena, California.

83. Ibid, 124.

84. DuPlessis, *A Man Called Mr. Pentecost* (1977), 175.

85. Harrell, *All Things are Possible* (1975), 20. See for example, Stanley Frodsham's dismissal from the Assemblies of God for his support of the Latter Rain movement.

86. Demos Shakarian, *The Happiest People* (1975), 129.

87. This aspect of the relationship between Demos and Rose Shakarian came to light through a series of interviews the author conducted with their daughter, Geraldine Shakarian Scalf in Colorado Springs, CO on January 8, 9, and 11, 2008. In addition,

Demos Shakarian's personality profile, submitted to Management By Strengths, Incorporated (Olathe, KS), September 20, 1989, reflects this same entrepreneurial outlook.

88. Demos Shakarian, personality profile, submitted to Management By Strengths, Incorporated (Olathe, KS), September 20, 1989.

89. Demos Shakarian, "How our Fellowship Came into Being," *Voice*, February 1953, 4–5.

90. See Synan, *Under His Banner* (1992), 50.

91. Demos Shakarian, *The Happiest People* (1975), 129.

92. "Norwalk Center has New Store," *Los Angeles Times*, May 11, 1952, F5.

93. "Ground Broken for Norwalk Goodwill Store, *Los Angeles Times*, November 11, 16.

94. See Demos Shakarian, *The Happiest People* (1975), 110–115.

95. Ibid, 64.

96. Demos Shakarian, *The Happiest People* (1975), 130–131.

97. See the six display ads in the *Los Angeles Times* running from June 30 until August 4, 1951 advertising his tent crusades.

98. Demos Shakarian-Synan interview, October 5, 1987, 4.

99. See Tommy Hicks, "Argentina," *Voice*, May 1954, 4–5; and Tommy Hicks, "Trips to Argentina and Russia," *Voice*, December 1954, 17.

100. Demos Shakarian, *The Happiest People* (1975), 131–132.

101. Ibid, 37.

102. Demos Shakarian, *The Happiest People* (1975), 132–133.

103. Ibid, 133–134.

104. Ibid, 134.

105. Ibid, 135.

106. Ibid.

107. Ibid, 138.

108. Thomas Nickel, *Voice*, June 1955, 9.

109. Oral Roberts, "His Works do Follow Him," *Voice*, January 1965, 15; and Demos Shakarian, "God's Dairyman," (1955), 51.

110. See Demos Shakarian, *The Happiest People* (1975), 131–134; Demos Shakarian, *The Vision*, DVD (Costa Mesa, CA: FGBMFI, n.d.); and Demos Shakarian, "How our Fellowship Came into Being," *Voice*, February 1953, 3.

111. See Vinson Synan, *Under His Banner* (1992), 56; also Demos Shakarian, *The Happiest People* (1975), 129. One other minor discrepancy occurred in the oral recording of Shakarian's vision, *The Vision*, DVD (Costa Mesa, CA: FGBMFI, n.d.) in which Demos Shakarian recalled that Tommy Hicks stayed in Richard Shakarian's bedroom while Richard was away at Southern California College. *The Happiest People on Earth* recorded that Richard was away at a youth retreat which he was leading (131). The story as recorded in Shakarian's autobiography is more probable since Richard would not have been away at college over Christmas vacation.

112. See Thomas R. Nickel, "The Amazing Shakarian Story," *Voice* 1:7, 1:8, 1:9, 1:10, 2:1, 2:2 (October, 1953–April 1954) for the earliest recorded version of the Shakarian immigration to America, and Demos Shakarian, "How Our Fellowship Came into Being," *Voice*, February 1953, 3–5 for the earliest version of the vision of Shakarian. In a recent Full Gospel Business chapter meeting the author attended on January 8, 2005 in Garden Grove, California, the chapter president briefly recounted both stories during the meeting.

113. See Synan, *Under His Banner*, (1992), 52. The rug on which Shakarian received his vision while praying is still kept in the FGBMFI headquarters in Irvine, California, but it currently resides on the floor of the board room on the second floor.

114. Stan Perumean-Tallman interview, March 26, 2006.

115. Demos Shakarian, *The Happiest People* (1975), 38 and 73.

116. Ibid, 50, 88, and 89.

117. These and the remaining reflections in this paragraph were collected from a series of interviews conducted with his daughter, Geraldine, his son-in-law Gene Scalf, his granddaughters Karen, Renee, and Michelle, and some close FGBMFI associates of his during the week of January 6, 2008, in Colorado Springs, CO.

118. Gene Scalf, interview with Matthew Tallman, Colorado Springs, CO, January 9, 2008.

119. Demos Shakarian, *The Happiest People* (1975), 134.

120. These observations were made by Shakarian's daughter and her family and friends at the same location in Colorado Springs, CO on January 9, 2008. Added to these observations were the impressions of the author on the one occasion that he had to personally meet Demos Shakarian at a FGBMFI convention in Portland, Oregon at the Red Lion Jantzen Beach Motor Inn in late May 1979.

121. See Demos Shakarian, *The Happiest People* (1975), 37. Also Gene Scalf made this observation in one of the author's interviews with him on January 12, 2008.

122. Demos Shakarian, *The Happiest People* (1975), 51.

123. Geraldine Shakarian Scalf, interview with Matthew Tallman, Colorado Springs, CO, January 11, 2008.

124. Demos Shakarian, *The Happiest People* (1975), 90 and 101.

125. Brad Tuttle, interview with Matthew Tallman, Colorado Springs, CO, January 9, 2008.

126. Geraldine Scalf-Tallman interview, January 9, 2008.

127. See Demos Shakarian, *The Happiest People* (1975), 162–165; and Donald Gee, "World Pentecostal Conference Held in Jerusalem," *Voice*, September 1961, 34 for an account of this healing miracle.

128. Demos Shakarian, *The Happiest People* (1975), 145; and especially the Demos Shakarian-Synan interview, May 27, 1992.

129. Geraldine Scalf-Tallman interview, January 9, 2008.

130. See Demos Shakarian, *The Vision*, DVD (Costa Mesa, CA: FGBMFI, n.d.). Mordecai Ham had also been a spiritual mentor to Billy Graham, and he came to Demos Shakarian just as the fellowship was beginning to grow and gave Demos Shakarian a prophetic utterance regarding the future global impact of the organization that Shakarian had just founded.

131. Tommy Hicks, "Marvelous Start for the Sioux Falls Chapter," *Voice*, March 1953, 10–11.

132. Thomas Nickel, ed., "Tommy Hicks in Sweden," *Voice*, October 1955, 3–18; and Nickel, "Hicks in Norway," *Voice*, January 1956, 10–16.

133. Thomas R. Nickel, "International Chapters Busy on all Fronts," *Voice*, September 1953, 3–4.

134. See Thomas R. Nickel, ed., "God's Mighty Power Manifested at our First Annual Convention," *Voice*, November 1953, 10.

135. Harrell, *All Things are Possible* (1975), 58.

136. Ibid, 59.

137. Thomas R. Nickel, ed., "Annual Convention in Washington, D.C.," *Voice*, September 1955, 12.

138. Harrell, *All Things are Possible* (1975), 61.

139. Ibid, 61.

140. Ibid, 16.

141. Ibid, 16.

142. See Thomas R. Nickel, ed., "God's Mighty Power Manifested at our First Annual Convention," *Voice*, November 1953, 9–10.

143. Demos Shakarian, "Our Movement is Spreading," *Voice*, July–August 1953, 3, 5.

144. See Demos Shakarian, *The Happiest People* (1975), 118–119.

145. For an example see the doctrinal statement in *Voice*, February 1953, 16.

146. Ibid.

147. See Lee Braxton, *Voice*, May–June 1953, 8–10.

148. See George Gardner, *Voice*, March 1953, 13. Also Thomas R. Nickel, *Voice*, February–March 1955, 14, 18.

149. See Thomas R. Nickel, *Voice*, February 1953, 8–11.

150. FGBMFI Articles of Incorporation, 1977, as cited in Vinson Synan's *Under His Banner* (1992), 54, and 57.

151. Bradfield, *Neo-Pentecostalism* (1979), 25.

152. Demos Shakarian, *The Happiest People* (1975), 83, 118.

153. Articles of Incorporation, 1977, as cited in Synan's *Under His Banner* (1992), 54.

154. James Priddy, interview by Matthew Tallman, Ocean City, MD, May 17, 2005.

155. See Demos Shakarian, *The Happiest People* (1975), 81.

156. Ibid, 54 and 76.

157. See Margaret Poloma's *The Assemblies of God at the Crossroads: Charisma and Institutional Dilemmas* (Knoxville, TN: University of Tennessee Press, 1989) for a more thorough discussion of this development in the Assemblies of God. See Jeffrey Burton Russell's *A History of Medieval Christianity: Prophecy and Order* (Arlington Heights, IL: AHM Publishing Company, 1968) for a more thorough discussion of this topic in earlier church history.

158. For an excellent review of this tension between prophecy and order, see Jeffrey Russell's *Prophecy and Order* (1968). Stanley Burgess' trilogy on *The Holy Spirit* also offers an excellent historical account of this tension and the continuity of the charismatic Christian tradition.

159. See *Voice*, November 1962, 19 for the best explanation of Shakarian's policy toward churches.

160. See "Full Gospel Business Men of America," *Healing Waters* (January 1952), 12.

161. See Demos Shakarian, *The Happiest People* (1975), 123.

162. Val Fotherby, *The Awakening Giant*, (London: Marshall Pickering, 2000), 11, 21; and Jimmy Rogers-Tallman interview, Washington, D.C., February 22, 2008.

163. See *Voice*, January 1955, 14–19.

164. See *Voice*, March 1956, 3–9.

165. See *Voice*, June 1956, 3, 9–10.

166. See *Voice*, May 1956, 3.

167. Demos Shakarian, *The Happiest People* (1975), 124.

168. David DuPlessis, *A Man Called Mr. Pentecost* (1977), 175.

169. Ibid, 176–180.

170. Demos Shakarian, *The Happiest People* (1975), 133–134.

171. Even though David DuPlessis does not mention Demos Shakarian in his autobiography, he quickly became interested in the FGBMFI and was frequently found at early FGBMFI meetings and conventions. At his very first Full Gospel Business Men's meeting, DuPlessis encouraged Shakarian, explaining to him that "he was really on to something... Each man a missionary to the people he works with every day!" (Demos Shakarian *The Happiest People* (1975), 122).

172. Demos Shakarian, *The Happiest People* (1975), 121.

173. Thomas Nickel, "Catholic Helps Protestants," *Voice*, January 1954, 3–5.

174. Thomas Nickel, "From the Editor's Mail," *Voice*, May 1955, 18.

175. Thomas Nickel, "Our Banner is Love," *Voice*, July 1956, 12; and *Voice*, May 1955, 36.

176. Demos Shakarian, *Life Lifters* (1984), 3:17. Shakarian does not identify this individual in the article, but in his interview with Vinson Synan, February 2, 1988, 5, Shakarian identified a later individual, Dr. Howard Hendricks, who, in 1965, tried to persuade Shakarian to preach against Roman Catholics just before the Catholic Charismatic renewal began.

177. "God's Mighty Power in our First Annual Convention," *Voice*, November 1953, 8–14.

178. Demos Shakarian, *Life Lifters* (1984), 3:12.

179. Demos Shakarian, "Our God is Moving, *Voice*, July–August 1954, 3–9.

180. Vinson Synan, *The Century of the Holy Spirit* (2001), 135–136.

181. Synan, *Under His Banner* (1992), 72. Also see *Voice*, October 1955, 3–18; and January 1956, 10–16.

182. Synan, *Under His Banner* (1992), 73. Also see Irvine J. Harrison, "Latin America Needs the Peace of God," *Voice*, December 1959, 16–19.

183. Geraldine Shakarian Scalf-Tallman interview, January 8, 2008.

184. See Demos Shakarian, "Official Dedication of Full Gospel Men's Voice," *Voice*, March 1953, 3.

185. Gene Scalf-Tallman interview, January 9, 2008; and Jerry Jensen-Synan interview, February 15, 1992, 7. Jensen recalled that some business men bought as many as 1,000 copies at a time for distribution in their communities.

186. Geraldine Shakarian Scalf-Tallman interview, January 9, 2008.

187. Demos Shakarian, *Life Lifters* (1984), 3:47.

188. Gene Scalf-Tallman interview, January 8, 2008 and Demos Shakarian, *Life Lifters* (1984), 3:3, 32.

189. Asamoah-Gyadu, "'Missionaries without Robes,'" *Pneuma* (Fall 1987): 183.

190. See "Earl Prickett Remembered," *Voice*, October 1990, 9; and James Priddy, interview by Matt Tallman, Ocean City, Maryland, May 17, 2005.

191. Brad Tuttle-Tallman interview, January 9, 2008.

192. Dian Scott, phone interview by Matthew Tallman, January 14, 2008; also Gene Scalf-Tallman interview, January 9, 2008.

193. Nkusi Sebujisho Josiah, interview by Matthew Tallman, Kigali, Rwanda, July 26, 2005.

194. Demos Shakarian, *The Happiest People* (1975), 150; and Demos Shakarian, *Life Lifters* (1984), 1:20–21.

195. Demos Shakarian, *The Happiest People* (1975), 150.

196. Asamoah-Gyadu, "'Missionaries without Robes,'" (1987): 170.

197. Walter J. Hollenweger, "Charismatic Renewal in the Third World: Implications for Missions," *Occasional Bulletin of Missionary Research* 4 (April 1980): 69. While the

term "third world" may be a more familiar reference to the third of the world that is under-developed and impoverished, Hollenweger rightly recognized that the Charismatic movement has also seen rapid growth in the third of the world's population that would be considered "developing nations" with rapidly growing economies. Thus he recognized that the greatest growth in the Charismatic movement has not been relegated or isolated to one specific socio-economic class or distinction.

198. Thomas, Nickel, "A Concise History of Our Fellowship," *Voice*, November 1955, 4.

199. Ibid.

200. Thomas Nickel, "First FGBMFI Chapter Still Extra Active," *Voice*, August 1955, 14.

201. Demos Shakarian, *Life Lifters* (1984), 2:43.

202. Demos Shakarian, "Together," February 1981, 17; and Karen Linamen Scalf-Tallman interview, January 9, 2008.

203. John W. Caughey, *California: A Remarkable State's Life History* (Englewood Cliffs, NJ: Prentice Hall, 1970), 556.

204. Andrew Rolle and John Gaines, *The Golden State: A History of California* (Northbrook, IL: AHM Publishing, 1965), 221.

205. Demos Shakarian, *Life Lifters* (1984), 2:23–24; and Gene Scalf, interview with Matthew Tallman, Colorado City, CO, January 8, 2008.

206. "Pentecostal Laymen to Lead Revival Today," *Los Angeles Times*, September 22, 1956, B10.

207. "The Golden Jubilee will Continue in our Hearts," *Voice*, October 1956, 3–5.

208. "Pentecostal Laymen to Lead Revival," *Los Angeles Times*, September 22, 1956, B10.

209. Glenda Parton, "Fourth Annual Convention a Great Success," *Voice*, July 1956, 12–14.

210. Harold Herman, "German Lutherans Receive Holy Ghost Baptism," *Voice*, August 1957, 10.

211. David DuPlessis, "All Barriers Submerged," *Voice*, September 1957, 9.

212. Demos Shakarian, "Calling Business Men Back to God," *Voice*, August 1957, 23.

213. Theodore Hegre, "Lutheran Minister Tells of Pentecostal Experience," *Voice*, October 1957, 22–24.

214. Demos Shakarian, "President's Report of Nation-wide Tour," June 1958, 9.

215. Ibid.

216. Demos Shakarian, *Life Lifters* (1984), 1:18–19.

217. *Voice*, September 1958, 6; and "Full Gospel Group Ready for Convention," *Los Angeles Times*, June 27, 1959, B2.

218. See Demos Shakarian, *Life Lifters* (1984), 3:12 for further discussion of how Shakarian interpreted Price's prophecy.

219. Demos Shakarian, "A Decade of Divine Destiny," *Voice*, October 1963, 6–7.

220. Darlene Janoian-Tallman interview, January 13, 2008. Darlene's brother Paul Janoian also contributed information regarding Shakarian's teen-age years.

221. See Demos Shakarian, *The Happiest People* (1975), 53, 77, 80–82, and 87–89.

Chapter Nine

In the Wake of Demos Shakarian's Vision—
The Growth of the FGBMFI (1959–1974)

In the late 1950s, Shakarian refined and renewed his commitment to the dairy industry and the Reliance Diary his family owned by using the latest techniques of artificial insemination and even creating a patented milking process. At the same time, his speaking engagements, ministry opportunities, and leadership responsibilities for the FGBMFI placed greater demands on his time and his family. Indeed, the FGBMFI was about to enter a new phase of influence in the realm of global Christianity, and Shakarian was about to see the vision he experienced in December 1952 become a reality. However, the causes for this exponential growth and influence cannot be completely credited to Shakarian's vision, his charisma, or even the sacrificial nature and evangelistic fervor of the laymen in his organization. Shakarian mostly offered providential explanations for the spectacular growth of the FGBMFI in the 1960s and 1970s, but he also occasionally offered economic and sociologic reasons. These and other factors offer possible explanations for Shakarian's growing influence as the founder of the FGBMFI, but sometimes just being in the right place at the right time makes the difference.

The Expansion of Reliance Dairies

In 1959, the Reliance Dairy operation continued to rebuild and expand its operations, its products, and its output. With a new 500 acre calving ranch in Modesto, California, a new 800 acre dairy operation in Delano, California, and 400 productive dairy cows sired by Pabst Leader Crusader, Shakarian was able to expand his dairy business through a variety of products and venues.[1] Construction on a third drive-in dairy was started in East Los Angeles, on Atlantic Boulevard, in October 1959.[2] By 1965, the Shakarian's operated fourteen different drive-in dairies throughout the greater Los Angeles area.[3]

The expansion of Reliance Dairies was also enabled by the increased output of its dairy cows. When Isaac Shakarian began his dairy in 1912 with three Holstein cows, each cow produced an average of two and a half gallons of milk per day. By 1943, through breeding and agricultural science, Isaac and Demos Shakarian had increased the average daily milk production over one hundred percent to six or seven gallons from each cow. With the acquisition of his prize bull, Pabst Leader Crusader, in 1954, Shakarian planned to replenish his dairy herd of one thousand cows and he estimated his milk production would increase eight percent.[4] By 1960, Crusader's offspring helped add 900 cows to the Shakarian herd.[5] In 1964, the Shakarian herd had once again increased to 3,000 cattle, and some of Crusader's offspring were already producing eleven and a half gallons of milk daily.[6] The efficiency of the Shakarian dairy operation was also improved by Demos Shakarian's creative mind as he invented a procedure to improve the stimulation and cleaning process of a cow's udder. Shakarian filed his invention with the United States Patent Office on October 20, 1964.[7]

Through artificial insemination, Pabst Crusader's offspring continued to multiply, and Shakarian saw a need to expand the calving ranch in Modesto. Demos Shakarian turned to prayer and invited his son Stephen to pray with him that they might be able to expand the size of the property in Modesto. Soon 300 acres adjoining the south end of the property was sold to the Shakarians, and before the end of 1964, Demos Shakarian had two 800 acre ranches in northern California.[8] In addition, he introduced his son, Stephen, to his own appreciation for prayer and his holistic spiritual approach to business.

As Shakarian purchased more property in northern California for his dairy business, he continued to reap the benefits of the commercial property he owned in southern Los Angeles County and the profits he garnered from the sale of former Reliance Dairy property he sold in the Downey and Norwalk, California, area. Shakarian also found time to volunteer as a philanthropist when he was re-elected for another three-year term as a director on the board of Goodwill Industries in Orange County, California, in 1962.[9] He had already served on the board of Goodwill Industries for over a decade.[10]

Demos Shakarian's work load at Reliance Dairies was lightened by the promotion of his son Richard to general manager of the Dairy and Shakarian's sister Florence, who became the vice president.[11] In addition, Demos Shakarian's son-in-law, Gene Scalf, oversaw the property management portfolio of the Shakarian enterprise, and Shakarian and Scalf would meet weekly at Foxy's Restaurant in Downey, California, to discuss future purchases and the liquidation of current property investments.[12] Shakarian also utilized the services of a realtor named Frank Foglio (1921–1989) who began helping him with the purchase and sale of various properties in California in 1961.[13] Richard Shakarian continued to follow Isaac and Demos Shakarian's example with his ministry obligations as youth director of the FGBMFI and his endeavors in evangelistic youth rallies.[14] Richard also found time to embark on a few extra-curricular activities of his own in 1962 when he joined a team in Turkey who climbed Mount Ararat in search of Noah's ark.[15]

Demos Shakarian's dairy duties still commanded much more of his time than did his leisure time or his civic duties to the greater Los Angeles area. With the increased dairy output, the Shakarians added a creamery and an ice cream plant to their expanding dairy business.[16] The added dairy variety was utilized both in the Shakarian's exclusive contract with Ralph's Grocery Stores, and also with the increasing consumer demand from their drive-in dairies. The Reliance Drive-in Dairies offered eggs, cottage cheese, buttermilk, and fruit punch when they began advertising their first drive-in location in Downey, California, in 1953, but in 1965, they also began to regularly feature a half gallon of banana fudge ice cream for forty-nine cents, a half gallon of ice milk for twenty-five cents, extra large eggs for thirty-nine cents a dozen, and orange juice for forty-nine cents a half gallon.[17]

With increased dairy output from their herd and increased revenue and profits in the direct sale of their dairy products at the Reliance Drive-in Dairies, the Shakarians decided to multiply the potential benefits of their drive-in business by selling the concept as a franchise to potential business owners. In 1968, Richard and Demos Shakarian ran a series of eight announcements in the *Los Angeles Times'* franchise opportunity section of the classified advertisements.[18] After the success of the McDonald's franchise operation, beginning with the opening of the third McDonald's restaurant in Shakarian's home town of Downey, California, in 1953, the Shakarians saw a formula for future financial growth.[19] However, Shakarian was not the only business man who saw opportunities for financial success in selling a franchise business. Other businesses such as International House of Pancakes, Orange Julius, 7-Eleven Stores, Denny's Restaurants, and Western Auto Supply vied for the attention of regional Southern Californian and national business owners. The success of these other businesses ultimately garnered the attention and financial backing of a large consortium of future franchise owners to the detriment of any potential franchise opportunities the Shakarians had to offer in 1968.[20] Nevertheless, in the 1960s, Demos Shakarian began to attract the regional, national, and international attention of business men and business owners through a non-profit, spiritually oriented franchise called the FGBMFI.

The Emergence of the Charismatic Movement

In 1959, the FGBMFI convened for their seventh annual international convention at the Ambassador Hotel in Los Angeles, California from June 27 through July 3.[21] Demos Shakarian invited two of his most popular Pentecostal speakers from previous conventions, Oral Roberts and William Branham. [22] Shakarian also invited Presbyterian professor of theology, James Brown, as a featured speaker for a second consecutive year. In addition, Gerald Derstine (1928–), an evangelist with the Mennonite Church of America, spoke of how God was moving with a pneumatic emphasis among Mennonites, and John Osteen (1921–1999), pastor of a large Baptist congregation in Houston, Texas, shared his personal testimony of Spirit baptism.[23] Every speaker agreed that God's Spirit was moving across ecclesiastical boundaries. Added to this pneumatic excitement at the convention was an eschatological energy fueled by the discussion of an article published in *Voice* six months earlier titled "Bible Prophecies Coming True in Israel."[24]

James Brown published an article in *Voice* two months after the convention titled "Every Christian Must Become a Pentecostal."[25] While the title of the article could have been construed ecclesiastically, Brown wrote experientially of his own encounter with the Holy Spirit. Brown was able to share more of his pneumatic experience when he was invited by Demos Shakarian to come and speak at the Ambassador Hotel on Wilshire Boulevard in Los Angeles on September 20, 1959.[26] On Thursday, September 17, 1959, the Ambassador Hotel suddenly cancelled Shakarian's reservation without an explanation. Shakarian was able to find a smaller venue for the rally at Clifton's Cafeteria, but both Shakarian and the *Los Angeles Times* suggested that the cancellation had something to do with Nikita Khrushchev's (1894–1971) departure from the Ambassador Hotel one hour after the rally began.[27] The Ambassador Hotel denied that the cancellation had anything to do with Khrushchev's visit, the State Department, or security concerns, but a large Christian rally, featuring guest speaker Carl McIntire (1906–2002), gathered in the Rose Bowl in Pasadena, California on Friday evening, September 18 to protest Khrushchev's visit. They believed Khrushchev was selling "communist peaceful co-existence."[28] While this large rally at the Rose Bowl might have motivated the State Department to cancel the FGBMFI breakfast, Demos Shakarian interpreted the cancellation and Khrushchev's visit to mean "that there are forces in America today that, as Christians, we should be on the lookout for."[29]

While Shakarian construed this imposition politically and perhaps eschatologically, on April 3, 1960, Shakarian focused his attention on pneumatic events as Father Dennis Bennett (1917–1991), rector of St. Mark's Church in Van Nuys, California, publically announced his experience of Spirit baptism to his congregation.[30] *Time* and *Newsweek* featured articles about Dennis Bennett's charismatic experience bringing national media attention to glossolalic experiences which crossed over from traditional Pentecostal confines to mainline Protestant churches in North America.[31] The article in *Time* stated, "Now glossolalia seems to be on its way back in U.S. churches — not only in the uninhibited Pentecostal sects but even among Episcopalians, who have been called 'God's frozen people.'"[32]

After Dennis Bennett was ousted from his position as rector of St. Mark's Episcopal Church as a result of his public announcement, he was given an opportunity to pastor a small Episcopalian congregation in Seattle. With the media coverage Bennett received in August 1960, a chapter of the FGBMFI in Spokane, Washington invited Bennett to come and share his pneumatic experience. Two hundred and twenty-five attendees listened to Bennett's testimony of Spirit baptism.[33] The October cover of *Voice* featured an article by Dennis Bennett in which he proclaimed, "No one needs to leave the Episcopal Church in order to have the fullness of the Spirit."[34]

Other notable early leaders in the Charismatic movement wrote articles in *Voice* and spoke regularly at FGBMFI chapter meetings and regional conventions soon after Bennett's media attention began. Jean Stone (1924–), a publisher and a member of Dennis Bennett's former congregation, was an active participant at Los Angeles area FGBMFI chapter meetings and a regular contributor to *Voice* magazine.[35] Harald Bredesen (1918–), a Dutch Reformed minister who was an early leader in the Charismatic movement, became a regular speaker at FGBMFI chapter meetings and conventions.[36] Pat Robertson (1930–) first became involved with the FGBMFI at a regional conference in Washington, D.C. in 1959. Robertson became a featured speaker at several conventions in the early 1960s, and he was featured on the cover of *Voice* in April 1962.[37] In 1963, Robertson started the Norfolk, Virginia, chapter of the FGBMFI.[38] Oral Roberts remained a regular fixture at regional conventions and the annual international conventions in the 1960s, and even Billy Graham shared the stage with Oral Roberts and Demos Shakarian at the tenth annual international convention in 1962, where he stated to the listening audience, "I need your prayers that God will give me an infilling of his Holy Spirit."[39]

An experience Demos Shakarian had on May 20, 1961 helped broaden the leadership and influence of the Charismatic movement beyond professional clergy. Shakarian attended the World Pentecostal Conference held in Jerusalem in May 1961 and on the second night of the convention, James Brown was the guest speaker. Miriam Rapaport (d.b.a. 1910–d.d.a. 1980), a Christian worker from Jerusalem, brought a Jewish man to the conference who had converted to Christianity in 1956.[40] As James Brown and Shakarian talked in the lobby of the conference building, Miriam Rapaport called out Demos Shakarian's name in the crowded vestibule and asked if Shakarian could pray for the crippled man. According to Shakarian, the man walked slowly with the assistance of a cane and his torso was misshapen and bent parallel to the floor. Shakarian prayed for the crippled man and the man slowly began to straighten his posture as Shakarian heard an occasional popping sound come from the man's body.[41] As the man declared that he was healed, a significant commotion occurred in the lobby of the Pentecostal conference meeting, and the man's healing experience was repeated by the guest speaker at the conference, James Brown, and in two separate articles in *Voice*.[42]

Shakarian had prayed for various people in the past who proclaimed a healing experience including his sister Florence.[43] More recently, in 1956, he had prayed for Myrtle Danner (d.b.a. 1910–d.d.a. 1980) at a FGBMFI chapter meeting, who had a healing experience.[44] However, at the World Pentecostal Conference in Jerusalem, Shakarian was surrounded by professional pastors, evangelists, and ministerial leaders, and Shakarian questioned why God would ask him to pray for this man rather than any of these "high-powered Pentecostal leaders from all over the world?"[45] Shakarian's early reliance upon Pentecostal healing evangelists to spread his organization now seemed superfluous. On later reflection, Shakarian believed the emphasis on healing in the FGBMFI did not become a priority until after this experience at the World Pentecostal Conference in Jerusalem.[46] After returning from Jerusalem, Shakarian was convinced, more than ever, that laymen were going to play a significant role in this emerging Charismatic movement.[47]

However, as this new Charismatic renewal spread beyond its Pentecostal origins, some ecumenists and scholars within the Pentecostal movement were concerned that the expressions of charisma outside of Pentecostalism threatened the Pentecostal hierarchy. Donald Gee, as early as 1960, warned fellow Pentecostals not to misjudge or misconstrue charismatic expressions outside of Pentecostal denominations.[48] Walter Hollenweger was blunt in his assessment of the Assemblies of God when they removed David DuPlessis' ministerial credentials in 1962 because of DuPlessis' ecumenical cooperation with the WCC. "It seems that the Assemblies of God were chagrined because the Holy Spirit had used this false channel and not extended the baptism of the Spirit to the traditional churches by means of the official committees of the Assemblies of God."[49] Demos Shakarian was also concerned about the response of traditional Pentecostal denominations towards the Charismatic renewal other denominations were experiencing in the 1960s. Shakarian stated that any opposition he faced came "mainly from those we believe should support us. None from liberal Christians."[50] Perhaps this perception harkened back to the earlier objections of his own Armenian Pentecostal elders when he began his tent crusades in 1940.[51]

In contrast to the sectarianism of some Pentecostal groups, Shakarian and the FGBMFI provided a catalyst and a place for charismatic renewal to touch all of Christendom by regularly and approvingly publicizing what was happening in different denominations. In addition to offering numerous testimonies of individuals touched among different denominations and backgrounds, a series of booklets was published beginning in 1963 highlighting the Charismatic renewal that was happening in different denominations. The first booklet came out in 1963 entitled *Methodists and the Baptism in the Holy Spirit*. Further volumes offered testimonies of those touched by charismatic renewal in Episcopalian, Baptist, Catholic, Presbyterian, Nazarene, Disciples of Christ, Church of Christ, and Lutheran denominations.[52] The FGBMFI also offered one of the first theological and pastoral symposiums on the renewal which took place in November, 1963 in New York City.[53] In 1963, the term "Charismatic revival" was used for the first time to describe this movement in a *Voice* special report.[54]

This same ecclesiological diversity was reflected both in the leadership and the overall membership of the FGBMFI. Steve Durasoff (1922–) estimated in 1972 that as much as eighty percent of the Full Gospel members in many U.S. cities were from a non-Pentecostal background.[55] Cecil Bradfield's study found an even higher percentage in his 1979 survey when he discovered that only three percent of the chapter in Harrisonburg, Virginia was from a Pentecostal background, while the largest constituencies were from Lutheran, Presbyterian, Methodist, or Mennonite backgrounds.[56] The FGBMFI continued to cross ecclesiastical boundaries throughout the 1960s, but it ultimately saw its greatest growth internationally as the final part of Demos Shakarian's vision came to fruition.

The International Growth of the FGBMFI

Before 1959, international FGBMFI chapters were almost exclusively started in the aftermath of evangelistic crusades led by various healing evangelists the organization sponsored in the 1950s. Evangelistic crusades in Europe, South America, and Asia led by Tommy Hicks, William Branham, A.C. Valdez, Harold Herman, and T.L. Osborn helped initiate chapters and create an increasing interest of the organization's appeal internationally.[57] Their evangelistic efforts in Europe allowed for the growth of a German publication of *Voice* in October 1960, and the first European FGBMFI convention in Zurich, Switzerland, represented eighteen nations in 1961.[58] Their efforts in the Caribbean and Latin America led to the introduction of FGBMFI chapters in Puerto Rico, Monterrey, Mexico, and the publication of *La Voz*, a Spanish language edition of *Voice* magazine.[59]

In 1959, Demos Shakarian and the business leaders in the FGBMFI began initiating their own international outreaches. Miner Arganbright and Thomas Nickel toured Europe and Asia and established six new FGBMFI chapters.[60] Dr. Irvine Harrison (1909–1972) expanded their international mission by including larger numbers of business men as "Squadrons of Commandos" to evangelize parts of Mexico in 1959.[61] Demos Shakarian took a small team of business men on an evangelistic mission to Cuba in 1959, where they successfully established a FGBMFI chapter in Havana.[62] While staying at the Cuba Libre Hotel, Shakarian said he met with Fidel Castro (1926–) and told Castro he did not desire to become involved in politics. In addition, Shakarian told Castro that he "had learned from many that he had brought a great liberation to Cuba."[63] During the conversation, Castro responded by saying, "I like what you men are doing."[64] Castro confided to Shakarian during an impromptu meeting of over thirty minutes at the hotel restaurant that he listened to television broadcasts of Oral Roberts and Billy Graham.[65] On later reflection, Shakarian observed, "Here was a great man with a deep hunger in his heart for God."[66]

Shakarian met another head of state in 1960 as the FGBMFI began utilizing another means of evangelism they called airlifts. The first airlift occurred in February 1960 when twenty-five FGBMFI members boarded a plane to Haiti under the invitation of President François Duvalier (1907–1971).[67] The airlift was actually part of a three island tour with regional FGBMFI conventions planned in Kingston, Jamaica; San Juan, Puerto Rico; and Port au Prince, Haiti.[68] The visit to Haiti was preceded by a $2,000 donation in April 1959, from the FGBMFI, in cooperation with CARE, for food distribution to drought stricken areas of Haiti.[69]

The evangelistic crusade in Haiti started well, but on the third night, 300 voodoo priests disrupted the meetings and the Haitian military threatened to intervene with force if necessary.[70] Shakarian pleaded with the commanding general attending the meetings to avoid violence, but then a man and woman ran towards the platform claiming their young son had miraculously recovered his sight. Senator Arthur Bonhomne, a Haitian member of the FGBMFI, lifted the child up to the podium, claiming he knew the young boy's family. He added that the boy was born blind, and the apparent miracle drew the attention of the audience away from the voodoo priests. Five thousand people including many voodoo priests came to the front of the stadium for prayer.[71] By the end of their time in Haiti, Demos Shakarian and the business men who accompanied him estimated they witnessed 100,000 Christian conversions and distributed over 80,000 pounds of food in cooperation with CARE.[72]

The next airlift did not take place until 1965. Hundreds of FGBMFI from the United States, enough to fill two large commercial jets, and thousands of European members of FGBMFI and curious onlookers convened in London as Oral Roberts spoke at the Royal Albert Hall.[73] Hundreds of FGBMFI members talked to business men and young people on the streets of London, inviting them to the evening meetings that ran from November 24 through November 27, 1965. [74] Beatniks received haircuts at the hands of Full Gospel Business Men after their conversion. At this point, "the airlift became a hair lift," and *Voice* magazine editor, Jerry Jensen, reported thousands of new Christian converts.[75] Val Fotherby suggested that as large scale as that event was, it was not until almost a decade later, when some men in England eventually "caught the vision" of Demos Shakarian, that FGBMFI chapters began to multiply in the United Kingdom.[76]

With the short term success of the London airlift, in 1966 additional airlifts went into Asia and Europe and in 1967 into South America and South Vietnam.[77] Val Fotherby suggested that members of the young FGBMFI Seattle chapter became the primary coordinators for these airlifts throughout their history in the organization.[78] Soon other airlifts followed the London crusade, as Simon Vikse (1917–1979), Henry Carlson (d.b.a. 1925–), and Enoch Christofferson each led numerous airlifts to Europe and Asia.[79] Christofferson in particular, organized airlifts in Asia for over a decade, sacrificially paying for most of the costs himself.[80] These airlifts were popular and effective for the next several decades in the organization.

Demos Shakarian also travelled with Oral Roberts to the Soviet Union in September 1966. Under the auspices of the Oral Roberts Evangelistic Association, Roberts and Shakarian seemed limited by the religious restrictions of the Soviet system. The successful tent crusades Roberts and Shakarian were familiar with in the United States were not allowed in Russia. Nevertheless, Shakarian had success meeting with agricultural officials because of his experience in the dairy industry.[81] Shakarian also had the opportunity to tell the ancestral story of his grandfather's introduction to charismatic Christianity through Russian pneumatics on Moscow radio and in front of a large congregation at a church in Moscow.[82]

By July 1964, there were 335 chapters in 25 different nations.[83] In 1966, *Voice* magazine circulation increased to 300,000, and continued to be a vehicle of growth for the FGBMFI.[84] As international and domestic growth continued, Shakarian and his board deemed it necessary to expand their organizational structure to include nine foreign directors of the FGBMFI.[85]

As the FGBMFI began to expand internationally, the ingenuity and sacrifice of its members continued to create new venues to spread their message domestically. In 1961, the first television program produced by the organization was sponsored by the Camden, New Jersey chapter of the FGBMFI.[86] In May 1965, Southern California chapters of the FGBMFI joined together to sponsor additional television programming.[87] More significant television production followed after the initial success of these two programs beginning in February 1970.[88]

Beyond evangelistic venues or organizational programs, the irrepressible personality of Demos Shakarian broadened the outreach of the FGBMFI far beyond any sociological, political, or ecclesiastical barriers. In early July 1961, the international FGBMFI world convention was held in Miami, Florida at the same time the Teamsters were having a national union conference. Shakarian invited Jimmy Hoffa (1913–d.d.a. 1975), the president of the Teamster's Union, to address the FGBMFI convention attendees.[89] Shakarian met with other Teamster leaders during the conference, and three leaders of the union became Christian converts through his evangelistic efforts.[90] Other business men at the FGBMFI convention followed Shakarian's example and invited more Teamsters to their gospel meetings.[91]

Shakarian continued inviting political luminaries to offer impromptu addresses at various regional and national FGBMFI conventions in the 1960s. A young congressman from Illinois, Donald Rumsfeld (1932–), attended the Eastern Regional FGBMFI Convention in Washington, D.C. in February 1963 and he briefly addressed the audience.[92] In early July 1965, Shakarian invited Mayor Richard Daley (1902–1976) to address the business men attending the international FGBMFI convention in Chicago, Illinois.[93] James Watt (1932–) also became involved in the FGBMFI in the early 1960s, long before he became United States Secretary of the Interior.[94]

In July 1964, the FGBMFI received more media coverage when a *New York Times* journalist ran a feature article on their organization.[95] *Voice* magazine also created more international attention when it was published in French, Japanese, Spanish, and Swedish, in addition to German and English.[96] Plans were also made to publish *Voice* in Italian, Dutch, Mandarin, and Finnish before the end of 1966.[97] In addition, the FGBMFI began to publish a quarterly youth magazine called *Vision* and a quarterly magazine for pastors and scholars named *View*.[98] In early July 1962, at the Seattle, Washington FGBMFI convention, Demos Shakarian fired his original editor, Thomas Nickel.[99] In spite of this setback, the FGBMFI publications office quickly recovered and expanded due to the efforts of the new editor, Jerry Jensen, who was hired in late 1962.[100] Demos Shakarian would not recover as quickly from personal challenges and losses he faced during the early 1960s.

The Death of Isaac Shakarian

With the pace and pressures of running a large dairy corporation and a growing ministry, it was surprising Shakarian remained as healthy and vigorous as he did during the first decade of existence for the FGBMFI. Nevertheless, in late February 1962, Shakarian developed a heart condition from a viral infection he contracted which required hospitalization.[101] He remained ill until May, 1962.[102] While the illness forced Shakarian to miss some activities with the FGBMFI and some oversight at Reliance Dairies, he was healthy enough to moderate the tenth annual FGBMFI world convention in Seattle, Washington while sharing the stage with Billy Graham and Oral Roberts.[103]

Demos Shakarian and the Reliance Dairies were not able to recover as quickly from the next two losses that occurred in the Shakarian household. Isaac Shakarian died in his home at 8431 Lexington Road in Downey on Friday night, November 6, 1964 at the age of seventy-two.[104] A funeral service for Isaac was held at Downey Presbyterian Church at 1:30 PM on Tuesday, November 10, 1964, and Isaac was interred next to his first wife, Zaroohi Shakarian, at Rose Hills Memorial Park in Whittier, California.[105] Traffic was congested for miles by people trying to reach Downey Presbyterian Church, and the building was filled to capacity as the mourners listened to Oral Roberts preside over the memorial service.[106] Oral Roberts also named a recently constructed dormitory at his new university in Isaac Shakarian's honor.[107] In addition, most of the January 1965 edition of *Voice* was devoted to several tributes written about his life.[108]

Only ten months later, Demos Shakarian's sister Florence died on Friday, September 10, 1965, after a prolonged illness caused by a rare form of cancer.[109] Services were held at Downey Presbyterian Church at 1:30 PM on Monday, September 13, 1965.[110] In less than one year, Reliance Dairies had lost both its founder and its vice president. Demos Shakarian had lost his sister and his father. In addition, beginning in early 1966, Shakarian accrued estate and inheritance tax problems related to the death of his father and his sister.[111] Significant events in the Charismatic movement related to the FGBMFI would give him some solace in 1967.

The Birth of Catholic Charismatic Renewal

On February 18, 1967, members of the Roman Catholic Church at Duquesne University in Pittsburgh, Pennsylvania began experiencing the pneumatic fervor of Charismatic renewal.[112] They quickly shared their new spiritual experience with students at the University of Notre Dame. These students at Notre Dame sought someone who might know about the baptism in the Holy Spirit. They came upon Ray Bullard, president of the South Bend, Indiana FGBMFI chapter and a janitor at a local junior high school, who introduced them to Spirit baptism.[113] From Bullard's basement emerged most of the early leadership in the Catholic Charismatic renewal.[114] In addition, from that basement they decided to stay within the Catholic Church and share their pneumatic experience within their denomination.[115]

Voice magazine first mentioned the early history of Charismatic renewal in the Roman Catholic Church in July 1967, just a few months after the movement began.[116] In October 1967, Jerry Jensen devoted an entire issue of *Voice* to the Catholic Charismatic revival with articles by Kevin Ranaghan (1940–) and Bert Ghezzi (d.b.a. 1945–).[117] An early leader in the Catholic Charismatic renewal, Kevin Ranaghan claimed that "the greatest Protestant Pentecostal contribution to the charismatic renewal in the Catholic Church has come through the agency of the Full Gospel Business Men's Fellowship International."[118]

Shortly before the Catholic Charismatic movement began, Shakarian's ecumenical standards were challenged again by a prominent Baptist teacher who visited the FGBMFI offices on Figueroa Street in downtown Los Angeles probably in November 1965.[119] For nearly an hour, Dr. Howard Henricks (1924–) sat in Shakarian's office insisting that Shakarian should use his influence with the FGBMFI as a platform to speak against the Roman Catholic Church which Hendricks told Shakarian was "the great whore of Babylon."[120] Shakarian acknowledged Hendricks' intelligence and his experience as a minister, but Shakarian insisted that Hendricks was wrong. Instead Shakarian said "I'm going to love the Catholics into the doctrine of the Holy Spirit."[121]

Demos Shakarian quickly embraced this new movement in the Roman Catholic Church, and a FGMBFI world convention was organized to be held in Rome, Italy, from May 16–23, 1969. Richard Shakarian was the chairman for the event, and the convention was extended to include a trip to Jerusalem, Athens, and London.[122] Shakarian also visited the Notre Dame campus in April 1970, to meet with the leaders of this new movement in the Catholic Church.[123] Peter Hocken (1932–) summarized Shakarian's contribution to the Catholic Charismatic movement in one sentence: "by welcoming Catholics as members and speakers, Shakarian's group provided an important platform for the spread of the renewal throughout the world."[124] With the participation of Cardinal Suenens (1904–1996) in this movement and the blessings of Pope Paul VI (1897–1978) and Pope John Paul II (1920–2005) for this movement, Roman Catholics quickly filled the ranks of the Charismatic movement.[125]

Demos Shakarian's Armenian ecumenism was reinforced by the experience of these Roman Catholic Charismatics. However, in the early part of the Charismatic renewal, Shakarian rejected ecclesiastical efforts of the formal ecumenical movement by suggesting they were in league with the Anti-Christ.[126] His ecumenism was based on the pneumatic experience of his own background which he shared with these new Charismatic participants and the collegial relationships he shared with a broad spectrum of ecclesiastical participants inside and outside of the FGBMFI. In addition, Charles Price and Oral Roberts, Demos Shakarian's spiritual mentors, shared his broad ecumenism. The ecumenism of Charles Price may have been influenced by his own eclectic religious experience beginning with his Methodist upbringing and ordination and climaxing with his introduction to Pentecostalism at an Aimee Semple McPherson meeting.[127] Oral Roberts' own ecumenism was likely shaped by the rejection of his own Pentecostal Holiness denomination early in his ministry, eventually causing him to join the Methodist Church.[128]

Occasionally, one of the more popular Pentecostal evangelists of that era, such as Jimmy Swaggart (1935–), would discredit or critique what was happening among Catholic Charismatics, but Demos Shakarian rarely associated with Swaggart and he never featured him in *Voice* magazine.[129] Ironically, many of the groups that initially rejected the Charismatic movement were from a Pentecostal background. Some of the rejection was a result of theological distinctions, but much of the dismissal also came from lifestyle differences between many Pentecostal groups who had strong convictions against alcohol, tobacco, dancing, theaters, and other assorted taboos. However, many mainstream Protestants and Catholics who entered into the Charismatic movement had none or very few restrictions about the aforementioned taboos. Instead of working with Jimmy Swaggart, Shakarian served on the boards of several Pentecostal and Charismatic organizations whose leaders shared his broader ecumenism. These boards included the Oral Roberts Evangelistic Association, Paul Crouch's Trinity Broadcasting Network, and Jim Bakker's PTL ministry board, but he refused to adhere to those who would detract from the Charismatic movement or criticize any groups that desired to participate in it.[130]

Full Gospel Business Women— the Beginning of Women's Aglow

In 1967 at the end of a FGBMFI meeting in Seattle, Washington, four women, Joyce Doerflein, Virginia Blankenship, Ruth Gothenquist, and Rose Collins, stayed behind and prayed for a full gospel fellowship for women. They held their first convention in the Meany Hotel in Seattle, Washington, with one hundred women in attendance. By 1972, Women's Aglow had grown to include sixty chapters, and by 1973, it expanded internationally to Canada and New Zealand.[131] By 1990, Women's Aglow had grown to 2,600 fellowships in 88 countries.[132] The international growth of the movement has continued unabated with over 4,600 groups meeting in 171 different nations by 2008.[133]

Unfortunately, one factor that has not been considered is how the exclusion of women from membership in the FGBMFI may have affected the growth of the organization. Women were never actually barred from participating in conventions or chapter meetings, and Demos Shakarian modeled this co-ed participation by bringing his wife Rose along with him on most of his Full Gospel speaking engagements.[134] Women regularly participated in the monthly dinner meetings and the occasional regional, national, and world conventions. They offered logistical assistance, shared testimonies, and even expressed charismata, or prayed for other men and women during the meetings.

In addition, the same year Women's Aglow started, Shakarian invited a popular female evangelist, Kathryn Kuhlman (1907–1976), to speak at the FGBMFI annual international convention in Miami, Florida, in early July.[135] In 1968, Kuhlman was inducted as an honorary member of the greater New York City FGBMFI chapter.[136] Shakarian maintained a friendship with Kuhlman, inviting her to speak at several international conventions in the 1970s.[137] After Kuhlman's death in 1976, Shakarian asked her assistant, Dian Scott, to become his personal secretary.[138]

Shakarian's decision to exclude women from membership in the FGBMFI may have been influenced in part by the tide of patriarchal conservatism that swept the United States at the end of WWII when millions of men came back to North America from overseas expecting to come back to the jobs that were filled by women while they were in Europe or Asia. However, Shakarian did not exclude women from participation in ministry and featured women such as Kathryn Kuhlman as featured speakers at FGBMFI conventions. In addition, Shakarian did not accept a model of female subjugation suggested by some conservative Christian groups and their interpretation of Ephesians 5:21–28 but instead spoke of the importance of partnership in marriage.[139]

Shakarian stated that his motivation for starting a men's organization was instigated by the lack of male participation he observed in local Southern Californian churches.[140] However, the fact that women were excluded from membership and leadership positions within the FGBMFI minimized the organization's effectiveness in reaching the overall business community during and after WWII as that community became increasingly more integrated. As a result, it excluded potentially half of the participants in the FGBMFI from the membership roles. While female exclusion may have initially held some appeal to the men in the organization, the FGBMFI could not continue to maintain the status quo.

Ironically, while the FGBMFI excluded females from membership and leadership roles, it was this exclusion of women who were actually involved in the FGBMFI that drove them to start Women's Aglow. However, as Aglow grew and expanded, it continued to work complementarily and cooperatively in an amiable relationship with FGBMFI in many parts of the world.[141] As such, it could be considered part of the legacy of Demos Shakarian, albeit an indirect one.

In 1975, at the twenty-second annual international FGBMFI convention in Anaheim, California, leaders of Women's Aglow attended the convention when Kathryn Kuhlman was a featured speaker. During the meetings, the Women's Aglow directors met with Demos Shakarian and asked if the FGBMFI was interested in providing oversight and leadership to Aglow in a ministry merger. Shakarian declined the offer and suggested that Women's Aglow had a unique ministry and calling that needed to remain separate and distinct from what Shakarian felt God was calling him to do.[142] Nevertheless, both Demos Shakarian and his son Richard eventually recognized the negligence towards women in their organization, at least partially. In response to this neglect, the FGBMFI eventually adopted a new program called "Ladies of the Fellowship" or "Women of the

Fellowship" in some of the countries which allowed women in the group increased participation and a certain amount of self-governance.[143]

The Symbiotic Relationship between the FGBMFI and the Charismatic Movement

With the rapid growth of the FGBMFI, there was very little reflection on how this dramatic expansion was taking place other than frequently offering the explanation that it was providential. Occasionally, some FGBMFI leaders listed socioeconomic reasons for their rapid growth, such as the disillusionment caused by Watergate and the recession of the 1970s. Demos Shakarian was quoted as stating that present conditions had prompted many business men to "realize they can't put trust in material things."[144] Steve Shakarian, son of founder Demos Shakarian, said the phenomenal growth of the FGBMFI in the 1970s might be related to the similar growth in the Charismatic renewal occurring at the same time.[145] Val Fotherby, a popular author who cited the growth of the FGBMFI from a European perspective, concurred with Steve Shakarian's analysis by stating that the growth of the FGBMFI in the United Kingdom did not occur until the Charismatic renewal began.[146] By 1970, David Barrett estimated there were over three million participants in the Charismatic movement, and both this movement and the organization which helped launch it, the FGBMFI, continued to fuel the growth of both groups.[147]

A similar symbiotic connection that spurred early growth was the relationship between the FGBMFI and the healing evangelists invited to their regional and annual conventions in the 1950s.[148] Demos Shakarian had a knack for being in the right place at the right time. His own personality profile suggested he was "intuitively oriented."[149] As discussed earlier, whether it was his keen sense of business or his eye for opportunity, he excelled at a variety of business ventures. Some of his Christian peers suggested that he had an incredible gift of discernment which allowed him to identify opportunities or people beyond the natural means or ability of ordinary people.[150] His involvement with the most significant healing evangelists of the twentieth century was impeccably timed as he helped support and organize some of the largest Christian crusades in United States history. His financial support and his business savvy were crucial to the success of these healing evangelists, and in turn, they enthusiastically endorsed and advertised his fledgling organization. As such, this became a symbiotic relationship that mutually benefited both groups, and as one group prospered, so did the other.

Shakarian saw the need for a Christian men's organization that was not available to most people from a Pentecostal persuasion in the 1950s.[151] What he could not foresee, except in his pneumatic vision, was how the organization he founded would play such a crucial part in the Charismatic movement. The FGBMFI preceded the Charismatic renewal by almost a decade, but it served as a bridge between traditional Pentecostalism and modern Charismatic and neo-Charismatic groups and movements throughout the world.[152] When David DuPlessis went out from the early FGBMFI meetings and conventions, his ecumenical dialogue laid the foundation for a movement far beyond any single ecclesiology. When Dennis Bennett gave his open admission of glossolalia in 1960, the publicity and reaction from his charismatic confession caused people to attend Full Gospel Business Men's meetings before they would ever consider going to a Pentecostal church. When Catholics began seeking a charismatic experience, Ray Bullard of the FGBMFI was there to lead them into the experience.

Other Reasons for the Success of the FGBMFI

From June 30 until July 5, 1969, 50,000 people gathered for the sixteenth annual international FGBMFI convention in Washington, D.C. to hear speakers such as Senator Mark Hatfield (1922–), James Watt, Secretary of Labor George Schultz (1920–), Oral Roberts, Bob Mumford (1930–), Earl Prickett, and Demos Shakarian.[153] An ambassador's breakfast featured representatives from at least twenty nations and over twenty-five nations were represented at the largest and most international FGBMFI world convention in its eighteen year history.[154] Pat Robertson televised the 1969 convention on his burgeoning Christian Broadcasting Network.[155]

By the summer of 1969, Demos Shakarian reported that the FGBMFI had 577 chapters in the United States, 15 chapters in Canada, and 91 additional chapters internationally.[156] Domestically, the organization continued to gain influence politically as Shakarian moderated a Sacramento, California, rally with then Governor Ronald Reagan on Thursday, February 5, 1970.[157] Internationally, the FGBMFI continued to expand in Asia, Africa, Europe, and South America, initiating their first chapters in Nigeria in 1969 and 1970, a nation which would eventually boast the largest number of FGBMFI chapters.[158]

The symbiotic relationship between the growing Charismatic movement and the expanding FGBMFI was one factor that contributed to the success of Shakarian's organization, but other factors contributed to their growth as well. One likely cause was Shakarian's growing eschatological urgency. In 1964, Shakarian wrote "when Israel became a nation in 1948 it was another sign fulfilled…The Jewish people have always been known as God's Time-Clock."[159] As the FGBMFI continued to multiply in 1969, Shakarian urged members of the FGBMFI to evangelize the world because "time is of the essence…We must do it now, while the doors are open…Let us live this year of 1969 as though it were our last."[160] In 1970, Demos Shakarian saw mounting Middle Eastern tensions after the Six Day War (1967) as a further sign of eschatological urgency. "The signs are all about us. The prophets of old told us what would happen in the Middle East. Upon the stage of the world, against the backdrop of eternity, we are seeing scenes enacted in Egypt and Israel and in the north country."[161]

Economic factors likely supplemented the eschatological influences that spurred growth in the FGFBMFI. The rising affluence of a rapidly growing middle class was propitious both for the business ventures of Demos Shakarian and also for his spiritual outreach to business men. Thus, once again, Shakarian's timing was impeccable. Pentecostal business men and the general population in the United States were prospering economically, and consequently, wealth and affluence needed to be reinterpreted theologically in light of those circumstances. Similar to the "gospel of wealth" that had been preached in many pulpits in the Gilded Age eighty years earlier, now a group of Christian business men could freely discuss how God had blessed them after WWII. Similar to books that were published during the Gilded Age such as *Acres of Diamonds* by Russell H. Conwell (1843–1925), business men were being offered books like *A New Wave of Revival: In Your Finances* (1992) by Demos Shakarian while simultaneously being encouraged to sow a seed faith offering with the promise of financial blessing.[162] Just as important, much like readers in the Gilded Age loved to hear a rags-to-riches Horatio Alger story, now people were getting the opportunity to read hundreds of testimonies in *Voice* magazine on how God had financially blessed one business man or miraculously provided for another individual.[163]

For most of his time as founder and president of the FGBMFI, Demos Shakarian regularly promoted and featured some of the most popular preachers and advocates of the prosperity gospel. In 1969, Kenneth Hagin (1917–2003) spoke at a Pittsburg, Pennsylvania, chapter meeting in March 1969 and the New York regional FGBMFI convention in November 1969.[164] In 1971, Shakarian prominently featured both Hagin and Kenneth Copeland (1937–) as speakers at the eighteenth annual international FGBMFI convention in Denver, Colorado.[165]

Interestingly, at least one direct link between the gospel of wealth of the Gilded Age and the prosperity gospel that emerged with a burgeoning middle class and age of affluence after WWII can be attributed to Napoleon Hill (1883–1970). He interviewed some of the most famous people from the Gilded Age including Andrew Carnegie (1835–1919) and the extravagantly wealthy John D. Rockefeller (1839–1937), who was himself a devout Baptist. After interviewing these and hundreds of more contemporary successful leaders and business men, Hill summarized his formula for success in his best seller *Think and Grow Rich* in 1937. [166] Shortly after this, Oral Roberts pored through this book and gleaned its pages to synthesize his own formula for spiritual success, subsequently passing it on to his slightly older protégé, Demos Shakarian.[167]

However, the gospel of wealth had its critics in this age of affluence. While Pentecostal leaders offered the FGBMFI a criticism of silence, perhaps out of fear of losing offerings or members, some Pentecostal scholars criticized the FGBMFI openly for being an elitist organization, at odds against the poor and disenfranchised founders of its Pentecostal predecessors.[168] However, Synan suggested that it was both the Christological emphasis of the organization and "the American dream of prosperity for those who served the Lord" that appealed to many, both in the United States and abroad.[169] Simply by the name of their organization the FGBMFI targeted a specific gender and socioeconomic level of society. Asamoah-Gyadu suggested these same politicians, business men, doctors, lawyers, university professors, and policy makers have had a much greater influence on forming, shaping, and growing Christianity within any given nation than the actual membership of the FGBMFI reflected.[170]

As the influence of this pneumatic, non-sectarian group began to escalate in the 1970s, several outside observations began to emerge about its identity and beliefs. One newspaper article suggested that the FGBMFI reflected conservatism and patriotism in its preaching and its praxis.[171] In addition, the journalist went on to add that "the groups are predominantly white, Protestant, male, and evangelical."[172] While the first observation was largely true, the second observation was becoming less accurate, especially from an international perspective.

The organization did espouse patriotism by regularly inviting politicians to speak at conventions and meetings. Early in the history of the FGBMFI, Vice-President Nixon was invited to speak at the annual FGBMFI convention in Washington, D.C. where he stated that America has a profound advantage over the communists because "this nation has a fundamental belief in God."[173] Other politicians already mentioned include Governor Ronald Reagan (1911–2004), Mayor Richard Daley (1902–1976), Donald Rumsfeld (1932–), Pat Robertson (1930–), George Schultz (1920–), and James Watt (1938–), as well as Senator Mark Hatfield (1922–) who gave the closing address at the twenty-second annual FGBMFI convention in Anaheim, California.[174] All of these politicians, with the exception of Richard Daley, were or are conservative Republican politicians.

The majority of politicians who spoke at FGBMFI meetings and conventions in the United States were conservative Republicans, but Shakarian still showed a universal concern to reach out to people regardless of their political affiliation. In 1972, when Richard Nixon was running for re-election, Shakarian took a non-partisan approach before the election by saying "He loves everyone, whether Democrat, Republican, or whatever...He is the only one with a peace plan that will work...He is the only one who can set the POWs free...I urge you to cast your vote for Jesus Christ."[175]

Shakarian and the FGBMFI seemed more concerned with gaining spiritual rather than political influence. In July 1971, at the eighteenth annual international FGBMFI convention in Denver, Colorado, the convention delegates submitted a proposal to ask Congress and President Nixon to establish a national day for prayer, fasting, and repentance.[176] On December 20, 1973, with the Watergate scandal dominating newspaper headlines, Senator Mark Hatfield proposed a resolution for a national day of prayer and fasting, and the resolution passed both houses of Congress.[177] On Tuesday, April 30, 1974, approximately three months before Richard Nixon resigned from office, churches and religious venues throughout the United States honored this resolution.[178]

FGBMFI members also did not hesitate to use their charismatic style of Christianity in reaching out to politicians. In another meeting with Ronald Reagan on September 20, 1970, seven months after the FGBMFI had sponsored a governor's rally in Ronald Reagan's honor, George Otis, Sr. (1917–2007), a FGBMFI member, prophesied that Reagan would become president of the United States.[179] In addition, at a FGBMFI conference in July 1978, Herb Ellingwood (d.b.a. 1925–), legal affairs secretary to Reagan, told FGBMFI members in Anaheim, California, that a small group of Christians at the governor's office prayed for Reagan to be healed of stomach ulcers.[180] Later, Reagan confirmed that his stomach ulcers disappeared after the group prayed for him.[181]

Shakarian recognized that his goal of spiritual influence could sometimes be met through political influence. In some cases, especially internationally, Demos Shakarian and the FGBMFI utilized important and sometimes controversial figures such as François Duvalier to gain important evangelistic access to those nations.[182] Through influential leadership internally, and important political leadership externally, the FGBMFI has continued to gain evangelistic access in places often inaccessible to traditional Christian organizations and denominations.[183]

Critics of Demos Shakarian's political pandering for evangelistic purposes point to the 1960 Haitian airlift as an example of Shakarian's "complete ignorance of the social role of religion."[184] Shakarian expressed some concern in meeting with Duvalier during his visit to Haiti because he was aware of Duvalier's reputation as a ruthless dictator, but he did not criticize Duvalier or exhort him to change certain policies. Shakarian only offered Duvalier prayer when he privately met with him.[185] While Shakarian's approach to political leaders was uncritical, Paul Gifford (1944–) suggests that his approach may have bordered on naivety and Duvalier may have used the FGBMFI and other evangelical agencies "to counter the rise of liberation theology" in Haiti.[186]

Nevertheless, what historically concerned Shakarian and the FGBMFI was to convey the importance of their message across political boundaries. Although Shakarian himself may have been hesitant at first to reach out to communists, fascists, or tyrants, it was Rose who challenged him: "In your vision, Demos were any parts of the world left out because of the government they had?"[187] Demos Shakarian himself never seemed to see any walls – whether they be political, sociological, racial, or ecclesiological.[188]

Other causes of growth in the FGBMFI have been credited to the location of FGBMFI meetings in restaurants and the location of their conventions in hotel ballrooms.[189] In July 1974, Oral Roberts dubbed the members of the FGBMFI "God's ballroom saints"[190] due to the location of their regional and annual conventions. At these meetings and conventions, ordinary laymen felt free to invite their friends from various denominational or unchurched backgrounds without the constraints or labels of any ecclesiastical authority. Once again, Shakarian's eye for opportunity spotted the need and the most suitable location to meet that need was in convention centers and restaurants throughout the United States. Perhaps his experience in the Lions Club or his experience with the Christian Business Men's Committee helped prepare him for such a venture, but he excelled far beyond these humble beginnings. In 1978, Shakarian estimated that the organization had become one of the top ten renters of convention center and hotel space in the United States.[191] In 1962, just as the early Charismatic movement began to expand, Shakarian offered a non-providential explanation for the Charismatic movement by stating, "You can trace the breakthrough of the denominational churches receiving the Holy Spirit as a direct result of FGBMFI testimonies in hotels."[192]

The pneumatic nature of these full gospel meetings created a common bond of experience that went beyond theological creed or dogma. There were certain basic beliefs that were held as a minimum requirement for membership, but they were rarely taught and never preached in meetings.[193] What were kept as priorities were the testimony of lay people and the expression of charismatic gifts. Both of these aspects were practiced and emphasized in the life of Demos Shakarian and became the very fabric and ethos of FGBMFI praxis.

More Growth and Setbacks

By early 1974, the FGBMFI had chartered 1,300 chapters worldwide.[194] Shakarian moved the original chapter of the FGBMFI to the Rodger Young Center Auditorium on Washington Boulevard in downtown Los Angeles to accommodate the size of the first group.[195] *Voice* magazine now printed 500,000 copies monthly.[196] In addition, Shakarian estimated that nearly four million people had met together at various FGBFMI chapter meetings, conventions, and outreaches in 1973.[197]

The television venue which the FGBMFI had occasionally experimented with in the 1960s had become a linchpin of the growing ministry by the end of 1972. Shakarian spoke of the need for a new television ministry to a FGBMFI audience at the Riviera Hotel in Palm Springs, California, in September 1971, and he began pleading his case for the funds necessary to begin such a venture. In addition, Shakarian initiated a department of stewardship for the new television ministry.[198]

The program, called "Good News," focused on the testimonies of various individuals. Interviews with nearly 200 people from 13 different cities in the United States were videotaped by the production crew for the "Good News" program, and the long range goal was to broadcast a FGBMFI television series on 100 television stations reaching a potential audience of 20,000,000 people.[199] By early 1972, the television show was already transmitted in twenty cities, and by the fall of 1972, the program was advertised in forty-nine cities in the United States.[200] Stephen Shakarian began working as the associate producer of the program and he eventually became the producer of the series.[201] By early 1973, Shakarian had already reached his goal of broadcasting in one hundred cities when the "Good News" program began airing on sixty-seven stations in the United States and forty-seven stations in Canada.[202] In 1972, Pat Boone (1934–), a popular actor and singer, began speaking at FGBMFI chapter and convention meetings, and he often hosted the "Good News" program in the 1970s and 1980s.[203] In 1974, Shakarian hosted specially syndicated broadcasts of "Good News" in the top 100 television markets featuring the testimonies of James Edward Johnson, Undersecretary of the Navy, and other business men and celebrities.[204]

The rapid growth in the new television venue was also reflected in the continuing growth of almost all other facets of the FGBMFI. By the summer of 1973, Shakarian estimated that the FGBMFI was starting a new chapter every day. In addition, 250,000 business men gathered at various chapter meetings and conventions every month.[205] Before the end of 1973, Shakarian calculated that the FGBMFI sponsored at least two airlifts every year, employed twenty-five full time staff at their headquarters, and had over 4,000 officers worldwide. In addition, the "Good News" television program aired in 129 cities.[206] By 1974, Shakarian explained to his constituents that the FGBMFI had already communicated the message of Christ to 138,000,000 people, but he was not satisfied. He set a new goal to reach 1.25 billion people, nearly one third of the world's population in 1974, with the gospel of Jesus before the end of the decade.[207]

In spite of the rapid growth in the FGBMFI in the 1960s and 1970s, there were some setbacks. Many of the reversals took place in the late 1960s and early 1970s with the deaths of founding FGBMFI members such as Jewel Rose (1900–1968) and Henry Krause (1887–1972). In addition, healing evangelists popular in the early history of the FGBMFI such as Raymond T. Ritchie (1893–1968), Tommy Hicks (1909–1973), and Gordon Lindsay (1906–1973) all passed away during this period. Their deaths were all followed by memorial articles in *Voice*.[208]

With rapid growth, the FGBMFI also faced other challenges. In 1974, external suspicions from churches that saw the FGBMFI as a competitive threat forced Shakarian to carefully explain again, "We never have, do not now, nor ever will advocate any man leaving his church. Nor do we advocate the giving of tithes to the Fellowship."[209] There were also some reversals internally within the FGBMFI. Shakarian initially interpreted these losses as related to heterodox teachings of some FGBMFI members who were inexperienced or new to traditional Christian doctrine. In addition, Shakarian also theorized that some organizational deficiencies led to internal dissensions within the FGBMFI. Some of these challenges led to the demise and reorganization of early FGBMFI chapters such as the Philadelphia, Pennsylvania, group in 1971.[210] A larger challenge occurred in Europe when the European director of the FGBMFI, Adolf Guggenbühl (d.b.a. 1936–), separated from the FGBMFI, and joined a newer, competing organization in Europe called the Internationale Vereinigung Christlicher Geschäftsleute (IVCG – 1958–).[211] Demos Shakarian and George Otis, Sr. went back to Germany in October 1973, to recapture some of their losses and encourage remaining chapters to stay in the FGBMFI at a regional convention in Braunschweig, Germany.[212]

With the challenges Shakarian faced in the FGBMFI, he sought the counsel of his mentor, Oral Roberts.[213] Roberts was concerned that Shakarian was allowing preachers to dominate the chapter meetings and conventions, and he encouraged Shakarian to re-emphasize the testimonies of business men in their meetings.[214] With some of the doctrinal challenges the FGBMFI encountered, Shakarian sought the assistance of the Society for Pentecostal Studies (SPS –

1970–).[215] Nevertheless, bigger challenges and reversals occurred before the end of the 1970s because of the significant involvement of leaders in the Shepherding movement who were featured in *Voice* and FGBMFI conventions as early as 1963.[216]

In spite of the factions and disputes Shakarian faced as the FGBMFI experienced some inversion and reorganization, Shakarian remained an incessant visionary and an optimist with an infectious attitude. In May 1974, Shakarian held a special three day conference in Chicago, Illinois, for international directors. He laid out a six-point plan which included literature translation, weekly radio broadcasts translated in twenty-five different languages, international evangelism, international regional conventions on every continent, national FGBMFI headquarters in every nation, and a full time director for each continent.[217] Shakarian prepared for a period of unprecedented growth within the FGBMFI.

Challenges and Milestones for the Shakarian Household

Concurrent with some of the factions and frictions in the FGBMFI, the Shakarian household also faced some illnesses and financial setbacks from the late 1960s into the 1970s. Rose Shakarian suffered from an extended illness in late 1968, and Demos Shakarian asked the men in the FGBMFI to pray for her rapid recovery. Rose Shakarian recovered by the end of the year, and she joined her husband at the ninth annual regional FGBMFI conference in Phoenix, Arizona, in January 1969.[218] In late July 1971, the Shakarian's faced additional health problems as Demos Shakarian had to undergo a serious operation. Nevertheless, he recovered quickly, and he and Rose spoke at a FGBMFI chapter meeting in Hayward, California on August 27, 1971.[219]

Shakarian also encountered serious financial and legal challenges related to the death of his father Isaac in 1964, and his sister Florence in 1965. Significant estate and tax problems continued until Demos Shakarian's lawyer informed Shakarian in January 1971 that he did not know how Shakarian's business could be saved.[220] With internal and external challenges in the FGBMFI, and recent illnesses in the Shakarian household, Shakarian felt overwhelmed by the circumstances he faced. However, he felt encouraged later that same month by the responsiveness of the men at the regional FGBMFI convention in Phoenix, Arizona.[221] Shakarian had a renewed sense of hope for the future as he shared the challenges he was facing at a Philadelphia, Pennsylvania, FGBMFI chapter meeting in March 1971.[222] While the estate and tax problems were eventually resolved, other financial problems occurred in 1974 after the bankruptcy and dissolution of White Front Stores, which had a lease agreement as an anchor store on one of Demos Shakarian's properties in Norwalk, California.[223]

In spite of the financial challenges Shakarian faced, Reliance Dairies continued to expand their operations in the early 1970s. The drive-in dairies increased their menu options by including bacon, hot dogs, potato chips, juice, sausage, and of course, milk. By 1974, the Reliance Drive-in Dairies had become a small super market or convenience store, adding variety, and consequently, adding revenue to the business.[224] Richard Shakarian continued to manage the drive-in dairies and eventually expanded to twenty-eight retail outlets with three hundred employees. Reliance Dairies now claimed to be the largest dairy retailer in California.[225] With Richard Shakarian as general operations manager of Reliance Dairies and Demos Shakarian's surgery in 1971, Shakarian decided to divest and delegate most of his time in the dairy business to his son and other investors in 1972 so he could devote most of his time to his growing responsibilities as the president of a rapidly growing international business men's organization.[226]

With the rapid growth of the FGBMFI, Shakarian's time and money were devoted to reaching and recruiting business men in the early 1970s. As new chapters opened nationally and internationally, more demand was placed on Shakarian's time, but with ninety-eight international directors by the end of 1973, Shakarian delegated most of his responsibilities to these FGBMFI officials.[227] In addition, the executive committee of the FGBMFI hired Art Nersasian (d.b.a. 1934) as an administrative assistant to Shakarian after the July 1972 FGBMFI World Convention in San Francisco, California.[228] Nersasian helped run the international office, oversee the Los Angeles FGBMFI chapter, and deliver the weekly radio broadcast from Los Angeles in Shakarian's absence.[229] Nersasian's assistance helped provide Shakarian the freedom to travel domestically and internationally for the FGBMFI.

In the 1960s and 1970s, Richard Shakarian's involvement with the FGBMFI was mostly confined to leading the youth rallies at FGBMFI world conventions.[230] Occasionally, he chaired a convention, such as the Rome convention of 1969, but Richard Shakarian was more interested in working as an evangelist.[231] However, Richard's evangelistic endeavors were not restricted by FGBMFI boundaries. In the early 1970s, he worked full time as the vice president of world evangelism for Morris Cerullo   (1931–).[232] In 1973, Richard created his own evangelistic organization, "Youth Crusades of America," and planned evangelistic crusades in El Paso, Texas; Phoenix, Arizona; Fresno, California; and Portland, Oregon.[233]

Steve Shakarian became increasingly involved with the FGBMFI beginning in 1973 as the producer of "Good News". He also ran an advertising agency called Omega Advertising, but his attention and time became increasingly focused on the media outreach of the FGBMFI. He also displayed his talent in other areas by playing the trumpet at the FGBMFI World Convention in Denver, Colorado in July 1971, and advertising his virtuosity on the trumpet in a solo album in 1969.[234]

Demos and Rose Shakarian also offered their talent to an album featuring Rose's skills at playing the organ.[235] Rose Shakarian was already widely known in FGBMFI circles for leading worship on the organ at various conventions so her skills were advertised in a featured album in *Voice* in early 1971.[236] Shakarian also accompanied his wife on the album by singing the words to "Job's God" and narrating the words for "The Storm."[237] While it is not clear if Shakarian was boastful about his vocal performance in 1971, he was clearly proud of his seven granddaughters whom he paraded in front of the audience at the Denver convention in 1971, declaring they were all saved and filled with the Holy Spirit.[238] However, like the Shakarian generations who lived in Karakala, Armenia, before Isaac was born, Shakarian did not have any male grandchildren yet. That would come later.

Conclusion

In late 1972, as the Charismatic movement grew exponentially and the FGBMFI expanded internationally, Demos Shakarian reflected upon the advice of his late mentor, Charles Price. During one of their weekly visits in the 1940s, Shakarian had asked about the success of Price's evangelistic crusades. Price responded by saying "You never ride the crest [of the wave] in God's work. There is always another billow rolling in higher than the one before. If a man rests on his oars, he is apt to be swamped."[239]

Shakarian took his mentor's advice to heart and worked incessantly to accomplish the vision he had experienced in 1952 and the goals he had established for the FGBMFI as a result of that vision. The FGBMFI did face some challenges as they grew, such as an internal schism in Europe and the external suspicions of ministers and churches who thought the FGBMFI was trying to steal their members to create its own denomination. Shakarian also received unfavorable remarks for his uncritical attitude towards the various heads of state, including tyrants, fascists, and communists, whom he interacted with, and who assisted him with his goals of fulfilling his international vision. In addition, the Shakarian family faced internal crisis first as Rose and then Demos Shakarian developed health problems, and later when mounting legal and financial problems due to estate and tax problems brought Demos Shakarian to the brink of bankruptcy.

Nevertheless, Shakarian's indefatigable personality would not allow him to let these personal circumstances "swamp his boat." He kept working tirelessly on behalf of the FGBMFI, and by the end of 1974, the FGBMFI had chapters in locales as remote as Burns, Oregon, and as cosmopolitan as New York City.[240] Shakarian's creative mind, the sacrificial efforts of the business men who followed him, the evangelistic venues he initiated, the passionate testimonies of people from all walks of life, and the eschatological urgency with which they accomplished their goals created a spiritual supernova that spread far beyond the original confines of Clifton's Cafeteria. In the wake of Demos Shakarian's vision, the FGBMFI would never be the same. However, Demos Shakarian was never satisfied with the status quo, and his energy and optimism would carry the FGBMFI to far greater heights than they had already accomplished at the end of 1974.

Notes

1. Gene Scalf-Tallman interview, January 8, 2008; Ed Ainsworth, "A Lot of Faith: A Lot of Cows," May 8, 1960; and "Downey Dairy Owner Isaac Shakarian Dies," *Los Angeles Times*, November 8, 1964, A2.

2. "Drive-in Sales Facility Begun," *Los Angeles Times*, October 4, 1959, F4.

3. Display Ad, *Los Angeles Times*, August 11, 1965, D13.

4. "Downey Dairy Farm Buys $4000 Prize Bull," *Los Angeles Times*, July 18, 1954, F4; and Demos Shakarian, "God's Dairyman" (1956), 51.

5. Ed Ainsworth, "A Lot of Faith," May 8, 1960.

6. "Downey Dairy Owner Isaac Shakarian Dies," November 8, 1964, A2; and Display Ad, *Los Angeles Times*, August 11, 1965, D13.

7. United States Patent Office, "Method of Milking Cows," for Demos Shakarian, patent number 3,301,215, patented January, 31, 1967.

8. Demos Shakarian, *Life Lifters* (1984), 2:23–24; and "Downey Dairy Owner," *Los Angeles Times*, November 8, 1964, A2.

9. "Goodwill Industries Seats New Officers," *Los Angeles Times*, March 1, 1962, E2.

10. "Ground Broken for Norwalk Goodwill Store," *Los Angeles Times*, November 11, 1952, 20.

11. "Services Set for Mrs. Lalaian," *Los Angeles Times*, September 11, 1965, 14; Display ad, *Los Angeles Times*, August 11, 1965, D13; and Richard Shakarian-Tallman interview, January 16, 2008.

12. Gene Scalf-Tallman interview, January 11, 2008.

13. Demos Shakarian-Synan interview, October 5, 1987, 6.

14. Display ad, *Los Angeles Times*, October 1, 1960, 11; Demos Shakarian, *The Shakarian Story* (1999), 34–35; Richard Shakarian, "Outasight," *Voice*, October 1971, 35; and Richard Shakarian-Tallman interview, January 16, 2008.

15. Demos Shakarian, "Is it God's Time?" *Voice*, May 1970, 27; and Richard Shakarian-Tallman interview, January 16, 2008.

16. "Downey Dairy Owner Isaac Shakarian Dies," November 8, 1964, A2.

17. Display ad, *Los Angeles Times*, October 30, 1955, J5; and Display ad, *Los Angeles Times*, July 22, 1965.

18. Classified Ad, *Los Angeles Times*, March 18, 1968, D14; also see advertisements on March 28, F9; April 10, E12; April 19, E9; April 23, D12; April 24, E13; May 3, D8; and May 6, 1968, E14.

19. For more information on this historic McDonald's Restaurant visit the City of Downey web site, http://www.downeyca.org/visitor_mcdonalds.php (accessed September 25, 2008). The City of Downey web site also mentions that Glenn Bell opened the first Taco Bell restaurant in Downey, California in 1962.

20. For an example of the advertisements of these various companies, see the franchise opportunity section of the classified ads, *Los Angeles Times*, March 18, 1968, D14.

21. Thomas R. Nickel, "Convention Report," *Voice*, July/August 1959, 11, 20–29; and "Businessmen Gospel Convention Slated," *Los Angeles Times*, June 20, 1959, B8.

22. "Full Gospel Group Ready for Convention," *Los Angeles Times*, June 27, 1959, B2; and Nickel, "Convention Report," July/August 1959, 11.

23. Thomas R. Nickel, "Convention Report," *Voice*, July/August 1959, 20–29. John Osteen founded the church that his son, Joel Osteen, a popular author, pastors presently. Lakewood Church, in Houston, Texas, is currently the largest church in North America.

See David Van Bema and Jeff Chu, "Does God Want You to be Rich?" *Time*, September 10, 2006.

24. Thomas R. Nickel, "Bible Prophecies Coming True in Israel," *Voice*, November 1958, 13–16.

25. James Brown, "Every Christian Must Become a Pentecostal," *Voice*, September 1959, 7–8.

26. Display ad, *Los Angeles Times*, September 12, 1959, 11.

27. "Gospel Businessmen's Rally Set at Cafeteria," *Los Angeles Times*, September 19, 1959, 13.

28. Display ad, *Los Angeles Times*, September 12, 1959, 11.

29. "Gospel Businessmen's Rally Set at Cafeteria," *Los Angeles Times*, September 19, 1959, 13.

30. Dennis J. Bennett, *Nine O' Clock in the Morning* (Plainfield, NJ: Logos International, 1970), 17.

31. "Rector and a Rumpus," *Newsweek*, July 4, 1960; and "Speaking in Tongues," *Time*, August 15, 1960.

32. "Speaking in Tongues," *Time*, August 15, 1960, 52.

33. Eleanor Klause, "Spirit-Filled Episcopalian Thrills Spokane Chapter," *Voice*, October 1960, 13.

34. Dennis Bennett, "They Spoke with Tongues and Magnified God!" *Voice*, October 1960, 8.

35. Jean Stone, "A High Episcopalian becomes Pentecostal," *Voice*, October 1960, 15.

36. Harald Bredesen, "Glorious Events Coming; FGBMFI Moves with God!" April 1961, 22.

37. Pat Robertson, "We All can be Directed of the Lord!" *Voice*, April 1962; and Thomas R. Nickel, "Plans Completed for Washington, D.C. Convention," *Voice*, January 1962, 10–11.

38. Demos Shakarian, *Life Lifters* (1984) 2:9; and "Chapter Reports," *Voice*, March 1963, 28.

39. Billy Graham, "Something is Happening," *Voice*, October 1962, 6–7.

40. Demos Shakarian, *The Happiest People* (1975), 162–163; and Thomas R. Nickel, "Jesus Healed a Crippled Hebrew in Jerusalem!" *Voice*, July 1961, 18.

41. Demos Shakarian, *The Happiest People* (1975), 162–163; Thomas R. Nickel, "Jesus Healed a Crippled Hebrew," July 1961, 18; and Donald Gee, "World Pentecostal Conference Held in Jerusalem," *Voice*, September 1961, 34.

42. Demos Shakarian, *The Happiest People* (1975), 162–163; Thomas R. Nickel, "Jesus Healed a Crippled Hebrew," July 1961, 18; and Donald Gee, "World Pentecostal Conference Held in Jerusalem," *Voice*, September 1961, 34.

43. Demos Shakarian, *The Happiest People* (1975), 38–39.

44. Myrtle Danner, "Healed of Cancer by Business Man's Prayer," *Voice*, January 1956, 27.

45. Demos Shakarian, *The Happiest People* (1975), 163–165.

46. Demos Shakarian, *The Ultimate Dimension* (Costa Mesa: Full Gospel Business Men's Fellowship International, 1988), 26.

47. Demos Shakarian, interview with Vinson Synan, Downey, CA, May 27, 1992.

48. Donald Gee, "Let's Not Condemn the Independents!" *Voice*, November 1960, 20–22.

49. Walter Hollenweger, *The Pentecostals: The Charismatic Movement in the Churches*, trans. by R.A. Wilson (Minneapolis, MN: Augsburg Publishing House, 1972), 7.

50. *Christian Life*, August 1967, 22 and 42.

51. See Demos Shakarian, *The Happiest People* (1975), 58.

52. See Jerry Jensen, *Methodists and the Baptism in the Holy Spirit* (Los Angeles: Full Gospel Business Men's Fellowship International, 1963); Jensen, *Presbyterians and the Baptism in the Holy Spirit* (Los Angeles: Full Gospel Business Men's Fellowship International, 1963); Jensen, *Baptists and the Baptism in the Holy Spirit* (Los Angeles: Full Gospel Business Men's Fellowship International, 1964); Jensen, *Episcopalians and the Baptism in the Holy Spirit* (Los Angeles: Full Gospel Business Men's Fellowship International, 1964); Jensen, *Lutherans and the Baptism in the Holy Spirit* (Los Angeles: Full Gospel Business Men's Fellowship International, 1966); Jensen, *The Acts of the Holy Spirit among the Disciples of Christ Today* (Los Angeles: Full Gospel Business Men's Fellowship International, 1974); and Jensen, *Catholics and the Baptism in the Holy Spirit* (Los Angeles: Full Gospel Business Men's Fellowship International, 1976).

53. See Jerry Jensen, "FGBMFI Views the Charismatic Renewal," *Voice*, December 1963, 10–12, 20 for more thorough coverage of this New York seminar.

54. Ibid.

55. Steve Durasoff, *Bright Wind of the Spirit* (1972), 150.

56. Bradfield, *Neo-Pentecostalism* (1979), 15.

57. See Tommy Hicks, "My Second World-Wide Mission Tour," *Voice*, October 1955, 3–18; Harold Herman, "German Lutherans Receive Holy Ghost Baptism," *Voice*, August 1957, 10; and William A. Caldwell, "One of the Greatest Spiritual Awakenings of All Time," *Voice*, April 1959, 12–16.

58. Thomas R. Nickel, "Full Gospel Men's Voice has New German Child," *Voice*, November 1960, 17; and Nickel, "European Convention," *Voice*, July/August 1961, 1–6.

59. See Thomas R. Nickel's report of A.C. Valdez's influential crusades, *Voice*, April 1957, 4, 10, 13, and 17, simultaneously featured in Spanish so it could quickly and cost effectively be distributed to the growing Hispanic members of the FGBMFI. In 1964, *La Voz*, was first advertised and distributed (*Voice*, October 1964, 30).

60. Thomas R. Nickel, *Voice*, November 1959, 16.

61. Irvine Harrison, "Latin America Needs the Peace of God," *Voice*, December 1959, 16–19.

62. Thomas R. Nickel, "New FGBMFI Chapter Established in Havana, Cuba," *Voice*, March 1959, 19–21; and Demos Shakarian, *The Happiest People* (1975), 175–177.

63. Nickel, "New FGBMFI Chapter," March 1959, 21.

64. Nickel, "New FGBMFI Chapter," March 1959, 21; and Demos Shakarian, *The Happiest People* (1975), 177.

65. Demos Shakarian, *The Happiest People* (1975), 177.

66. Nickel, "New FGBMFI Chapter," March 1959, 21.

67. Demos Shakarian, *The Happiest People* (1975), 151–152; and Irvine Harrison, "Report of the Caribbean Crusade," *Voice*, March 1960, 19.

68. Harrison, "Caribbean Crusade," March 1960, 20.

69. Thomas R. Nickel, "FGBMFI Co-Operating with CARE in Haiti," *Voice*, April 1959, 17; and "$2,000 Gift Given CARE for Drought-Stricken Haiti," *Los Angeles Times*, April 25, 1959, 11.

70. Irvine Harrison, "Caribbean Crusade," March 1960, 20; and Demos Shakarian, *The Happiest People* (1975), 154.

71. Demos Shakarian, *The Happiest People* (1975), 155–157.

72. Irvine Harrison, "Caribbean Crusade," *Voice*, March 1960, 21; and Irvine Harrison, "A Loaf of Bread Won a Nation," *Voice*, May 1960, 13.

73. See Jerry Jensen, "London Convention," *Voice*, January/February 1966, 1–2.

74. Ibid.

75. Ibid, 1–16. The "hair lift" quote was suggested by Vinson Synan based on his observations of the London Airlift.

76. Fotherby, *Awakening the Giant* (2000), 53.

77. Jerry Jensen, "The Far East" *Voice*, November 1966, 8–15; Jensen, "Europe" *Voice*, December 1966, 8–17, 22; Jensen, "South America" *Voice*, January–February 1968, 22–27; and Jensen, "South Vietnam" *Voice*, November 1967, 8–17.

78. Fotherby, *The Awakening Giant* (2000), 19.

79. See *Voice*, March 1966, 20; April 1966, 16–17; November 1966,: 8–15; December 1966, 8–17, 20–22; July–August 1967, 17–19; November 1967, 8–17, 27; January–February 1968, 8–15, 23; September 1968, 12–13; and November 1968, 8–11, 11–13.

80. Synan, *Under His Banner* (1992), 79.

81. "Speaker to Tell of Contact with Soviet Officials," *Los Angeles Times*, December 10, 1966, B5.

82. Demos Shakarian, *The Happiest People* (1975), 178.

83. "Paul L. Montgomery, "Businessmen's Religious Group Strives for Speaking in Tongues," *New York Times* July 5, 1964, 45.

84. "Full Gospel Business Men to Convene Here," *Los Angeles Times* June 4, 1966, B7.

85. See "International Board of Directors," *Voice*, October 1963, 3.

86. Ralph Marinacci, "New Jersey Chapter has First Television Program," *Voice*, October 1961, 1.

87. Jerry Jensen, "Charismata in the Twentieth Century," *Voice*, June 1965, 3.

88. See *Voice*, May 1970, 36–37.

89. Cover of *Voice*, October 1961; also see Robert B. Burkley, "I Baptized Teamsters in a Swimming Pool," *Voice*, October 1961, 11; and Demos Shakarian, *Life Lifters* (1984), 1:15.

90. Demos Shakarian, *Life Lifters* (1984), 1:15.

91. Burkley, "I Baptized Teamsters," October 1961, 11.

92. Jerry Jensen, "Capital Commentary," *Voice*, April 1963, 16.

93. Jerry Jensen, "Chicago 1965," *Voice*, September 1965, 4.

94. James Watt, "I Was a Candidate," *Voice*, July/August 1965, 9.

95. Paul Montgomery, "Businessmen's Religious Group Strives for Speaking in Tongues," *New York Times*, July 5, 1964, 45.

96. Jerry Jensen, "Growth of the Fellowship," *Voice*, June 1966, 11.

97. Ibid.

98. See ad in *Voice*, April 1966, 13.

99. There is some speculation regarding why Shakarian fired Thomas Nickel. Jerry Jensen suggested that Shakarian and Nickel had a difference of opinion regarding how the publications office should be run, and eventually Shakarian told Nickel that he should look elsewhere to manage another publications office (Jerry Jensen-Synan interview, February 15, 1992, 5). After leaving the FGBMFI, Nickel founded another magazine called *Testimony* (*NIDPCM* [2002], 931).

100. Jerry Jensen, interview by Vinson Synan, Costa Mesa, CA, February, 15, 1992.

101. Jerry Jensen, "President Shakarian Ill from Virus Infection," *Voice*, March 1962, 24.

102. See *Voice*, May 1962, 35.

103. Jerry Jensen, "Seattle Convention Report," *Voice*, September 1962, 2–10.

104. Jerry Jensen, "Isaac Shakarian: Son of Promise," *Voice*, January 1965, 7; and "Downey Dairy Owner Isaac Shakarian Dies," *Los Angeles Times*, November 8, 1964, A2.

105. "Isaac Shakarian Dies," *Los Angeles Times*, November 8, 1964, A2; and "Isaac Shakarian Rites Set Today," *Los Angeles Times*, November 10, 1964, 26.

106. Oral Roberts-Synan interview, October 10, 1991.

107. Oral Roberts, "His Works Do Follow Him," *Voice*, January 1965, 15.

108. Jerry Jensen, "Isaac Shakarian," *Voice*, January 1965, 3–7; Oral Roberts, "His Works Do Follow Him," *Voice*, January 1965, 12–15; and Edna Shakarian, "Go Over Jordan," *Voice*, January 1965, 8–11. Additional tributes and comments were made in the same January 1965 edition of *Voice*, 2, 16–19.

109. Demos Shakarian, *The Happiest People* (1975), 184.

110. "Services Set for Mrs. Lalaian," *Los Angeles Times*, September 11, 1965, 14.

111. Demos Shakarian, "President's Message: Take Your Stand," *Voice*, October 1968, 37–38; and Demos Shakarian, *Life Lifters* (1984), 3:54.

112. Peter Hocken, "The Catholic Charismatic Renewal," in Vinson Synan's *The Century of the Holy Spirit* (Nashville, TN: Thomas Nelson Publishers, 2001), 209.

113. Demos Shakarian, *The Happiest People* (1975), 143; and Edward O'Connor, "Pentecost at Notre Dame," *Voice*, July/August 1967, 25.

114. Synan, *Under His Banner*, (1992), 91; also see Kevin and Dorothy Ranaghan's *Catholic Pentecostals* (New York: Paulist Press, 1969), 6–16, 41; and Edward O'Connor's *The Pentecostal Movement in the Catholic Church* (Notre Dame, Indiana: Ave Maria Press, 1971), 24–47 for a more thorough account of the beginnings of the Catholic Charismatic Renewal.

115. Kevin Ranaghan, "Dedication Under the Dome," *Voice*, October 1967, 8–30.

116. O'Connor, "Pentecost," July/August 1967, 25–29.

117. Kevin Ranaghan, "Dedication," *Voice*, October 1967, 8–11, 15, 18–19, and 30; and Bert Ghezzi, *Voice*, October 1967, 12–14.

118. Kevin Ranaghan, *Logos Journal* 39:10 (November–December 1971): 22.

119. "Display ad," *Los Angeles Times*, October 30, 1965, B9. The only time that Howard Hendricks was advertised to speak in the Los Angeles area while the FGBMFI offices were on Figueroa Street was during a Baptist Sunday School Conference at First Baptist Church in Los Angeles from November 4–6, 1965. Hendricks has been an instructor at Dallas Theological Seminary for over fifty years, a popular speaker for the Promise Keepers, and a mentor for other well known Christian leaders including Chuck Swindoll, Tony Evans, and David Jeremiah.

120. Demos Shakarian-Synan interview, February 2, 1988, 5.

121. Ibid.

122. "Rome World Convention," *Voice*, January 1969, 3 and 39.

123. See *Voice*, September 1970, 4.

124. Hocken, "Catholic Renewal," (2001), 213.

125. David Barrett estimates that by 2000, Catholic Charismatics totaled nearly 120 million participants (*World Christian Encyclopedia* [New York: 2001], 1:24).

126. Demos Shakarian, "In This Generation," *Voice*, January 1964, 15.

127. Price, *And Signs Followed* (1972), 45–49.

128. See David Harrell, *Oral Roberts* (1985), 158–159 for some details regarding the rejection and controversy surrounding Roberts' relationship with the Pentecostal Holiness denominational leaders. See 293–295 for a good summary of Roberts' acceptance as an elder into the Methodist Church. Also consult Vinson Synan's *Old Time Power: A Centennial History of the International Pentecostal Holiness Church* (Franklin Springs, GA: LifeSprings Resources, 1998).

129. One exception was the 1979 FGBMFI World Convention in New Orleans, Louisiana, when Jimmy Swaggart was invited to be a guest speaker ("When the Saints Go Marching In," *Voice*, March 1979, 24–25).

130. Dian Scott-Tallman phone interview, January 14, 2008; also Geraldine Shakarian Scalf-Tallman interview, January 9, 2008.

131. Aglow International, "History," Women's Aglow, http://www.aglow.org, (accessed January 19, 2008); and Asamoah-Gyadu, "'Missionaries without Robes'" (Fall 1997): 175.

132. Asamoah-Gyadu, "'Missionaries without Robes'" (Fall 1997): 175.

133. Aglow International, "History," Women's Aglow, http://www.aglow.org, (accessed January 19, 2008). While it currently has fewer chapters than the FGBMFI, it is actually in more countries.

134. Karen Linamen-Tallman interview, January 11, 2008; and Demos Shakarian, "Together," *Voice*, February 1981, 15.

135. "1967 FGBMFI Convention July 3–8, Miami, Florida," *Voice*, June 1967, 20.

136. "New York, N.Y.," *Voice*, January 1969, 30.

137. See "Fellowship's Founder to be Head Delegate," *Los Angeles Times* June 27, 1970, 18; and Russell Chandler, "Gospel Fellowship Draws Charismatics," *Los Angeles Times* July 5, 1975, A27.

138. Dian Scott-Tallman phone interview, January 14, 2008.

139. Demos Shakarian, "Together," *Voice*, February 1981, 15–16.

140. Demos Shakarian, *The Happiest People* (1975), 80–81.

141. In many regions and nations, Women's Aglow leadership and chapters have maintained a close but informal relationship with the FGBMFI. See Asamoah-Gyadu, "'Missionaries without Robes'" (Fall 1997): 176. Christina Darko, the head of Women's Aglow in Ghana is married to Kwabena Darko, the African president of FGBMFI. Also in an interview with James and Betty Priddy by Matt Tallman, May 19, 2005, Betty Priddy, wife of James Priddy (international vice-president of FGBMFI), has founded several chapters of Women's Aglow on the East Coast.

142. Dian Scott-Tallman phone interviews, January 14 and August 25, 2008.

143. For example, see Full Gospel Business Men's Fellowship International, "Welcome to Women's Support," FGBMFI in the UK, http://www.fgbmfi.org.uk/fgbmfi/ladies/asp, (accessed February 20, 2008). Val Fotherby, who has authored several books on the history of the FGBMFI, helps lead the women's ministry in Great Britain.

144. Kenneth A. Briggs, "Religion is Now an Important Part of Business," *The New York Times*, May 11, 1975, E10.

145. Russell Chandler, "Gospel Fellowship Draws Charismatics," *Los Angeles Times*, July 5, 1975, A27.

146. Fotherby, *Awakening the Giant* (2000), 53.

147. David Barrett, *World Christian Encyclopedia* (2001), 1:25.

148. Harrell, *All Things are Possible* (1975), 146.

149. Demos Shakarian, Personality Profile, submitted September 20, 1989.

150. Gene Scalf-Tallman interview, January 11, 2008; also Dian Scott-Tallman phone interview, January 14, 2008. See Demos Shakarian *The Happiest People* (1975), 88–89 for an example of this kind of spiritual discernment.

151. See Demos Shakarian, *The Happiest People* (1975), 80–81, 83, 88, and 89.

152. Margaret Poloma, *The Charismatic Movement* (1982), 14. Poloma apparently derived this analysis from David DuPlessis' early observations on the movement. See David DuPlessis, "A Report on the Full Gospel Business Men's Fellowship International," *Christianity Today*, November 24, 1967, 39.

153. Convention ad, *Voice*, April 1969, 20–21; and "16th World Convention," *Voice*, October 1969, 24–25.

154. "16th World Convention," *Voice*, October 1969, 4, 24–25.

155. Ibid, 12.

156. Demos Shakarian, "We have Come This Far by Faith...," *Voice*, October 1969, 14.

157. "Governor's Luncheon Highlights Sacramento Rally," *Voice*, April 1970, 37.

158. "Chapter Reports," *Voice*, December 1970, 31–32.

159. Demos Shakarian, "In This Generation," *Voice*, January 1964, 14.

160. Demos Shakarian, "President's Message: Time to Serve," *Voice*, January 1969, 34.

161. Demos Shakarian, "The Prophetic Rerun," *Voice*, June 1970, 34.

162. See Russell H. Conwell, *Acres of Diamonds* (New York, NY: Harper & Brothers, 1915); Oral Roberts, *A Daily Guide to Miracles, and Successful Living through Seed Faith* (Old Tappan, NJ: F.H. Revell, 1975); and Demos Shakarian, *A New Wave of Revival: In Your Finances* (Costa Mesa, CA: FGBMFI, 1992).

163. For a few examples from early *Voice* magazines see C.C. Ford, "Prosperity," *Voice*, September 1955, 17–19; E.W. Kenyon, "Provision," *Voice*, August 1958, 29–31; Charles Price, "Provision," *Voice*, December 1958, 26; Henry Krause, "The Krause Story," *Voice*, October 1953, 3–5 and December 1953, 5–7; E.N. Richey, "Provision," *Voice*, May 1956, 22–25; William G. Roll, "Provision," *Voice*, February 1956, 21–22; and *Voice*, February 1957, 11–12.

164. "Pittsburgh, Pennsylvania," *Voice*, July/August 1969, 40–41; and "New York Regional," *Voice*, October 1969, 3.

165. "Outasight," *Vision*, October 1971, 36.

166. See Napoleon Hill, *Think and Grow Rich* (New York, NY: Fawcett Crest, 1960).

167. While Oral Roberts does not cite Napoleon Hill in either of his autobiographies, this author and Vinson Synan have both witnessed Roberts publically cite Hill on numerous occasions at Oral Roberts University, respectively as a student and a professor at the university.

168. See Walter Hollenweger, *Pentecostalism: Origins and Developments* (1997), 211.

169. Synan, *Under His Banner* (1992), 83.

170. Kwabena Asamoah-Gyadu, "Missionaries without Robes," (Fall 1997): 185.

171. Kenneth A. Briggs, "Religion is Now an Important Part of Business," *The New York Times*, May 11, 1975, E10.

172. Ibid.

173. Associated Press, "Nixon Speaks to Gospel Fellowship," *The Washington Post and Times Herald*, June 25, 1954, 29.

174. Russell Chandler, "Gospel Fellowship Draws Charismatics," *Los Angeles Times*, July 5, 1975, A27.

175. Demos Shakarian, "Your Vote is Important," *Voice*, November 1972, 21.

176. "Nixon Urged to Proclaim Day of Fasting," *Los Angeles Times*, July 10, 1971, 25.

177. "Introduction of a Resolution for a National Day of Humiliation, Fasting, and Prayer," *Voice*, April 1974, 28–29; and Art Buchwald, "The Day We All Eat Humble Pie," *Los Angeles Times*, January 6, 1974, D2.

178. Russell Chandler, "Tuesday Designated as National Day of Prayer," *Los Angeles Times*, April 27, 1974, 29.

179. Paul Gifford, *The New Crusaders: Christianity and the New Right in Southern Africa*, rev. ed. (Concord, MA: Pluto Press, 1991), 55; "Governor's Luncheon Highlights Sacramento Rally," *Voice*, April 1970, 37; John Herbers, "Reagan Beginning to Get Top Billing in Christian Bookstores for Policies," *New York Times*, September 28, 1984, A23; and Bob Slosser, *Reagan Inside Out* (Waco, TX: Word Books, 1984), 1.

180. "Reagan was Healed of Ulcers by Prayer Group, Ex-Aide Says," *Los Angeles Times*, July 15, 1978, A28.

181. Ibid.

182. See Demos Shakarian, *The Happiest People* (1975), 151–152, 175–177; and Richard Shakarian-Tallman interview, January 10, 2005 to see how François Duvalier, Fidel Castro, and Daniel Ortega were used to open doors in Haiti, Cuba, and Nicaragua respectively.

183. In David Barrett's *World Christian Trends AD 30 – AD 2200: Interpreting the Annual Christian Megacensus* (Pasadena, CA: William Carey Library, 2001), 814, he estimated that the FGBMFI is the only Christian organization or church that has an established Christian outreach in some religiously restricted Muslim nations on the Persian Gulf and broke new evangelistic barriers in Eastern Europe in the 1990s.

184. Gifford, *The New Crusaders* (1991), 57.

185. Demos Shakarian, *The Happiest People* (1975), 151, 159–160.

186. Gifford, *The New Crusaders* (1991), 57.

187. Demos Shakarian, *The Happiest People* (1975), 151.

188. Geraldine Shakarian Scalf-Tallman interview, January 9, 2008.

189. Richard Shakarian-Tallman interview, January 10, 2005.

190. "God's Ballroom Saints," *Voice*, February 1975, 3; and Synan, *Under His Banner* (1992), 95.

191. Jerry Jensen, "Anaheim Convention," *Voice*, September 1978, 24.

192. Demos Shakarian, *Voice*, November 1962, 19.

193. One doctrinal requirement that eventually may have caused some contention between Pentecostals, Charismatics, and neo-Charismatics was the Pentecostal insistence upon a glossolalic manifestation of Spirit baptism (Nelson Melvin, *FGBMFI Chapter Manual* [Costa Mesa, CA: FGBMFI, 1983] 11).

194. Demos Shakarian, "Now God Says Europe," *Voice*, April 1974, 16.

195. "Los Angeles Chapter Celebrates 21st Year!" *Voice*, January 1974, 33.

196. Demos Shakarian, "Ten Thousand Voices," *Voice*, May 1974, 25.

197. Demos Shakarian, "Eight Memorable Days," *Voice*, February 1975, 20–21.

198. Demos Shakarian, "Expanded Horizons," *Voice*, January 1972, 20–21, 37.

199. *Voice*, February 1972, 32.

200. *Voice*, July/August, 1972, 15; and *Voice*, November 1972, 31.

201. Demos Shakarian, *Life Lifters* (1984), 3:30; and *Voice*, December 1972, 35.

202. *Voice*, April 1973, 23.

203. *Voice*, September 1972, 36; and "Conventions," *Voice*, May 1973, 36.

204. See "Saturday's TV Programs," *Los Angeles Times*, April 7, 1974, M29; and "Thursday's TV Programs," *Los Angeles Times*, December 5, 1974, H29.

205. Demos Shakarian, "Businessmen for Christ," *Voice*, November 1973, 7.

206. Ibid, 9.

207. Demos Shakarian, "World Wide Outreach," *Voice*, September 1974, 19, 24.

208. See "My God can do Anything: The Story of Jewel Rose," *Voice*, May 1968, 17–18; "Raymond Ritchie," *Voice*, June 1968, 34; for Henry Krause's death see "A Man Fit for the Kingdom," *Voice*, February 1973, 17; for Tommy Hick's death see, "Closing Time, Gentlemen: A Memorial Tribute to the Man who Stirred Argentina for Christ," *Voice*, April 1973, 20–21; on Gordon Lindsay see "Christ for the Nations," *Voice*, July/August 1973, 26–27.

209. Demos Shakarian, "We are not Interested in Starting New Churches," *Voice*, November 1974, 29.

210. Demos Shakarian, "Demos Shakarian at Philadelphia," *Voice*, October 1971, 31.

211. Walter Hollenweger, *The Pentecostals* (1972), 7, 17. Also see the web site for the IVCG at http://www.ivcg.org (accessed October 6, 2008). IVCG lists quite a number of cooperating agencies that work with them including the Christian Business Men's Committee and Campus Crusade for Christ, but not the FGBMFI.

212. "FGBMFI: Kindling the Fires of Revival in Germany," *Voice*, April 1974, 34–37.

213. Oral Roberts-Synan interview, October 10, 1991, 9–11.

214. Ibid, 10.

215. William Menzies, phone interview by Matthew Tallman, September 24, 2008.

216. See Derek Prince, "I Wanted to Find my Solution to Life's Problems," *Voice*, June 1963, 22–25; Bob Mumford and Charles Simpson speaking at the 1967 Miami FGBMFI world convention, "1967 FGBMFI Convention July 3–8, Miami, Florida," *Voice*, June 1967, 20; Don Basham, "Keeping a Divine Appointment," *Voice*, December 1967, 24–28.

217. Demos Shakarian, "The Eight Memorable Days," *Vision*, February 1975, 21.

218. "Phoenix: A Time to Remember," *Voice*, April 1969, 37–38.

219. Sandy Weldon, "A Happening in Hayward," *Voice*, November 1971, 27.

220. Demos Shakarian, *Life Lifters* (1984), 2:3; Demos Shakarian, *Life Lifters* (1984), 3:54; and "Demos Shakarian at Philadelphia," *Voice*, October 1971, 31.

221. Demos Shakarian, *Life Lifters* (1984), 2:4.

222. "Demos Shakarian at Philadelphia," *Voice*, October 1971, 31.

223. Demos Shakarian, *Life Lifters* (1984), 2:49; Display Ad, *Los Angeles Times*, July 22, 1973, 14; "Interstate to Ask Court for Bankruptcy Shelter," *Los Angeles Times*, May 22, 1974, D12; and "Interstate Gets Bank Loan for Surviving Toys-R-Us Unit," *Los Angeles Times*, August 2, 1974, D15.

224. See display ads, *Los Angeles Times*, May 26, 1970, A6; and May 15, 1974, D8.

225. Richard Shakarian, "A Life Long Commitment to Jesus," *Voice*, October 1993, 10.

226. John Dart, "Group Pushes Prison Program," *Los Angeles Times*, July 10, 1982, B5; and Demos Shakarian, *Life Lifters* (1984), 3:30.

227. *Voice*, December 1973, 39. Also see "FGBMFI Chapters Recently Chartered," *Voice*, December 1973, 27–30 for some examples of how various international directors spoke at new chapter meetings, accepted new charters, and helped meet with potential new chapter leaders and chapter presidents to help expand the FGBMFI.

228. "Called According to His Purpose," *Voice*, January 1973, 41.

229. Ibid, 41–42.

230. See, for example, "Outasight!" *Voice*, October 1971, 35; and also Richard Shakarian's own account of his involvement with the FGBMFI in its early years in Richard Shakarian, "A Life-Long Commitment to Jesus," *Voice*, October 1993, 10–14.

231. "Rome World Convention," *Voice*, January 1969, 3 and 39.

232. "Outasight!" *Voice*, October 1971, 35.

233. "Youth Crusades of America in El Paso," *Voice*, April 1973, 31; "31,000 Attend Richard Shakarian Youth Crusades," *Voice*, October 1973, 35; and Richard Shakarian, "A Life Long Commitment to Jesus," *Voice*, October 1993, 10–14.

234. "Outasight," *Voice*, October 1971, 36; and a display ad in *Voice*, May 1969, 33–34.

235. Display ad in *Voice*, January–February 1971, 38.

236. See Demos Shakarian, *The Happiest People* (1975), 107 and 132 for examples of her musical skills.

237. Display ad in *Voice*, January–February 1971, 38.

238. "Outasight," *Voice*, October 1971, 38.

239. Demos Shakarian, "FGBMFI: Twenty Years of Charisma," *Voice*, January 1973, 2.

240. "Chapter Reports," *Voice*, September 1974, 34.

Early Leaders of the FGBMFI with Demos Shakarian in the front row (fourth from left) and William Branham (third from left) and Isaac Shakarian (second from left).

Clifton's Cafeteria in 2005

The First Edition of *Voice Magazine*

The interior of Clifton's Cafeteria - the same today as it was in 1951

Demos and Rose in 1964

Demos and Rose Enroute to the 1965 London Airlift

Demos Shakarian with Four of His Granddaughters:
Denice, Cindy, Karen, and Renee

*Demos Shakarian Speaking at an Early FGBMFI Banquet
with Rose Shakarian Playing an Organ behind Him*

Demos Shakarian in 1965

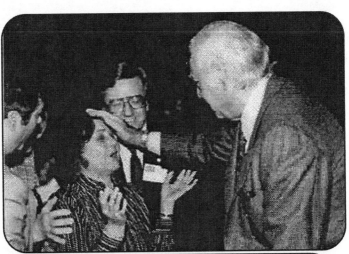

Demos Shakarian Praying for His Wife Rose
at a FGBMFI Convention

Chapter Ten

The Golden Years of Demos Shakarian (1975–1984)

At the age of sixty-five when Demos Shakarian was approaching retirement, he wrote an article in *Voice* magazine announcing that he was not planning to retire, but rather he would be "refiring."[1] After all, he was still vibrant, healthy, energetic, and still consumed by the divine vision he had received more than twenty-five years earlier. Prophetic words from fellow FGBMFI members and ministers confirmed his continuing leadership role.[2] The church of his heritage and the example of his father dictated that he not retire from the ministry or pastoral calling but to serve in that role for life.[3] He was able to witness the continuation of some of the greatest growth of the fellowship over the next decade as both the fellowship and the Charismatic movement reached a crescendo in the United States.

By 1975, there were 1,500 chapters worldwide and a mailing list of 780,000 recipients in the FGBMFI.[4] The Charismatic movement was at the height of its influence in North America and it was garnering further growth internationally. Demos Shakarian had become one of the most prominent leaders in the Charismatic movement, and he would enjoy accolades and recognition as the founder of the FGBMFI and a pioneer in the Charismatic movement as it continued to expand nationally and internationally for the next decade.

At the Home Front

Even though Shakarian actively left the dairy business in 1972, he kept his farm in Delano, California, where he raised alfalfa, cotton, and cattle and continued to produce champion bulls until 1978.[5] In 1978, Shakarian sold the remainder of his cattle and his farm, but he kept most of his real estate holdings, and he relied financially on the money generated from leases and the sale of property for the remainder of his life.[6] One piece of real estate that continued to create financial strain for Demos Shakarian and the Shakarian Corporation was a piece of property in Downey, California at the corner of Pioneer and Firestone Boulevard. After the White Front stores went bankrupt in 1974, Demos Shakarian lost the additional lease payments from the vacant White Front store on that property.

Shakarian thought about subordinating the lease on the property, but he claimed he felt directed by the Holy Spirit to halt this process and help this company even though they had no reason or capabilities to respond with any financial assistance of their own. Two years later, the company assumed a loss of 1.1 million dollars and gave him the White Front building on his property.[7] Shortly after this, Trinity Center Church in Lynwood, California, negotiated a contract with Shakarian to lease the building with an option to purchase the vacant Downey White Front store in May 1976 for 2.6 million dollars.[8] Ultimately however, another church, Downey Calvary Chapel, purchased the property and became one of the largest churches in the United States under its current pastor, Jeff Johnson (d.b.a. 1950).[9]

In 1975, Shakarian completed his autobiography, *The Happiest People on Earth* (1975), with the assistance of John (1923–) and Elizabeth Sherrill (1928–), and by November of that same year *Voice* began advertising his life story.[10] The book used an uncritical inspirational approach to tell Shakarian's story beginning with his ancestral home in Karakala, Armenia, progressing to their immigration to the United States, climaxing with the introduction and early history of the FGBMFI, and concluding with a few anecdotal stories of his involvement in the FGBMFI in the 1960s and early 1970s. By 1979, the book had already sold over one million copies, it was eventually translated into over twenty-five different languages, and Pope John Paul II was even presented a copy of Shakarian's autobiography in late 1979.[11]

For their service to the community as civic leaders and their commitment to the FGBMFI, Demos and Rose Shakarian were honored at an international breakfast in Anaheim, California in late 1975 with 500 people in attendance. The remarks of their children demonstrated both their commitment to Christian faith and their hard work and dedication towards promoting the FGBMFI. Their daughter Geraldine said, "Often I would awaken late at night or early in the morning hours. I would hear Dad in the living room praying. That meant so much to me and still does."[12] Richard Shakarian was grateful since this was the first time in years the whole family had been together because of Shakarian's extensive travel schedule.[13] Demos and Rose Shakarian were honored once again in late 1975 to observe the marriage of their youngest son Steve to Debra Abbott.[14]

However, sometimes Demos and Rose Shakarian's travel schedule separated them from the rest of their family during important holidays. They spent Thanksgiving of 1976 in Anchorage, Alaska, speaking at a conference from November 25–27.[15] Nevertheless, most of their Thanksgivings were spent with their family in Downey, California, enjoying a traditional turkey dinner with pumpkin pie.[16]

As Shakarian became more recognized through the sale of his autobiography, the promotion of the FGMBFI, and the production of his television show, more public demands were placed upon him. However, Shakarian's appeal was not in his oratory skills but in his ability to empower others or in his ability to be a "helper" to others as he suggested in his autobiography.[17] In 1976, Shakarian reflected upon a previous conversation he had with A.C. Valdez in which Valdez wondered why people flew and drove from great distances to come and hear Demos Shakarian speak even though Shakarian did not claim to be a communicator. Shakarian answered Valdez by saying, "Albert, that's why men come – because I let them speak and witness for the Lord. It hurts me to see men sitting in a meeting and not being used."[18]

As Shakarian's schedule intensified in 1978, he expressed his satisfaction and his hectic schedule in his work with the FGBMFI by stating, "It seems as though the more I work for the Lord, the better I feel. This year I've been to Europe; had four conferences in four weeks; flew back to California; then to Toronto for five days of interviewing; back home; flew to Dallas to speak; then the World Convention in Anaheim; and so it continues. But I have never felt better and my business is better than it has ever been. Now we must move ahead because God has given us another plan."[19]

Apparently, business was better for Shakarian in 1978 than it had been in previous years. With the weight of tax and inheritance problems resolved and the responsibility of running a dairy or overseeing a ranch no longer Shakarian's concern, he could focus more exclusively on his spiritual passion of expanding the FGBMFI. In addition, he had recently sold seventy acres of his property holdings to a railroad company at a premium price. The profit from this sale enabled Shakarian to pay off all of his mortgages and personal debt.[20] At the age of sixty-five, Shakarian could now enjoy his "retirement" by devoting all of his time to promoting and fulfilling the vision he received in 1952.

Across the Airwaves

Shakarian started doing radio broadcasts on behalf of the FGBMFI from Clifton's Cafeteria in 1951, but in 1975, the FGBMFI expanded its evangelistic influence to 148 television stations in the United States and Canada, along with radio programs broadcast in eighteen languages, in fifty nations.[21] The "Good News America" broadcasts in 1975, co-hosted by Pat Boone and Demos Shakarian, were seen by twenty million people in North America.[22] The television show and the distribution of Shakarian's new autobiography that same year began to make Demos Shakarian a household name in the Christian community and beyond.

Television production within the FGBMFI was overseen by Omega Advertising, a wholly owned subsidiary of the FGBMFI. Steve Shakarian was the president of Omega Advertising and the producer for FGBMFI telecasts.[23] According to Steve Shakarian, in 1976, the FGBMFI produced more Christian television programs for broadcast than any other religious organization of its kind.[24] In addition, "Good News America" won an Emmy for "Special Achievement in Technical Arts" in 1976.[25]

In July 1975, the FGBMFI partnered with the Trinity Broadcasting Network (TBN) to televise the FGBMFI World Convention in Anaheim, California.[26] While the proprietary agreement between the FGBMFI and TBN did not create any controversy, during that convention, the *Los Angeles Times* ran an article on

Kathryn Kuhlman (1907–1976), one of the featured speakers at the Anaheim meetings, mentioning that her pianist, Dino Kartsonakis (1942–), was suing her for breach of contract.[27] In the article, Dino claimed that Kuhlman lived an extravagant lifestyle and accumulated a personal jewelry collection worth over one million dollars, including a fifteen carat diamond ring.[28] Her untimely death only seven months later, on February 20, 1976, squelched any further controversy.[29]

Shakarian also cooperated and collaborated with the efforts of other Christian television productions in the 1970s. He was a guest for a national production that Pat Robertson and the Christian Broadcasting Network aired in major cities in September 1976 which included President Gerald Ford (1913–2006) and then Governor Jimmy Carter (1924–).[30] He also appeared on a Thanksgiving Telethon a few months later on behalf of Paul (1934–) and Jan Crouch (d.b.a. 1940–) and the Trinity Broadcasting Network.[31] In 1978, "Good News" telecasts began to air daily after prime time telecasts of Jim Bakker's (1940–) PTL Show.[32] In addition, the FGBMFI entered into a cooperative agreement with TBN to underwrite the cost of local translator stations, so that the FGBMFI "Good News" broadcasts were aired on TBN.[33]

Because of the introduction of satellite telecasts in 1978, satellite receivers now offered broadcasts of "Good News" twenty-four hours every day.[34] Plans were made by the FGBMFI executive committee to place 300 satellite translators in North America and 1,000 translators worldwide.[35] Before the end of 1978, there were 300 "Good News" television outlets in North America, and there were 425 satellite translators applied for by local FGBMFI chapters.[36]

"Good News" television programs also began to air internationally in Australia in 1977, reaching a potential audience of 13.5 million people.[37] While regular television broadcasts continued domestically in North America through most of the 1980s, occasionally the FGBMFI continued to produce a special feature which was aired on major networks. In 1981, the FGBMFI began production on a new television special called "The Happiest People on Earth" with taped interviews and testimonies. The special was broadcast in sixty-one cities by August 1982.[38] As regular "Good News" broadcasts continued in the early 1980s, the FGBMFI received several broadcasting awards in 1983 including eight Halo Awards and a number one ranking in the religious broadcasting category by *People Magazine*.[39]

In the 1970s and 1980s, Shakarian's television productions continued to promote the mission of the FGBMFI and elevate Shakarian's status as a leader in the Charismatic movement. However, internationally, the FGBMFI continued to gain its largest audience on the radio. As early as 1974, the FGBMFI signed contracts to broadcast on radio with Far East Broadcasting Company. These broadcasts were translated into sixty-eight different languages in fifty different nations with a potential audience of two billion listeners.[40]

Across the Globe

Continued global expansion occurred in 1975 with the advent of international offices in Brussels, Singapore, and New Zealand and John Andor predicted that the introduction of a new office in Europe would double the number of FGBMFI chapters on that continent within the next year.[41] Eventually, other offices sprang up in Australia, Canada, Hong Kong, Malaysia, Singapore, Indonesia, Nigeria, and Rwanda, and others have been developed in different nations as the FGBMFI leadership of that nation saw fit.[42] FGBMFI Continental Conventions in Brussels, Belgium, and in Africa were scheduled for 1976.[43] The conference in Brussels from May 8–10, 1976, drew business men from twenty-six different nations.[44]

To consolidate growth in the United States and internationally, the FGBMFI began providing teaching seminars for eager disciples of the burgeoning Charismatic movement. In 1975, the FGBMFI hired J. Robert Ashcroft (1911–1995) as their director of teaching and prayer ministries, and he began coordinating university level teaching seminars called "Institutes for Charismatic Living" at various locations throughout North America.[45] By 1976, the FGBMFI estimated it had tripled its outreach and shared the gospel with 1.25 billion people.[46]

One of the reasons for this meteoric rise in the evangelistic efforts of the FGBMFI was its continued collaboration with popular healing evangelists of the 1970s. In late 1975 or early 1976, the FGBMFI began cooperating with T.L. Osborn to incorporate people from his crusades into new chapters of the organization. In early 1976, ten new chapters of the FGBMFI were started in Nigeria after one of Osborn's crusades there.[47]

Because of the initial response at Osborn's crusades, in late 1975, Demos and Rose Shakarian travelled with several other leaders and international FGBMFI directors to Africa for thirty-one days, speaking and praying with over twenty thousand people in various nations including Kenya, Nigeria, and South Africa. While in South Africa, Rose and Demos Shakarian visited a gold mine where they were impressed with the size of the operation, which employed 12,800 Black Africans and 2,200 White Afrikaners.[48] Upon later reflection, Shakarian seemed so impressed by the interracial population of this company that he wrote, "Yes, God loves every soul – black, white, yellow and red – they are more precious to Him than gold."[49] However, he made no comments about apartheid in this or any article in *Voice*. In fact, he promoted Caucasian South African business leaders such as Robert Trench (1927–), a FGBMFI director and vice-president, who claimed his corporate enterprises in South Africa, saw a thirty percent increase in sales in 1981 in spite of trade sanctions.[50] Paul Gifford cites this as an example of his criticism towards the FGBMFI if not necessarily for its overt support of apartheid, then for its silence towards those business men, corporations, and politicians who perpetuated it.[51]

In North America in some areas of the country, some FGBMFI chapters were started to help target African-American business men in the community.[52] While these efforts may have alleviated some of the perceptions of racism directed towards the leadership of the FGBMFI, it did not silence the critics of the organization as the FGBMFI began to expand domestically and internationally. One newspaper reporter for the *Los Angeles Times* suggested that the FGBMFI was "heavy on personal testimonies and light on business ethics."[53]

In spite of some criticism, the FGBMFI continued to grow internationally. By 1978, the organization had already established chapters in sixty six nations.[54] But Shakarian was not satisfied. He sent out a clarion call to his constituent chapters reminding them of his original vision. "We're reaching a point in history when God will change the course of nations and the faces of continents. God showed me how He would change the faces of every continent on earth from a look of death and discouragement to a look of praise and brotherhood. Now is the time it will happen."[55] The vision of Demos Shakarian was now more urgent than ever. Chapters began to be organized in areas of the world closed to the gospel. The actual appeal that Shakarian sent out had been spurred on by the first airlift to Eastern Europe in 1978, where a spontaneous spiritual response from people in Budapest, Hungary, allowed Shakarian to see how the curtain that separated Eastern Europe from the rest of the continent was not as "iron" as he had previously thought.[56] Three hundred people became Christians shortly after that impromptu street meeting, and Shakarian reported that the country of Hungary remained open to them as long as they did not speak against Socialism.[57]

While the FGBMFI was just beginning to forge new paths and opportunities in Eastern Europe, the organization continued to expand in the Caribbean and Latin America since its first airlift to Haiti in 1960. Jean Claude Duvalier (1951–), son of François Duvalier, and President of Haiti (1971–1986), purportedly claimed to watch the "Good News" telecast on a weekly basis.[58] In San Juan, Puerto Rico, a meeting was held with the governor of Puerto Rico, Carlos Romero Barcelo (1932–) and other Caribbean ambassadors in 1978.[59] The FGBMFI also gained some political and popular appeal in Guyana shortly after the Jonestown Massacre on November 18, 1978. Shakarian and other FGBMFI members organized an airlift to Guyana. During the airlift, Shakarian met with Prime Minister Linden Forbes Burnham (1923–1985) of Guyana and soon, Burnham began attending FGBMFI meetings in Guyana through the efforts of Shakarian and Sir Lionel Luckhoo (1914–1997).[60]

Luckhoo was the legal counsel for Jim Jones (1931–1978), the religious leader of the People's Temple in Jonestown, but Luckhoo had a dramatic religious experience after he interpreted that he was providentially spared from the tragedy of the Jonestown mass suicide. A short time after his conversion experience, Luckhoo helped start a local chapter of the FGBMFI in Guyana, and he befriended Demos Shakarian and became a popular speaker internationally in the organization.[61]

Perhaps the most successful and influential expansion the FGBMFI made in this region began in Central America in the 1970s. 1978 became a bellwether year for the FGBMFI in Central America. In 1978, President-elect Rodrigo Carazo Odio (1926–) of Costa Rica attended a FGBMFI meeting and a banquet was held in his honor by the FGBMFI on October 5, 1978.[62] John Carrette (d.b.a. 1950–) became involved in the FGBMFI after attending the World Convention in Anaheim, California, in July 1978, and he went back to Guatemala and started the first FGBMFI chapter in that country.[63] Business men in Guatemala became more responsive to the evangelistic efforts of the FGBMFI after Demos Shakarian donated $15,000 towards an agency providing relief for indigenous Guatemalans still suffering from the effects of a 1976 earthquake. President Rios Montt (1926–) also responded to Shakarian's generosity and started attending FGBMFI meetings in Guatemala City in the early 1980s.[64] Other presidents of Guatemala, Costa Rica, and El Salvador continued to be actively involved in the FGBMFI throughout the 1980s.[65]

In the late 1970s, the FGBMFI became involved in Nicaragua and several leading figures in the Sandinista political movement began participating in Bible studies and private prayer meetings with FGBMFI members including Daniel Ortega (1945–).[66] Apparently a sizeable population of Pentecostal and other scripturally oriented Christian groups became involved with the Sandinista movement in the 1970s[67] Demos Shakarian visited Nicaragua in the early 1980s, and presented a prize bull as a gift to one of the leading generals in the Sandinista army.[68] However, relationships between the FGBMFI in North America and the Sandinistas subsided for a period of time after a Charismatic evangelist popular within FGBMFI circles named Morris Cerullo (1931–) and his anti-communist rhetoric prevented Cerullo from entering Nicaragua in May 1981.[69] The fact that Pat Robertson's "Operation Blessing" relief program raised two million dollars in aid to Contra-run refugee camps in Honduras in the 1980s did not help this relationship between the Sandinistas and the FGBMFI.[70] In 1989, the FGBMFI listed having only one active chapter in Nicaragua.[71]

Many of these political leaders in the Caribbean and Central America who affiliated themselves with the FGBMFI were controversial political leaders accused of human rights violations and atrocities. Paul Gifford suggested that the FGBMFI alliance with these political leaders was used as a protective shield against communism "in those parts of the world where the United States has strong interests, or where the United States is fearful of civil disturbance or Soviet influence."[72] Shakarian's relationship with communist or socialist leaders such as Fidel Castro, Linden Burnham, and Daniel Ortega run counter to Gifford's argument. Nevertheless, whether or not the FGBMFI had any political ambitions or whether Demos Shakarian was unknowingly used as a pawn by the United States Department of State, there was no record that Shakarian questioned the political affiliation or actions of any of these politicians except for François Duvalier.[73] In spite of accusations of genocide against Rios Montt and his subsequent removal as President of Guatemala in August 1983, Demos Shakarian invited Montt to speak at the FGBMFI World Convention in Anaheim, California in July 1984.[74] Shakarian's vision for the FGBMFI did not exclude any business man or politician, regardless of his political persuasion or perception.[75]

In spite of Shakarian's uncritical approach, or perhaps because of it, the FGBMFI continued to grow internationally at an exponential rate in the late 1970s and into the 1980s. By the end of 1978, there were 1,723 chapters in sixty-six nations. The FGBMFI also sponsored a total of 134 rallies, conventions, and seminars in 1978.[76] Before the end of 1979, thirty of the top FGBMFI leaders from Europe visited the new international headquarters in Costa Mesa, California. While meeting with Shakarian, these leaders developed a plan to start 1,000 new chapters in Europe by November 1980.[77]

In May 1980, *Voice* advertised fourteen global regional conventions from Winnipeg, Canada, to Stuttgart, Germany, and beyond.[78] By 1980, there were 2,000 chapters worldwide in seventy countries. In addition, the new building dedicated in the same year boasted 100 full time employees.[79] From May 31 until June 5, 1982, Shakarian spoke at an Asian FGBMFI regional convention in Singapore in which attendance ranged from 35,000 to 47,000 participants.[80] At the thirtieth annual FGBMFI World Convention in Anaheim, California, in July 1982, Shakarian said, "If I were to choose one word to characterize this unique difference it would be international."[81] As international chapters and regions of the FGBMFI continued to grow, their stature and influence necessitated new international strategies and a new structure for the organization. Preliminary meetings were held with the international directors on January 24–29, 1983, and a culminating series of international strategy sessions was held from April 17–21, 1983. Shakarian asked Khoo Oon Theam (d.b.a. 1940–), an owner of a consulting firm in Singapore, to facilitate the meetings.[82]

Within the next few years, other opportunities began to develop in countries that restricted Christian expression. As early as 1976, the FGBMFI began to initiate chapters in the Middle East when they had their first regional convention in that part of the world in Jerusalem from October 15–25, 1976, and Shakarian spoke at the conference while joining a number of FGBMFI members from North America on a tour of Israel.[83] By the middle of the next decade, many nations in the Middle East had active FGBMFI chapters, and in some cases these were the only expression of Christianity in those nations.[84]

Demos Shakarian played a large part in the success of the FGBMFI internationally. In addition to his extensive travel schedule, he had a unique mixture of charm, charisma, amiableness, tenacity, and garrulousness that allowed him to mix comfortably with heads of state, presidents, kings, popes, and even tyrants. Val Fotherby recounts a somewhat humorous anecdote in which Shakarian accompanied a United States government delegation to Egypt during which Shakarian readily conversed with Egyptian generals, the Egyptian ambassador, and the Pope of the Coptic Church and managed to seemingly garner more attention than the entire government delegation.[85] This trip was planned by the United States government to commemorate the transfer of the Sinai Peninsula from Israel to Egypt after a peace treaty was signed on March 26, 1979. After Shakarian's visit to Egypt, President Anwar Sadat (1918–1981) returned the favor by sending an Egyptian representative, Kamal Badir (d.b.a. 1935–), to speak on his behalf at the official dedication of the new FGBMFI headquarters on January 27, 1980.[86]

Demos and Rose Shakarian felt comfortable meeting with dignitaries and heads of state from a variety of cultures in Asia, Africa, the Americas, and the Middle East. In June 1980, they had dinner with Madame Soong Mei-Ling (1897–2003), the widow of Chiang Kei-Shek (1887–1975). As they enjoyed their meal, the Shakarians proceeded to share their Christian faith with Madame Soong, and she invited them to return and celebrate their fiftieth wedding anniversary with her in 1983.[87]

Global Headquarters

While Shakarian's personality attracted a wide variety of business men and political leaders to the FGBMFI, his visionary leadership and the vision he received in 1952 brought a divine urgency to their cause of international expansion and global evangelism. In May 1974, at the first FGBMFI international directors' board meeting in Chicago, Illinois, it became clear that a larger facility was needed for such ambitious growth. Paul Toberty (d.b.a. 1930–), as a successful Southern California developer and builder, chaired a committee to find a new, larger site to replace the site in downtown Los Angeles where the FGBMFI was headquartered since 1959. The presentation was made on May 2, 1975, at the board meeting, and there apparently was some debate and concern about the cost of a new six-acre site with extensive architectural structures proposed. However, during the meeting, the charismata of tongues and interpretation of tongues verbally expressed what was interpreted as divine approval for the project. Consequently, the board of directors unanimously voted to approve the site.[88]

On July 5, 1975, a large group of FGBMFI members and attendants gathered to dedicate the newly purchased property in Costa Mesa, California.[89] While the permanent headquarters in Costa Mesa were being built, the international headquarters moved from downtown Los Angeles to Irvine, California. In July 1976, the FGBMFI expected the permanent site in Costa Mesa to be completed sometime in 1977.[90]

With the significant sum of money needed to build this site, several new items were advertised through *Voice* to generate revenue. These included an audio-recorded version of the New Testament on cassette tapes for a one hundred dollar donation and a hardback edition of *The Happiest People on Earth* for a ten dollar donation.[91] More ambitious fundraising efforts began after the July 1977 FGBMFI World Convention in Chicago, Illinois. At the convention, a charismatic gift of glossolalia and the interpretation of that gift exhorted members of the FGBMFI to prepare to reach two billion people with the gospel in the near future.[92] Shakarian and the executive leadership of the FGBMFI responded to this pneumatic message as a mandate for quickly raising the funds necessary to complete the FGBMFI headquarters, hopefully in sixty days. The executive board created a Founder's Circle Plan in which donors would be sent a certificate and their names would be prominently displayed in a book at FGBMFI headquarters.[93] It was explained that a donation of twenty-five dollars or more would allow an individual to become a member of the Founder's Circle.[94]

Only six months after the charismatic gift expressed at the Chicago Convention exhorted FGBMFI members to prepare to minister to two billion people, Shakarian predicted that the FGBMFI would accomplish that goal before the end of 1977.[95] The urgency of these evangelistic ambitions encouraged Shakarian to avoid any further delay in the construction of their international headquarters. At the Phoenix Regional Convention from January 25–29, 1978, the executive FGBMFI board voted to begin immediately with construction on the new headquarters site. In addition, at the convention, the organization gathered the largest offering in its history, collecting a total of $850,000 in cash and pledges for the construction of the headquarters building. However, the FGBMFI still needed to raise an additional one million dollars in order to complete the project.[96] Nevertheless, on Friday, March 13, 1978, an official groundbreaking ceremony finally took place at the future FGBMFI headquarters site in Costa Mesa.[97] An additional $500,000 was raised at the FGBMFI 1978 World Convention for the completion of the headquarters building project.[98] Still more fundraising was deemed necessary, so a FGBMFI Bible correspondence course was advertised in *Voice* for $24.[99] Completion of the new headquarters was now expected in the spring of 1979.[100]

Before the end of 1978, construction workers had completed sixty percent of the headquarters building.[101] By the spring of 1979, the headquarters building was almost completed and Steve Shakarian was appointed director of ministries and chief executive officer of FGBMFI headquarters.[102] On August 1, 1979, the staff at FGBMFI international headquarters moved into their new building.[103] Unfortunately, before the building was completed, the construction cost had increased to five million dollars, thus creating a significant debt for the FGBMFI.[104] Before the end of 1979, the FGBMFI international directors met at the new headquarters and devised a plan to retire the additional debt on the new building by asking each chapter in the United States to give $1,500 to $3,000. At the special meeting of international directors, $26,000 was given immediately towards meeting this goal.[105] However, the debt on the building was not eliminated by the end of 1980, so other fundraising measures were initiated in 1981 to help establish a solid financial future for the FGBMFI.[106]

Finally, the new headquarters was officially dedicated on January 27, 1980, at 2:30 PM. International FGBMFI directors, the FGBMFI executive board, and dignitaries from across the globe attended the event, and Oral Roberts was the keynote speaker.[107] One *Voice* article described the new FGBMFI headquarters, "as a silent but powerful witness next to a great California freeway where thousands pass daily; its architectural lines unique; its east and west wings stretched like arms of love to a lost world. Encircling its rotunda, snapping in seasonal breezes, flags of the nations symbolize the scope of the ministry linked within its walls."[108] The FGBMFI international headquarters had become a concrete per-sonification of Shakarian's vision. It also provided the logistical and administrative structure under which Shakarian's vision could hopefully be completed. The building also signified how influential, expansive, and powerful the FGBMFI had become.

Washington for Jesus

As the FGBMFI became more pervasive in North American society, politicians frequently appeared at conventions, and they were often invited to speak at FGMBFI banquets held in their honor. Democratic Governor George Wallace (1919–1998) spoke at the FGBMFI Alabama State Regional Convention on November 7, 1975.[109] Sometimes a politician such as Republican Congressman William Dannemeyer (1929–) would use the FGBMFI as a platform during election season.[110] Shakarian spoke on September 15 and 16, 1978, at a South Carolina Regional FGBMFI Rally attended by Democratic Lieutenant Governor of South Carolina, Brantley Harvey, Jr. (d.b.a. 1932–).[111] However, the organization appeared non-partisan in its support for both Democrat and Republican politicians in the United States during the 1970s.

Nevertheless, members of the FGBMFI were excited when a politician who identified himself as a "born again" Christian was elected as president of the United States in 1976. In the midst of their political and spiritual euphoria, the FGBMFI Washington, D.C. Regional Convention drew a record crowd of 18,000 people in January 1977.[112] They had more reason to celebrate upon finding out that the sister of President Jimmy Carter (1924–), Ruth Carter Stapleton (1929–1983), identified herself as a Charismatic Christian. Ruth spoke at the Florida State FGBMFI Convention and was interviewed by the editor of *Voice* for a feature article in September 1977.[113] In the article, Stapleton explained how she had received Spirit baptism through the prayers of a popular Charismatic Methodist evangelist named Tommy Tyson (1922–2002).[114]

Demos Shakarian usually remained non-partisan and avoided any public endorsement of candidates either individually or on behalf of the FGBMFI.[115] Shakarian may not have overtly or publicly expressed his political opinions, but his sister Roxana was not afraid to write about her support for a Republican politician when she stated, "If Richard Nixon runs for President in 1980, I would vote for him. There are many more of us who believe in him than you think!"[116] Just as telling is the fact that she used her full married name as Roxana Shakarian Vahan rather than her abbreviated name as Roxana Vahan, so that readers of the *Los Angeles Times* would know that it was a Shakarian writing this remark.

While Shakarian remained silent regarding any public endorsement of candidates, he did believe that prayer could be a powerful force in the political arena. In July 1978, Shakarian's mentor, Oral Roberts, spoke at the annual FGBMFI world convention at the Anaheim Convention Center in California about the possibility of prayer overcoming political resistance. Roberts described how he believed his battle with the Oklahoma Health Planning Council in gaining approval to establish the City of Faith medical facility was won through the prayers of his supporters.[117]

Shakarian and some of his Christian peers decided to take this theory of prayer to a much larger constituency. In the February 1980 issue of *Voice*, Shakarian began advertising the Washington for Jesus Rally to be held April 29, 1980.[118] However, the rally had been in the planning stages for two years, initiated by John Gimenez (1931–2008), a prominent pastor from Virginia Beach, Virginia; Pat Robertson; Bill Bright (1921–2003); and Demos Shakarian. A previous rally was attempted in Washington, D.C. in 1979, by a Los Angeles pastor named John Hinkle (1917–1999), but he excluded the Charismatic segment of Christianity and only succeeded in garnering 10,000 participants to attend his rally.[119]

With over 1,500 FGBMFI chapters in the United States in 1980, the organization had enough groups scattered throughout the nation to act as a major coordinating structure for planning and promoting the rally.[120] The FGBMFI was a primary sponsor, and Shakarian was a featured spokesman at the Washington for Jesus Rally.[121] As the FGBMFI began preparing for the rally, Shakarian considered the potential influence his organization had accumulated in twenty-eight years. In terms of economic influence alone, Shakarian estimated that the cumulated wealth of the FGMBFI executive board was in excess of $200,000,000.[122] On April 29, 1980, at least 200,000 people gathered for "what was then the largest ever political gathering of born-again Christians."[123] While the FGBMFI estimated that the event drew as many as 700,000 participants, news media reports of the event gave more conservative estimates based on information given by the National Park Service.[124]

The rally was seen as a high-water mark in the quest for inter-denominational cooperation but it also came about just one year after the Christian Right became openly organized.[125] The rally also created the establishment of 380 organizing offices in most United States Congressional Districts, creating a ready made structure for political activism.[126] In addition, the event drew severe criticism from some religious groups such as the National Council of Churches who called the event an "arrogant attempt to press one group's religious views on the Government and other people."[127] In response to the criticism, the organizer of the rally, John Gimenez, said "It's almost like no one believes a group of Christians can come (to Washington) with a proper motive…We came to pray."[128] Demos Shakarian added "we went there to pray for our nation…believing God would hear our prayers."[129]

After the success of this rally, another rally was planned on the West Coast in Pasadena, California in the Rose Bowl on October 3, 1980.[130] Other rallies were also held in Chicago, Illinois; St. Louis, Missouri; and Miami, Florida earlier that same year. A FGBMFI member, Peter Congelliere (1921–2007), chaired the event in California and Demos Shakarian was one of the primary speakers. However, invitations for Jerry Falwell (1933–2007) and several United States Senators to speak at the rally were rescinded after the political overtones of the Washington for Jesus Rally were heavily criticized.[131]

In late 1982, Shakarian was invited to the White House in Washington, D.C., and James Watts, Secretary of the Interior, personally expressed his gratitude towards Shakarian and the FGBMFI for influencing his life and allowing him to come to a Christian conversion experience at a regional FGBMFI convention in Washington, D.C. while he was a young legislative aide.[132] Watts spoke at the FGBMFI World Convention in July 1983 delivering a jingoistic address he titled "Battle for America."[133] Among other things, Watts stated "How appropriate that we who have committed our lives to Christ also rededicate ourselves to America."[134] Watts spoke again at the FGBMFI World Convention in July 1984 in Anaheim, California, and *Voice* magazine featured a cover story on James Watts which was the largest printing of *Voice* in its history.[135]

Paul Gifford suggested that the FGBMFI not only promoted political conservatism through speakers such as James Watts but also promoted the militaristic goals of some Republicans and supported the military industrial complex through their association with such prominent FGBMFI members as Sanford McDonnell (1922–), chairman of the board for McDonnell Douglas.[136] In support of this thesis, General John Vessey, Jr., Chairman of the Joint Chiefs of Staff, (1922–) spoke at a FGBMFI banquet in San Antonio, Texas, on March 17, 1984, suggesting that people should consider military duty as a method of avoiding the "sinful nature... sinful nature is the cause of war and requires nations be strong."[137]

Nevertheless, the political preference of the FGBMFI or Demos Shakarian was never exclusively Republican during the Reagan era of the 1980s. In many regions of the United States and other parts of the world, invitations from the FGBMFI were extended to politicians regardless of their political persuasion. Politicians were especially welcome to speak at FGBMFI conventions and banquets if they had a testimony; that testimony was received with enthusiasm if a particular politician expressed his own experience with Charismatic Christianity. On August 12, 1983, Kentucky Governor Julian Carroll (1931–) a Democrat, spoke at the FGBMFI Kentucky Regional Convention and later wrote an article in *Voice* sharing his testimony of Charismatic Christian experience in March 1984.[138] In addition, after the 1980 Washington for Jesus Rally, the FGBMFI and Demos Shakarian were careful to avoid public partisan political controversy. They were already facing enough internal challenges within the Charismatic movement by this time that further controversy seemed frivolous and excessive.

The Struggle with the Shepherding movement

An issue that caused a certain amount of confusion and consternation in the FGMBFI was the Shepherding movement of the 1970s and 1980s. In early 1975, Demos Shakarian and the FGBMFI executive board formally decided to reject the teachings of the Shepherding movement and the leaders who espoused and directed it.[139] Initially, Shakarian welcomed the leaders of the movement and invited them to be guest speakers at conferences and conventions. As early as 1963, Derek Prince (1915–2003) was already a popular speaker at FGBMFI conventions and banquets, and Prince wrote a featured article in *Voice*.[140] Charles Simpson (1937–) and Bob Mumford (1930–) were both featured speakers at the FGBFMI World Convention in Miami, Florida, from July 3–8, 1967.[141] However, as early as 1970, Demos Shakarian expressed some concern to Charles Simpson about the loose knit association even before it became a formal Shepherding movement.[142]

In fact, by nature, Shakarian was rarely, if ever, critical of another organization or individual in ministry. Yet ultimately, the Shepherding movement violated at least one of the primary mores of the FGBMFI and, as such, Shakarian defended his organization against what he perceived as a growing threat to the FGBMFI and the future of the Charismatic movement.[143] Until the emergence of the Shepherding movement, the Full Gospel Business Men were the avatars of the burgeoning Charismatic movement and *Voice* magazine was their oracle. Suddenly, a new organization was not just competing with the FGBMFI, but this new organization was experimenting with a new form of ecclesiology that threatened to unravel the ecumenical ethos of the Charismatic renewal.[144] For various reasons, the Shepherding movement actually did begin to siphon off or divert the growth of the Charismatic movement away from the FGBMFI, and even away from the variety of churches both Pentecostal and neo-Pentecostal that had successfully harnessed the energy of the Charismatic renewal at its height.

Just as important, the leaders of this movement were encouraging people to tithe to their emerging, independent cell-based churches, and they were discouraging them from donating to most of the healing evangelists and television evangelists that the FGMBFI frequently endorsed and featured in their conventions and on their "Good News" television programming. In particular, Kathryn Kuhlman and Pat Robertson both felt the monetary diversion of the Shepherding movement most acutely.[145] Pat Robertson, in particular, became the most vocal opponent of the Shepherding movement. Frequently and with vitriol, he protested against the teachings of the Shepherding leaders.[146]

Various leaders in the Charismatic movement attempted to stop any further misunderstanding, confusion, or division caused by the Shepherding movement and called for a meeting between leaders of the Shepherding movement and other leaders in the Charismatic movement in order to provide an opportunity for reconciliation between the various factions of the broader Charismatic movement. Thirty-eight leaders met in Oklahoma City, Oklahoma, for five days in March 1976, in an effort to heal the rift between the two movements.[147] Noticeably absent from those meetings were Demos Shakarian and Pat Robertson.[148] In addition, Pat Robertson found an important ally in Demos Shakarian. Robertson barred the leaders of the Shepherding movement from the 700 Club and the Christian Broadcasting Network. Shakarian followed suit by not only banning the Shepherding leaders and their teachings from any local FGBMFI chapter or regional convention meeting, but he also threatened to revoke the charters of any local chapters that continued to endorse the Shepherding movement.[149]

While Shakarian's edict against the Shepherding movement was followed by a majority of FGBMFI members and chapters in North America, his ban was not followed unanimously. Certainly members of both the FGBMFI and the Shepherding movement had to make a decision to stay in one organization and leave the other.[150] As early as 1983, North American membership in the FGBMFI had stalled, and in 1984, for the first time, membership actually decreased.[151] Accordingly, the FGBMFI headquarters in Costa Mesa, California, reduced their staff from one hundred to seventy-five full time employees in 1984.[152]

With growth in the FGBMFI lagging in North America, Shakarian and the executive board considered other options for growth. As early as 1979, with the success of Women's Aglow, the FGBMFI began to reconsider the exclusion of women as members of the organization. However, the executive board was only willing to consider the creation of an auxiliary ministry because as Shakarian explained, "If we have women equal with men in the fellowship with full rights, I think women will dominate the fellowship because men are timid."[153] Eventually, an auxiliary ministry called "Ladies of the Fellowship" was instituted as part of the functional ministry of the FGBMFI.

To what extent the controversy surrounding the Shepherding movement or the exclusion of women actually affected this decrease in FGBMFI membership in North America is unknown. Although these were critical factors, they were not the only ones that led to decline and fluctuation within the FGBMFI. Some losses in the FGBMFI occurred from attrition and the aging population of members in North America. As growth in North America peaked in the early 1980s, one of the most important losses the FGBMFI faced was the death of Lee Braxton, one of the founding executive board members of the FGBMFI, on November 18, 1982.[154]

Ever Expanding Circles

In spite of these set backs and lagging growth in North America, the FGBMFI continued to create new venues of ministry and penetrate untapped arenas of the business world and society in general. One example was a new publication issued in 1975 called *Convicts for Christ* in which Shakarian and the executive board began to advocate a new emphasis upon prison ministry.[155] By 1982, the FGBMFI had established nineteen chapters in North American prisons.[156] Also in 1982, a Braille edition of Shakarian's autobiography was published through the generous efforts of FGBMFI members in New Zealand.[157]

The FGBMFI continued to use unique methods of evangelism to get their message across, such as the riders in 1982 who carried packets of *Voice* magazines while following the pony-express route from St. Louis, Missouri, to Sacramento, California.[158] The sixty-nine chapters in North and South Carolina sponsored a float in the Carolina's Christmas Carousel and handed out 10,000 copies of *Voice* to parade watchers in December, 1983.[159] Occasionally, the FGBMFI invited unorthodox guests to speak at chapter meetings and conventions such as Larry Flynt (1942–), publisher of *Hustler* magazine, who spoke at a FGBMFI rally in Montgomery, Alabama, in November 1977, accompanied by Ruth Carter Stapleton.[160] By June 1981, the FGBMFI announced it had exceeded 2,300 chapters.[161] In addition, business men in the organization had infiltrated a wide variety of sociologic and economic groups in North American society with their full gospel Christian message. These groups included prostitutes, pimps, Wall Street executives, homeless children, convicts, and even pornographers.[162]

Shakarian also continued to emphasize and encourage the participation of lay ministry as the FGBMFI vacillated and variegated in the 1970s and 1980s. Upon visiting a FGBMFI convention in Auckland, New Zealand, Shakarian retold his experience of praying for an older Jewish man in Jerusalem in 1961. Shakarian explained, "Unlike men with the specific gift of healing, I had not sought the experience. I had not spent hours and days fasting and preparing myself. The best I'd be able to tell the people in Auckland is that healing is one of the normal functions of the Body of Christ."[163]

At the July 1980 FGBMFI World Convention in Anaheim, California, Shakarian modeled this mantra of personal participation in the charismatic gift of healing while Ralph Wilkerson (1927–) was conducting healing prayer meetings. Shakarian was not satisfied with sitting on the sidelines. He prayed with the sick and participated actively in the healing ministry alongside Wilkerson.[164] Later that same year, Shakarian visited a hospital in December 1980 on behalf of one of his friends and competitors in the dairy industry, Norm Frost (1916–2007). Frost's grandson Sam was seriously ill with health complications resulting from Reyes Syndrome. Shakarian prayed for the young boy and Sam's convulsions stopped, and later he regained his appetite. The boy was able to go back to school and eventually became "a straight A university student and a computer wiz."[165]

After these experiences with the charismatic gift of healing, in 1982 Shakarian began to encourage FGBMFI chapters to initiate local and regional laymen's healing and evangelistic crusades without the assistance of healing evangelists to pray for the sick. While Shakarian still relied on well-known healing evangelists to draw crowds at the larger annual FGBMFI conventions, he insisted that business men were just as capable of praying for the sick, and Shakarian continued to publicly pray for infirmed and ill individuals at regional, national, and international conventions that he attended.[166] In addition, Shakarian encouraged business men in his organization to express other charismatic gifts such as prophecy by reminding them how prophecy had led Shakarian and the FGBMFI thus far.[167]

In spite of lagging growth in North America, in July 1982, Shakarian announced that the FGBMFI exceeded 2,646 chapters with 700,000 people attending weekly meetings. The majority of chapters were still in the United States with 1,800 chapters, but the organization had now spread to seventy-seven nations with the second and third largest concentrations being in Europe and

Canada respectively.[168] By the end of 1982, Shakarian estimated there were at least 3,000 FGBMFI chapters worldwide.[169] At the FGBMFI World Convention in Detroit, Michigan, in July 1983, 15,000 people attended the meetings each night, and over 2,000 individuals experienced Christian conversion throughout the entire conference.[170]

At the 1983 FGBMFI World Convention, Shakarian and the international directors adopted a five year plan of reaching every nation on earth by 1988 by enlisting an army of 1,000,000 Spirit-filled lay men and establishing 40,000 FGBMFI chapters in that same time period.[171] As some popular eschatologists began to predict that the parousia would occur by 1988, this was not likely a random timetable, but an eschatological mandate that Demos Shakarian and the international FGBMFI directors initiated to reach the world with the gospel of Jesus Christ before the end of that decade.[172]

Another speaker at that Detroit convention in 1983, John Wimber (1934–1998), spoke about the next wave of revival that would sweep through seminaries, universities, and upper society, thus foretelling the impact of an emerging neo-Charismatic movement which had already begun to appear in the early 1980s.[173] At the same time, Wimber recognized the significance of the past twenty-five years of Charismatic renewal in which he estimated two hundred million people had been influenced by the movement or identified with it.[174] Wimber, Shakarian, and other participants at this conference all sensed, implied, or stated that God was bringing one last great global renewal before the parousia, and they believed they were going to be a part of it.[175]

At the end of the July 1983 Detroit conference, the participants publicly celebrated with Demos and Rose Shakarian in anticipation of their fiftieth wedding anniversary on August 6, 1983.[176] A second milestone that occurred at this time was the birth of Demos Shakarian's one and only grandson, Steven Shakarian, Jr.[177] Demos and Rose Shakarian realized they had a lot to be thankful for as they gathered later that year with their extended family at Christmas for a tranquil holiday celebration. The Shakarian family gathered at what once was Isaac Shakarian's farm home in Downey, California. Shakarian helped decorate the home and his wife cooked seasonal Armenian dishes. They mixed their traditional family decorations with Christmas decorations they had accumulated from the many countries they had visited on behalf of the FGBMFI, and the living room was filled with greeting cards from friends around the world.[178] As the extended family gathered on Christmas Eve, they exchanged gifts and sang Christmas carols, and Shakarian told the Christmas story to his children and grandchildren. Demos and Rose Shakarian typically also invited people who would otherwise be alone on Christmas to join them for their Christmas festivities.[179]

After a quiet ending to 1983, on February 2–4, 1984, Shakarian met with the FGBMFI executive committee and the international directors in Dallas, Texas and they proposed ideas and goals for completing their five year plan instituted in July 1983. A separate national constitution and by-laws for the United States FGBMFI was adopted and approved, and ambitious benchmarks for growth were set for nations and continents over the next four years.[180] The Canadian FGBMFI set one of the most aspiring goals by calling for 10,000 new members and 1,000 chapters of the FGBMFI in Canada by 1988.[181] The FGBMFI also began having executive leadership training seminars, beginning in January 1984, at their international headquarters in Anaheim, California, to meet their five-year goals. Demos Shakarian and his son Steve were very involved in the planning and implementation of these seminars.[182]

In spite of these ambitious plans, March 1984 brought two major setbacks to the FGBMFI. On March 4, 1984, Miner Arganbright, one of the last surviving members of the original FGBMFI board of directors, died. Shakarian delivered the eulogy at his friend's service.[183] It was the last time most FGBMFI members or executive board members would see Shakarian publicly for four months because the same edition of *Voice* also carried some tragic news about the founder of the FGBMFI.[184]

Conclusion

From 1975 until 1984, the FGBMFI saw unprecedented growth and influence. Demos Shakarian's autobiography and his nationally syndicated television program made him a recognizable figure in North American culture. With Shakarian as the president of the FGBMFI, the organization became a force to be reckoned with in the 1970s and 1980s.

Shakarian retired from the dairy business in 1972 and sold his farm and ranching property in 1978 so he could devote more of his time to promote the organization he founded in 1951. While he remained in business as a property owner and landlord, he spent the remainder of his life speaking on behalf of the FGBMFI and working as an ambassador for the Charismatic movement. As the FGBMFI continued to expand internationally, Shakarian and the executive board saw fit to invest in a facility that could symbolize their influence and evangelistic efforts and coordinate their efforts in promoting the Charismatic movement and global evangelism.

As their chapters multiplied and their financial largesse expanded, the FGBMFI also drew the attention of politicians. Perhaps politicians and Demos Shakarian both saw benefits in their affiliation, as politicians sought elected office and the FGBMFI sought new converts and new evangelistic fields. Nevertheless, Demos Shakarian and the FGBMFI began to receive criticism for their affiliation with various politicians in the United States and internationally. While Shakarian attempted to remain non-partisan and non-sectarian in his evangelistic efforts, inevitably, his association with a wide range of political leaders and his participation with gatherings such as the Washington for Jesus Rally generated criticism about the FGBMFI and Shakarian's motives.

Nevertheless, Shakarian's personable nature and irresistible charm brought him before people to whom even the most powerful politicians rarely, if ever, had access. His expertise and financial acumen as a business man allowed him to introduce the FGBMFI to societies and nations that restricted or completely excluded any other Christian expressions or ecclesiologies.[185] Shakarian's optimism and his leadership allowed the FGBMFI to penetrate segments of society that were ignored or overlooked by church men and business men alike.

However, the Shepherding controversy winnowed away some FGBMFI membership in North America, and the exclusion of women from FGBMFI membership prevented the possibility of any expansion beyond the male gender. Unfortunately, the vision of Shakarian and his eschatological mandate would not allow him to see the financial reality of numerical decline in the United States. Finally, in early 1984, Shakarian was forced to significantly reduce the staff at the FGBMFI headquarters.[186] However, that was a minor problem compared to the challenges and realities that the FGBMFI were about to face as Demos Shakarian drove down a Southern California freeway in January 1984.

Notes

1. Demos Shakarian, "Refired – Not Retired," *Voice*, May 1978, 23.

2. See ibid, 23, for an example.

3. Demos Shakarian's father, Isaac, served from 1952 until his death in 1964 as pastor of the Armenian Pentecostal Church. (Jeff Janian, *God at Our Side*, DVD, 2005). Of the other pastors who served at First Armenian Pentecostal Church in its 100 year history, only one, Harding Mushegian, did not serve for life, but he might have been considered only an interim pastor at the time. (Harding Mushegian-Tallman interview, January 14, 2008; and Darlene Janoian-Tallman interview, January 13, 2008).

4. Kenneth A. Briggs, "Religion is Now an Important Part of Business," *The New York Times*, May 11, 1975, E10.

5. Demos Shakarian-Synan interview, February 2, 1988, 16; and John Dart, "Group Pushes Prison Program," *Los Angeles Times*, July 10, 1982, B5.

6. Demos Shakarian-Synan interview, February 2, 1988, 16–17; and John Dart, "Group Pushes Prison Program," *Los Angeles Times*, July 10, 1982, B5.

7. Demos Shakarian, "Victory Through Obedience," *Voice*, November 1977, 16.

8. "Lynnwood Church Plans Move to Downey Story," *Los Angeles Times*, May 30, 1976, SE4.

9. "Pastor Jeff Johnson and Calvary Chapel of Downey," Downey Calvary Chapel, http://www.ccdowney.com/church_info/history.html (accessed November 6, 2008); and Mark Maciel and J. Jacquart, *The Seeker: Jeff Johnson's Search for the Clear Light* (Costa Mesa, CA: Calvary Chapel Publishing, 2005), 159–162.

10. "The Long Awaited Personal Story of Demos Shakarian," *Voice*, November 1975, 20–21.

11. "The Happiest People on Earth," *Voice*, March 1980, 16; Demos Shakarian, foreword to Synan's, *Under His Banner* (1992) 8; and "The Demos Shakarian Story," *Voice*, October 1993, 10.

12. "Shakarians Honored at International Breakfast in Anaheim, California," *Voice*, March 1976, 38.

13. Ibid.

14. *Voice*, March 1976, 39.

15. *Voice*, February 1977, 30.

16. Demos Shakarian, *Life Lifters* (1984), 1:5.

17. Demos Shakarian, *The Happiest People* (1975), 101.

18. Demos Shakarian, "Divine Fire," *Voice*, May 1975, 7–8.

19. Demos Shakarian, "Love is the Answer," *Voice*, December 1978, 6–7.

20. Demos Shakarian-Synan interview, October 5, 1987, 7.

21. Russell Chandler, "Gospel Fellowship Draws Charismatics," *Los Angeles Times*, July 5, 1975, A27.

22. "Dateline: World Report," *Voice*, January 1976, 15.

23. "Dateline: World Report," *Voice*, January 1976, 16.

24. *Voice*, April 1976, 11.

25. "Dateline: Fellowship Highlights," *Voice*, November 1976, 39.

26. *Voice*, June 1975, 23; also see "Good News America – Display Ad," *New York Times*, December 2, 1975, 79; and "Good News America – Display Ad," *The Washington Post*, December 2, 1975, C6.

27. Russell Chandler, *Los Angeles Times*, July 3, 1975, C1.

28. Ibid, C2.

29. Russell Chandler, "No 'Second Miss Kuhlman' Apparent," *Los Angeles Times*, March 1, 1976, C1.

30. "Its Time to Pray, America – Display Ad," *The Washington Post*, September 17, 1976, B9.

31. "Thanksgiving Telethon – Display Ad," *Los Angeles Times*, November 14, 1976, B31.

32. "FGBMFI Dateline," *Voice*, July/August 1978, 11.

33. Russell Chandler, "Crusaders Look to Heavens: Space Race on to Broadcast Gospel via Satellites," *Los Angeles Times*, March 11, 1978, A23.

34. Demos Shakarian, "Love is the Answer," *Voice*, December 1978, 6–7.

35. Ibid.

36. "FGBMFI Dateline," *Voice*, January 1979, 18.

37. "Australians Launch Good News," *Voice*, March 1977, 10.

38. "Update," *Voice*, September 1982, 24.

39. "FGBMFI Captures Coveted Awards," *Voice*, July/August 1983, 28; and "Man to Man," *Voice*, June 1983, 7.

40. *Voice*, March 1975, 38; and Demos Shakarian, "100 Men and God," *Voice*, May 1975, 31.

41. Russell Chandler, "Gospel Fellowship Draws Charismatics," *Los Angeles Times* July 5, 1975, A27.

42. See http://www.fgbmfi.org.au for Australian office; http://www.fgbmfi.org.ca/ for Canadian office; http://www.fgbmfi.or.id/national.php for Indonesian office; http://www.fgb.com.my/ for Malaysian office; http://www.fgbmfi-nigeria.org/ for Nigerian office; and http://www.fgbmfi.org.uk for the offices in the United Kingdom. There are numerous other offices that could be mentioned in this study if time and space allowed including the Rwandan office. (Nkusi Sebujisho Josiah-Tallman interview, July 26, 2005). Josiah started an office in 1998 in Kigali, just four years after the FGBMFI started its first chapter in Rwanda in 1994.

43. "Dateline: World Report," *Voice*, April 1976, 10.

44. "The Fellowship in Europe," *Voice*, September 1976, 20–21.

45. Display Ad, *Los Angeles Times*, July 18, 1975, C8.

46. "Dateline: World Report," *Voice*, January 1976, 15.

47. "Dateline: World Report," *Voice*, May 1976, 10.

48. Demos Shakarian, "More Precious than Gold," *Voice*, March 1976, 24.

49. Ibid, 25–26.

50. Carol McGraw, "The Keys to Success: An Unlimited Partner," *Los Angeles Times*, July 8, 1982, OC-C1A.

51. Gifford, *The New Crusaders* (1991), 35.

52. "Faith through Fate," *Voice*, November 1979, 18–20.

53. John Dart, "Full Gospel Fellowship Will Dedicate Building," *Los Angeles Times*, January 26, 1980, B2.

54. Synan, *Under His Banner* (1992), 112.

55. Demos Shakarian, "Dark Horizons," *Voice*, January 1979, 3–7, 12.

56. Fotherby, *The Awakening Giant* (2000), 101–102; and Demos Shakarian, "Dark Horizons," *Voice*, January 1979, 4.

57. Demos Shakarian, "Dark Horizons," *Voice*, January 1979, 5–6.

58. "FGBMFI Dateline," *Voice*, February 1979, 15.

59. Ibid.

60. "The Shadows in Guyana," *Voice*, July/August 1979, 2, 6; *Voice*, September 1979, 18; and Demos Shakarian, *Life Lifters* (1984), 2:15 and 55.

61. "The Shadows in Guyana," *Voice*, July/August 1979, 2, 6; *Voice*, September 1979, 18; and Demos Shakarian, *Life Lifters* (1984), 2:15 and 55.

62. "FGBMFI Dateline," *Voice*, November 1978, 12; and "FGBMFI Dateline," *Voice*, February 1979, 30.

63. John Carrette, "Equipping for Action," *Voice*, May 1981, 7.

64. John Dart, "Religion Notes: Churches Plan Relief Aid to Guatemala," *Los Angeles Times*, October 23, 1982, B4.

65. Gifford, *The New Crusaders* (1991), 56.

66. Richard Shakarian-Tallman interviews, January 10, 2005 and January 16, 2008; and David Stoll, *Is Latin America Turning Protestant? The Politics of Evangelical Growth* (Berkeley, CA: University of California Press, 1990), 226.

67. Stoll, *Is Latin America Turning Protestant?* (1990), 224–230.

68. Richard Shakarian-Tallman interview, January 16, 2008.

69. Stoll, *Is Latin America Turning Protestant?* (1990), 228–229.

70. Myra MacPherson, "The Pulpit and the Power: '700 Club's Pat Robertson, Preaching Gospel and Eyeing the White House," *The Washington Post*, October 18, 1985, D1.

71. Jerry Jensen, *FGBMFI 1988–89 World Chapter Directory* (1989), 52.

72. Gifford, *The New Crusaders* (1991), 56.

73. Demos Shakarian, *The Happiest People* (1975), 151.

74. Bruce Horovitz, "Business Group has Investment with the Lord," *Los Angeles Times*, July 4, 1984, OC-CA.

75. Demos Shakarian, *The Happiest People* (1975), 151–152.

76. "FGBMFI Dateline," *Voice*, January 1979, 18.

77. "Dateline," *Voice*, December 1979, 24–25.

78. "Conventions," *Voice*, May 1980, 14.

79. John Dart, "Full Gospel Fellowship Will Dedicate Building," *Los Angeles Times*, January 26, 1980, B2.

80. "Singapore Convention," *Voice*, October 1982, 16.

81. Demos Shakarian, "Coming Together," *Voice*, September 1982, 17–18.

82. "World Strategy," *Voice*, July/August 1983, 27.

83. "FGBMFI 1st Jerusalem Regional Convention and Holy Land Pilgrimage October 15–25, 1976," *Voice*, June 1976, 38.

84. Synan, *Under His Banner* (1992), 106; also see David Barrett, "A Chronology of Renewal in the Holy Spirit," in *The Century of the Holy Spirit: 100 Years of Pentecostal and Charismatic Renewal*, ed. Vinson Synan (Nashville, TN: 2001), 431; and consult Barrett's *World Christian Encyclopedia* (2001).

85. Fotherby, *The Awakening Giant* (2000), 181–182; also see Demos Shakarian, "The World Changers," *Voice*, May 1980, 2.

86. Demos Shakarian, "The World Changers," *Voice*, May 1980, 2.

87. Demos Shakarian, "Together," *Voice*, February 1981, 14; and Demos Shakarian, *Life Lifters* (1984), 2:27–28.

88. "New FGBMFI World Headquarters Site and Building Approved in 2nd Historic Director's Meeting in Chicago, May 1–3," *Voice*, September 1975, 37.

89. "Escrow Closes on New Headquarters Location," *Voice*, November 1975, 36.

90. "International Headquarters Moves to Temporary Site," *Voice*, July/August 1976, 10.

91. "The Word is out to Grow," *Voice*, November 1976, 20–21.

92. "Founder's Circle Plan Formulated for Funding New Headquarters," *Voice*, September 1977, 10.

93. Ibid, 11.

94. "Construction of World Layman's Headquarters to Begin Soon," *Voice*, October 1977, 10.

95. Ibid, 11.

96. "Dateline: World Headquarters," *Voice*, April 1978, 13.

97. "FGBMFI Dateline," *Voice*, June 1978, 15.

98. "1978 World Convention and Silver Anniversary Celebration," *Voice*, September 1978, 24.

99. "FGBMFI Bible Correspondence Course," *Voice*, October 1978, 15.

100. "FGBMFI Dateline," *Voice*, November 1978, 12.

101. "FGBMFI Dateline," *Voice*, February 1979, 15.

102. "Dateline," *Voice*, June 1979, 14; Demos Shakarian, *Life Lifters* (1984), 3:30; and Steve Shakarian, "Ministers in the Marketplace," *Voice*, June 1981, 25.

103. "Dateline," *Voice*, July/August 1979, 19.

104. John Dart, "Full Gospel Fellowship Will Dedicate Building," *Los Angeles Times*, January 26, 1980, B2.

105. "Dateline," *Voice*, December 1979, 25.

106. "Could You Benefit from an Income Deduction? God Needs 1000 Partners," *Voice*, December 1985, 27.

107. "The Dedication in God's Tears," *Voice*, May 1980, 14–17; and John Dart, "Full Gospel Fellowship Will Dedicate Building," *Los Angeles Times*, January 26, 1980, B2.

108. "A Spiritual Cape Canaveral," *Voice*, July/August 1981, 24.

109. "Old Fashioned Faith," *Voice*, May 1976, 17–19, 22.

110. Don Smith, "Doubleheader Debate Scheduled," *Los Angeles Times*, October 9, 1976, OC11.

111. "FGBMFI Dateline," *Voice*, January 1979, 18.

112. "Regional Convention Highlights," *Voice*, July/August 1977, 37.

113. Raymond Becker, "Voice Editor Interviews Ruth Carter Stapleton," *Voice*, September 1977, 37.

114. Ibid.

115. One example of this non-partisan approach already mentioned occurred during the 1972 residential campaign between Richard Nixon and Eugene McGovern when Shakarian suggested that the FGBMFI had already declared which candidate they would endorse in the presidential race: "Jesus Christ." (Demos Shakarian, "Your Vote is Important," *Voice*, November 1972, 9).

116. Roxana Shakarian Vahan, "Letter to the Editor 10," *Los Angeles Times*, July 10, 1978, C6.

117. Russell Chandler, "Roberts Describes Power of God's Will," *Los Angeles Times*, July 15, 1978, A28–29.

118. "Washington for Jesus," *Voice*, February 1980, 10.

119. Marjorie Hyer, "Evangelistic Leaders Plan Rally to Draw Million Followers Here," *The Washington Post*, February 17, 1980, B8.

120. John Dart, "Group Pushes Prison Program: Business Men's Fellowship Adds Convicts to Ranks," *Los Angeles Times*, July 10, 1982, B4.

121. "Washington for Jesus," *Voice*, July/August 1980, 24.

122. "The World Changers," *Voice*, May 1980, 2.

123. Sara Diamond, *Not by Politics Alone: The Enduring Influence of the Christian Right* (Guilford Press: New York, 1998), 68.

124. "Washington for Jesus in '88," *Voice*, March 1988, 27; and Penny Girard and Sean Dunnahoo, "Christian Rally Draws 200, 000," *Los Angeles Times*, April 30, 1980, A17.

125. Sara Diamond, *Roads to Dominion: Right Wing Movements and Political Power in the United States* (Guilford Press: New York, 1995), 175.

126. Ibid, 233.

127. "Religious Rally on Mall in the Capital Draws Support and Criticism: Political Focus Denied Organizers are Listed," *New York Times*, April 27, 1980, 64.

128. Penny Girard and Sean Dunnahoo, "Christian Rally Draws 200, 000," *Los Angeles Times*, April 30, 1980, A17.

129. John Dart, "Group Pushes Prison Program," *Los Angeles Times*, July 10, 1982, B4.

130. "Southern California America for Jesus Rally – Display Ad," *Los Angeles Times*, October 2, 1981, F16.

131. John Dart, "Rose Bowl's 'America for Jesus' Rally Avoids 'Political' Tag," *Los Angeles Times*, October 3, 1981, B4.

132. "Update," *Voice*, April 1983, 26.

133. James G. Watt, "Battle for America," *Voice*, October 1983, 2–7.

134. Ibid, 3–4.

135. "The 31st World Convention," *Voice*, September 1984, 16–17; and Jerry Jensen interview with Vinson Synan, Costa Mesa, CA, February 15, 1992, 17.

136. Gifford, *The New Crusaders* (1991), 56; also see *Voice*, August 1986, 3–9 for McDonnell's featured testimony.

137. Chuck Conconi, "Personalities," *The Washington Post*, March 19, 1984, C3.

138. "Kentucky Regional Convention," *Voice*, November 1983, 30; and Juliann Carroll, "The Fifty-Fourth Man," *Voice*, March 1984, 2–6.

139. Vinson Synan, *Under His Banner* (1992), 136; and David Moore, *The Shepherding Movement: Controversy and Charismatic Ecclesiology* (New York, NY: T&T Clark International, 2003), 91–92. Moore's text in particular, offers the most comprehensive analysis of the Shepherding movement and gives complete details about the many

connections and leaders who were involved in both the FGBMFI and the Shepherding movement.

140. Derek Prince, "I Wanted to Find My Solution to Life's Problems," *Voice*, June 1963, 22–25.

141. "1967 FGBMFI Convention July 3–8, Miami, Florida," *Voice*, June 1967, 20.

142. Charles Simpson phone interview with David Moore, February 5, 1996 as cited in Moore's *The Shepherding Movement* (2003), 32.

143. Throughout the history of the FGBMFI, Demos Shakarian repeatedly emphasized that the FGBMFI did not exist to create new churches or encourage people to leave churches, but rather encouraged people to remain in their respective churches as a pneumatic witness of their own Charismatic experience (see Demos Shakarian, "We are not Interested in Starting New Churches," *Voice*, November 1974, 29–30). Even as early as 1962, Shakarian recognized how this stance helped enhance rather than hinder the burgeoning Charismatic renewal (see *Voice*, November 1962, 19). Perhaps his admonition was partially influenced by the suspicions of Demos Shakarian's Pentecostal clerical peers; these same pastors often speculated whether the FGBMFI was trying to create its own church.

144. The concept of this experimental ecclesiology is best explained in David Moore's *The Shepherding Movement: Controversy and Charismatic Ecclesiology* (New York, NY: T&T Clark International, 2003). In particular, chapter four of his work most succinctly describes this experiment and the growing suspicion of Demos Shakarian and the FGBMFI towards this ecclesiological enterprise. Moore offers the only thorough examination of the Shepherding movement to date. While he proposes the formulation of this experiment in ecclesiology, he does not necessarily propose that it was a threat to the Charismatic renewal or its ecumenical influence. However, he does agree that Demos Shakarian *perceived* the Shepherding movement as a threat to the growth and influence of the Charismatic movement.

145. David Moore, *The Shepherding Movement* (2003), 106–111.

146. See ibid, 99–124.

147. Russell Chandler, "Charismatics Close 'Shepherding' Gap," *Los Angeles Times*, March 20, 1976, A26.

148. Ibid.

149. Moore, *The Shepherding Movement* (2003), 106–108. Moore suggests that Shakarian's concern may have been prompted by financial concerns of FGBMFI members who were redirecting the majority of their funding away from the FGBMFI and towards Shepherding leaders.

150. Ibid, 107–108. Moore cites John Heard, a Houston attorney and FGBMFI member, who wrote Demos Shakarian about his concerns in 1975. Other FGBMFI members shared Heard's concern, especially after the Odessa-Midland chapter of the FGBMFI in West Texas had its charter revoked in 1976.

151. See Steve Shakarian, "Organizational Assessment," *Voice*, November 1984, 4. In the spring of 1982, Shakarian estimated that the number of chapters in the United States was at an all time high of 1,800 chapters (see Demos Shakarian, "A Prophecy Fulfilled," *Voice*, July/August 1982, 20), but by the end of that year, the organizational estimates were tempered by a more precise estimate of 1,677 chapters in the United States (see "Update," *Voice*, December 1982, 31).

152. Bruce Horovitz, "Business Group has Investment with the Lord," *Los Angeles Times*, July 4, 1984, OC-CA.

153. John Dart, "Group Pushes Prison Program," *Los Angeles Times*, July 10, 1982, B5.

154. "The Braxton Story," *Voice*, July/August 1983, 33.

155. "FGBMFI Prison Ministry Magazine 'Convicts for Christ,'" *Voice*, December 1975, 27; and John Dart, "Group Pushes Prison Program," *Los Angeles Times*, July 10, 1982, B4–5.

156. John Dart, "Group Pushes Prison Program," *Los Angeles Times*, July 10, 1982, B4.

157. "Happiest People in Braille," *Voice*, September 1982, 25.

158. "FGBMFI Riders on Horseback," *Voice*, October 1982, 31.

159. "Update," *Voice*, December 1984, 33.

160. Jennings Parrott, "Newsmakers," *Los Angeles Times*, November 21, 1977, C2.

161. Steve Shakarian, "Ministers in the Marketplace," *Voice*, June 1981, 25.

162. Ibid, 26.

163. Demos Shakarian, "The Golden Chain," *Voice*, October 1976, 22–23; and Demos Shakarian, *The Happiest People* (1975), 162–165.

164. "By My Spirit," *Voice*, September 1980, 14.

165. Norman Frost, "The Missing Ingredient," *Voice*, December 1982, 6; Demos Shakarian, *Life Lifters* (1984), 2:28–29; and Demos Shakarian, "Will God Provide," *Voice*, January 1988, 4.

166. Demos Shakarian, "A Prophecy Fulfilled," *Voice*, July/August 1982, 18–20.

167. Ibid.

168. Demos Shakarian, "A Prophecy Fulfilled," *Voice*, July/August 1982, 20.

169. Demos Shakarian, *A New Wave of Revival: The Vision Intensifies* (Costa Mesa, CA: FGBMFI, 1992), 9.

170. "Detroit 83," *Voice*, September 1983, 23.

171. Ibid.

172. Ibid. See Hal Lindsey, *Planet Earth – 2000 A.D.: Will Mankind Survive?* (Palos Verdes, CA: Western Front, Ltd., 1994), 143–144. Lindsey had previously predicted that the parousia would occur a generation after the establishment of the state of Israel, roughly calculating Christ's return around the year 1988 in his best selling book, *The Late Great Planet Earth*, 2nd edition (Grand Rapids, MI: Zondervan, 1977). Also see Edgar Whisenant's *The Rapture: Rosh Hash Ana, 1988, and 88 Reasons Why* (Little Rock, AR: Whisenant, 1988), 34 for the boldest prediction that Jesus would return between September 11–13, 1988.

173. Ibid. Also see David Barrett, "Appendix: A Chronology of Renewal in the Holy Spirit," in Vinson Synan's *The Century of the Holy Spirit: 100 Years of Pentecostal and Charismatic Renewal* (Nashville, TN: Thomas Nelson Publishers, 2001), 429, 438 for further explanation regarding when the neo-Charismatic movement began. Although Barrett suggested that the origins and earlier manifestations of this later renewal movement began as early as 1656, 1783, and 1937, (429) he mentioned that it formally began in earnest in 1980 (438). In addition, Barrett proposed that all three Pentecostal, Charismatic, and neo-Charismatic movements are collectively three waves of one broader cohesive movement of Spirit renewal within Christianity for the past 450 years (393).

174. Ibid. Also see David Barrett's *World Christian Encyclopedia* (2001) for a more accurate estimate of how many people had been impacted by the Charismatic movement by 1983. Although Barrett gave no precise figures for 1983, by 1970, Barrett estimated that the total number of participants who had been impacted by the Pentecostal, Charismatic, and neo-Charismatic movements was approximately 72,000,000. By the time of Barrett's

publication of his encyclopedia in 2001, he estimated that number had increased to 523,000,000.

175. Ibid.

176. Ibid.

177. Geri Scalf-Tallman phone interview, August 25, 2008.

178. Demos Shakarian, "Christmas – A Reminder," *Voice*, December 1981, 12.

179. Demos Shakarian, "Christmas Tradition," *Voice*, December 1980, 13.

180. "Encouraging Growth Noted," *Voice*, May 1984, 25.

181. Ibid.

182. "Update," *Voice*, May 1984, 27.

183. "The Man Who Changed His Mind," *Voice*, June 1984, 12.

184. "For Immediate Release," *Voice*, June 1984, 19.

185. David Barrett suggests that by 1986, the FGBMFI had already gained access to such restricted nations as Russia and Czechoslovakia, and it was perhaps the only expression of Christian faith in countries such as Saudi Arabia at that time. (David Barrett, "A Chronology of Renewal in the Holy Spirit," in Vinson Synan's *The Century of the Holy Spirit* (2001), 431.

186. Bruce Horovitz, "Business Group has Investment with the Lord," *Los Angeles Times*, July 4, 1984, OC-CA.

Chapter Eleven

The Denouement and Death of Demos Shakarian (1984–1993)

In early 1984, at the age of seventy, Demos Shakarian was apparently healthy, and the FGBMFI was larger and more influential than ever. He had retired from the dairy business, but he remained active in property investments, purchasing, leasing, and selling property to provide for his family. With the additional free time during his retirement years, Shakarian remained consumed with growing and expanding his original vision for the FGBMFI as an international ministry that would reach the world with the Christian gospel before the parousia. However, in March 1984, Shakarian's life was unexpectedly altered by a stroke that left him physically and spiritually changed for the rest of his life.

Demos Shakarian's Stroke

Driving home on a Los Angeles freeway in January 1984 with his wife Rose, Shakarian temporarily lost his vision. Rose asked her husband to pull the car over to the emergency lane on Interstate 605, and they briefly prayed for Shakarian's condition. Rose drove the remainder of the journey home, and she insisted that Shakarian undergo a thorough physical examination the next day. Unfortunately, the stroke he suffered was not immediately diagnosed by the doctor. However, friends and co-workers noticed that Shakarian seemed confused at times and occasionally his judgment was halted or slightly impaired.[1] Two months later, Demos Shakarian was seated at home reading an edition of the *Golden Wheat* series from his former mentor Charles Price when he collapsed, unconscious in his black chair in the den.[2] Rose Shakarian called 911, and paramedics rushed her husband to the hospital on March 26, 1984.[3] Shakarian had symptoms of a progressive stroke on the left side of his body. Ultimately he suffered a series of three strokes as he was rushed to Daniel Freeman Memorial Hospital in Inglewood, California. After assessing the serious nature of his condition, the hospital sent Shakarian to the UCLA Medical Center in Los Angeles, California for emergency surgery to remove an obstruction from his right carotid artery.[4] He was only given a fifty percent chance of surviving the procedure.[5]

After recovering from surgery, the FGBMFI reported that Shakarian's intellect and speech control centers were unaffected by the stroke.[6] While slowly recuperating from surgery, Shakarian received a note from his granddaughter Renee suggesting that God had his purposes in the circumstances that Shakarian was facing and that God still desired to use him.[7] The note encouraged Shakarian, and he was released from the hospital on April 21, 1984, and sent to a Southern Californian rehabilitation center for physical therapy.[8]

Shakarian then began to go through physical therapy, but at his lowest point of despondency, he was wheeled into a physical therapy group session where a group of disabled stroke victims gathered in a circle of wheelchairs and shared their feelings. Shakarian did not want to participate, but in the midst of his discouragement and depression an African-American woman in the support group began to sing "Pass me not, O gentle Savior."[9] The woman's song lifted Shakarian out of his depression, and soon he was asked to pray for other sick individuals in the hospital. This became a source of encouragement to him as he interpreted his stroke as God's way of "pruning him to bear more fruit."[10]

In vintage Full Gospel fashion, the men of the fellowship continued to regularly pray for Shakarian's healing and recovery. Every time the men of the fellowship prayed for him, his family and friends declared that he would improve.[11] By May 10, 1984, Shakarian was beginning to walk without the aid of a cane.[12] He remained lucid, alert, and active in the fellowship even though his diminished physical capacity reduced his ability to travel abroad.[13] Thomas Ashcraft fulfilled Shakarian's duties as head of the FGBMFI while Shakarian recuperated from his stroke and surgery.[14] However, perhaps one of his greatest disappointments about his physical limitations was his inability to walk upstairs and serve his wife coffee in bed as he had been accustomed to doing for over fifty years.[15]

A few months later, from July 3–7, 1984, the FGBMFI celebrated its thirty-first annual world convention in Anaheim, California featuring speakers such as James Watt, Paul Crouch, Sir Lionel Luckhoo, James Robison (1943–), R.W. Schambach (1926–), and of course, Oral Roberts.[16] Even with such popular speakers, the high point of the annual convention was when Demos Shakarian walked onto the platform with his arm lifted in victory with Rose by his side. He gave a short speech on the future of the FGBMFI, reminding the business men and various participants in the audience of the original vision of the FGBMFI to reach a lost world.[17] It was the first time that most of the audience had seen Shakarian since his stroke, and they gave him an enthusiastic and prolonged standing ovation.[18] At the end of the convention, Oral Roberts asked Shakarian, his wife, and his three children to come to the podium; Roberts conferred an honorary Doctor of Law degree from Oral Roberts University upon Shakarian.[19]

After his stroke and his rapid recovery, Shakarian reflected upon his past thirty-three years with the FGBMFI and his recent experiences in the hospital, and he became a prolific writer over the next eight years. He began with a three volume inspirational and devotional book titled *Life Lifters*.[20] In 1987, Shakarian wrote a book titled *An Unexpected Miracle* in which he reflected upon his experience in the hospital and the theological implications of understanding human suffering when prayer does not bring an immediate response.[21] Shakarian also wrote *God's Answer to Twenty Tough Questions* (n.d.), a brief ethical and theological treatise on Shakarian's opinions regarding suffering, depression, finances, miracles, stress, and homosexuality.[22] Other books soon followed including *Behold the Glory of God* (1988), *The Ultimate Dimension* (1988), *Divine Life* (1991), *Come Let Us Exalt Him* (1992), *A New Wave of Revival: In Your Finances* (1992), and *A New Wave of Revival: The Vision Intensifies* (1992).[23]

Success Breeds Competition

The size of the FGBMFI began to decline in the United States early in 1984.[24] By 1989, the organization had lost at least 10,000 members in North America from a peak of over 43,000 to approximately 33,000 registered participants in the FGBMFI.[25] However, the organization continued to grow internationally as did the Charismatic movement. One reason for the decline in North America was the symbiotic relationship between the FGBMFI and the Charismatic movement. Peter Hocken (1932–) suggested that the Charismatic movement in America had peaked in the early 1980s thus confirming a parallel relationship of growth and decline between the two movements.[26] Nevertheless, there were a variety of factors responsible for the decline beyond this symbiotic relationship between the FGBMFI and the Charismatic movement.

Some of the fluctuation in growth was possibly due to the increasing popularity of specialized Christian business fellowships including the Fellowship of Christian Airline Personnel, the Christian Legal Society, and the Christian Medical Society.[27] These were specialized Christian business organizations that appealed to a particular targeted constituency. While their specialized nature limited their growth, these organizations were extremely effective at harnessing loyal membership within their respective fields. However, the FGBMFI often effectively countered this type of competition by creating auxiliary ministries under the auspices of the FGBMFI such as "Peace Officers for Christ" which focused on connecting with people in law enforcement.[28]

Some sources cited the growth of popular competing groups like the Promise Keepers as another reason for the decline of the FGBMFI.[29] The Promise Keepers started in 1990 under the leadership of Bill McCartney (1940–) and excelled at harnessing men into large gatherings and conventions in public sports arenas and stadiums throughout America. In 1996, they had gathered 1.1 million men at twenty-two stadium events.[30] The group reached its apex with a Stand in the Gap rally at the Washington Mall on October 4, 1997. While there are no precise measurements of how many men attended this rally, it was estimated that at least hundreds of thousands gathered at the Mall in one of the largest rallies recorded in United States history, and it certainly exceeded the Million Man March that occurred two years earlier on the Mall.[31]

It is likely that some of the Promise Keepers' broad appeal developed from its name and its leadership which came from a broad spectrum of scripturally oriented ecclesiologies including many Pentecostal and Charismatic groups while the FGBMFI, because of its name, tended to attract a more Charismatic constituency. In addition, the racial diversity of its leadership helped attract a more multiracial constituency in many parts of the country.[32] Unfortunately, the organization ran into financial trouble in 1998, and consequently, several hundred employees of Promise Keepers were laid off.[33] The organization continues to operate stadium events and smaller venue endeavors; however, it only managed to operate seven major stadium events in 2007.[34] While the Promise Keepers likely took away attendance from many FGBMFI conventions in the United States in the 1990s, Promise Keepers has never gained the international recognition or success that the FGBMFI has achieved over the past fifty years. In addition, while the Promise Keepers was enormously successful at large scale stadium events, it failed to organize or galvanize the support of men or churches on a smaller scale. In contrast, the FGBMFI relied upon their chapter meetings as a core aspect of their growth and structure in a variety of venues and settings.

However, one final arena of competition would erode the effectiveness and growth of the FGBMFI in many parts of the world. This challenge came from the local churches with whom Demos Shakarian and the FGBMFI had vowed never to compete.[35] Pastors from these churches began to recognize that the FGBMFI was meeting a niche in the Christian community that local churches were neglecting, and so churches all over the United States established men's ministries to help fill that gap.[36] Unfortunately, the success of the FGBMFI was its own downfall, as the organization had effectively trained hundreds of thousands of laymen all over the world for decades about the practical aspects of ministry. Consequently, thousands of these same men eventually decided to close or sell their businesses and launch their own churches.[37] These same churches and their pastors emphasized and included men's ministry as a prominent part of their programming.

Other Challenges for the FGBMFI

In addition to the competition the FGBMFI faced in the 1980s and 1990s, other challenges may have contributed as much or more to their decline. Some of the controversial people that Shakarian associated with may have contributed to the deterioration or decline of the fellowship. Of course, Shakarian had associated with a number of controversial communist leaders and tyrants such as François Duvalier and Fidel Castro. However, the diversity of political leaders he associated with probably did not contribute to the decline of the organization. Actually, Shakarian's association with this diverse collection of political leaders may have actually added to his appeal. As he suggested, his intentions in associating with these leaders were not politically motivated but were merely in the interest of obeying and expanding the vision he had received.[38]

However, Shakarian's association and friendship with some of the evangelists that the FGBMFI sponsored and promoted may have helped lead to the decline of the organization. While Shakarian was a very discerning person with excellent business instincts, he occasionally had a lapse in judgment with evangelists he sponsored. In his own autobiography, he offered a glaring example of one such scoundrel, which left an indelible mark on his memory. Shakarian did not reveal the name of the evangelist, but rather called him "Bob Smith".[39]

Perhaps Shakarian's own trusting, gentle nature overcame his discernment at times, as this was not the only time he encountered and associated with controversial individuals, some of whom were also proven to be scoundrels.[40] Although William Branham was certainly not a scoundrel, he was controversial. His character or his ethics were never in question, but his predictions of the parousia, his Oneness theology, his angelic visitations, and his followers who made his prophetic utterances sacerdotal made him controversial in many Christian circles.[41] Nevertheless, Branham's healing crusades were extremely popular and influential during the 1950s and early 1960s before his death in 1965, and Shakarian admired his life and ministry.[42] In addition, even though Shakarian and Branham admired each other, Branham's premature death in 1965 from a car accident probably was too early to have any negative effect on Shakarian or his contribution to the Charismatic movement.

However, this was not the case with Oral Roberts. Obviously, the close relationship and respect that Roberts and Shakarian had for each other has been documented. Both of these men made enormous contributions to the burgeoning Charismatic renewal, but it is possible that Robert's vision of a 900 foot Jesus in 1977 or certainly Roberts' fundraising death proclamation might have tarnished the image of both their ministries.[43]

Nevertheless, the controversy surrounding Oral Roberts was relatively insignificant compared to the downfall of Jim Bakker (1940–) and Jimmy Swaggart (1935–) in 1987 and 1988 respectively. Newspapers and tabloids throughout the United States and the world caught hold of their salacious stories and ran headlines of their escapades for years.[44] While Shakarian had no formal ministry relationship with Jimmy Swaggart, he was on the board of the *PTL Club*. That, coupled with his relationship with Jim Bakker, may have damaged the image of the FGBMFI.[45] More importantly, the downfall of these two televangelists sent a chilling blow to the Charismatic movement globally. Their scandals were most devastating in North America; although the newly emerging neo-Charismatic or Third Wave movement was able to distance itself internationally from Swaggart and Bakker.[46]

Financial challenges also beset the FGBMFI as membership declined in North America. The revenue the FGBMFI received in 1988 had decreased thirty percent in two years.[47] In 1987, Shakarian pledged "to increase and intensify" his personal ministry to members of the FGBMFI. He established an initiative in 1984 called the "120 Club" to improve communication with his constituency. In addition, the club was initiated to help increase financial revenue that had declined with falling membership. For a donation of ten dollars every month, each member of this club received a monthly audio-taped message from Shakarian, and he promised to read the prayer requests of club members and pray for the members and their requests on a regular basis.[48]

An earlier initiative, called the "International 1,000 Club" was designed to provide a nucleus of 1,000 men who could each give $1,000 to support the FGBMFI and eliminate their debt load. As people signed up to become members of this club, they received a certificate and a fourteen carat gold lapel pin. Ironically, in 1985, *Voice* tried to promote this initiative by advertising a display ad titled "Could You Benefit from an Income Deduction?"[49] While they meant to suggest the advantages of receiving a tax deduction for their gifts to the FGBMFI, the organization was beginning to feel the further effects of a reduction in income. To exacerbate financial problems within the FGBMFI, Abraham Boldt (d.b.a. 1940–), a FGBMFI member and popular speaker within the organization, was involved in a Ponzi scheme which conned at least 600 investors from various churches and FGBMFI chapters in the United States out of over $10,000,000.[50]

Facing a severe financial deficit, the FGBMFI was forced to sell some of its properties in 1987 and 1988 in order to remain solvent.[51] The FGBMFI also attempted to raise additional income by featuring a variety of products in *Voice*. In 1991, a Christian trivia board game called "Move by Faith" was advertised in *Voice* for $15.95.[52] The display ad in *Voice* advertised the game by suggesting, "When you move by faith the Scriptures come alive!"[53] In 1992, the FGBMFI featured a more traditional product: a fortieth anniversary FGBMFI pocket planner for $4.95.[54]

In spite of financial decline in the ministry, Shakarian's diminished physical capacity suffered after his stroke, and medical bills incurred from his hospitalization and rehabilitation, Shakarian felt very blessed in his business and his personal finances. During the 1980s, Shakarian received most of his income from leases on commercial property he owned and the sale of other properties he had previously purchased. In 1987, he sold some property in Fontana, California, for $1.8 million, and he estimated that he was netting $18,000 every month in lease and rental payments from other properties that he owned.[55] At the end of 1990, Shakarian claimed "God shows me what property to buy, how to handle my deals. I am better off than I was years ago."[56]

The FGBMFI also faced sociologic and economic challenges beyond their control in the 1980s. By 1980, the labor force growth rate in the United States marketplace had peaked, and it began to decline for the first time since WWII.[57] Consequently, the average worker began to work longer hours so that sixty-three percent of the workforce exceeded the forty-hour standard set by the Fair Labor Standards Act in 1938, and forty percent of the labor force in the United States began to work more than fifty hours per week by 2000.[58] The reduction of leisure time for workers and professional business men in the United States probably contributed to the decline in FGBMFI membership in the United States. In addition, the amount of leisure time available for the typical laborer in the United

States was significantly less when compared to nations in Europe, Asia, Latin America, and Africa.[59] This fact may have helped sustain and continue growth in the FGBMFI internationally. Nevertheless, Shakarian recognized this sociological trend early in the 1980s, and he was concerned about declining FGBMFI membership in the United States. In the *1983 FGBMFI Chapter Manual*, he encouraged chapters to keep guest speakers limited to thirty minutes for lunch and dinner meetings.[60]

The FGBMFI also faced several theological challenges in the 1980s. For several decades, the organization had featured popular proponents of the prosperity gospel including Kenneth Hagin (1917–2003) and Kenneth Copeland (1937–). Both of these speakers were widely popular at FGBMFI world and regional conventions, but Shakarian challenged some of the teaching of the prosperity gospel by suggesting, "We do not serve a formula God. There is no place in scripture where it says, 'Give a dime and get a dollar,' but that's what is being taught."[61] He further added, "Our precious Heavenly Father is not some magical vending machine in the sky."[62] Instead Shakarian deftly proposed, "God makes many marvelous financial promises in Scripture for those who give to His purpose, but none of these promises will ever be fulfilled when they are taken out of the context of relationship."[63] Nevertheless, in spite of Shakarian's disagreements with the leading proponents of the prosperity gospel, he recognized their popularity within the organization and invited Kenneth Hagin to be a featured speaker at the 1987 and 1992 World Conventions.[64]

However, the FGBMFI faced a more serious theological challenge in 1986. At one of the FGBMFI international directors' meetings, a heated debate ensued on whether or not the FGBMFI doctrinal statements on the initial evidence of glossolalia should be removed or restated. Pentecostal traditionalists in the organization and many Charismatics insisted on keeping the statement intact because of their experience of receiving glossolalia during Spirit baptism and their theological emphasis upon the need to express glossolalia in their meetings. However, many neo-Charismatics and other Charismatics in the meeting debated whether the doctrine was necessary or biblical.[65] Ultimately, the traditionalists prevailed in the meeting, and the doctrine of initial evidence remained intact as part of the theology and praxis for the FGBMFI. However, it is probable that this theological challenge led to later schisms within the FGBMFI.[66]

The FGBMFI also faced a political challenge in the 1980s when one of their members had presidential aspirations. Pat Robertson's presidential ambitions brought some focus to the FGBMFI and the Charismatic movement when he began to explore the possibility of running for political office in 1985.[67] In particular, a video tape of Pat Robertson speaking at the twenty-eighth annual FGBMFI World Convention in Philadelphia, Pennsylvania, in July 1981 was a popular topic in some political circles that wanted to portray Robertson as a charismatic mystagogue and a Pentecostal preacher.[68] However, Robertson's political advisers attempted to distance themselves from what they considered a narrow, stereotypical portrayal of Robertson. Instead, they emphasized that he was "a man of great depth."[69]

As a FGBMFI member, former chapter president, and featured speaker in the organization, Robertson was a popular candidate among FGBMFI constituents. Chapter presidents and members became involved in Robertson's campaign as precinct party chairmen and volunteers for his campaign.[70] Some pundits suggested that the Republican Party in the Reagan era attempted to keep the Religious Right content but unobtrusive.[71] However, Robertson was no longer content with sitting on the back pew of the political scene. Robertson invited his friend Demos Shakarian to Virginia Beach, Virginia, in early 1987, and he asked Shakarian what he thought about his running for the President of the United States. Shakarian said he did not have any prophetic word or sense of God's providence in the matter, but he assured Robertson that he would pray for him.[72]

While Shakarian and Robertson considered each other allies and friends in the Charismatic movement, Shakarian did not openly endorse Robertson's campaign. It is plausible that Shakarian avoided official approval of his friend's political ambitions because of his concern for the non-profit status of his organization, but it is possible that two other reasons motivated Shakarian. Robertson was traditionally a pre-millennialist, but his dispensational pessimism was muted by his optimistic musings as a post-millennialist who "was convinced that Christians can change the world" as he prepared for his presidential aspirations in the 1980s.[73] In contrast, Shakarian was a pre-millenialist who believed that terrible suffering and tribulation would come upon the earth before the parousia.[74] In spite of theological differences, Shakarian may have been more motivated by the possibility of alienating members of the FGBMFI whose politics deviated from the platform of the Religious Right. Nevertheless, Demos Shakarian and the FGBMFI were willing to take that risk as they invited Pat Robertson and Kenneth Hagin to be featured speakers at the July 1987 FGBMFI World Convention in Anaheim, California.[75]

Schism within the Full Gospel family

While a variety of factors and challenges may have contributed to declining membership in the United States within the FGBMFI, internal conflicts caused as much or more decline as any other factor. After Shakarian had his stroke in 1984, the board decided to temporarily install executive vice president Thomas Ashcraft as acting president until Shakarian recovered.[76] The temporary change in power within the FGBMFI seemed to work well. After all, Demos Shakarian trusted Ashcraft implicitly and considered him one of his closest friends.[77] However, some tension between Shakarian and the FGBMFI executive board began to develop when Thomas Ashcraft began to develop health problems and Ashcraft asked Norman Norwood (d.b.a. 1930–) to complete his term as acting executive vice-president of the FGBMFI in January 1987.[78] In May 1987, at a FGBMFI board meeting at the Hilton Hotel in Chicago, Illinois, Thomas Ashcraft and other

FGBMFI leaders, including Norman Norwood, Lynwood Maddox (d.b.a. 1938–), and Gerald Walker (1925–2005), felt Shakarian was incapable of leading the organization due to his diminished health and the decreased size of the FGBMFI in the United States. They said that the board wanted Shakarian to resign, and Norman Norwood volunteered to replace Shakarian as president of the organization.[79] The board even offered Shakarian a salary of $60,000 to remain as chairman of the board with no acting power. However, Shakarian refused their retirement package because his health was stable, and he had never accepted a salary from the organization.[80] In spite of their efforts, the international directors unanimously re-elected Shakarian as the president of the FGBMFI at the world convention in Anaheim, California in July 1987.[81] However, they also voted for Norman Norwood to begin a new term as executive vice-president of the FGBMFI by a narrow margin. In addition, the international directors voted to create a corporation called the FGBMFI, U.S.A. as a separate entity from the FGBMFI.[82]

Perhaps the person who hurt Shakarian the most was Tommy Ashcraft because Shakarian considered him one of his dearest friends. However, any animosity or misunderstanding between Shakarian and Ashcraft was short-lived as Ashcraft passed away on September 1, 1987.[83] Indeed, before Ashcraft died, Jimmy Rogers heard Tommy encourage others to continue following Shakarian and not bring further division to the FGBMFI.[84] As Ashcraft lay dying on a hospital bed, that appeal for unity went unheeded when the FGBMFI, U.S.A. called for a special meeting of the executive board at 9:00 A.M., August 22, 1987 at the Marriott Hotel in St. Louis, Missouri. At the meeting the board agreed to transfer all funds and assets of the international FGBMFI to the FGBMFI, U.S.A. As a result, Demos Shakarian and the international board of directors for the FGBMFI no longer had control of the finances for the FGBMFI. In addition, a variety of financial questions and accusations at this meeting were directed against Demos Shakarian by Peter Taylor (d.b.a. 1935), the controller at FGBMFI headquarters.[85]

As a result of this meeting, Norman Norwood convened a special meeting of the FGBMFI executive board in Houston, Texas on October 3, 1987, and he charged Shakarian with financial irregularities for expenses he charged to the organization. Ironically, until his later years, Shakarian had not received reimbursements for the expenses incurred in almost three decades of travel.[86] Nevertheless, the board temporarily removed him as president of the organization until an investigation could be conducted. In particular, the investigation focused on $276,000 he supposedly received for benefits which should have been declared as taxable income.[87] Of this amount, $168,000 was received for unauthorized insurance benefits, and $108,000 was spent on undocumented travel and entertainment expenses.[88] The FGBMFI board's audit committee, headed by Gerald Walker, reported this income to the Internal Revenue Service.[89]

On October 10, 1987, the FGBMFI international board of directors met at FGBMFI headquarters in Costa Mesa, California, and ratified the decisions made by the executive board in St. Louis, Missouri, a week earlier.[90] The $168,000 in insurance benefits pertained to a $500,000 life insurance policy and a health insurance policy that the board had approved for Demos and Tommy Ashcraft in 1981. Ashcraft's policy was never enacted because he failed the medical exam, but Shakarian's policy was approved, and the health insurance policy became quite useful in 1984 when Shakarian's medical expenses dramatically increased due to hospital and medical costs as he recovered from his stroke.[91] The international board eventually agreed that Shakarian's insurance premiums paid for by the FGBMFI since 1981 had been authorized by the board.[92]

The question regarding the undocumented travel and entertainment expenses remained unresolved for more than a year. Some members who were supportive of Shakarian, such as Ronny Svenhard, admitted that Shakarian was not an administrator or an organizer by suggesting, "His head was in the clouds, but his feet were firmly on the ground."[93] Other executive board members who were not as supportive, such as Bill Weaver (1928–1998), stated that Shakarian's "bookkeeping is atrocious."[94]

The relationship between Demos Shakarian and his board continued to become increasingly acrimonious over the next few months. The board gave executive power for daily operations to executive vice-president, Norman Norwood, leaving Shakarian only as a spiritual advisor to the FGBMFI.[95] After this transfer of executive authority, Shakarian suspected that the headquarters building was bugged by his opponents on the executive board. Shakarian hired a company to investigate his suspicions, and evidence of electronic surveillance was found, but the investigation found no equipment used in the surveillance.[96] Shakarian also suspected that his controller, Peter Taylor, was conspiring to send confidential information to members of the FGBMFI executive board who were opposed to Shakarian's leadership.[97] Shakarian tried to fire Taylor, but the executive board did not allow Taylor's termination.[98]

During this time, Shakarian was also accused of sexual harassment by a female employee at FGBMFI headquarters in Costa Mesa, California.[99] Supporters of Shakarian and other employees at the headquarters office denied the charge and questioned the woman's sanity.[100] Shakarian insisted that he was a virgin before he got married and that he had never touched any woman except Rose after his marriage.[101] Although it was a topic of discussion among the executive board members, opponents of Shakarian apparently agreed that there was no substantiation to the woman's claim of harassment and never made any public accusations regarding this incident.[102] However, revenue at the FGBMFI headquarters in Costa Mesa, California, continued to decline, especially after the controversy and schism began in May 1987. FGBMFI, U.S.A., had already sold some of the assets of the organization, and now they were considering selling the headquarters building in Costa Mesa and moving the FGBMFI headquarters to Texas.[103]

Demos Shakarian was devastated, discouraged, and disoriented over the treatment he received after thirty-six years of sacrifice to the organization he founded. In 1988, he and the FGBMFI were also under tremendous financial pressure as membership in the United States dropped from a high mark of 43,000 and revenue declined by $2.5 million dollars in the previous two years.[104] Two leaders in the Charismatic movement, Jack Hayford (1934–) and John Wimber (1934–1998), came into Shakarian's office on separate occasions to encourage him to stop worrying about the assets of the ministry and focus on the ministry that God had given him.[105] At one regional FGBMFI convention in Joplin, Missouri, Shakarian sought solace and comfort from a Full Gospel Business Man named John Schmook (d.b.a. 1924–), sitting down in his hotel room and praying with him. Schmook said Shakarian wept profusely for at least twenty minutes, and the two shared a cathartic experience, even if Shakarian was still discouraged.[106] It took another prophetic word to release Shakarian from his despondent state and gain the encouragement he needed to recapture the vision he had received thirty-six years earlier.[107] Even though the controversy was not over, Shakarian was now convinced that "God is going to bring good out of this. He's already made me a better man because of the fire I've been through. He has me at a place I can hear His voice. The important thing is not to become bitter, because bitterness can control your life."[108]

In July 1988, a few days before the next FGBMFI world convention, Shakarian drove to the headquarters office in Costa Mesa, California, and knelt in prayer on the old Turkish rug where he had received his original vision early in the morning of December 27, 1952. Shakarian asked for God's guidance and God's help to enable him to complete the vision God had given him thirty-six years earlier.[109] While the executive board was divided and some political infighting took place, at the closing banquet of the Toronto Convention, July 9, 1988, Shakarian was once again re-elected as president, and he gave a challenging message on forgiveness, dedication, and opportunity. Gene Ellerbee (d.b.a.1935–) was voted in as the new executive vice president, replacing Norman Norwood in that office.[110] Shakarian prayed with members, weeping in the arms of FGBMFI directors such as Gene Arnold (d.b.a. 1935–) as the convention concluded, sensing that the emotional ordeal was nearly over.[111]

However, matters were still not concluded until the executive FGBMFI board convened a special meeting of international directors from Friday, January 27 until Sunday, January 29, 1989, in Palm Springs, California.[112] At first the group was deeply divided, and out of concern, Shakarian stated, "We are on the brink of a split."[113] However, on the last day, Mark Bellinger presented a box of documents and receipts that he said accounted for all but $6,000 of $108,000 in missing travel expense receipts. Bill Moretti (d.b.a. 1945–), a former tax accountant, was at the meeting and said he had reviewed the contents of the box and confirmed Bellinger's suspicions that Shakarian had been wrongly accused.[114] Bellinger's evidence was convincing enough that seventy-nine members of the board voted to exonerate Shakarian of any financial improprieties.[115] Bellinger further explained that the box of missing receipts was given to him by an assistant to Peter Taylor, the FGBMFI controller. The assistant claimed she was instructed by Taylor to hide the receipts, but she eventually felt remorse after receiving a prophetic word from a friend at her church, so she surrendered the materials to

Bellinger.[116] Peter Taylor denied these allegations, but he was accused of purpose-fully undermining Shakarian's credibility and promptly dismissed from his employment with the FGBMFI.[117]

Not everyone on the board agreed with Mark Bellinger's presentation or the assessment of Shakarian's innocence as seventeen members voted against Shakarian's innocence and two members abstained.[118] Treasurer Gerald Walker stated that he felt "very badly about the whitewashing of...Demos without any documentation. He will have to answer to God and to the IRS, not necessarily in that order."[119] Norman Norwood defended his actions by stating that he was sim-ply trying to bring some stability back to the FGBMFI "but when you have a fel-low who is a founder of a thing and it's religious, people look to him as a kind of deity."[120] Consequently, other significant leadership changes took place on the FGBMFI executive committee as Hank Lackey (d.b.a. 1935–) replaced Lynwood Mattox as secretary, Ronny Svenhard (d.b.a. 1942–) replaced Gerald Walker as treasurer, and Reginald Elliott (1946–2006), Carlin Nash (d.b.a. 1929–), and Jimmy Rogers (d.b.a. 1940–) were added as members of the executive board.[121] At the national convention for the United States FGBMFI in Nashville, Tennessee, from July 4–8, 1989, the remaining dissenters, nearly one-third of the international directors, were removed from the FGBMFI board, and the FGBM-FI, U.S.A. corporation was dissolved and all assets relinquished to the interna-tional FGBMFI.[122]

In 1990, some questions and discussion began regarding the possibility of succession, and Gene Ellerbee's position and respect within the FGBMFI made him the most likely candidate to replace Shakarian as president of the organiza-tion.[123] However, as a result of this controversy, Shakarian's son, Richard, lobbied for a change in the by-laws that would allow Shakarian to serve as president for life.[124] In addition, true to his nature, Demos Shakarian openly forgave his board for temporarily removing him, even if many of his constituents disagreed with his gracious attitude.[125] Nevertheless, several key members on the executive board of the FGBMFI resigned or were removed after Shakarian was found innocent of these charges, and they immediately started a competing organization called the International Fellowship of Christian Businessmen (IFCB). Ultimately, many of the international directors who were dismissed by the FGBMFI became involved in the new competing organization.[126] This organization adopted several key ideas and strategies of the original fellowship including airlifts, conventions, chapter meetings, and the value of testimonies. However, they did not include any refer-ences to Demos Shakarian, his vision, or his legacy in the formation of their organization.[127] While this organization never came close to rivaling the size and influence of its parent organization, the IFCB currently retains headquarters in Tulsa, Oklahoma and has had some success in establishing chapters in South America, particularly Columbia.[128]

In the aftermath of this schism, United States membership continued to decline, and the organization went further into debt.[129] Some further discussion ensued regarding the possibility of selling the international headquarters in Costa

Mesa in order to relieve the debt. One interested buyer was a well known Christian author and radio talk show host, Hank Hanegraaf (1950–), but Richard Shakarian opposed selling the property to an individual with such an anti-Charismatic position, so he began potential negotiations with other potential Charismatic leaders such as Roberts Liardon (1966–) and Paul Crouch.[130] In addition, Steve Shakarian resigned his position as chief executive officer of the FGBMFI international headquarters and moved to Tulsa, Oklahoma, in 1991.[131] At the 38th annual FGBMFI World Convention in Orlando, Florida, only 3,500 members attended the conference in spite of speakers such as Mario Murillo (d.b.a. 1950–), Oral Roberts, Dick Mills (d.b.a. 1932–), and Marilyn Hickey (1931–).[132]

A New Anointing

In spite of this domestic turbulence and decline, the FGBMFI continued to grow and expand internationally in the 1980s and 1990s. To accommodate this growth, the FGBMFI began to celebrate some of their annual world conventions in international locations. In October, 1984, the FGBMFI announced their 32nd annual world convention in Melbourne, Australia from March 26–30, 1985. Featured speakers included Demos Shakarian, Reinhard Bonnke (1940–), Jack Hayford (1934–), and Sir Lionel Luckhoo.[133] Crowds as large as 7,000 people attended the meetings every night, and over 5,000 participants sought Christian salvation or prayer by the end of the convention.[134] However, in order to accommodate their constituents in the United States, the FGBMFI celebrated their first annual national convention in Dallas, Texas, from July 2–6, 1985 where Shakarian, Bonnke, and R.W. Schambach were featured speakers.[135]

The FGBMFI continued to expand into new areas and new countries internationally in the 1980s. In 1985, the FGBMFI started a chapter in Leon, Nicaragua, while a team of FGBMFI members did some outreach in Honduras and Nicaragua.[136] This country's openness to the FGBMFI had been precipitated by the gift of a prize bull that Shakarian had given one of the Nicaraguan government leaders.[137] Humberto Aguilar (d.b.a. 1950–) first participated in a FGBMFI world convention in Rio de Janeiro, Brazil, from August 29–September 2, 1989 as a representative from Nicaragua.[138] Aguilar's participation with the FGBMFI and Shakarian's gift helped launch what would become the most successful FGBMFI program per capita in any nation in the organization's history.[139]

Shakarian also continued to interact with heads of state internationally after his stroke. In February, 1985, Shakarian and the FGBMFI sponsored a head-of-state banquet in Los Angeles, California on behalf of King Taufa'ahau Tupou IV of Tonga (1918–2006). King Tupou was introduced to Spirit baptism through a FGBMFI team that had visited the island in November 1984.[140] In addition, King Tupou became interested in Christian spirituality through reading Shakarian's book and watching "Good News" television programs.[141]

In 1985, the FGBMFI launched a new television special called "Turning Point" and hosted by Pat Boone.[142] However, with declining revenues, this would be the last major television program that the FGBMFI produced in the 1980s.[143] Nevertheless, Shakarian continued to receive accolades as a leader in the Charismatic movement. In the fall of 1986, the North American Congress on the Holy Spirit and World Evangelism honored Demos Shakarian, David DuPlessis, and Oral Roberts for their role in initiating and leading the Charismatic renewal.[144]

Shakarian's stroke and the physical disabilities and weakness caused by his cerebrovascular accident in March 1984 did not deter him from remaining actively involved in the ministry of the FGBMFI nor did it discontinue his charismatic praxis of praying for the sick. In fact, after his stroke and for the remainder of his life, his supporters claimed that Shakarian received "a new anointing to pray for the sick."[145] This began at a FGBMFI convention from November 22–24, 1984, when Shakarian had his first full speaking engagement after his stroke and rehabilitation. The Southern California FGBMFI chapters gathered for their first regional convention in six years as Demos Shakarian spoke and ministered with a renewed emphasis upon prayer for the sick. Hundreds of members waited in line for hours to have Shakarian pray for them. The conference was so successful and demand was so great that another regional conference was scheduled for November 2005. One participant said, "Those who have known him for years agreed that they have never seen such an anointing upon Demos."[146] At the Phoenix Regional Convention from January 16–20, 1985, Shakarian stood on his feet for nearly three hours as he prayed for hundreds of people eager to receive a healing experience.[147]

At the Dallas National Convention in July 1985, Shakarian explained that there were two parts to the original vision of the FGBMFI. According to Shakarian, the first part of this vision included an outpouring of the Holy Spirit, but this would be followed by an outpouring of healing.[148] In 1986, Shakarian further explained that he was not referring to the vision he received in 1952 but rather to the prophecy that Charles Price had given to him at some point before Price's death in 1947. Shakarian further explained Price's prophecy by mentioning that a period of great spiritual revival led by healing evangelists would be followed by a period of spiritual renewal led by laymen who would pray for the sick.[149]

This renewed emphasis upon a new healing anointing continued into the early 1990s. In January 1991, Shakarian prayed for people several times during the FGBMFI Georgia Men's Advance. By popular demand, the advance was scheduled over two consecutive weekends as 3,000 FGBMFI members attended each conference and hundreds waited in line to be prayed for by Shakarian.[150] With this attention focused upon Shakarian's healing ministry, some leadership in the FGBMFI began to be concerned about inappropriate attention given towards him.[151] However, Shakarian never considered this healing anointing as something he innately possessed by his own power. Ultimately, Shakarian was reminded after forty years of leading the fellowship that "Nothing man could do made any difference. No amount of careful planning, enticements, or even personal effort could launch the fellowship…only God, and the power of His Holy Spirit, can make the fellowship alive and vital."[152]

In spite of schism and physical disability, with the encouragement of a new anointing and a resilient attitude, Shakarian estimated that there were 4,000 chapters in ninety-three countries by 1988.[153] With this surge in international growth, the FGBMFI held their 35th annual world convention in Toronto, Canada, in July 1988. Jerry Jensen estimated that ninety percent of the speakers at the convention were not from the United States.[154] In 1989, the FGBMFI held their 36th annual world convention in Rio de Janeiro, Brazil, from August 29–September 2.[155] The FGBMFI held a separate convention for members in the United States in Nashville, Tennessee from July 4–8.[156]

At the end of the 1980s, the international impact of the FGBMFI was staggering as the FGBMFI and its affiliated ministries estimated they had reached 1.5 billion people with their full gospel message.[157] In addition, the FGBMFI had six international regional offices and twenty-four national offices in Asia, Africa, Australia, South America, North America, and Europe.[158] This growth continued in 1990, when the FGBMFI calculated that it was in 106 countries and forty percent of the international directors were from outside of the United States.[159] At the end of 1991, the FGBMFI was in 112 countries.[160]

By 1992, significant growth was seen in some Asian nations such as Indonesia with eighty FGBMFI chapters, Malaysia with forty-one chapters, and the Philippines with thirty-two chapters.[161] The FGBMFI also continued to grow in Africa with 100 chapters in Zaire, 177 chapters in Nigeria, and 82 chapters in Ghana by 1992.[162] The President of Gabon was so concerned about rapid FGBMFI growth in his country that he temporarily banned the organization from Gabon fearing "they were becoming too powerful."[163] By 1993, Shakarian estimated that the FGBMFI was now active in 120 nations representing a forty percent increase in global representation within five years.[164]

In 1990, the movement went full circle when Demos Shakarian was invited to Armenia. In the 1950s, Shakarian had requested to visit the Soviet Union when the Armenian Anastas Mikoyan (1895–1978), Deputy Premier of the Soviet Union, was visiting the United States, but nothing came of Shakarian's request at that time.[165] However, as the iron curtain softened, and Armenia was on the brink of sovereignty, government officials from Armenia began to explore the possibility that Shakarian might come and help establish FGBMFI chapters and speak at a convention in the late 1980s.[166] In addition, a severe earthquake struck Yerevan, Armenia, in 1988, creating an immediate need for financial assistance and aid.[167] However, having suffered a series of strokes, Shakarian was not physically able to travel, and so in 1990, he sent his son Richard, along with Richard's wife Vangie, in his place.[168]

Eight other FGBMFI members accompanied Richard and Vangie, and upon arriving in Yeravan, they were allowed to speak to the entire nation on Armenian television.[169] In spite of the fact that the country was still under Communist rule, Richard's entourage was given royal treatment; meeting halls, stadiums, and arenas were offered to them free of charge. Richard requested the largest sports arena in the region, and on the first evening, May 27, 1990, he made reference to the prophetic words of Gregory the Illuminator, the ancient apostle of Armenia. Over 3,000 people were in attendance, and over half of them responded positively towards this invitation to become Christians. The National Guard of Russia, which had recently been sent to Armenia to provide aid after the earthquake, knelt down on the ground and wept. Red Army soldiers, still stationed in Armenia, laid down their weapons in the arena and lifted their hands towards heaven. In all, approximately 10,000 Armenians and Russians responded to Richard's gospel message that week, and several FGBMFI chapters were established in the country.[170] It was a marvelous sight and an enormous source of encouragement to both Richard and the ailing Demos Shakarian, as what had originally come from Armenia to America, what was spreading exponentially throughout the world, had now come full circle back to Armenia.

As Shakarian reflected on this incident, he saw that much of the world was changing in 1990. "This year has been a turning point for the entire world. We've been praying for years to see the Gospel go behind the Iron Curtain and suddenly...the walls have been coming down."[171] By 1992, with ten chapters in Armenia, ten chapters in Romania, ten chapters in Czechoslovakia, and twenty chapters in Hungary, the FGBMFI was opening a new chapter in Eastern Europe every week.[172] Even though Christ did not return in 1988, Shakarian speculated whether the socio-political events of 1990 might preclude the parousia. "We are entering into the last ten years of this millennium. Many Christians have looked for the coming of Christ at the end of this millennium."[173]

As Demos Shakarian perceived that the parousia was imminent, he started negotiating to see if he could acquire the unopened prophetic scroll written by Efim Klubnikin over a century earlier. Shakarian and others within the Armenian Molokan and Russian Molokan community believed that this second scroll, written by Klubnikin, was a prophetic document, revealing an oracle of eschatological judgment that could only be opened by an anointed prophet selected by God. The Molokan community also believed anyone else except the prophet attempting to open the scroll would die.[174] The scroll had been in the possession of the Klubnikin family for three generations, and Shakarian discussed the possibility of taking possession of the prophetic oracle for several years. Ultimately, the negotiations failed, and the scroll remained in the possession of Klubnikin's grandson.[175]

Nevertheless, even though the parousia did not come by the end of the millennium, time had already run out for some of Shakarian's closest friends and associates in the FGBMFI. Earl Prickett passed away on June 11, 1990.[176] He had spent most of the past thirty years travelling up and down the East Coast of the United States establishing over one hundred chapters of the FGBMFI.[177] Enoch Christoffersen passed away on October 10, 1990 after an extended illness.[178] He had helped establish many of the first international airlifts for the FGBMFI, paying his own expenses, and promoting new chapters throughout Asia.[179] On March 2, 1993, Thomas R. Nickel, the original editor of *Voice*, passed away.[180] By 1993, time was also running out for Demos Shakarian.

Wrapping up Demos Shakarian's Affairs

By 1993, Shakarian knew that his health was failing. In addition to the after effects of the stroke, his doctor informed him that he had prostate cancer and he was suffering from severe aortic stenosis. In 1992, his physician also told Shakarian that he had developed atherosclerotic heart disease.[181]

Even before 1992, Shakarian began to think about the process of succession in the FGBMFI. In preparation for the future, starting in 1990, Shakarian began grooming his oldest son Richard to lead the organization. Richard Shakarian began travelling more on behalf of the FGBMFI after the trip to Armenia. He was a featured speaker at a FGBMFI conference in Ireland in late 1990.[182] Richard also helped host two Armenian FGBMFI chapter presidents when they came to do a series of meetings in the United States in December 1990.[183] In addition, Richard Shakarian represented his father at a European tour of FGBMFI conventions and banquets in 1991 including a convention in Helsinki, Finland, and a banquet in St. Petersburg, Russia.[184] Richard also was a featured speaker at the eleventh annual FGBMFI Asian Convention in early 1992.[185]

In 1992, while considering the possibility of officially making his son Richard his successor, Shakarian went to see his pastor at the First Armenian Pentecostal Church in La Habra Heights, California. As they prayed about the future, Harding Mushegian began to deliver a prophetic utterance to Shakarian. In the prophecy, Harding told Shakarian, "If your legacy will continue, appoint Gene Scalf as your successor."[186] Both Mushegian and Shakarian were surprised by the pronouncement since Mushegian only knew Scalf as a distant acquaintance while Shakarian knew Gene Scalf as his son-in-law. Then Shakarian began to weep and rejected Harding's pronouncement as he explained that he had already decided who he was going to appoint, and he could not reject his son.[187] Whether the cultural dictates of appointing a first-born son, the natural affinity of a father for his son, the spiritual discernment of a charismatic leader, or a combination of those factors was involved in Shakarian's response to this prophetic pronouncement, ultimately, Shakarian tested and rejected the prophecy of his pastor.

The process of Richard's succession started becoming more apparent when a motion was made and accepted by the FGBMFI executive committee to accept Richard Shakarian and Ralph Marinacci (d.b.a. 1916–) as vice presidents on the committee at the 1991 FGBMFI World Convention in Orlando, Florida.[188] At the 39th annual FGBMFI World Convention in San Francisco, California, Richard's presence became much more noticeable as he prayed with people during healing and prayer services.[189] After the convention was over, one week later, 400 hundred people gathered at the Crystal Cathedral in Garden Grove, California, to celebrate Shakarian's seventy-ninth birthday. Rose, Richard, Steve, and Gerri joined with leaders of the FGBMFI to share in the festivities and letters were read from various national and world leaders congratulating Shakarian. At the end of the gathering, Shakarian officially announced that his son Richard would take his place as the new president of the FGBMFI.[190]

On December 24, 1992, Shakarian spent his final Christmas with his extended family. The family typically celebrated the holiday on Christmas Eve and sometimes including grandchildren and great-grandchildren, the crowd of family and relatives approached fifty. Shakarian greeted the family and doted over the grandchildren and great-grandchildren. Occasionally he teased the children by jokingly bulging out his eyes and contorting his face but always with a smile and a chuckle. Sometimes his facial contortions terrified the great-grandchildren, but Shakarian lured them back with a piece of candy or gum. The pile of Christmas presents for the children filled up the area around the tree and spilled out into half of the room as family gathered around the dinner table and partook of Armenian pilaf and *shakar lokoom*.[191] As the dishes were being cleaned up, Steve Shakarian, dressed as Santa Claus, gave out the presents to the children. Christmas caroling followed with Rose at the organ and Geri on the piano as they led the family in singing. Finally, Shakarian concluded the evening by retelling the Christmas story about the birth of Jesus, and he closed the festivities with a prayer.[192]

On January 23, 1993, Shakarian signed a succession agreement, leaving his son Richard in charge of the fellowship.[193] He continued to speak at meetings and conventions and in June 1993, he spoke at his last chapter meeting at Knott's Berry Farm. After eating one of their famous chicken dinners, Shakarian spoke and all eyes were on him. According to accounts of the evening, as he began to speak, he "looked like death warmed over, but, as he segued into his testimony, his face lit up like a candle as he regaled the men with stories from his own life."[194]

In early July 1993, Shakarian attended his final world convention in Boston, Massachusetts, celebrating the fortieth anniversary of the organization.[195] He was going to speak at the convention, but as the patriarch of the organization began his oracle, he halted, and said, "You've heard enough of me for forty years. Now you need to hear this guy."[196] Shakarian handed the microphone to Dave Duell (1944–2006), the guest speaker, and that was the last time the fellowship heard from him. At the end of the meeting, several men gathered around Shakarian to pray for him including Ron Weinbender (d.b.a. 1942–) and Shakarian's son Richard. As they prayed, Shakarian rolled onto the floor and lay as though he was "slain in the spirit" (a common manifestation or phenomenon in Charismatic and neo-Charismatic Christian services). His body began to shake, and he began to move his paralyzed right leg back and forth. Someone prophesied over him, saying, "You haven't crossed over the Jordan River yet, but you have seen the Promised Land."[197] His son Richard looked on and began to weep, sensing that Demos Shakarian was about to cross over.

Demos and Rose Shakarian came home from the convention, and he was thrilled about the souls that had been saved. However, Rose had a dream that something terrible was going to happen.[198] Nevertheless, Shakarian was more concerned about the fact that he had lost his wedding band at the convention, and he insisted that he and Rose go and buy a new ring since their sixtieth wedding anniversary was going to be in less than a month. They went to Tiffany's and bought a beautiful eighteen carat wedding band. After doing some additional shopping, they decided to eat at a local restaurant. While talking over dinner, Shakarian remarked, "I'm ready to go."[199] The next day, July 14, 1993, Shakarian felt weak and his family rushed him to Downey Community Hospital where he was diagnosed with acute subendocardial myocardial infarction.[200]

On July 21, 1993, Shakarian's eightieth birthday, his old mentor Oral Roberts and another friend, Ralph Wilkerson (1927–), came to the hospital and visited Shakarian. Shakarian could only acknowledge the presence of Roberts by squeezing his hand, and Oral prayed for his friend before they departed.[201] On July 23, 1993, Shakarian's vital signs began to deteriorate at about 3:00 PM.[202] The family gathered in the room to spend their last few hours with Demos Shakarian. Richard and Geri began to sing gospel songs as the grandchildren joined in.[203]

The Death of Demos Shakarian

Demos Shakarian died on July 23, 1993, at 9:00 PM from cardiogenic shock due to the myocardial infarction that had occurred nine days earlier and the atherosclerotic heart disease that had afflicted him for a year.[204] He was laid to rest at Rose Hill Cemetery in Whittier, California on July 28, 1993, and a memorial service was held at Calvary Chapel in Downey, California.[205] Interestingly, the church where the services were held existed on land formerly owned and operated by Reliance Dairies.[206] A young minister named Jeff Johnson needed more space for his rapidly growing congregation. so Shakarian sold the property to Calvary Chapel in Downey, California for a bargain price and even helped the young church remodel and refit the property to suit their church's needs.[207] On the old Reliance Dairy property nearly 1,000 family members, friends, and Full Gospel Business Men paid their final respects.[208]

Shakarian's old mentor, Oral Roberts led a procession of delegates into the service to memorialize his life. As Oral entered the room, without the aid of electronic amplification, he bellowed out, "I am the resurrection and the life. Anyone who believes in me, though he dies, yet shall he live."[209] The room became electric with hope, as many in the room hoped that God would perform one last miracle for this Full Gospel Business Man.[210] Oral Roberts gave a fitting tribute to Shakarian when he said, "The sweetest spirited layman that I have ever known was Demos Shakarian."[211]

Demos Shakarian was buried at Rose Hill Cemetery on the afternoon of July 28, 1993, and Oral Roberts led the graveside service. As Oral concluded the service, 160 white doves were simultaneously released near the graveside. The flock of doves immediately converging overhead, circling around the cemetery, and flying by the onlookers who had gathered to pay their respects was a fitting metaphor both to Demos Shakarian's physical departure from the bonds of his earthly existence and his lasting contribution to the work of the Holy Spirit and the Charismatic renewal.[212] His father Isaac is buried to one side of him, and his beloved wife Rose joined him in 1996. There is no elaborate marker or fitting tribute to a man who arguably changed the face of global Christianity in the twentieth century. His grave stone only carries his name, the date of his birth, and the date of his death.

Conclusion

The last nine years of Shakarian's life were filled with bittersweet moments of illness and rehabilitation, strife and forgiveness, schism and reconciliation, personal fortune and corporate misfortune, discouraging decline domestically and exciting growth internationally, deflating defeat and the hope of a new anointing. In spite of the limitations caused by a cerebrovascular accident, Shakarian persisted in his role as the president and international ambassador for the FGBMFI. He required some additional assistance after his stroke, but Shakarian discovered a new anointing to pray for other people's sicknesses in spite of his own disability. He found God's strength in the midst of his own weakness to pursue what he perceived as God's destiny for his life in one last great charismatic revival that would sweep the earth before Christ's imminent parousia.

Ultimately, time ran out for Demos Shakarian, and he died on July 23, 1993, just two days past his eightieth birthday. His close friends prayed for his healing while he was still alive, and some members of the FGBMFI even hoped for his resuscitation after he had died. Nevertheless, the only possibility of resurrection for Demos Shakarian now rested in the Christian hope of resurrection at the parousia. Efim Klubnikin's prophetic scroll revealing eschatological judgment and deliverance remained unopened.

Perhaps one of the most important things revealed in Shakarian's last years was how human he really was. Yet, in spite of his human weakness, Shakarian persevered, and his vision has continued to live on in the lives of the millions of individuals that he met directly, and the 523,000,000 people that he touched indirectly. Since his death, Shakarian's followers have broadened and expanded his vision and carried it even further to new heights internationally.[213] Before this study draws to a conclusion, one final chapter will examine his lasting legacy.

Notes

1. Demos Shakarian, "Pruned to Profit," *Voice*, September 1984, 34; Mark Bellinger, *Demos: The Man of Fellowship* (1992), 38–39; and Richard Combs-Tallman interview, January 16, 2008.

2. Mark Bellinger, *Demos: The Man of Fellowship* (1992), 40.

3. There is some discrepancy about the date Demos Shakarian was rushed to the hospital. Mark Bellinger suggests that the stroke occurred on March 3, 1984 (40) and Vinson Synan concurs (155). However, every report in *Voice* (June 1984, 19; July 1984, 22; September 1984, 34–36; March 1985, 19) stated that the stroke occurred on March 26, 1984.

4. "The Power of Prayer," *Voice*, July 1984, 22; and "For Immediate Release," *Voice*, June 1984, 19.

5. Demos Shakarian, "Pruned to Produce," *Voice*, September 1984, 35.

6. "Update," *Voice*, July 1984, 22.

7. Demos Shakarian, *Life Lifters*, (1984), 1:30–31.

8. "The Power of Prayer," *Voice*, July 1984, 22; and Demos Shakarian, *Life Lifters*, (1984), !:41.

9. Demos Shakarian, "Pruned to Produce," *Voice*, September 1984, 36.

10. Ibid.

11. Geraldine Shakarian Scalf-Tallman interview, January 9, 2008.

12. "Update," *Voice*, July 1984, 22.

13. Ron Weinbender-Tallman interview, January 16, 2008.

14. "The Power of Prayer," *Voice*, July 1984, 22; and Demos Shakarian, *Life Lifters* (1984), 1:42.

15. Karen Linamen-Tallman interview, January 10, 2008.

16. "Convention Ad," *Voice*, January 1984, 31.

17. "The 31st World Convention," *Voice*, September 1984, 16–18.

18. Ibid.

19. Ibid, 34–35.

20. Demos Shakarian, *Life Lifters*, 3 vols. (1984).

21. "An Unexpected Miracle," *Voice*, July 1987, 29; and Demos Shakarian, *An Unexpected Miracle* (Nashville, TN: Thomas Nelson Publishers, 1987).

22. Demos Shakarian, *God's Answer to Twenty Tough Questions* (Costa Mesa, CA: FGBMFI, n.d.).

23. All of these books were published by the FGBMFI in Costa Mesa, CA.

24. Steve Shakarian, "Organizational Assessment of the Full Gospel Business Men's Fellowship International," *Voice*, April 1985, 4; Synan, *Under His Banner* (1992), 156–157; and John Dart, "Worldwide Christian Body Divided Over Funds, Power," *Los Angeles Times*, January 14, 1989, B1

25. John Dart, "Worldwide Christian Body Divided Over Funds, Power," *Los Angeles Times*, January 14, 1989, B1.

26. Peter Hocken, "The Charismatic Movement," in *The New International Dictionary of Pentecostal and Charismatic Movements* (eds. Stanley Burgess and Eduard Van der Maas; Grand Rapids, MI: Zondervan, 2002), 485. Richard Quebedeaux would probably consider this phase in the Charismatic movement a period of consolidation given the title of his second study on the movement (*The New Charismatics II: How a Christian Renewal Movement Became Part of the American Religious Mainstream.* (San Francisco: Harper & Row, Publishers, 1983).

27. Russell Chandler, "Corporations Increase Ties to Christianity," *Los Angeles Times* October 20, 1974, 23.

28. "Peace Officers for Christ," *Voice*, December 1987, 9.

29. See Mark I. Pinsky, "A Baptism by Fire for Ministry's Upbeat Heir; Richard Shakarian is Rebuilding the Gospel Group for Businessmen," *Orlando Sentinel*, August 8, 2001, A1.

30. "Promise Keepers to Lay Off Paid Staff," *Christian Century* 115:8 (March 11, 1998): 254.

31. Laurie Goodstein, "Hundreds of Thousands Gather on the Mall in a Day of Prayers," *The New York Times* October 5, 1997, 1, 24.

32. The current president of Promise Keepers, Dr. Tom Fortson, is African-American.

33. "Promise Keepers" *Christian Century* (March 11, 1998): 255.

34. Promise Keepers, "Promise Keeper's 2007 Conference Schedule," Promise Keepers, http://www.promisekeepers.org, (accessed January 19, 2008).

35. See Demos Shakarian, *Voice*, November 1962, 19.

36. One of the first denominations to start a competing men's ministry was the Assemblies of God. Thomas Zimmerman, director of the new Men's Fellowship for the Assemblies of God visited the Washington, D.C. chapter of the FGBMFI in early 1955 when Ralph Riggs, the general superintendent of the Assemblies of God at that time, was a guest speaker ("Many Visitors at Washington Chapter," *Voice*, April 1955, 19).

37. Richard Shakarian-Tallman interview, January 16, 2008. Also Brad Tuttle speculates that the success of training these men simultaneously furthered church growth but sometimes hampered growth within the FGBMFI (Brad Tuttle-Tallman interview, January 9, 2008).

38. Demos Shakarian, *The Happiest People* (1975), 151–152.

39. See *The Happiest People* (1975), 91–96.

40. Demos Shakarian, *The Happiest People* (1975), 96.

41. As Branham's healing ministry became more popular outside of Oneness Pentecostal circles, he downplayed this aspect of his theology. In addition, he only made a prediction about the date of the parousia, but stated that he could be wrong. For an excellent biography of his life see Douglas Weaver, *The Healer-Prophet, William Marrion Branham: A Study of the Prophetic in American Pentecostalism* (Macon, GA: Mercer University Press, 1987) or Branham's own autobiography, William Branham, *The Autobiography of William Marrion Branham* (Jeffersonville, IN: Spoken Word Publications, 1975).

42. Harrell, *All Things are Possible* (1975), 165.

43. See David Harrell's *Oral Roberts* (1985), 415–417 for more details about some of the specific controversies surrounding Oral Roberts life, ministry, and proclamations in the 1980s.

44. For good introductory information about Jim Bakker and Jimmy Swaggart, their lives, and the controversy that surrounded both of them in the 1980s, see Gary McGee, "James Orsen Bakker," in *NIDPCM* (2002), 352–354; and D. Hedges, "Jimmy Lee Swaggart," in *NIDPCM* (2002), 1111.

45. Dian Scott-Tallman interview, January 14, 2008.

46. For more statistical information on the neo-Charismatic movement globally see David Barrett's statistics in the *World Christian Encyclopedia* (2001).

47. John Dart, "Worldwide Christian Body Divided Over Funds, Power," *Los Angeles Times*, January 14, 1989, B1.

48. Demos Shakarian, "120 Club," *Voice*, March 1987, 19; and "The 120 Club," January 1985, 19–20.

49. "Could You Benefit from an Income Deduction? God Needs 1000 Partners," *Voice*, December 1985, 27.

50. James Bates, "Southland Financiers Quoted Bible, Engaged in Scams, SEC Claims," *Los Angeles Times*, March 3, 1986, E1, E5.

51. Demos Shakarian-Synan interview, February 2, 1988, 14–15; and Mark Bellinger, *Demos: The Man of Fellowship* (1992), 105.

52. "When You Move by Faith the Scriptures Come Alive!" *Voice*, October 1991, 19.

53. "When You Move by Faith the Scriptures Come Alive!" *Voice*, October 1991, 19.

54. "FGBMFI's 40th Anniversary 1992 Pocket Planner," *Voice*, February 1992, 31.

55. Demos Shakarian-Synan interview, October 5, 1987, 7.

56. Demos Shakarian, "Happy Holidays," *Voice*, January 1991, 9.

57. Mitra Toossi, "A Century of Change: The U.S. Labor Force, 1950–2050," *Monthly Labor Review* (May, 2002): 23.

58. Lee Ann Sandweiss, "The 40-hour Work Week – Dead or Alive?" Indiana University, http://www.homepages.indiana.edu/040904/text/workweek.shtml, April 9, 2004 (accessed November 21, 2008).

59. Ibid.

60. Nelson Melvin, ed., *FGBMFI Chapter Manual* (Costa Mesa, CA: FGBMFI, 1983), 10.

61. Demos Shakarian, *A New Wave of Revival: In Your Finances* (Costa Mesa: CA, FGBMFI, 1992), 5–6.

62. Ibid, 9.

63. Ibid, 9–10.

64. Bob Armstrong, "39th Annual FGBMFI World Convention Report!" *Voice*, September 1992, 21; and Convention ad," *Voice*, June 1987, 33–35.

65. Oral Roberts-Synan interview, October 10, 1991, 21–22. Also see David Barrett's discussion on neo-Charismatics and their reduced emphasis upon glossolalia in "Global Statistics," *NIDPCM* (2002), 291.

66. Peter Redding-Tallman interview, January 6, 2005. As a Roman Catholic and a national director within the FGBMFI, Redding disagreed with the doctrinal stance of glossolalic initial evidence in the FGBMFI, but he remained a director until 2006, when he helped start a competing Christian men's organization.

67. Myra MacPherson, "The Pulpit and the Power: '700 Club's' Pat Robertson, Preaching Gospel and Eyeing the White House," *The Washington Post*, October 18, 1985, D1.

68. See John Balzar, "Faith-Healing-Service Video Dogs Robertson; Tape Replayed on TV as Republicans Attempt to Downplay His Evangelical Past," *Los Angeles Times*, October 3, 1987, A14; Myra MacPherson, "The Pulpit and the Power: '700 Club's' Pat Robertson, Preaching Gospel and Eyeing the White House," *The Washington Post*, October 18, 1985, D1; and "Philadelphia," *Voice*, March 1981, 20–21. This videotape had been discussed in the media for at least two years before he made his official announcement to run for president.

69. See John Balzar, "Faith-Healing-Service Video Dogs Robertson; Tape Replayed on TV as Republicans Attempt to Downplay His Evangelical Past," *Los Angeles Times*, October 3, 1987, A14.

70. David Maraniss, "Oklahoma and the Robertson Difference; Political Disaffection, Fear for Nation's Future Motivate Converts," *The Washington Post*, February 29, 1988, A1.

71. Myra MacPherson, "The Pulpit and the Power: '700 Club's' Pat Robertson, Preaching Gospel and Eyeing the White House," *The Washington Post*, October 18, 1985, D1.

72. Mark Bellinger, *Demos: The Man of Fellowship* (1992), 97.

73. David Edwin Harrell, Jr., *Pat Robertson: A Personal, Religious, and Political Portrait* (San Francisco, CA: Harper and Row, Publishers, 1987), 149.

74. Demos Shakarian-Synan interview, February 2, 1988, 2.

75. "Convention ad," *Voice*, June 1987, 33–35.

76. Demos Shakarian-Synan interview, February 2, 1988, 20–25. Also see Synan, *Under His Banner* (1992), 140–141 for a summary of the events that occurred in 1987. In addition, Mark Bellinger's book, *Demos: The Man of Fellowship* (Long Beach, CA: Upright Enterprises, 1992) offers a thorough account of these events.

77. Demos Shakarian, *Life Lifters* (1984), 2:32.

78. *Voice*, May 1987, 39.

79. John Dart, "Schism Hits Worldwide Fellowship Amid Bickering Over Funds, Power," *Los Angeles Times*, January 14, 1989, B6; Demos Shakarian-Synan interview, October 5, 1987; Demos Shakarian-Synan interview, February 2, 1988, 21; and Jerry Jensen-Synan interview, February 15, 1992, 21.

80. Mark Bellinger, *Demos: The Man of Fellowship* (1992), 61–63; Jensen-Synan interview, February 15, 1992, 23; Richard Combs-Tallman interview, January 16, 2006; and John Dart, "Pentecostals Back Founder on Finances," *Los Angeles Times*, January 14, 1989, B6.

81. "A New Wave of Revival," *Voice*, September 1987, 16.

82. Mark Bellinger, *Demos: The Man of Fellowship* (1992), 69–71; and Gene Scalf-Tallman interview, January 11, 2008.

83. "Tommy Ashcraft is Called Home," *Voice*, December 1987, 39.

84. Jimmy Rogers, interview with Matthew Tallman, Arlington, VA, February 22, 2008.

85. Gene Scalf-Tallman interview, January 11, 2008; John Dart, "Schism Hits Worldwide Fellowship Amid Bickering Over Funds, Power," *Los Angeles Times*, January 14, 1989, B6; and Mark Bellinger, *Demos: Man of Fellowship* (1992), 79–81.

86. Gene Scalf-Tallman interview, January 9, 2008; Mark Bellinger, *Demos: The Man of Fellowship* (1992), 89–91; and John Dart, "Pentecostals Back Founder on Finances," *Los Angeles Times*, January 30, 1989, A7.

87. Myrna Oliver, "Demos Shakarian; Founded Religious Group," *Los Angeles Times*, July 30, 1993, A28; John Dart, "Southern California File," *Los Angeles Times*, February 4, 1989, B7; Mark Bellinger, *Demos: The Man of Fellowship* (1992), ; and Gene Scalf-Tallman interview, January 11, 2008.

88. John Dart, "Pentecostals Back Founder on Finances," *Los Angeles Times*, January 30, 1989, A7.

89. John Dart, "Southern California File," *Los Angeles Times*, February 4, 1989, B7

90. Mark Bellinger, *Demos: The Man of Fellowship* (1992), 94–96; John Dart, "Schism Hits Worldwide Fellowship Amid Bickering Over Funds, Power," *Los Angeles Times*, January 14, 1989, B6; and Jerry Jensen-Synan interview, February 15, 1992, 21.

91. Demos Shakarian-Synan interview, February 2, 1988, 25.

92. Demos Shakarian-Synan interview, February 2, 1988, 25; and Bellinger, *Demos: The Man of Fellowship* (1992), 151.

93. Ronny Svenhard, phone interview by Matthew Tallman, January 22, 2008; and John Dart, "Pentecostals Back Founder on Finances," *Los Angeles Times*, January 30, 1989, A7.

94. John Dart, "Pentecostals Back Founder on Finances," *Los Angeles Times*, January 30, 1989, A7.

95. Jerry Jensen-Synan interview, February 15, 1992, 23.

96. John Dart, "Schism Hits Worldwide Fellowship Amid Bickering Over Funds, Power," *Los Angeles Times*, January 14, 1989, B6.

97. John Dart, "Schism Hits Worldwide Fellowship Amid Bickering Over Funds, Power," *Los Angeles Times*, January 14, 1989, B6; and Gene Scalf-Tallman interview, January 11, 2008.

98. Jerry Jensen-Synan interview, February 15, 1992, 25; John Dart, "Schism Hits Worldwide Fellowship Amid Bickering Over Funds, Power," *Los Angeles Times*, January 14, 1989, B6; Mark Bellinger, *Demos: The Man of Fellowship* (1992), 81–82; and Gene Scalf-Tallman interview, January 11, 2008.

99. Dian Scott-Tallman interview, July 10, 2008; and Jimmy Rogers-Tallman interview, February 22, 2008.

100. Dian Scott-Tallman interview, July 10, 2008; and Jimmy Rogers-Tallman interview, February 22, 2008.

101. Oral Roberts, "The Righteous Man Who Flourished Like the Palm Tree," *Voice*, October 1993, 36.

102. Jimmy Rogers-Tallman interview, February 22, 2008.

103. Mark Bellinger, *Demos: The Man of Fellowship* (1992), 117; and John Dart, "Southern California File," *Los Angeles Times*, February 4, 1989, B7.

104. John Dart, "Schism Hits Worldwide Fellowship Amid Bickering Over Funds, Power," *Los Angeles Times*, January 14, 1989, B6.

105. Demos Shakarian-Synan interview, February 2, 1988, 14–15; and Mark Bellinger, *Demos: The Man of Fellowship* (1992), 134–136, 148–149.

106. John Schmook, interview by Matthew Tallman, Fort Lauderdale, FL, July 8, 2006.

107. Demos Shakarian-Synan interview, October 5, 1987, 1.

108. Mark Bellinger, *Demos: The Man of Fellowship* (1992), 139.

109. Ibid, 149–150.

110. "1988 World Convention Report," *Voice*, September 1988, 19; also see Synan, *Under His Banner* (1992), 121.

111. Gene Arnold, interview by Matthew Tallman, Orlando, FL, July 5, 2008.

112. John Dart, "Pentecostals Back Founder on Finances," *Los Angeles Times*, January 30, 1989, A7.

113. John Dart, "Schism Hits Worldwide Fellowship Amid Bickering Over Funds, Power," *Los Angeles Times*, January 14, 1989, B6.

114. John Dart, "Southern California File," *Los Angeles Times*, February 4, 1989, B7; Mark Bellinger, *Demos: The Man of Fellowship* (1992), 191–197 ; and Gene Scalf-Tallman interview, January 11, 2008.

115. John Dart, "Pentecostals Back Founder on Finances," *Los Angeles Times*, January 30, 1989, A7.

116. Mark Bellinger, *Demos: Man of Fellowship* (1992), 173–174.

117. John Dart, "Southern California File," *Los Angeles Times*, February 4, 1989, B7; Mark Bellinger, *Demos: The Man of Fellowship* (1992), 196 and 200; and Gene Scalf-Tallman interview, January 11, 2008.

118. John Dart, "Pentecostals Back Founder on Finances," *Los Angeles Times*, January 30, 1989, A7.

119. John Dart, "Southern California File," *Los Angeles Times*, February 4, 1989, B7.

120. John Dart, "Schism Hits Worldwide Fellowship Amid Bickering Over Funds, Power," *Los Angeles Times*, January 14, 1989, B6.

121. "Executive Committee," *Voice*, April 1989, 39; "Executive Committee," *Voice*, June 1989, 39; "Executive Committee," *Voice*, November 1989, 39; "Executive Committee," *Voice*, December 1989, 31; and "Executive Committee," *Voice*, January 1990, 31.

122. Jerry Jensen-Synan interview, February 15, 1992, 20, 26; and Bellinger, *Demos: The Man of Fellowship* (1992), 213.

123. James Autry, interview with Matthew Tallman, Portland, OR, April 1, 2009.

124. Mark I. Pinsky, "A Baptism by Fire for Ministry's Upbeat Heir; Richard Shakarian is Rebuilding the Gospel Group for Businessmen," *Orlando Sentinel*, August 8, 2001, A1; and James Autry, interview with Matthew Tallman, Portland, OR, April 1, 2009.

125. Gene Scalf-Tallman interview, January 11, 2008.

126. Oral Roberts-Synan interview, October 10, 1991, 36; and Bellinger, *Demos: The Man of Fellowship* (1992), 213.

127. International Fellowship of Christian Business Men, "Christ's Ambassadors in the World's Marketplace," IFCB, www.ifcb.org/index.php, (accessed February 29, 2008).

128. International Fellowship of Christian Business Men, "Christ's Ambassadors in the World's Marketplace," IFCB, www.ifcb.org/index.php, (accessed February 29, 2008); and Carlton Milbrandt, phone interview with Matthew Tallman, December 11, 2008.

129. Synan, *Under His Banner* (1992), 141; and John Dart, "Schism Hits Worldwide Fellowship Amid Bickering Over Funds, Power," *Los Angeles Times*, January 14, 1989, B6.

130. James Autry-Tallman interview, April 1, 2009.

131. Dian Scott, phone interview with Matthew Tallman, January 22, 2008.

132. Demos Shakarian, "Orlando '91," *Voice*, June 1991, 34; and "Moving in Unity to Victory!" *Voice*, September 1991, 19.

133. "Help Lift Jesus Up in the Land Down Under," *Voice*, October 1984, 34.

134. "32nd World Convention," *Voice*, June 1985, 34.

135. "His Banner Over Us is Love," *Voice*, February 1985, 20–21.

136. "Outreach: Antigua, Honduras, Nicaragua," *Voice*, August 1985, 19.

137. Brad Tuttle-Tallman interview, January 9, 2008; and Richard Shakarian-Tallman interview, January 16, 2008.

138. Humberto Aguilar, interview by Matthew Tallman, Orlando, FL, July 4, 2008.

139. With over 800 chapters of the FGBMFI in 2008 in a country with 5.5 million inhabitants, the Nicaraguan FGBMFI has permeated the business and politics of that nation (Richard Shakarian, "Report of all Nations," FGBMFI World Convention, Orlando, FL, July 4, 2008).

140. "Update," *Voice*, May 1985, 34.

141. Ibid.

142. "Turning Point," *Voice*, August 1985, 20–21.

143. John Dart, "Southern California File," *Los Angeles Times*, February 4, 1989, B7.

144. "Demos Shakarian Receives Award for Charismatic Leadership," *Voice*, January 1987, 28.

145. "Conventions," *Voice*, February 1985, 29.

146. "Conventions," *Voice*, February 1985, 29.

147. "Update," *Voice*, April 1985, 17.

148. Demos Shakarian, "New Marching Orders," *Voice*, September 1985, 17.

149. Demos Shakarian, "Focus on Healing," *Voice*, January 1986, 2.

150. "1991 Georgia Men's Advance Highlights," *Voice*, March 1991, 28; also see Mark Bellinger, *Demos: The Man of Fellowship* (1992), 78.

151. As already mentioned, Norman Norwood was concerned that Shakarian was becoming deified by many FGBMFI members (John Dart, "Schism Hits Worldwide Fellowship Amid Bickering Over Funds, Power," *Los Angeles Times*, January 14, 1989, B6). In addition, Bob Bignold mentioned that many FGBMFI members began to worship Demos Shakarian towards the end of his life (Bob Bignold, phone interview with Matthew Tallman, December 9, 2009).

152. Demos Shakarian, *A New Wave of Revival: The Vision Intensified* (Costa Mesa, CA: FGBMFI, 1992), 5.

153. Demos Shakarian, "Will God Provide," *Voice*, January 1988, 4. However, Asamoah-Gyadu made a more conservative calculation of 3,000 chapters worldwide in 87 countries before the end of 1988 (Kwabena Asamoah-Gyadu, "Missionaries without Robes: Lay Charismatic Fellowships and the Evangelization of Ghana," *Pneuma* 19:2 [Fall 1997]: 173).

154. "1988 World Convention Report," *Voice*, September 1988, 18.

155. "Behold the Glory," *Voice*, May 1989, 28–29.

156. "USA Convention," *Voice*, January 1989, 9.

157. Jerry Jensen, ed., *FGBMFI 1988–1989 World Chapter Directory* (Costa Mesa, CA: FGBMFI, 1989), 4.

158. Ibid, 17, 20–21.

159. "International Directors," *Voice*, January 1991, 29–30.

160. "Moving in Unity to Victory!" *Voice*, September 1991, 19.

161. "Asian Highlights," *Voice*, June 1992, 32. Indonesia in particular had grown from twenty-three to eighty chapters in just three years (Jerry Jensen, ed., *FGBMFI 1988–1989 World Chapter Directory* (Costa Mesa, CA: FGBMFI, 1989), 43–44.

162. "African Advance," *Voice*, June 1992, 33.

163. "African Advance," *Voice*, June 1992, 33.

164. Demos Shakarian, "Forty Years of Fellowship," *Voice*, July 1992, 3.

165. Durasoff, *Bright Wind of the Spirit* (1972), 162.

166. Fotherby, *The Awakening Giant* (2000), 103.

167. Richard Shakarian and Paul Toberty, "FGBMFI Airlift to Armenia and Russia," *Voice*, September 1990, 29.

168. Fotherby, *The Awakening Giant* (2000), 103.

169. Richard Shakarian and Paul Toberty, "FGBMFI Airlift to Armenia and Russia," *Voice*, September 1990, 29.

170. Richard Shakarian-Tallman interview, January 16, 2008; and Richard Shakarian and Paul Toberty, "FGBMFI Airlift to Armenia and Russia," *Voice*, September 1990, 29.

171. Demos Shakarian, "The Move of God Will be Mighty in the '90s," *Voice*, April 1990, 30.

172. "European Expansion," *Voice*, July 1992, 33.

173. Demos Shakarian, "The Final Countdown," *Voice*, May 1990, 30.

174. Demos Shakarian, *The Happiest People* (1975), 20.

175. Demos Shakarian-Synan interview, February 2, 1988, 17; and Paul Sobolew-Tallman interview, January 15, 2008.

176. "Earl Prickett Remembered," *Voice*, October 1990, 9.

177. "Earl Prickett Remembered," *Voice*, October 1990, 9.

178. "Enoch Christoffersen Remembered," *Voice*, January 1991, 22.

179. Enoch Christoffersen, "Remember Thy Creator," *Voice*, January/February 1969, 4–7, 22–25, 35; "Far East Airlift," *Voice*, November 1966, 9–14; and Vinson Synan, *Under His Banner* (1992), 79.

180. "In Memoriam," *Voice*, June 1993, 18.

181. Los Angeles County Bureau of Records, Death Certificate for Demos Shakarian, Los Angeles County, CA, filed July 22, 1993.

182. Richard Shakarian, "The All Ireland Conference," *Voice*, February 1991, 25.

183. "The Russians are Coming," *Voice*, December 1990, 26.

184. "FGBMFI News Briefs," *Voice*, February 1992, 32.

185. "Asian Highlights," *Voice*, June 1992, 32.

186. Harding Mushegian-Tallman interview, January 14, 2008.

187. Ibid.

188. "Executive Committee," *Voice*, November 1991, 39; and Jimmy Rogers-Tallman interview, February 22, 2008.

189. Bob Armstrong, "39th Annual FGBMFI World Convention Report!" *Voice*, September 1992, 22.

190. "Happy Birthday Demos!" *Voice*, January 1993, 32; Richard Combs, interview by Matthew Tallman, Irvine, CA, January 16, 2008; and Walt White, interview by Matthew Tallman, Colorado Springs, CO, January 9, 2008.

191. This description of a typical Christmas was given by Brenda Shakarian during the interview by Matthew Tallman, Irvine, CA, January 18, 2008. *Shakar lokoom* is a special Armenian sweet bread served predominantly during the Christmas season.

192. Ibid.

193. Ron Weinbender-Tallman interview, January 16, 2008.

194. Ibid.

195. While the FGBMFI first began to meet in 1951, it was not recognized legally as a non-profit corporation by the State of California until January 2, 1953. See *Voice*, February 1953, 16. Thus the organization celebrates its anniversaries based on the date of legal recognition.

196. Brad Tuttle-Tallman interview, January 9, 2008; and "Celebrating the Past – Launching the Future," *Voice*, September 1993, 16.

197. Ron Weinbender-Tallman interview, January 16, 2008.

198. Rose Shakarian, "His Family Reflects," *Voice*, October 1993, 23.

199. Ibid.

200. Los Angeles County Bureau of Records, Death Certificate for Demos Shakarian, Los Angeles County, CA, filed July 28, 1993; and Rose Shakarian, "His Family Reflects," *Voice*, October 1993, 23.

201. Oral Roberts, "The Righteous Man Who Flourished Like the Palm Tree," *Voice*, October 1993, 36.

202. Steve Shakarian, "His Family Reflects," *Voice*, October 1993, 27.

203. Richard Shakarian, "His Family Reflects," *Voice*, October 1993, 24.

204. Los Angeles County Bureau of Records, Death Certificate for Demos Shakarian, Los Angeles County, CA, filed July 28, 1993; and Steve Shakarian, "His Family Reflects," *Voice*, October 1993, 27.

205. Los Angeles County Bureau of Records, Death Certificate for Demos Shakarian, Los Angeles County, CA, filed July 28, 1993.

206. Gene Scalf-Tallman interview, January 9, 2008.

207. Geraldine Shakarian Scalf-Tallman interview, January 9, 2008.

208. Geraldine Shakarian Scalf-Tallman interview, January 9, 2008. Also in an interview with Jimmy Rogers by this author in Arlington, VA, on February 22, 2008, Rogers expressed his disappointment that thousands more did not attend this service. Perhaps the brevity of time between Shakarian's death and his memorial service (only four days) only

allowed local friends, relatives, and FGBMFI members from the Southern California area to attend.

209. Walt White, interview by Matthew Tallman, Colorado Springs, CO, January 9, 2008.

210. Ibid.

211. Oral Roberts, "Demos Shakarian – The Righteous Man Who Flourished Like the Palm Tree," *Voice*, October 1993, 32.

212. "Demos Shakarian Memorial Issue," *Voice*, October 1993, 18; and Los Angeles County Bureau of Records, Death Certificate for Demos Shakarian, Los Angeles County, CA, filed July 28, 1993.

213. This international growth is in contrast to the movement's North American diffusion and decline.

Chapter Twelve

The Legacy of Demos Shakarian

Most narrative biographies conclude their story with the death of the primary character and a brief summation of their life. A summary of the findings in this study will be discussed in the final chapter. However, a brief look at the history of Demos Shakarian's legacy since his death is important to evaluate the significance of his life. A brief overview of these aspects of Shakarian's legacy will also help evaluate his contribution towards the three things he loved most in his life: his family, his cattle, and the Full Gospel Business Men.

Demos Shakarian's Family Legacy

At the time of his death, Shakarian was survived by his wife Rose; their three children: Stephen, Geraldine, and Richard; eight granddaughters and one grandson, Stephen, Jr.; and five great-grandchildren.[1] Shakarian was surrounded by his extended family shortly before his death, and they honored him at his memorial service on July 28, 1993.[2] Only three short years after Shakarian's death, on June 15, 1996, Rose Shakarian died from a heart attack and was laid to rest next to her husband at Rose Hills Memorial Park in Whittier, California.[3]

Shakarian's son Steve Shakarian died of complications related to amyloidosis on December 5, 2004. His wife Debra succumbed to breast cancer in 2003. They are survived by two children: Stephanie and Stephen Jr., Shakarian's only grandson.[4]

In 2009, Shakarian's daughter Geri and her husband Gene Scalf resided in Colorado Springs, Colorado, on a piece of property with a panoramic view of Pike's Peak. Gene still successfully invests in property but admits that his father-in-law was much better at purchasing and selling property.[5] All three of their daughters reside in the Colorado Springs area. Michelle Scalf Willett (d.b.a. 1969–) is an emergency dispatch operator who also has one daughter.[6] Karen Scalf Linamen (1960–) is a successful author who has written seventeen books and contributed to three others mostly on the subject of marriage and family. She also has two daughters.[7] Renee Scalf Berge (d.b.a. 1964–) also resides in

Colorado Springs, and she is busy raising three sons and overseeing several small businesses that she founded. Her husband, Harald Berge is a pilot for United Airlines.[8]

Richard Shakarian followed his father's footsteps and currently serves as the president of the FGBMFI. His wife Vangie currently leads the Ladies of the Fellowship under the auspices of the FGBMFI. Richard and his wife Vangie celebrated their fiftieth wedding anniversary on August 6, 2005. They have four daughters: Denice, Cynthia, Suzanne, and Brenda. Most of Richard's daughters stay actively involved in FGBMFI conventions, and his daughter Brenda works in the FGBMFI headquarters overseeing an affiliated youth organization called Excellence International and developing some television programming for the FGBMFI.[9] Brenda Shakarian (d.b.a. 1969–) has just finished completing a television program for the FGBMFI called "FGBMFI No Borders."[10] Richard and Vangie also have three grandchildren: Blake, Rachel, and Brianna.[11]

Shakarian left a personal legacy through his family which has grown to include two sons, one daughter, nine grandchildren, and nine great-grandchildren. All of his descendents are gainfully employed, active in church or ministry, and continue to follow his charismatic brand of Christianity. Many of his descendents are entrepreneurs and industrious, creative members of society in their various crafts, and some are wealthy although none have likely exceeded Shakarian's wealth. In addition, all of his children, grandchildren, and the few great-grandchildren who remember him have fond memories of his gentle nature, his sense of humor, his discernment and common sense approach to business, and his leadership as the humble Christian patriarch of the Shakarian clan.[12]

Demos Shakarian's Commercial Legacy

At first glance, not much of Shakarian's commercial legacy remains except the financial inheritance that his children and his wife received after his death. The original Reliance Dairy in Downey, California, has been replaced by townhouses and a large Calvary Chapel Church.[13] None of the original Reliance Drive-in Dairies remain except at least two historical reminders of the Shakarian dairy empire on Paramount Boulevard in Downey, California and on Florence Street in Bell Garden, California where two drive-in dairy signs have survived modern commercial renovations.[14] Perhaps if Richard or Demos Shakarian had added coffee to the variety of items sold at their drive-ins, they would have had more success, but an entrepreneur from Seattle, Washington, would later discover the advantages of combining milk and coffee in a successful franchise operation.[15]

Shakarian did offer several innovations in the dairy industry that improved the productivity and profitability of the dairy industry in California. In addition to Shakarian's patent for milking cows that he submitted in 1964, he also devised a way to minimize deaths among young calves by rotating calving booths. Calve deaths were almost eliminated and other dairy operations in Southern California quickly replicated his innovations.[16] In the year that Demos Shakarian died,

California surpassed Wisconsin to become the leading dairy state in the United States. By 2003, California produced nineteen percent of the nation's dairy supply, was eighth in the world in total dairy production, and dairy farming had become the largest agricultural commodity in California with a four billion dollar industry.[17]

What was Demos Shakarian's great commercial legacy? Some of his closest supporters have suggested that his own cattle have left a significant legacy.[18] However, his dairy business is gone, sold off to various dairy companies and businesses more than thirty years ago, and one of the largest herds of dairy cattle in the United States was parceled out and sold off to the highest bidder. Nevertheless, one legacy of Shakarian is the offspring of his prize bulls. Some of Shakarian's bulls are still producing calves through sperm cryogenically frozen and artificially inseminated to produce some of the finest dairy cows in Southern California and throughout the world.[19] While this aspect of his life may not seem important to his spiritual legacy or vision, some of the prize bulls he gave as gifts to various national and world leaders have produced a lasting spiritual inheritance that complemented his pneumatic vision.[20]

Demos Shakarian's Spiritual Legacy: The FGBMFI

Shortly before Shakarian's death, he appointed his son Richard to lead the FGBMFI. Immediately after Shakarian's death, Oral Roberts affirmed Richard's leadership over the organization at Shakarian's funeral.[21] In October 1993, the FGBMFI published a lengthy memorial issue honoring their founder, Demos Shakarian.[22] The next month's issue of *Voice* devoted the magazine to Richard Shakarian's qualifications as the new leader of the FGBMFI. The magazine listed existing and new members of the executive board and produced an extensive list of prophecies that various Full Gospel Business Men and evangelists delivered to Richard Shakarian from 1990 to 1993 predicting and affirming his leadership over the organization.[23] Richard announced to his constituents, "I will never fill the shoes of my father, and I will not try, but he instructed me well in the Lord, and taught me to hear the voice of God."[24]

In spite of challenges that the FGBMFI faced after Demos Shakarian's death, since 1993, the organization has continued to grow under Richard's leadership. In 2007, the organization claimed to have at least 6,000 chapters in over 160 nations.[25] This represented an increase of approximately one hundred percent in both the organization's size and breadth when compared to the size of the organization in 1988 at the height of the Charismatic renewal in the United States. In 1988, the FGBMFI had 3,000 chapters in eighty-seven different nations, with nearly two-thirds of those chapters located in the United States.[26] This growth appears to reflect an ongoing symbiotic relationship between the explosive growth of the Charismatic renewal internationally and the FGBMFI abroad. However, the growth of the renewal movement in the United States has leveled off in the past two decades, and the FGBMFI has declined dramatically with 500 chapters in the United States today as compared to its high point of nearly 2,000 chapters in the mid 1980s.[27] The FGBMFI admitted this symbiotic relationship in 2003, when its editor wrote, "the life and course of FGBMFI was the best barometer of the growth and development of the renewal at large."[28]

The FGBMFI rose and fell in stride with the various fluctuations of the Charismatic renewal. While the Charismatic renewal has stalled or dissipated in large parts of North America and Europe in recent years, in the past fifteen years, the FGBMFI has also declined correspondingly. In similar fashion, as the Charismatic renewal has continued to expand internationally, especially in Latin America, Asia, and Africa, so has the FGBMFI. Much like the earlier relationship with the healing evangelists of the 1950s, the FGBMFI began a symbiotic relationship with the Charismatic movement that has lasted for five decades.

Technically, in the United States from 1986 until 2006, registered chapters had decreased over seventy percent and membership had declined by approximately sixty percent to 14,403 members and approximately 500 chapters.[29] Considering a broader period of three decades, there was a 330 percent increase in the combined Pentecostal, Charismatic, and neo-Charismatic movements in North America from 1970 until 2000 reflecting 55,448,259 additional constituents in the renewal movements.[30] While the United States experienced a significant increase in the growth of the renewal movements from 1970 until 2000, most of this increase appeared to occur during the first two decades from 1970 until 1990 when the Charismatic movement peaked in North America.[31] In contrast, much of the decline that occurred in the FGBMFI in North America during this period can be attributed to schisms, sociological shifts, and the success of competing organizations mentioned in previous chapters.

In Europe, there was a 468 percent increase in the combined renewal movements from 1970 until 2000 representing 29,550,520 participants added to the various renewal streams of the twentieth century.[32] European renewal movements had the most significant increase from 1970 until 1990 with an increase of 417 percent, but they still saw some moderate increase in the last decade of the twentieth century.[33] In the European FGBMFI, most regions declined or stalled after 1990. In 2006, Great Britain had 100 chapters and France had 45 chapters; however Britain had 241 chapters and France had 44 chapters in 1989.[34] In 2006, Finland had nine active chapters, the Netherlands had eleven chapters, and Sweden had five active chapters, representing a significant decline as compared to 1989.[35] Some Eastern European countries' membership grew slightly from 1989 until 2006, and Germany's membership grew slightly with over 100 FGBMFI chapters in 2006.[36]

In comparison to the decline the FGBMFI experienced in North America and Europe in the past two decades, on the continents of Africa, Latin America, and Asia, the FGBMFI has experienced a growth pattern in the past three decades that supports a symbiotic relationship with the Pentecostal, Charismatic, and neo-Charismatic movements on those continents. In Africa, there was a 739 percent increase from 1970 to 2000 with 108,982,182 participants added to the renewal movements by 2000.[37]

As the size and influence of the FGBMFI began to expand globally, nowhere was this more evident than on the continent of Africa. In much of Africa, and in particular, in nations such as Ghana and Nigeria, the FGBMFI has had enormous influence upon society and the growth of Christianity.[38] In 1989, Nigeria had only fifty-one chapters of the FGBMFI.[39] By 2006, there were 1,217 chapters in Nigeria, and the FGBMFI World Convention in Lagos in 2004 was perhaps the best attended FGBMFI convention in its history attracting as many as 60,000 people every night.[40] In 2008, the number of chapters in Nigeria had increased to 1,381 with an ambitious goal of attaining an accumulated goal of 4,000 chapters before the end of the year. Nigerian FGBMFI teams went to Dubai, Thailand, Malaysia, and throughout the continent of Africa in 2008. In addition, the Nigerian FGBMFI successfully planted a chapter in Dubai in 2007.[41]

The FGBMFI started its first chapter in Ghana in 1978, but by 1997, they had grown to 114 chapters.[42] In addition, in 1996, Ghanaian Full Gospel Business Men had done such an effective job of reaching their own people in other nations that the presidents of the FGBMFI organizations in Gambia, Guinea, Israel, Italy, and Senegal were all Ghanaians.[43] The Congo also had an enormous initial success developing hundreds of chapters in a short period of time and even planting chapters in other nations such as Rwanda.[44] At one point, Congo may have had as many 2,000 chapters, but civil war has reduced that number to 323 chapters in 2008.[45]

Asia has experienced the largest percentage increase of participants in the renewal movements from 1970 until 2000 with a 1,329 percent increase while adding 124,745,410 constituents to the various movements.[46] The growth of renewal movements continued to increase steadily throughout this period with 256 percent of that growth occurring in the 1990s.[47] The FGBMFI in some Asian nations has seen similar or even more dramatic growth during a shorter span of time. In 1989, Indonesia had only 23 chapters, but by 2008, reported 562 chapters – an increase of 2,443 percent.[48] The FGBMFI has only existed in Cambodia since 2003, but by 2006, there were already over sixty chapters.[49]

However, the most dramatic growth in the FGBMFI in the past two decades has occurred in Central America. The Pentecostal, Charismatic, and neo-Charismatic movements on the continent of Latin America have also reflected a significant 1,121 percent increase in renewal participants from 1970 until 2000, consequently adding 128,811,430 participants to the various renewal streams at the beginning of the twenty-first century.[50]

In particular, the Nicaraguan FGBMFI has seen spectacular growth since 1999. In January 1999, several key Central American leaders of the FGBMFI met with Richard Shakarian in Miami, Florida, and decided to plan a focused outreach to Nicaragua in early May of that year.[51] The 400 planned meetings multiplied into 925 meetings and speaking venues, and in five short days 97,000 people expressed a need to know more about Jesus. Sandinista leaders such as Daniel Ortega became involved again in the FGBMFI chapters that were organized as a result of that outreach.[52] Growth has continued unabated in Nicaragua with at least 800 active chapters of the FGBMFI and at least 2,000,000 people making a personal decision to embrace Christianity through the ongoing evangelism of the FGMBFI.[53]

Ironically, the story of FGBMFI's dramatic growth in Nicaragua may have started with one of Demos Shakarian's prize bulls that he shipped to Nicaragua in the early 1980s. Richard Shakarian recalls the humor in this connection when he first visited Nicaragua in 1999 on behalf of the FGBMFI.[54] He discovered that several members of the Sandinista party who came to greet him had already met his father. In the ensuing discussion, it was discovered that Demos Shakarian had sent a prize bull from his herd as a gift to one of the leading party members. Richard asked the man what happened with the bull, and the man replied, "For awhile, we used it to propagate more cattle, but eventually we ate that capitalist bull!" At that point the room erupted in laughter, but Richard, with a smile on his face, announced to the men in the room that they needed to be warned. He said, "My father anointed that bull to propagate the gospel, and now that you've eaten it, you need to know the gospel." Richard Shakarian claims that within a very short period of time, every man in that room became an active member of the FGBMFI.[55]

In Nicaragua, the membership of the FGBMFI often includes Sandinistas who have a decidedly Socialist or Marxist approach to politics.[56] Nevertheless, this political diversity did not concern Demos Shakarian, and his son Richard does not seem threatened by it either.[57] As Richard Shakarian said recently, "We don't try and change their politics; we leave that to the Lord."[58] In 2006, there were already 600 chapters in Nicaragua.[59] By 2008, there were 800 chapters and 27,000 FGBMFI members in Nicaragua.[60]

Honduras and Guatemala have also experienced significant growth in the past fifteen years. Honduras, in particular, experienced dramatic growth shortly after the devastation of Hurricane Mitch. One of the Honduran directors of the FGBM-FI, Jose Velasquez, almost single-handedly invited over 150,000 men to a variety of FGBMFI luncheons and dinners in a twelve-month period, and 100,000 people experienced Christian salvation.[61] In 2008, nearly one million Hondurans were prayed for by members of the FGBMFI through various Fire Team outreaches.[62] Currently, there are 362 active chapters of the FGBMFI in Honduras.[63] Guatemala and Costa Rica have also experienced rapid growth in their various FGBMFI meetings with 275 and 220 active chapters respectively.[64] In fact, by 2008, seven nations in Central America (Mexico, El Salvador, Guatemala, Panama, Costa Rica, Honduras, and Nicaragua) represented over 1,800 active chapters, nearly one-third of the FGBMFI chapters worldwide.[65]

The dramatic growth of the FGBMFI in Central America has been used as an example to inspire growth in other parts of the world. Nicaraguan FGBMFI leaders have been actively involved in training members in North America, Africa, Europe, and Asia in ways to expand their evangelistic influence and increase the number of FGBMFI chapters on those continents.[66] Central American FGBMFI leaders have also had direct impact on establishing chapters in other nations.

Through the influence of Honduran and Nicaraguan FGBMFI members, Cuba had fifty active chapters by 2008.[67]

Demos Shakarian's Spiritual Legacy: Challenges to That Legacy

The success stories that the FGBMFI has seen in Central America over the past decade has not been uniformly reflected in other parts of the world. As already mentioned, some parts of Africa and Asia continued to grow dramatically in the past two decades but with mixed results. In contrast, most European and North American FGBMFI chapters saw decline during this period. Much of this ongoing decline in North America and Europe can be attributed to sociological, theological, and political challenges already discussed in previous chapters.

In addition, financial problems continued to beset the organization after Demos Shakarian's death. In 1995, the FGBMFI executive board decided that significant financial cuts in the operating budget needed to be made and assets needed to be sold to keep the organization solvent. Negotiations began with Paul Crouch and the Trinity Broadcasting Network (TBN) to sell the FGBMFI international headquarters in Costa Mesa. In 1996, a contract was ratified and the headquarters building was sold for five million dollars, and a specified amount of free air time for the FGBMFI on the TBN network was included in the sales package.[68]

A transition in leadership in 1993 may have also contributed to the decline in North America and Europe. When Demos Shakarian transferred his authority as president of the FGBMFI to his son on January 23, 1993, Richard made some changes in the organization.[69] Almost immediately, Richard removed several international directors from Canada and Asia after he transitioned into his role as president of the FGBMFI.[70] Richard also operated under a different leadership style than his father. Demos Shakarian was a natural listener with an easy going, cooperative, and considerate personality while Richard tended to be more candid, direct, and results-oriented.[71]

The biggest internal challenge that Richard Shakarian and the FGBMFI faced after Shakarian's death was the emergence of a new Business Men's Fellowship (BMF – 1995). With all of the recent changes, challenges, and transitions in leadership, several key members of the FGBMFI met in Kansas City in 1995 to discuss the possibility of starting a new business men's ministry. Even though financial difficulties and transitions in leadership may have played a big part in their decision, ultimately, it was a disagreement over the vision of the FGBMFI that led to this schism within the ranks of the FGBMFI. Many of the leaders in the newly chartered BMF recognized Richard Shakarian's anointing for evangelism, but they wanted to renew an emphasis upon the chapter meetings, testimonies, and importance of business men finding genuine Christian fellowship.[72]

As discussed in chapter eleven, a schism had already occurred with the establishment of the IFCB in 1989 after Demos Shakarian and the FGBMFI went through some financial turmoil.[73] However, no offshoot of the FGBMFI has been more successful than the Business Men's Fellowship which started in Kansas City, Missouri, in 1995.[74] Currently, the organization has approximately 150 active chapters in the United States in twenty-three states with nearly half of those chapters in California.[75] Much like the FGBMFI in the United States, some of the BMF's international chapters trace their lineage to Demos Shakarian's original vision.[76] While the BMF is fairly widespread in the United States, it has excelled in certain international arenas, particularly in Brazil. Perhaps almost half of the BMF chapters exist in Brazil, with somewhere between 1,500 and 2,000 chapters globally.[77] Coincidentally, Pentecostalism and the Charismatic movement have both continued to thrive in Brazil reflecting that same symbiotic relationship between this organization, the FGBMFI, and the various streams of renewal movements in the twentieth century.

The BMF desires to emphasize the importance of local chapter meetings and creating an environment for Christian fellowship among business men in the marketplace. Much like its parent organization, BMF utilizes a monthly bulletin called *Answer* to communicate the testimonies of business men.[78] While the organization has many similarities to the FGBMFI including testimonies, local chapters, and a monthly magazine, the BMF insists that it has remained true to Demos Shakarian's original vision of gathering together local business men through the sharing of testimonies and experiencing the power of the Holy Spirit. However, the organization desires to distinguish itself from the FGBMFI by emphasizing an approach to growth based more on relationships while still recognizing the parent organization's emphasis upon evangelism.[79] The BMF's distinction of relationship is based on chapter meetings that provide interaction and prayer between business men, meetings that devote more time for men to give their testimonies, and meetings that provide a comfortable setting where men can build strong Christian relationships and friendships.[80]

Ronnie Svenhard (d.b.a. 1935) became the founder and first president of the BMF. He was a business man and entrepreneur who, with his father and brother, established one of the most successful bakeries on the West Coast.[81] Ronnie was a FGBMFI member since 1969, and he served as the international treasurer of the organization from 1989 until 1993.[82] Interestingly, Svenhard's leadership style and personality had similar traits to Demos Shakarian's personality profile; consequently, many FGBMFI members transferred their membership to the BMF.[83] However, other FGBMFI members transferred their membership to the BMF because of ongoing concerns regarding nepotism.[84] As early as 1988, when John Wimber had a meeting with Demos Shakarian, Wimber suggested these concerns of nepotism when he stated that "some of the people are believing the lies that Demos is incapacitated and trying to keep the fellowship in the hands of family."[85]

Sadly, the schism between the FGBMFI and the BMF extended to the Shakarian family as many key leaders in the FGBMFI and even members of the Shakarian family including Richard's brother Steve, his brother-in-law Gene

Scalf, and Richard's mother Rose, all pledged their support to the newly formed BMF.[86] Rose Shakarian even donated the first $1,000 to the new BMF; her gesture was significant and perhaps symbolic since a donation of $1,000 by Miner Arganbright in 1952 helped launch the FGBMFI immediately after Shakarian received his vision on December 27, 1952.[87]

The internal family schism did not disappear with the death of Rose Shakarian.[88] However, forgiveness was a trait that Shakarian demonstrated towards FGBMFI members and family members and encouraged in others. Perhaps reconciliation began with the grandchildren as Karen, Michelle, and Brenda reunited shortly after the beginning of the new millennium.[89] Relationships continued to mend after the premature deaths of Deborah and Steve Shakarian in 2003 and 2004 respectively. Gene Scalf certainly expressed regret for his part in creating any division within the Shakarian family or the FGBMFI.[90] In addition, Gene has recently been reinstated as a member of the FGBMFI.[91]

Nevertheless, challenges were still ahead for the FGBMFI. As recently as 2006, a small schism occurred in the FGBMFI in North America that resulted in a new organization named the Full Gospel Business Men's Fellowship in America (FGBMFA).[92] This new organization acknowledges its lineage from Demos Shakarian's vision and the original foundations and history of the FGBMFI. In addition, it includes several key former leaders in the FGBMFI including Bob Bignold (1932–) and Peter Reding (1926–).[93] While this new organization functions in only three states and is primarily located in the Pacific Northwest, it is indicative of the two decades of decline for the FGBMFI in North America and Europe that is due in part to schism and controversy within the original organization.[94]

The FGBMFI also faces financial scrutiny and potential schisms from other member countries. At the 2008 World Convention, a FGBMFI member from Canada announced that the Canadian delegation was refusing to pay dues to the international headquarters and was threatening to secede from the international organization.[95] Peter Reding suggested that much of the recent controversy stems from financial questions related to the international headquarters and the fact that the FGBMFI has not become a member of the Evangelical Council for Financial Accountability (ECFA).[96]

Nevertheless, these organizations trace their lineage to the historic foundations established by Demos Shakarian, and most claim to represent his original vision. They all acknowledge the remarkable growth, creativity, and influence of Demos Shakarian's original vision, and they all honor and admit a debt of gratitude to Demos Shakarian as the founder of this movement. As such, in spite of schisms that diminished the size and influence of the original FGBMFI, all of these organizations can be claimed as a part of the spiritual legacy of Demos Shakarian.

While this chapter in Demos Shakarian's life is certainly one that he never envisioned, it is still part of his legacy. Now there were not one but four business men's fellowships that he helped found, a women's fellowship that he helped found indirectly, thousands of trained ministers who consequently started their own churches and their own men's ministries, and a maturing Charismatic movement that would now spawn many new and varied neo-Charismatic groups and movements. In all of these organizations, churches, and movements, the vision of Demos Shakarian continued to expand as it evolved and shaped thousands of churches and ministries and millions of people.

Demos Shakarian's Spiritual Legacy: The Current Status of the FGBMFI

In the aftermath of Demos Shakarian's death, the financial struggles the organization faced, and the schisms that occurred, it is somewhat surprising, if not miraculous, that the FGBMFI is alive and well today. In fact, many inactive or former members of the organization are still surprised to find that the FGMBFI is still a vibrant, active, and growing ministry in the twenty-first century.[97] Perhaps the challenges of the 1980s and 1990s brought into question the viability or survival of the organization. Nevertheless, under the helm of Richard Shakarian, the organization has survived and thrived. Tenacity is a trait that Richard Shakarian inherited from his father as he picked up the pieces of the organization his father founded and trudged on to take the organization to new heights internationally – even if they have not regained their former glory in North America.[98]

Richard Shakarian has reorganized the leadership of the FGBMFI to reflect its international growth by adding new international directors from other nations. He has also encouraged the creativity of his members and has endeavored to foster new growth and longevity by nurturing younger members of the organization.[99] Finally, he has promoted rapid growth in the organization through his emphasis on evangelism.[100] As a result, currently there are approximately 6,000 chapters of the FGMBFI in at least 160 countries worldwide.[101]

The FGBMFI today continues to carry on the tradition of Demos Shakarian's innovative and creative influence through its constantly evolving venues of ministry. Airlifts, while still continuing to some degree, have largely been replaced with an emphasis upon Fire Teams who bring a concerted evangelistic outreach to a community.[102] Fire Teams usually consist of hundreds, and sometimes thousands, of Full Gospel Business Men, who fly or drive into a community and provide lay evangelism, prayer teams, and impromptu healing services, climaxing with a series of evening rallies. The organization has also become more inclusive by creating a female branch of the organization called "Ladies of the Fellowship" or in some countries, "Women of the Fellowship." These venues provide more opportunity and participation for women by including them in the ministry of the fellowship, the prayer meetings, the Fire Teams, and the healing services. Some nations and chapters even allow women to have official leadership and membership in the organization although the international office and the FGBMFI bylaws have not changed their stance on female membership.[103]

While the organization includes a variety of political constituents internationally including communists, socialists, and even fascists, the FGBMFI consistently expresses conservative Christian values, and its political orientation in the United States decidedly leans towards the right of the political spectrum. Every year some chapters in the United States have a regional meeting in Washington, D.C., perhaps as a nostalgic glance back at earlier world and national conventions held in the District, but more likely in recognition of the seat of power this community holds. Featured speakers typically include Jimmy Johnson (d.b.a. 1930–), former assistant secretary of the navy and a member of the FGBMFI, and often a representative from the White House. [104]

The organization has also been able to express diversity in its racial and ecclesiological expressions. In 1975, an article in *The New York Times* described the FGBMFI as being predominantly white and Protestant.[105] While this article may have accurately described the constituency of the New York City FGBMFI chapter in 1975, it certainly did not express the voice of the fastest growing segment of the FGBMFI and the Charismatic movement over the past three decades. Since 1975, the major segment of growth in both the FGBMFI and the Charismatic movement has been in Latin America, Asia, and Africa, more often than not among Roman Catholics.[106]

Even in North America, the FGBMFI still shows resilience and growth in some regions. The Georgia Men's Advance remains one of the most popular events in the FGBMFI in North America. The annual retreat in Georgia started in 1981 with 120 men but today as many as 3,000 men meet over two weekends every year.[107] Recently, a FGBMFI chapter in Lancaster, Pennsylvania, began reaching out to people in the Amish community, and some members of the Amish community have responded with their own brand of Charismatic Christianity: praying for the sick; attending an international reconciliation conference for Amish, Mennonites, and Anabaptists in Sweden; teaching Iraqi Kurds suffering from post-traumatic stress disorder about the importance of forgiveness; and even praying with border guards between Iraq and Turkey, inviting them to sip tea together.[108]

Other recent ministries include an outreach to youth led by Demos Shakarian's granddaughter, Brenda Shakarian. The organization Brenda founded, Excellence International, aims to reach youth and young business men with a creative gospel message and connect them through local groups and modern technology. She is starting to broadcast in the Good News Studios out of the FGBMFI headquarters and provide pod-casts and telecasts that will cater to a younger audience.[109] While this studio might utilize the same name as the "Good News" programs Demos Shakarian broadcast in the 1970s and 1980s, it offers a fresh new approach using the latest technology and hopefully drawing a much needed younger audience to the aging ranks of the FGBMFI.

Perhaps the single most important influence upon the current resurgence of the FGBMFI today is the evangelistic vision of Demos Shakarian's son, Richard. The one aspect of Demos Shakarian's vision that has most impressed his son

Richard is the burden for lost souls that need to be evangelized by the Christian message. In spite of challenges, financial difficulties, and schisms that have hindered the FGBMFI over the past twenty years, Richard Shakarian claims that the organization today is reaching more men that it ever did. Richard recalls that when the organization was handed over to him in 1993, the FGBMFI was only reaching about 800,000 people per year, but now at least 2,300,000 people receive Christian salvation every year directly through the ministries of the FGBMFI.[110]

This emphasis upon evangelism has always been part of the ethos of the FGBMFI and a central part of the vision of Demos Shakarian. However, the effectiveness of their evangelism has increased and accelerated under the leadership of Richard Shakarian. Richard Shakarian was trained and groomed as an evangelist both in his biblical education at Southern California Bible School (now Vanguard University), in his involvement with Youth for Christ, and in his first experiences preaching as a young evangelist on the radio at Clifton's Cafeteria at the age of eighteen during those early years of the first FGBMFI chapter. However, even before he preached on the radio, he was a successful youth evangelist who helped start approximately three hundred Youth for Christ chapters in Southern California.[111] Richard recognized his affinity for evangelism as did his family, friends, and even his critics.[112]

In spite of Richard Shakarian's emphasis upon evangelism, it is difficult to predict the exact future of the FGBMFI. Perhaps there will be more schisms or perhaps some of the splinter groups will decide to reconcile and rejoin or regroup. Even internationally, some regions have lost members and chapters due to civil unrest, such as the Democratic Republic of Congo, while other regions have lost members due to attrition, such as Grenada, where one national president complained, "We have become a club of old men."[113] Because of the apparent symbiotic relationship between the Charismatic movement and the Full Gospel Business Men, it is possible that the future of these different branches of Demos Shakarian's vision may depend largely on the future of the Charismatic movement, the neo-Charismatic movement, and how these various pneumatic streams continue to relate to the Church and to society.

Arguably, at least two of these organizations, the FGBMFI and the BMF, are firmly established worldwide and continue to grow internationally. Richard Shakarian's emphasis upon evangelism and the proclamation of the gospel is irrepressible, and he is convinced of the urgency of his task and the importance of continuing the vision that began with his father. He emphasizes the evangelistic outreaches, the Fire Teams, and the number of salvations that are regularly recorded through the various ministries and outreaches related to the FGBMFI.

The BMF is equally emphatic about the importance of reaching business men through local chapter meetings and sharing testimonies that reach and incorporate people in various marketplace settings. While their style of evangelism is more relational, they have still been successful in spreading their message and multiplying their chapters through the testimonies of business men and the Christian fellowship they provide. In fact, at least in North America and in some South American nations, they have been extremely effective in reaching their target audience.

For both of these organizations and for the Full Gospel Business Men globally, the future still looks promising. However, there are questions of succession and transition that will need to be answered eventually. Richard Shakarian turned seventy-five years old in October of 2009, and he is already a few years older than his father was when he faced the severe health problems that created a leadership crisis in the FGBMFI in the 1980s. However, there are currently no plans for a leadership transition in the FGBMFI. Ron Weinbender insists that when the time for a transition is right, God will let them know.[114] Inevitably a transition will take place, but unless Steve Shakarian's young adult son Stephen, Jr., becomes involved in the FGBMFI or a change in the bylaws allows women to become executive leaders, it is not likely that another Shakarian will follow Richard Shakarian at the helm of the FGBMFI.[115]

While the FGBMFI is hesitant to think about future leadership transitions, the BMF has already experienced a smooth leadership transition in its brief existence. Ronny Svenhard recently retired as president of the BMF, and Wendell Nordby has taken over that role.[116] Of course, Svenhard is still the chairman of the global network of BMF chapters, but at least the BMF leadership has successfully experienced a significant leadership transition which bodes well for future leadership changes in the organization.

Demos Shakarian's Spiritual Legacy and its Broader Implications

The rise of the neo-Charismatic movement and the rise of post-denominationalism are beyond the scope of this study, but they do present a broader sphere of influence for Shakarian's lasting legacy upon global Christianity. The fact that Shakarian had some significant interaction with John Wimber, one of the pioneers of the neo-Charismatic movement in North America, has already been established.[117] Since Wimber came to the FGBMFI World Convention in Detroit, Michigan, in 1983 and prophesied of this already emerging neo-Charismatic movement brings added weight to Shakarian's possible influence upon the neo-Charismatic movement.[118] In addition, while numerous other scholars have already established Shakarian's credentials as a pioneer and founder within the Charismatic movement, David Barrett places the beginning of the FGBMFI within the chronological emergence of the neo-Charismatic movement thus giving Shakarian significant credit for helping promote and establish the neo-Charismatic movement domestically and internationally.[119]

Interestingly, Barrett also compares the rise of the neo-Charismatic movement with post-denominationalism since, by Barrett's definition, neo-Charismatics tend to be independent post-denominationalists.[120] While the rise of post-denominationalism was not quite as significant as the combined renewal movements of the past century, 386,000,000 Christian constituents were outside of the confines of any traditional Christian ecclesiology by the year 2000, including the 65,000,000 members of the African Independent Churches.[121] Richard Shakarian admitted that the FGBMFI's direct contribution to post-denominationalism occurred when they trained thousands of laymen to perform practical ministry duties. Consequently, these FGBMFI members resigned their secular positions and devoted themselves to pioneering independent neo-Charismatic churches.[122]

To suggest that Demos Shakarian and the FGBMFI pioneered all of these movements, including post-denominationalism, would be an overstatement. However, Demos Shakarian did have significant influence upon the Pentecostal movement and post-denominationalism, he was a leading pioneer of the Charismatic movement, and he helped instigate the neo-Charismatic movement either directly, indirectly, or perhaps both. In addition, Demos Shakarian's spiritual legacy and his emphasis upon global Christianity should not be understated. As the FGBMFI and these renewal movements continue to grow internationally, Barrett predicts that the combined renewal movements of the past century will grow to represent 811,551,594 constituents by 2025.[123]

Conclusion

While only a few of his great-grandchildren have memories of Demos Shakarian, his grandchildren and his two surviving children remember Shakarian with affection. Some of the grandchildren fondly recall the way that Shakarian treated his wife Rose, and many of his descendants reflect his entrepreneurial spirit.[124] All of his children and grandchildren continue to faithfully participate in the Charismatic movement, and a few of them contribute to his legacy as leaders in that movement.

In addition to his family, Shakarian loved his cattle. In defining the life of Demos Shakarian, his son-in-law described Shakarian as a cattleman and a dairyman who had a life-long passion for his dairy cows.[125] His innovations, his inventions, and his prize bulls have all left a lasting legacy that continues to make the California dairy industry one of the largest milk producing provinces in the world.

Nevertheless, it was Shakarian's avocation, and not his vocation, which became his greatest spiritual legacy. However, to call the FGBMFI his avocation would become a misnomer shortly after he received his vision in 1952. His avocation eventually consumed his life, becoming his vocation as the organization he founded began to impact global Christianity. With perhaps more than 8,000 chapters of the Full Gospel Business Men meeting in a variety of venues, settings, and organizations throughout the world, the future of the various organizations that trace their roots back to Demos Shakarian and the vision he received in 1952 look bright indeed. While many of these same organizations may continue to fluctuate in different regions and nations, their overall global influence continues to increase, reach new arenas, and new horizons. In the twenty-first century, the Full

Gospel Business Men may face further challenges, schisms, and fluctuations, but their emphasis upon the Charismatic nature of Christianity will continue to leave a lasting impression upon the ecclesiastical, ecumenical, and pneumatic aspects of global religion for the foreseeable future.

Notes

1. Myrna Oliver, "Demos Shakarian; Founded Religious Group," *Los Angeles Times*, July 30, 1993, 28.

2. See the memorial issue of Demos Shakarian in *Voice*, October 1993.

3. Information gathered from Rose Hills Memorial Park and Mortuary, Whittier, CA; Rose Shakarian, Social Security Death Index (accessed December 1, 2008); and Dian Scott-Tallman phone interview, July 16, 2008.

4. Harald and Renee Berge-Tallman interview, January 9, 2008; Dian Scott-Tallman phone interview, July 16, 2008; and Karen Linamen-Tallman interview, January 9, 2008.

5. Gene Scalf-Tallman interview, January 9, 2008. Scalf suggests that Shakarian was better at his investment choices because of his ability to be directed by the Holy Spirit in the purchase and sale of various properties.

6. Michelle Willett, interview by Matthew Tallman, Colorado Springs, CO, January 10, 2008.

7. Karen Scalf Linamen-Tallman interview, January 11, 2008; and World Cat Search, December 3, 2008.

8. Harald and Renee Berge, interview by Matthew Tallman, Colorado Springs, CO, January 9, 2008.

9. Brenda Shakarian, interview by Matthew Tallman, Irvine, CA, January 18, 2008.

10. Brenda Shakarian, e-mail correspondence to Matthew Tallman, October 6, 2008.

11. Bob Armstrong, *Celebrate the 50th Year Jubilee Anniversary* (Lake Forest, CA: Full Gospel Business Men's Fellowship International, 2002), 38.

12. Geri Shakarian Scalf-Tallman interview, January 9, 2008; Karen Linamen Scalf-Tallman interview January 10, 2008; Renee Berge Scalf-Tallman interview, January 9, 2008; Michelle Willett Scalf-Tallman interview, January 10, 2008; Richard Shakarian-Tallman interview, January 16, 2008; and Brenda Shakarian-Tallman interview, January 18, 2008.

13. Geri Shakarian Scalf-Tallman interview, January 8, 2008.

14. The dairy sign in Downey, CA is in front of a vacant convenience store where the drive through dairy canopy still remains. The other location in Bell Garden, CA is in front of an existing convenience store whose current owner has no knowledge of the history of Reliance Dairies. In addition, the sign in front of the Bell Garden convenience store advertises "Rockview Drive-in Dairy" indicating that the local Rockview Dairy may have bought out some of the Reliance Drive-in Dairies when they closed.

15. For more information about the history of Starbucks see "Starbucks Timeline and History," Starbucks Coffee http://www.starbucks.com/aboutus/timeline.asp (accessed December 5, 2008).

16. Gene Scalf-Tallman interview, January 8, 2008.

17. "California Dairy Industry Facts," California Dairy Quality Assurance Program, http://www.cdqa.org/facts/ (accessed December 3, 2008).

18. This legacy was suggested by Andy Kaminski and Gene Scalf in a joint interview with the author in Colorado Springs, CO on January 9, 2008.

19. Andy Kaminski, interview by Matthew Tallman, Colorado Springs, CO, January 9, 2008; and Gene Scalf-Tallman interview, January 9, 2008.

20. Richard Shakarian-Tallman interview, January 16, 2008.

21. Oral Roberts, "The Crowning Triumph," *Voice*, October 1993, 17–18.

22. See *Voice*, October 1993.

23. *Voice*, November 1993, 1–32; the prophecies are listed from pp. 20–25.

24. Richard Shakarian, "A Word from Richard Shakarian," *Voice*, November 1993, 3.

25. Richard Shakarian, "An Introduction to the Full Gospel Businessmen's Fellowship International," FGBMFI, http://www.fgbmfi.org, (accessed November 4, 2007).

26. Asamoah-Gyadu, "'Missionaries without Robes'" (Fall 1997): 173.

27. Weinbender-Tallman interview, March 27, 2006; and Jim Priddy, "Report of All Nations," Ft. Lauderdale, FL, July 7, 2006. While Ron Weinbender suggests that the organization currently has 500 chapters in the United States, it is not certain if all of these chapters are active, but it is certain that many of these chapters are aging judging by the demographics of those attending regional and national FGBMFI conventions in the United States. At a recent regional FGBMFI convention in Washington, D.C., in a business meeting on February 23, 2008, a national director from California mentioned there were thirty-seven active chapters in California. Since California is still the center of activity and the most active region for the FGBMFI in the United States, it is likely that the 500 chapters Weinbender referred to may all be registered, but they might not all be active.

28. Bob Armstrong, *Celebrate the 50th Year Jubilee Anniversary* (Lake Forest, CA: Full Gospel Business Men's Fellowship International, 2002), 27.

29. Jim Priddy, "Report of All Nations," July 7, 2006.

30. Barrett, *World Christian Encyclopedia* (2001), 1:15.

31. Barrett, *World Christian Encyclopedia* (2001), 1:15. By 1990, North America had already seen a 278 percent increase. Also see Richard Quebedeaux, *The New Charismatics II: How a Christian Renewal Movement Became Part of the American Religious Mainstream* (San Francisco: Harper & Row, Publishers, 1983).

32. Barrett, *World Christian Encyclopedia* (2001), 1:14.

33. Ibid.

34. Richard Shakarian, "Report of All Nations," July 7, 2006; and Jerry Jensen *FGBMFI 1988–89 World Chapter Directory* (1989), 29 and 32.

35. Richard Shakarian, "Report of All Nations," July 7, 2006; and Jerry Jensen *FGBMFI 1988–89 World Chapter Directory* (1989), 30–32.

36. Richard Shakarian, "Report of All Nations," July 7, 2006; and Jerry Jensen *FGBMFI 1988–89 World Chapter Directory* (1989), 30–33. In 1989, West Germany had only sixty-seven chapters but there was no record of any chapters in East Germany before the two nations merged.

37. Barrett, *World Christian Encyclopedia* (2001), 1:13.

38. Asamoah-Gyadu, "'Missionaries without Robes,'" (Fall 1997): 168.

39. Jerry Jensen, *FGBMFI 1988–89 World Chapter Directory* (1989), 52–53.

40. Richard Shakarian-Tallman interview, January 10, 2005; Also Richard Shakarian, "Report of All Nations," FGBMFI World Convention, Fort Lauderdale, FL, July 7, 2006.

41. Richard Shakarian, "Report of All Nations," July 4, 2008.

42. Asamoah-Gyadu, "'Missionaries without Robes,'" (Fall 1997): 175.

43. Ibid, 184.

44. Josiah-Tallman interview, July 26, 2005.

45. Josiah-Tallman interview, July 26, 2005; and Richard Shakarian, "Report of All Nations," July 7, 2008.

46. Barrett, *World Christian Encyclopedia* (2001), 1:13.

47. Ibid.

48. Richard Shakarian, "Report of All Nations, July 4, 2008; and Jerry Jensen *FGBM-FI 1988–89 World Chapter Directory* (1989), 43–44.

49. Richard Shakarian, "Report of All Nations," July 7, 2006.

50. Barrett, *World Christian Encyclopedia* (2001), 1:14.

51. Fotherby, *The Awakening Giant* (2000), 167.

52. Ibid, 169.

53. Richard Shakarian-Tallman interview, January 10, 2005; and Richard Shakarian, "Report of All Nations," July 4, 2008.

54. Richard Shakarian-Tallman interview, January 16, 2008.

55. Ibid.

56. Humberto Aguilar-Tallman interview, July 4, 2008.

57. See Demos Shakarian, *The Happiest People* (1975), 151–152; Richard Shakarian-Tallman interview, January 10, 2005. and Richard Shakarian-Tallman interview, January 16, 2008.

58. Richard Shakarian, "Directors Meeting and Training," presentation given at the Washington, D.C. Full Gospel Business Men's International Regional Winter Conference, Arlington, VA, February 23, 2008.

59. Richard Shakarian, "Report of All Nations," July 7, 2006.

60. Richard Shakarian, "Report of All Nations, July 4, 2008.

61. Fotherby, *The Awakening Giant* (2000), 159–160.

62. Richard Shakarian, "Report of All Nations," Orlando, FL, July 4, 2008.

63. Richard Shakarian, "Directors Meeting and Training," presentation given at the Washington, D.C., Full Gospel Business Men's International Regional Winter Conference, Arlington, VA, February 23, 2008.

64. Ibid. Also see Richard Shakarian, "Reports of All Nations," July 7, 2006.

65. Ibid.

66. Richard Shakarian, "Directors Meeting and Training," February 23, 2008; and Richard Shakarian, Report of All Nations," July 4, 2008.

67. Richard Shakarian, "Report of All Nations, July 4, 2008.

68. Dian Scott-Tallman phone interview, January 22, 2008.

69. Ron Weinbender-Tallman interview, January 16, 2008.

70. Dian Scott-Tallman phone interview, July 16, 2008.

71. Demos Shakarian, personality profile, submitted to Management By Strengths, Incorporated, Olathe, KS, September 20, 1989; and Richard Shakarian, personality profile, submitted to Management By Strengths, Incorporated, Olathe, KS, December 23, 1986.

72. Dian Scott-Tallman phone interview, January 14, 2008.

73. For a more detailed account of that power struggle, see Mark Bellinger's *Demos: The Man of Fellowship* (1992).

74. See the organization's web site at http://www.bmfusa.com for more information. Information on this organization has also been supplied through interviews with the founder, Ronnie Svenhard, and Dian Scott, the Director of Administration for the organization.

75. Business Men's Fellowship, "Business Men's Fellowship Chapters and Meetings," BMF, http://www.bmfusa.com/chapter.html, (accessed February 15, 2008). The web site mentions that there are 150 chapters in the United States, but they only have links to 101 of these chapters. There are links to forty-five chapters in California alone. Interestingly, the parent organization, FGBMFI, also has a significant portion of its active chapters in

California where the organization was first birthed in 1951. However, demonstrating some of the success of the BMF, their organization exceeds the number of active FGBMFI chapters in California by a small margin (at the "Directors Meeting and Training," February 23, 2008, it was announced that the FGBMFI had only thirty-seven active chapters in California.).

76. See http://www.bmf-uk.com for an example of one of the international BMF organizations that traces its lineage to the original foundations of the FGBMFI. However, the BMF in the United States does not mention Demos Shakarian's vision on their web site.

77. Ronnie Svenhard, phone interview by Matthew Tallman, January 21, 2008. Svenhard estimates that fewer than 1,500 chapters exist globally, while Dian Scott estimates that as many as 2000 chapters exist worldwide (Scott-Tallman phone interview, January 14, 2008).

78. Business Men's Fellowship, "Who We Are," BMF, http://www.bmfusa.com/chapter.html, (accessed February 15, 2008).

79. This distinction was made by Dian Scott in her phone interview, January 14, 2008.

80. See Business Men's Fellowship, "Who We Are," BMF, http://www.bmfusa.com/chapter.html, (accessed February 15, 2008).

81. Ronnie Svenhard, "He Took It and Blessed It," *Voice*, November 1992, 24.

82. Ronnie Svenhard-Tallman interview, January 22, 2008.

83. See Ronnie Svenhard, personality profile, submitted to Management By Strengths, Incorporated, Olathe, KS, March 30, 1990; and Demos Shakarian, personality profile, submitted to Management By Strengths, Incorporated, Olathe, KS, September 20, 1989.

84. Dian Scott-Tallman interview, July 16, 2008; and Peter Reding-Tallman interview, December 5, 2008.

85. Mark Bellinger, *Demos: The Man of Fellowship* (1992), 135.

86. Pinsky, "A Baptism by Fire," August 8, 2001, A1; and Dian Scott-Tallman interview, January 14, 2008.

87. Dian Scott-Tallman interview, January 14, 2008.

88. Ibid.

89. Karen Linamen, *I'm not Suffering from Insanity…I'm Enjoying Every Minute of It!* (Grand Rapids, MI: Fleming H. Revell, 2002), 17–19.

90. Gene Scalf-Tallman interview, January 11, 2008.

91. Ibid.

92. For more information on this new organization see their website at http://www.fgbmfamerica.org. Interestingly, this is similar to the first title given to the original FGBMFI in 1951.

93. Full Gospel Business Men's Fellowship in America, "Minutes of the Organizational Meeting National Council of Directors," Full Gospel Business Men's Fellowship in America http://www.fgbmfamerica.org (accessed February 15, 2008).

94. Full Gospel Business Men's Fellowship in America, "Chapters," FGBMFA, http://www.fgbmfamerica.org (accessed February 15, 2008). In February 2008, the web site mentioned there were sixteen active chapters registered (ten chapters in Washington State, five chapters in Oregon, and one chapter in Florida). As recently as December 5, 2008, Peter Reding mentioned that there were now nineteen chapters (Peter Reding-Tallman interview, December 5, 2008).

95. Dennis Spenst, interview with Matthew Tallman, Orlando, FL, July 4, 2008.

96. Peter Reding-Tallman interview, December 5, 2008; also see the Full Gospel Business Men's Fellowship in America Articles of Incorporation which states that "it is the

intent of the Initial Directors of this organization to affiliate with the Full Gospel Business Men's Fellowship International at such time as it qualifies and becomes a member of the Evangelical Council of Financial Accountability." (Full Gospel Business Men's Fellowship in America, "Articles of Incorporation," Full Gospel Business Men's Fellowship in America, http://www.fgbmfamerica.org (accessed December 8, 2008).

97. In the introductory stages of researching this study, numerous individuals questioned whether the organization still existed. These included pastors, Christian leaders, and occasionally former members of the FGBMFI who had not kept informed of the organization's international growth. As an example, Harding Mushegian questioned whether the organization still existed during his interview with the author on January 14, 2008.

98. Richard Shakarian-Tallman interview, January 16, 2008; also consider Richard Shakarian's personality profile which lists tenacity as one of his primary characteristics (Richard Shakarian, personality profile, submitted to Management By Strengths, Incorporated, Olathe, KS, December 23, 1986).

99. Richard Shakarian-Tallman interview, January 10, 2005.

100. Richard Shakarian-Tallman interview, January 16, 2008.

101. Richard Shakarian, "An Introduction to the Full Gospel Businessmen's Fellowship International," FGBMFI, http://www.fgbmfi.org (accessed November 4, 2007).

102. Richard Shakarian-Tallman interview, January 10, 2005.

103. Weinbender-Tallman interview, January 16, 2008.

104. See Jim Johnson's testimony in *Voice*, December 1986, 36–37.

105. Kenneth A. Briggs, "Religion is Now an Important Part of Business," *The New York Times*, May 11, 1975, E10.

106. These statistics have already been mentioned earlier in this chapter, but for further clarification or information, consult David Barrett's *World Christian Encyclopedia* (2001).

107. Jimmy Rogers, *Victory Over Shattered Dreams: From Sharecropper to Successful Businessman* (Atlanta, GA: Jimmy Rogers, 2001), 140–141; and Jimmy Rogers-Tallman interview, February 22, 2008.

108. Gene Arnold, interview by Matthew Tallman, Orlando, FL, July 5, 2008. For more information about these Amish Charismatic Christians see www.lightofhopeministries.com and Paula Hornberger, "Amish Man Begins Healing Ministry," *Charisma*, August 2008, 14.

109. Brenda Shakarian, "Welcome to Excellence International," Excellence International, http://www.excellenceint.com, (accessed February 13, 2008).

110. Richard Shakarian-Tallman interview, January 16, 2008.

111. Richard Shakarian-Tallman interview, January 10, 2005.

112. Even those involved in the most significant schism to occur within the FGMBFI in 1995, including Dian Scott and Ronny Svenhardt, admit to Richard Shakarian's anointing and effectiveness at evangelism. (Dian Scott-Tallman phone interview, January 14, 2008; and Ronny Svenhardt-Tallman phone interview, January 20, 2008).

113. Richard Shakarian, "Report of All Nations," July 7, 2006.

114. Ron Weinbender-Tallman interview, January 16, 2008. He also added that he thought the 1980s transition led to problems and schism because people tried to accelerate or rush a transition of leadership prematurely. Weinbender felt that "neither Demos Shakarian nor God were ready to relinquish the leadership of the Full Gospel Business Men at that time."

115. The Shakarian most actively involved in the FGBMFI in the next generation after Richard Shakarian is Brenda Shakarian. She has taken a significant leadership role in min-

istering to the next generation of future Full Gospel members, but as already mentioned, unless the bylaws are altered at some point, she would be ineligible to become involved in the executive leadership of the organization.

116. Ronny Svenhard-Tallman phone interview, January 21, 2008.

117. See Demos Shakarian-Synan interview, February 2, 1988, 14–15; and Mark Bellinger, *Demos: The Man of Fellowship* (1992), 134–136.

118. "Detroit 83," *Voice*, September 1983, 23.

119. See David Barrett, "A Chronology of Renewal in the Spirit," in Vinson Synan's *The Century of the Holy Spirit* (2001), 429–433.

120. Barrett, *World Christian Encyclopedia* (2001), 1:29.

121. Ibid, 1:12.

122. Richard Shakarian-Tallman interview, January 16, 2008.

123. Barrett, *World Christian Encyclopedia* (2001), 1:4.

124. Karen Linamen Scalf and Michelle Willett Scalf both spoke fondly of the relationship between Demos and Rose Shakarian in their interview with the author on January 10, 2008.

125. Gene Scalf-Tallman interview, January 9, 2008.

Chapter Thirteen

Concluding Remarks

As this biographical sketch of Shakarian's life concludes, a few important questions need to be asked and answered. How has this study contributed to the academic fields of church history and renewal studies? Does the research in this project also correlate to any other academic arenas of inquiry? Has the information provided in this manuscript offered an accurate and thorough academic portrayal of Demos Shakarian's life, and if so, how? In conclusion, what is the life, legacy, and vision of Demos Shakarian?

The field of church history is filled with names such as Tertullian, Augustine, and Martin Luther; events such as the Ecumenical Council of Chalcedon, the Schism of 1054, and the Cane Ridge Revival of 1801; and movements such as Montanism, Pietism, and Methodism. While Demos Shakarian cannot be identified directly with any of these topics, he did identify with, contribute to, or correlate significantly to several movements in the twentieth century, including the Pentecostal movement, the Charismatic movement, the neo-Charismatic movement, and even post-denominationalism. As such, a biographical study of Demos Shakarian has hopefully contributed to a greater understanding of these movements and their historical significance in modern church history.

The field of renewal studies deals with the study of people, events, theology, and movements as they relate to the Spirit and the process of renewal within the world. Renewal studies intersects with church history in every event, movement, and person mentioned in the previous paragraph and a great many more in history, but it involves a narrower focus on how various people and movements have emphasized renewal, interpreted and identified with the Spirit, and interacted with the church in their understanding of the Spirit's interaction within human history. Demos Shakarian was arguably an instrument of renewal through the neo-Charismatic movement, a progenitor of renewal through the Charismatic movement, and an active participant of renewal through the Pentecostal movement. As such, this biographical study of Demos Shakarian has hopefully offered some additional insight to the understanding of these renewal movements for participants, students, and scholars alike. The events of his life intersected with all three movements and also provided some helpful insight towards the understanding of renewal in church history, the historical similarities with previous renewal movements in church history, and the historical continuity of renewal movements throughout church history.

The study of Demos Shakarian's life has also intersected with other fields of inquiry and hopefully contributed to some additional information and new areas of inquiry in those fields. Shakarian's own pneumatic background and the charismatic fervor of his Armenian Molokan ancestors has offered some additional material to consider in the field of pneumatology. How Shakarian's church in La Habra Heights, California contributed to the field of ecclesiology and a comprehensive analysis of the First Armenian Pentecostal Church are topics worthy of their own research. The Shakarian immigration to the United States is a topic which could contribute significantly to the study of human migration and sociology. The contrast between Shakarian's contribution to ecumenism during the Charismatic movement and the schismatic events which later occurred in his own organization can provide an interesting case study for the field of ecumenism. In addition, the sectarian nature of Shakarian's Molokan brethren and the larger conflicts which occurred in the Charismatic movement can add important impetus to any understanding of religious dialogue and broaden the scope of any case studies in the field of ecumenism.

This biography on Demos Shakarian's life offers new material to the study of his contribution to religion in several areas of academic research already mentioned. This study offers the first detailed attempt to narrate a detailed chronology of his life. In addition, this narrative involves a critical analysis of his life, including the remarks and concerns of both his critics and his supporters, thus attempting to dispense a fair and honest evaluation of his life. It is the hope of this author that this study will be considered seriously by a broad academic audience who has not previously considered or read about the life of Demos Shakarian. Hopefully in the process, all readers might gain a greater understanding of Shakarian's life, his vision, and his lasting contribution to renewal movements in the twentieth century.

In summary, Demos Shakarian began his life in a simple house on a small dairy farm in Southern California. He ended his life with a large extended family, a significant fortune made in the dairy industry and real estate, and an organization that continues to influence Christianity on a global scale. While the first half of Demos Shakarian's life, and the context that preceded it, helped shape his vision, the second half of his life was influenced largely by his vision. His own charismatic praxis and pneumatology was shaped by a group of Russian Molokans, some healing evangelists, and his own Armenian context. His ecclesiology was influenced by his First Armenian Pentecostal Church and the larger context of Armenian Church history. His ecumenism was forged from his own Armenian context and the mentors who influenced him. His life was largely directed by the prophetic word that saved his ancestors and led him into a new promised land of Christianity. His business acumen, creativity, and discernment served him well throughout his life and ministry. However, without his vision, his legacy would have been in question.

What was the vision of Demos Shakarian? First of all, Shakarian's vision was prophetic. In other words, as Shakarian perceived his vision in 1952, he did not simply observe a visual suggestion but a prophetic command that he believed was imperative to obey. In addition, he believed that this vision was a normal expression of his charismatic background, and as such, the organization he founded on this vision expressed a similar pneumatic emphasis. Thus he founded a ministry that was "full gospel."

His vision expressed a certain need to reach men, specifically business men, who were spiritually dead and seemingly disconnected from a relationship with God. Even before he ever received his pneumatic vision, his keen observational skills and discernment had already led him to the conclusion that business men were largely an untapped and unchurched segment of society that needed to be reconnected with the charismatic message of Christianity he was proposing. As a result of the prophetic words of Milton Hansen, Charles Price, and Oral Roberts, and Demos Shakarian's own vision, Shakarian became acutely aware of his own role in meeting this need.

The men Shakarian observed in his vision were not only spiritually disconnected from God, but they were also spiritually isolated from one another. As such, his vision included a desire to link these men together through a fellowship of business men. In addition, this Christian organization was not led by ministers but by business men who were empowered and linked together by the expression of their testimonies and their charismatic ministry for one another. As they empowered one another and allied with each other, they became a significant evangelistic force in global Christianity in the twentieth century.

The vision was not meant to be confined merely to a Full Gospel Business Men's Fellowship for America. The vision offered Shakarian a panoramic view of North and South America, Europe, Africa, Oceania, and Asia that would encompass the globe with the pneumatic gospel Shakarian saw and experienced. As a result, the FGBMFI became one of the most important factors in growing and spreading a global Charismatic movement that encompassed nearly every nation and almost every ecclesiology of Christianity.

How will Demos Shakarian be remembered in future generations? His family will remember him as a man devoted to God, his wife, his children, and his grandchildren. They will also remember him as a dairy man, an entrepreneur, and a visionary business man who loved his cattle and the thrill of finding a prize bull or increasing the butter fat content in his milk production.

Nevertheless, the legacy that his family and most of twentieth century Christianity will remember is the spiritual legacy Demos Shakarian passed on through the Pentecostal, Charismatic, and neo-Charismatic movements. He founded the largest Christian business men's organization in the world with over 6,000 chapters worldwide. In addition, he indirectly helped start at least three more Christian business men's organizations, and one Christian women's organization which rivals the FGBMFI in chapters and membership and exceeds it in international diversity. He sponsored thousands of ministries and evangelists domestically and internationally who would not have survived financially without the support of Demos Shakarian and the FGBMFI. His organization trained thousands of business men who ultimately became involved in active full time ministry and hundreds of thousands more who continue to be involved in lay evangelism in various capacities. Some of these business men are now household names in modern global Christianity, including Pat Robertson of the 700 Club and the Christian Broadcasting Network, who started as a chapter president of the FGBMFI in 1960 just as he began his fledgling television ministry.[1] Other names include Kenneth Copeland who started in ministry as an active member of a local FGBMFI chapter and Paul Crouch of the Trinity Broadcasting Network, who was largely supported by Demos Shakarian early in his ministry when Shakarian sat on his board.[2] Of course the dozens of internationally known healing evangelists he supported would never have likely had adequate financing or organizational support without his leadership and business acumen. Most notable among these was Oral Roberts.

Shakarian's name is mentioned among the most influential innovators of the modern Charismatic movement along with David DuPlessis, Dennis Bennett, and Oral Roberts. His organization far exceeded the influence of any other ministry or denomination in sparking this pneumatic renewal that changed the face of modern global Christianity. As such, he fulfilled his divine mandate, and his vision lives on in the hearts and minds of hundreds of millions of Pentecostal, Charismatic, and neo-Charismatic Christians today who owe a debt of spiritual gratitude to the legacy he left behind

Notes

1. David Harrell, *Pat Robertson* (1987), 53.
2. Ronny Svenhard, phone interview by Matthew Tallman, January 22, 2008.

Demos Shakarian at the FGBMFI Headquarters

Demos Shakarian in His Home

Demos and Rose Shakarian Celebrating their
Fiftieth Wedding Anniversary

Demos Shakarian celebrating His Seventy-Fifth Birthday

Demos Shakarian on His Seventy-Fifth Birthday
with His Wife, Daughters, and Grandchildren

292

Celebrating a Shakarian Family Christmas

Pallbearers Placing Demos Shakarian's Casket in His Grave

Family and Friends at the Burial Ceremony of Demos Shakarian

Demos Shakarian's Headstone

FGBMFI Current Headquarters

Bibliographical Essay

Most individuals familiar with Demos Shakarian have read at least one primary source about his life. *The Happiest People on Earth*, first published in 1975 and co-authored by John (1923–) and Elizabeth Sherrill (1928–), sold millions of copies in the next few years, and it is still widely distributed by the FGBMFI. As important as this source is for understanding Shakarian's life, the document has several shortcomings as a primary source. The editorial work in the book presented by the Sherrills, popular authors in the Charismatic movement, revealed their occasional biases when writing about the history of the FGBMFI or the history of Demos Shakarian and his family.[1] The Sherrills also called these Armenians and charismatic Molokan Christians "Pentecostal" before the movement started, in spite of the fact that they shared many similar characteristics to classical Pentecostalism.[2] In addition, the Sherrill's editorial interpretation of Shakarian's life credited almost all of the growth and influence of the FGBMFI to providential causes while neglecting any possible sociological, historically genetic, or anthropological explanations.[3] Finally, Shakarian's autobiography does not include important information pertaining to the last two decades of his life.

Fortunately, other important primary sources assist in offering a more complete portrait of Shakarian's life and legacy. Among these sources, the most important material can be found in the complete collection of *Voice* magazine (1953–), published by the FGBMFI, and seven inspirational books which Shakarian published between 1984 and 1992.[4] Audio-taped interviews provided additional information regarding how Demos Shakarian worked to help launch and sustain the FGBMFI as it expanded internationally. Vinson Synan provided the transcripts of interviews conducted with Demos Shakarian in 1987, 1988, and 1992.[5] Oral interviews conducted for the past four years with Shakarian's immediate family helped to examine his personal life, the challenges he faced later in life, as well as the schisms and fluctuation that his organization faced as his health began to deteriorate. In addition, these interviews and sources written in the last decade are offered to consider the current state of Shakarian's legacy, the FGBMFI.

Demos Shakarian gave two alternate accounts of his early life story which help give an excellent alternative to the account given in his autobiography.[6] First the *Voice* magazine and second, a lengthy list of oral interviews, have been crucial in confirming the latter half of Demos Shakarian's life. Both of these accounts were given consideration when triangulating the accuracy of Shakarian's version of events.

Vinson Synan wrote the first scholarly book on the growth and influence of the FGBMFI. However, he urged further scholarship concerning this organization and its founder.[7] Val Fotherby (d.b.a. 1940–) wrote a popular tribute to the FGBMFI in 1989 which was somewhat useful, especially from a European perspective.[8] In addition, she added a more recent account of the organization which offered the most current status of the FGBMFI.[9] Subsequently, Mark Bellinger (1955–1999) wrote a popular account of Demos Shakarian and the FGBMFI. It offered one of the only accounts of the schism that occurred in the 1980s, but its focus was limited to the challenges Demos Shakarian faced during that schism and the book tends to be primarily inspirational.[10] There is only one scholarly journal article available on the FGBMFI; nevertheless, the article from Asamoah-Gyadu (d.b.a.1950–) is quite helpful in analyzing the influence and growth of this movement in Africa.[11] Beyond this, there are several popular articles appearing in *Christianity Today*, *The Pentecostal Evangel*, and *Charisma*. The only other scholarly citations of the FGBMFI are found in approximately twelve different books, two dissertations, and a few encyclopedias and dictionaries examining the Charismatic renewal, ranging from Margaret Poloma's tome to David Harrell's examination of the renewal.[12] Hollenweger offers both the most emphatic recognition of the influence of the FGBMFI and the most critical analysis of its shortcomings. Even though his analysis is critical, his sociological observations regarding the FGBMFI in Latin America may give some simple clues to its global growth and influence far beyond its numerical growth.[13]

The other primary sources directly pertaining to Demos Shakarian include the entire collection of the FGBMFI's *Voice* magazines and two dozen books and evangelistic pamphlets written by Demos Shakarian and the FGBMFI, archived at the Regent University Library in Virginia Beach, Virginia.[14] The significance of *Voice* magazine as an important primary source cannot be underestimated since Demos Shakarian left no personal journal or diary. *Voice* magazine records significant details about where and what Shakarian did for the last half of his life.[15] *Voice* was first published in February 1953, edited by Thomas R. Nickel (1900–1993), and distributed as an inspirational magazine to promote the activities and testimonies of the FGBMFI. It was generally distributed monthly, ranged in size from twenty-four to forty pages in length, and remains currently the official magazine of the FGBMFI.

Additional primary sources included a personality profile that Demos Shakarian submitted on September 20, 1989 to Management By Strengths, Incorporated (MBS).[16] MBS used psychological benchmarks and common characteristics to evaluate Shakarian's personality and categorize his leadership and personality traits. The United States Patent Office recorded a patent that Demos Shakarian submitted in 1964 for improving the process of milking his dairy cows.[17] In the last decade of his life, Shakarian wrote some mostly inspirational works, but they give some helpful insight into his theology.[18] In addition, there are two smaller archives of audio-taped FGBMFI sermons available at the University of North Carolina at Chapel Hill and Asbury Theological Seminary.

As already mentioned, Vinson Synan provided the transcripts of three interviews he conducted with Demos Shakarian shortly before Shakarian died. In addition, Synan shared one interview he had with Oral Roberts pertaining to Roberts' part in the formation of the FGBMFI and an interview Synan had with Jerry Jensen (1924–), a former editor for *Voice*. These interviews are supplemented by dozens of interviews of past and current living leaders of the FGBMFI and family members of Demos Shakarian whom this author had the privilege of meeting with over the past several years. The following tables describe the most pertinent people interviewed for the production of this book, and the relationship these people had with Demos Shakarian.

Interviews with Family Members			
Person	**Relationship to Demos**	**Date of Interview**	**Location of Interview**
Berge, Renee	Granddaughter	January 9, 2008	Colorado Springs, CO
Janoian, Darlene	Cousin	January 13, 2008	La Habra Heights, CA
Janoian, Paul	Cousin	January 13, 2008	La Habra Heights, CA
Lalaian, Al	Brother-in-law	January 13, 2008	La Habra Heights, CA
Linamen, Karen	Granddaughter	January 8-11, 2008	Colorado Springs, CO
Mushegan, Harding	Cousin	January 14, 2008	San Dimas, CA
Perumean, Stan	Cousin	March 26, 2006	La Habra Heights, CA
Scalf, Geraldine and Gene	Daughter and son-in-law	January 8-11, 2008	Colorado Springs, CO
Shakarian, Brenda	Granddaughter	July 8, 2006 and January 18, 2008	Fort Lauderdale, FL and Irvine, CA
Shakarian, Richard	Son & current president of the FGBMFI	January 10, 2005 and January 16, 2008	Costa Mesa, CA and Irvine, CA
Willett, Michelle	Granddaughter	January 10, 2008	Colorado Springs, CO

Interviews with Members of the FGBMFI and Other Individuals

Persons	Relationship to Demos	Date of Interview	Location of Interview
Aguilar, Humberto	Current director of FGBMFI in Nicaragua	July 4, 2008	Orlando, FL
Antakin, Komo	Regional vice-president of FGBMFI in Asia	July 4, 2008	Orlando, FL
Armstrong, Bob	Current editor of *Voice*	July 8, 2006	Fort Lauderdale, FL
Autry, James	Former employee at FGBMFI headquarters in Costa Mesa, CA	April 1, 2009	Portland, OR
Bedley, Gene	Former employee of Reliance Dairy	August 29, 2008	Phone interview
Bignold, Bob	Past international vice president of FGBMFI	December 9, 2008	Phone interview
Bittke, Brian	Former executive with Ralph's Grocery	September 2, 2008	Portland, OR
Bond, Mike	Executive leader in U.S. FGBMFI	February 22, 2008	Arlington, VA
Brume, Senator Fred	Executive leader in Nigerian FGBMFI	July 8, 2006	Fort Lauderdale, FL
Bundy, David	Scholar of Pentecostalism	March 11, 2005	Virginia Beach, VA
Chakarian, Mark	FGBMFI chapter president	January 8, 2005	Garden Grove, CA
Combs, Richard	FGBMFI member	January 16, 2008	Irvine, CA
Duggan, George	Executive member of FGBMFI	February 18, 2006	Arlington, VA
Herman, Mildred	Widow of evangelist Harold Herman — friend of Demos	January 6, 2005	Eugene, OR
Josiah, Nkusi Sebujisho	Former director of FGBMFI in Rwanda	July 26, 2005	Kigali, Rwanda
Kaminsky, Andy	Executive director FGBMFI	February 17, 2005 and January 9, 2008	Arlington, VA and Colorado City, CO

Interviews with Members of the FGBMFI and Other Individuals (con't)

Manning, Norma Lee	Wife of former FGBMFI state director	January 9, 2008	Colorado Springs, CO
McDougal, Rob	FGBMFI member	July 8, 2006	Fort Lauderdale, FL
Menzies, Robert	Pentecostal scholar	October 27, 2007	Hampton, VA
Menzies, William	Pentecostal scholar	September 24, 2008	Phone interview
Milbrandt, Carlton	Past executive vice president of FGBM-FI and chairman of IFCB	December 11, 2008	Phone interview
Nash, Carlin	Past international director of FGBMFI	December 11, 2008	Phone interview
Ostrom, Don	Past executive and international director of FGBMFI	December 9, 2008	Phone interview
Priddy, James and Betty	Executive vice-president of FGBMFI	May 17, 2005	Ocean City, MD
Raborg, Jeanie	Daughter of former FGBMFI treasurer, Carl Williams	January 9, 2008	Colorado Springs, CO
Reding, Peter	Oregon state director of FGBMFI	January 6, 2005 and December 5, 2008	Portland, OR
Robeck, Cecil M.	Pentecostal scholar	January 10, 2005	Pasadena, CA
Rogers, Jimmy	Executive member of FGBMFI	February 22, 2008	Arlington, VA
Rosenthal, Bernard and Margaret	Friends of Demos	January 9, 2008	Colorado Springs, CO
Schmook, John	Former executive member of FGBM-FI	July 8, 2006	Fort Lauderdale, FL
Scott, Dian	Personal secretary of Demos	January 14, 2008, January 22, 2008, March 15, 2008, July 16, 2008, and August 25, 2008	Phone interviews
Sobolew, Paul	Russian Molokan friend of Demos	March 26, 2006 and January 15, 2008	La Habra Heights, CA and Los Angeles, CA

Interviews with Members of the FGBMFI and Other Individuals (con't)			
Spenst, Dennis	FGBMFI national director for Canada	July 4, 2008	Orlando, FL
Sun, Wey	FGBMFI member	February 23, 2008	Arlington, VA
Svenhard, Ronny	Former executive FGBMFI member and founder of BMF	January 21, 2008	Phone interview
Synan, Vinson	Pentecostal scholar and friend of Demos	February 27, 2008	Virginia Beach, VA
Tuttle, Brad and Juneal	Former FGBMFI chapter president	January 9, 2008	Colorado Springs, CO
Weinbender, Ron	Executive Director of FGBMFI	January 10, 2005, March 27, 2006, and January 16, 2008	Costa Mesa, CA and Irvine, CA
White, Walt	FGBMFI member	January 9, 2008	Colorado

The sources available on the Russian pneumatic sect that likely influenced Shakarian's ancestors are limited, but some recent scholarship illuminated some of the dark recesses of Russian mysticism. One candidate who caused some charismatic fervor in early nineteenth century Russia was Seraphim of Sarov (1759–1833). Archimandrite Lazarus Moore (1902–1992) offers the most comprehensive biography of this Russian mystic.[19] However, while Seraphim may have been a contributing influence, there is no direct correlation between him and the Russian pneumatics that arrived in Karakala, Armenia in the nineteenth century and interacted with the Shakarian family. Nicholas Breyfogle's (d.b.a.1962–) study identifies some of the primary dissident religious groups in Russia in the nineteenth century and how they would have likely arrived in Armenia.[20] In his book, William Fletcher (1926–2008) analyzes the variety of Russian charismatic groups that existed in the modern period, but he relies heavily on the primary research of A.I. Klibanov (d.b.a.1900–d.d.a.1992) who interviewed and analyzed many of these groups, albeit from a perspective that was obviously biased against sectarian religious movements in Russia.[21] However, Vinson Synan is the only scholar who attempts to identify the specific group that interacted with the Shakarian family in the nineteenth century.[22] While several scholars have begun researching the Priguny Molokans, John Berokoff (1898–1972), a descendant of the Russian Molokans who came to Los Angeles, does the greatest service, by offering a comprehensive history of their origins and their introduction into America.[23] While Berokoff offers a partial translation of the Molokan sacred text into English,[24] there is also a privately printed, full English translation, including the writings of Efim Klubnikin, which has proven invaluable for this study.[25] In addition, these same Molokans immigrated to Los Angeles at the same time Shakarian's family arrived in Southern California.[26] Nikolai Kol'tsov (d.b.a.1921–) may provide critical and independent Russian confirmation of the Russian prophecy that drew these Russian and Armenian sectarians to the United States.[27] Kol'tsov also suggests that the early Molokan immigrants were the original progenitors who brought classical Pentecostalism to the United States.[28]

Research regarding the history of Armenia and its diaspora in America is fairly widespread and diverse, but Redgate (d.b.a.1944–) offers one of the most thorough, up-to-date histories of Armenia, including an account of the tensions between the Armenians and the Ottoman Turks that led to the flood of Armenian immigrants who sailed to America in the period leading up to the genocide in World War I (WWI).[29] Some primary materials from the Western Prelacy of the Armenian Apostolic Church in addition to some secondary discussion on the historic ecumenical role of the Armenian Church have proven helpful.[30] Burgess (1937–) presents the most thorough analysis of the historic contributions of Eastern Christianity towards pneumatological development,[31] and Rybarczyk (d.b.a.1957) offers a helpful comparison between Eastern Orthodoxy and modern Pentecostalism.[32]

Sources for the Armenian Pentecostal Church in which Demos Shakarian was a member are scarce. Vinson Synan briefly looked at the beginnings of this church in his study of the FGBMFI,[33] but the most helpful sources for an examination of this church are the primary sources available from the church itself, including a songbook, a doctrinal statement, and a centennial anniversary videotape of the history of the church.[34] In addition, recent interviews with two former pastors of the Armenian Church and Vinson Synan's transcripts of his interviews with Demos Shakarian have proven invaluable for research on this subject. Finally, several visits to this church offered premier interview opportunities with living relatives and friends of Demos Shakarian and his family.

Other sources important to the study of Shararian's ancestors are the *Apostolic Faith* newsletter, which confirms the presence of Armenians at Azusa Street,[35] and numerous articles in the *Los Angeles Times*. While the press was not always favorable to the burgeoning Pentecostal movement, at least one article confirms the presence of pneumatic Priguny Molokan Russians in Los Angeles in 1906 and compared these Russians to the participants of the Azusa Street Mission.[36] Other sources include Frank Bartleman's (1871–1936) account of the Azusa Street Revival, but these and other sources generally overlook the Armenian Pentecostal Church or assume that it was launched into Pentecostalism from Azusa Street.[37] Robert Mapes Anderson (1929–) suggested that Anna Hall, from the Azusa Street Mission, visited the Armenian Pentecostal Church when it was on Boston Street in 1906 and Hall claimed that the members of the congregation had spoken in tongues for decades back in their homeland.[38] However, a closer look at the primary source he used reveals that she visited a Russian Church in Los Angeles which was receptive to her message, but the Russian Church did not claim to speak in tongues previously.[39] Other scholars such as Margaret Poloma (d.b.a.1948) lay claim to the pre-existing indigenous nature of Armenian Pentecostalism before Azusa Street[40]

Sources for the healing evangelists who influenced Shakarian's early life are numerous. The two evangelists who most profoundly shaped his life were Charles Price and Oral Roberts. While very little has been written about Charles Price, the best resource available is his autobiography which, interestingly, makes no mention of Demos Shakarian.[41] Apparently, Charles Price made a much bigger impression upon Shakarian.[42]

Fortunately, much more has been written about Demos Shakarian's other evangelistic mentor, Oral Roberts. Numerous primary sources point to the enormous influence Roberts had upon Shakarian. The most important comprehensive examination of Roberts' life is offered in David Harrell's biography, *Oral Roberts: An American Life*.[43] While Shakarian's organization gets much of the credit for launching the modern Charismatic movement, Harrell suggests that Oral Roberts played a more significant role in initiating the neo-Pentecostal renewal. Harrell states his case through numerous citations of Roberts' interaction with Shakarian among other contributions that Roberts and other healing evangelists made to popularize the modern Charismatic renewal. According to Harrell, "it was the vision of Shakarian and the backing of Oral Roberts that launched one of the most powerful parachurch organizations in modern history."[44] Guzanov (d.b.a.1919–) offers a critical account of Oral Robert's first crusade in Russia, sponsored and promoted by Demos Shakarian, even though Guzanov does not acknowledge or was not aware of Shakarian's support.[45] Indeed, most other scholars writing on the Charismatic movement fail to mention the connection between Demos Shakarian and Oral Roberts.[46]

Harrell's other book on the Charismatic movement, *All Things are Possible,* demonstrates thoroughly how the healing evangelists of the 1950s helped launch the modern Charismatic renewal, in addition to demonstrating how many of these same evangelists helped promote the fledgling FGBMFI.[47] Other sources on the influence of these early healing evangelists are still scarce, but the early editions of *Voice* illustrate the symbiotic relationship between these preachers and the FGBMFI. Early editions of *Voice* featured the success of Tommy Hicks' (1909–1973) crusades in Argentina[48] and reported that William Branham (1909–1965) was connected with the FGBMFI in its infancy. It was recorded that Branham helped with the formation of early chapters, was the keynote speaker at two or three of the early FGBMFI international conventions, and was also a featured evangelist in several *Voice* magazine editions.[49]

The ecumenical influences upon Demos Shakarian and the fledgling FGBMFI lie primarily within the context of Shakarian's Armenian background and the influence of early mentors and associates, including Oral Roberts, Charles Price, and David DuPlessis. Most of these influences have been previously discussed in this review, and the influence of David DuPlessis is well documented in Demos Shakarian's autobiography.[50] However, though David DuPlessis is widely recognized as a tireless ecumenist and catalyst for the modern Charismatic movement, DuPlessis never mentioned Shakarian or the FGBFMI in his own autobiography.[51]

Sources providing the political context of Demos Shakarian or the FGBMFI are scarce, but certainly the fellowship included and invited a long list of politicians, beginning with then Vice President Richard Nixon, to its second national convention in June 1954 in Washington, D.C.[52] The early involvement or affiliation of Pat Robertson (1930–), Donald Rumsfeld (1932–), Ronald Reagan (1911–2004), and James Watt (1938–) helped secure the reputation of the FGBMFI as a conservative force in North America.[53] Sara Diamond (1958–), Paul Gifford (1944–), and David Stoll (1952–) all offer critical outside perspectives on the politics of Demos Shakarian and the FGBMFI.[54]

While the organization has often attracted Republican politicians in the United States, it has interacted with a wide variety of politicians on an international scale, including dictators such as Juan Peron (1895–1974) of Argentina[55] and François Duvalier of Haiti (1907–1971),[56] and communist leaders like Fidel Castro (1926–) of Cuba[57] and Daniel Ortega (1945–) of Nicaragua.[58] While the discrepancy between these different political spectrums has been largely ignored and unexamined, Rose Shakarian (1917–1996) did remind her husband of his global vision for the movement he had started, a movement in which "political divisions didn't enter into it."[59]

The theological context surrounding Demos Shakarian's Pentecostal background and the origins of the FGBMFI has been explored a little further than his political context. Donald Dayton (1942–) offers the most succinct analysis of Pentecostal theology in North America by looking at the four-fold and five-fold theological roots of early Pentecostalism.[60] However, when looking at the broader context of global Pentecostalism, Allan Anderson (d.b.a.1950) suggests a much more variegated theological portrait.[61] While Anderson may be more helpful in understanding the various congruities and incongruities of the variety of FGBM-FI chapters throughout the world, perhaps Vinson Synan's analysis of the Holiness and Pentecostal movements[62] and William Fletcher's analysis of the origins of Russian Pentecostalism[63] prove most helpful for an understanding of Shakarian's brand of Armenian Pentecostalism.

One additional theological impulse important for this discourse is the influence of the Latter Rain movement which began in 1948. Richard Riss (d.b.a.1932–) offers the most comprehensive analysis of this movement, but the influence it had on Shakarian or the FGBMFI is largely unexplored.[64] William Faupel also offers a more thorough examination of the Latter Rain movement but does not offer any correlations or connections with Demos Shakarian or the FGBMFI.[65] David Harrell also contributes to the understanding and impact of the Latter Rain movement in his cursory examination of the early Charismatic movement.[66]

The eschatological impulses that may have influenced Shakarian and led to the origins of the FGBMFI have also been largely unexplored, but the significance of the Latter Rain movement might pale compared to the evangelical ferment instigated by the creation of Israeli statehood in 1948. Two of the best sources on this subject are Ernest Sandeen's (d.b.a.1930–) excellent summary of the origins of modern millenarianism and Peter Prosser's (d.b.a.1943–) analysis of dispensational eschatology.[67] However, works such as Douglas Jacobsen's (d.b.a.1952–) *Thinking in the Spirit* and Grant Wacker's (1945–) *Heaven Below* examine the broader theological context and eschatological impulses of early Pentecostalism that may have directed Shakarian and certainly most of the early pioneers of the FGBMFI.[68]

Finally, the sociological impulses surrounding Demos Shakarian and the beginnings of the FGBMFI are best examined within the context of a rising affluent middle class after WWII, the acceleration of the Cold War with the loss of an American nuclear monopoly, and the origins of a burgeoning Pentecostal movement within America and abroad. Robert Mapes Anderson probably offers the most comprehensive sociological analysis of the early Pentecostal movement,[69] but Wacker suggests a broader, more nuanced glance at early Pentecostalism by simultaneously looking at both its pragmatic and primitivistic impulses.[70] Margaret Poloma probably gives the most detailed sociological evaluation of both the Charismatic and neo-Charismatic movements offering a helpful paradigm for understanding the influence of the FGBMFI.[71] Finally, in a lesser known work, Cecil Bradfield (d.b.a.1928–) offers the only known sociological analysis of the early FGBMFI, albeit from a rather limited case study of one FGBMFI chapter in Harrisonburg, Virginia.[72]

Of course, the two best primary sources for examining the expansion and growth of the FGBMFI are Shakarian's autobiography and the hundreds of *Voice* magazines in the archival collection at Regent University. In addition, Vinson Synan provides the only comprehensive and scholarly summary of this information in *Under His Banner* (1992). David Harrell gives a slightly different emphasis in *All Things are Possible* (1975) by shifting the focus of the organization's growth toward the efforts of the healing evangelists who were some of its best spokespeople. Added to these various impulses are the dozens of interviews given for this study from various early leaders in the FGBMFI, revealing the urgency and sacrifice demonstrated by some of its earliest practitioners.

A few explanations have been offered for the international growth of the FGBMFI. Asamoah-Gyadu offers the only scholarly analysis of the organization's growth in West Africa, but virtually no research has been done on the growth of the FGBMFI in the rest of Africa, its outreach to many nations in Asia, or its recent significant growth in Central America.[73] Walter Hollenweger's critique of the sociologic, economic, and political status of FGBMFI members also suggests a political explanation for the growth of the movement internationally.[74] Synan considers a sociologic and economic explanation for the organization's expansion and influence in spreading the Charismatic movement.[75] Using another approach, Harrell suggests that the growth of the FGBMFI may be viewed as a theological protest against the increasing institutionalization and structure within the older Pentecostal denominations.[76] In the midst of this possible laymen's rebellion, Demos Shakarian led his army of business men into an era of unprecedented global expansion and evangelism. However, this expansion was not without its challenges and growing pains.

For the first three decades of its existence, the FGBMFI quickly grew into a worldwide movement, but in the early 1980s, the growth of the organization had leveled off. The late 1980s and early 1990s saw decline in the FGBMFI in North America due to a variety of factors, perhaps most notably the declining health of the organization's founder, beginning with his first stroke in 1984. Some of the fluctuation in growth may have been due to the increasing popularity of specialized Christian business fellowships such as the Fellowship of Christian Airline Personnel, the Christian Legal Society, and the Christian Medical Society.[77] Several sources cite the growth of popular competing groups like the Promise Keepers as another reason for the decline of the FGBMFI.[78] On the other hand, Asamoah-Gyadu discusses the interaction between the FGBMFI and Women's Aglow (1967–) suggesting both a cooperative and complementary relationship between the two groups.[79]

Internal conflicts in the organization have also been left largely ignored as causes for decline in the FGBMFI. Synan is the only scholar who has even mentioned the first schism that took place in 1987, and more recent controversies have yet to be considered in any scholarly material.[80] Mark Bellinger offers the most thorough account of this first schism in his inspirational account of Shakarian's life after Shakarian suffered his stroke.[81] The only other mention of later controversies is in a newspaper article in the *Orlando Sentinel*.[82]

Demos Shakarian's declining health and ultimate death are part of the public record and details on his death and internment can be found in his obituary in the *Los Angeles Times* and the public records for Rose Hill Memorial Park and Mortuary.[83] Vinson Synan's transcripts of his interviews with Demos Shakarian, given just a few short years before Shakarian's death, offer some valuable insight into Shakarian's perspective in his twilight years.[84] Information into the resurrection of the FGBMFI after the death of Demos Shakarian is available in a brief article on the growth of the organization in 2001,[85] and in an updated and edited version of Val Fotherby's book written in 2000.[86] In addition, the most recent statistics available on the growth of the movement were reported by Richard Shakarian at the FGBMFI International Conventions in Fort Lauderdale, Florida, in July 2006 and in Orlando, Florida, in July 2008.[87]

Notes

1. One example is found in the account of Shakarian's grandfather and his Spirit baptism. Sherrill states that the Shakarian patriarch spoke in tongues when he was baptized in the Holy Spirit. (See page 19 of *The Happiest People on Earth*). However, later oral interviews of Shakarian given to Vinson Synan reveal that Shakarian's family supposedly never spoke in tongues until their interaction with the Azusa Street Mission in 1906. (See Demos Shakarian, interview by Vinson Synan, Los Angeles, California, October 5, 1987, 5).

2. See Demos Shakarian, *The Happiest People* (1975), 15.

3. For a further explanation of these other historical views, consult Augusto Cerillo and Grant Wacker's article on "Bibliography and Historiography" in the *New International Dictionary of Pentecostal and Charismatic Movements* (*NIDPCM*), eds. Stanley M. Burgess and Eduard Van der Maas, rev. ed. (Grand Rapids, MI: Zondervan, 2003), 390–405.

4. Demos Shakarian, *Behold the Glory of God!* (Costa Mesa, CA: Full Gospel Business Men's Fellowship International, 1988); *Come Let Us Exalt Him* (Costa Mesa, CA: Full Gospel Business Men's Fellowship International, 1992); *Divine Life* (Costa Mesa, CA: Full Gospel Business Men's Fellowship International, 1991); *Life Lifters*, 3 vols. (Costa Mesa, CA: Gift Publications, 1984); *A New Wave of Revival: In Your Finances* (Costa Mesa, CA: Full Gospel Business Men's Fellowship International, 1992); *A New Wave of Revival: The Vision Intensifies!* (Costa Mesa, CA: Full Gospel Business Men's Fellowship International, 1992) *The Ultimate Dimension* (Costa Mesa, CA: Full Gospel Business Men's Fellowship International, 1988).

5. Demos Shakarian, interviews by Vinson Synan, Downey, CA, October 5, 1987, February 2, 1988, and February 15, 1992.

6. See Demos Shakarian, "God's Dairyman," in *God's Formula for Success and Prosperity*, edited by Oral Roberts and G.H. Montgomery (Tulsa, OK: Oral Roberts, 1956), 39–53; also Demos Shakarian, "The Amazing Shakarian Story," *Voice*, October 1953, 3–4; November 1953, 6–7; December 1953, 8–10; January 1954, 11–13; February–March 1954, 4, 11; April 1954, 10–11.

7. Synan, *Under His Banner* (1992), 12.

8. See Val Fotherby, *Catching the Vision* (Eastbourne: Kingsway, 1989).

9. Val Fotherby, *The Awakening Giant*. (UK: Marshall Pickering, 2000).

10. Mark Bellinger, *Demos: The Man of Fellowship* (Long Beach, California: Upright Enterprises, 1992). In addition, he changes the names of many of the primary characters in his account either to protect the innocent or avoid slander. However, doing this sometimes leads to confusion about the factual account of the schism.

11. See J. Kwabena Asamoah-Gyadu, "'Missionaries without Robes': Lay Charismatic Fellowships and the Evangelization of Ghana," *Pneuma* 19:2 (Fall 1997): 167–188.

12. See Charles E. Jones, *The Charismatic Movement: a Guide to the Study of Neo-Pentecostalism* (Metuchen, New Jersey: Scarecrow Press, 1995), 419–425, and 843 for a fairly comprehensive list of articles, studies, and books written by or about the Full Gospel Business Men's Fellowship International. The two studies: Cecil Bradfield, "An Investigation of Neo-Pentecostalism" (Ph.D. diss., American University, 1975), and Robert Heath, "Persuasive Patterns and Strategies in the Neo-Pentecostal Movement" (Ph.D. diss., University of Oklahoma, 1973), make some reference to the FGBMFI (especially Bradfield's study). Bradfield later published a book, *Neo-Pentecostalism: A Sociological Assessment* (Washington: University Press of America, 1979), which offers a very helpful analysis of the sociological shift of Pentecostals in the 1950s with a focus upon the FGBMFI and its contributions to this shift. In addition, his book offers the only sociological analysis of the FGBMFI, albeit from a perspective limited to one chapter in northwestern Virginia. However, the most helpful, thorough books written about the FGBMFI, or making reference to them, in addition to Vinson Synan's book, are Margaret Poloma's *The Charismatic Movement*, Steve Durasoff's *Bright Wind of the Spirit*, and especially David Harrell's two books: *All Things are Possible* (1975) and *Oral Roberts: An American Life* (1985).

13. Hollenweger, *Pentecostalism: Origins and Development* (1997), 211.

14. This is the largest archive available on the organization. It includes the entire collection of *Voice* magazines, approximately three dozen books published by Shakarian and the FGBMFI, a collection of photographs from the Shakarian family and the FGBMFI, and an uncatalogued collection of videos from the FGBMFI television show "Good News."

15. Both Shakarian's daughter, Geri Scalf, and his secretary, Dian Scott, have confirmed in phone interviews on June 26, 2008 and July 10, 2008 respectively that Shakarian left no journal or personal diary.

16. Demos Shakarian, personality profile, submitted to Management By Strengths, Incorporated (Olathe, KS), September 20, 1989.

17. United States Patent Office, "Method of Milking Cows," for Demos Shakarian, patent number 3,301,215, patented January, 31, 1967.

18. Demos Shakarian, *Behold the Glory of God!* (Costa Mesa, CA: Full Gospel Business Men's Fellowship International, 1988); *Come Let Us Exalt Him* (Costa Mesa, CA: Full Gospel Business Men's Fellowship International, 1992); *Divine Life* (Costa Mesa, CA: Full Gospel Business Men's Fellowship International, 1991); *Life Lifters* (Costa Mesa, CA: Gift Publications, 1984); *A New Wave of Revival: In Your Finances* (Costa Mesa, CA: Full Gospel Business Men's Fellowship International, 1992); *A New Wave of Revival: The Vision Intensifies!* (Costa Mesa, CA: Full Gospel Business Men's Fellowship International, 1992); *The Ultimate Dimension* (Costa Mesa, CA: Full Gospel Business Men's Fellowship International, 1988).

19. Archimandrite Lazarus Moore, *St. Seraphim of Sarov: A Spiritual Biography* (Blanco, TX: New Sarov Press, 1994).

20. Nicholas Breyfogle, "Heretics and Colonizers: Religious Dissent and Russian Colonization of Transcaucasia" (Ph.D. diss., the University of Pennsylvania, 1998), 1. Breyfogle offers the best explanation of why these Russian charismatic Christians dispersed throughout the Caucasus.

21. William C. Fletcher, *Soviet Charismatics: The Pentecostals in the USSR.* (New York: Peter Lang, 1985); A.I. Klibanov, ed. *Kritika religioznogo sektantsva* [A critique of religious sectarianism] (Moscow: Mysl' Press, 1974 and *Religioznoe sektantstvo i sovremennost'* [Religious sectarianism and contemporaneity], (Moscow: Nauka Press, 1962. Fletcher gives the most comprehensive analysis of Russian charismatic sects, and he uses an abundance of primary sources.

22. Synan, *Under His Banner* (1992), 20.

23. John Berokoff, *Molokans in America*, 2nd reprint (Buena Park, CA: Stockton Trade Press, Inc., 1987).

24. John K. Berokoff, ed., *Selections from the Book of Spirit and Life Including the Book of Prayers and Songs by Maxin G. Rudametkin*, trans. John K. Berokoff (Whittier, California: Stockton Trade Press, 1966), 23. This book is the only publicly published English translation of the Molokan prophecies. Berokoff received criticism from the Molokan community even though he only translated about fifteen to twenty percent of the Molokan text, and some branches of the Molokan Diaspora ostracized Berokoff for his work because they have tried to keep this text, also titled *Book of the Sun*, as an exclusive and sacred text confined to the Molokan community.

25. Shubin, Daniel H., ed. *Spirit and Life – Book of the Sun: Divine Discourses of the Preceptors and the Martyrs for the Word of God, the Faith of Jesus, and the Holy Spirit, of the Religion of the Spiritual Christian Molokan-Jumpers*, trans. by John Volkov from the 1928 2nd Russian ed. (Privately published, 1983). With the exception of Berokoff's partial translation, this book has never been published outside of the Molokan community and is rarely made available to anyone outside of this secluded pneumatic group.

26. In particular, Paul Sobolew of the Russian Molokan community proved to be extremely helpful, generous, and gracious in gathering much of this information. Harding Mushegian and Darlene Janoian, as cousins of Demos Shakarian, also offered alternative theories for the immigration of the Shakarian family to the United States.

27. Nikolai Vasil'evich Kol'tsov, *Kto takie piatidesiatniki* [Who are the Pentecostals] (Moscow: Znanie Press, 1965), 9–10.

28. Ibid, 5.

29. A.E. Redgate, *The Armenians* (Malden, MA: Blackwell Publishers, 1998).

30. Shahan Sarkissian, "Ecumenism in the Armenian Catholicosate of Cilicia," *Ministerial Formation* (October, 2000): 7–9; and Moushegh Mardirossian, *The Armenian Church: Celebrating Seventeen Hundred Years* (Los Angeles, CA: Western Prelacy of the Armenian Apostolic Church of America, 2000).

31. Burgess, Stanley M. *The Holy Spirit: Eastern Christian Traditions*. Peabody, MA: Hendrickson Publishers, 1989.

32. Ed Rybarczyk, *Beyond Salvation: Eastern Orthodoxy and Classical Pentecostalism on Becoming Like Christ* (Carlisle, UK: Paternoster Press, 2004).

33. Synan, *Under His Banner* (1992), 21–23.

34. Jeff Janoian and Mark Perumean, *God at Our Side: 100 Years* (DVD. La Habra Heights: Hillside Pentecostal Church, 2005); First Armenian Pentecostal Church. *Armenian Songbook* (La Habra Heights, CA: First Armenian Pentecostal Church, n.d); First Armenian Pentecostal Church, "Credo" (La Habra Heights, CA: First Armenian Pentecostal Church, n.d.).

35. Fred T. Corum, *Like as of Fire*, (Wilmington, Massachusetts: Fred T. Corum, 1981; a reprint of *The Apostolic Faith* from September 1906 to May 1908), February–March 1907, 7.

36. "Death Dance of 'Priguni,'" *Los Angeles Times*, October 9, 1906, 17.

37. Frank Bartleman, *How Pentecost Came to Los Angeles*, 2nd ed. (Los Angeles, CA: Frank Bartleman, 1925); Bartleman makes no mention of the Armenian Pentecostal Church but see Corum, *Like as of Fire*, April 1907, 2.

38. Robert Mapes Anderson, *Vision of the Disinherited: The Making of American Pentecostalism*, reprint (Peabody, MA: Hendrickson Publishers, 1992), 70–71. This could be in dispute because there was also an Armenian Molokan Church on Pecan Street which started as a result of an early schism within the Armenian Molokan community that originated out of the Armenian Pentecostal Church now residing in La Habra Heights, CA.

39. Corum, *Apostolic Faith* (1981), September 1906, 4.

40. See Poloma, *The Charismatic Movement* (1982), 24.

41. Charles S. Price, *And Signs Followed: The Life Story of Charles S. Price*, rev. ed. (Plainfield, NJ: Logos International, 1972).

42. See Demos Shakarian, *The Happiest People* (1975), 70–71, 74, 82, and 83.

43. David Edwin Harrell, Jr., *Oral Roberts: An American Life* (Bloomington, IN: Indiana University Press, 1985).

44. David Harrell, *Oral Roberts* (1985), 153.

45. Vitalii Grigor'evich Guzanov, *Izuvery* [Fanatics] (Moscow: Znanie Press, 1962), 84–85.

46. Hollenweger and Quebedeaux mention no connection; Poloma fails to even mention Oral Roberts in her book which is a significant omission.

47. See for example David Harrell, *All Things are Possible: The Healing and Charismatic Revivals in Modern America* (Bloomington, IN: Indiana University Press, 1975), 61, 77–78, 135, 146–147, 161.

48. Thomas R. Nickel, ed., "The Historic Argentina Revival," *Voice*, February 1955, 4–5; and "The Greatest Revival in all History" *Voice*, May 1955, 4–7.

49. For examples see Nickel, ed., "Many Meetings Scheduled for William Branham," *Voice*, February 1958, 21 and F.F. Bosworth, "Branham Meetings in Germany and Switzerland," *Voice*, September 1955, 3–11.

50. See Demos Shakarian, *The Happiest People* (1975), 122–124.

51. David DuPlessis, *A Man Called Mr. Pentecost* (Plainfield, New Jersey: Logos International, 1977), 91, and 170. While DuPlessis does go into some detail about attending the World Pentecostal Conference, he does not mention Shakarian or his organization. However, DuPlessis' archival material available at Fuller Theological Seminary's library in Pasadena, California, especially his date book, does contain frequent references to meeting with Shakarian or speaking at early local and national FGBMFI conferences.

52. Demos Shakarian, "Our God is Moving," *Voice*, July–August 1954, 3–9; and also Richard Nixon, "The Minds and Hearts and Souls of Men," *Voice*, September 1954, 4–7, 11.

53. See for example, Pat Robertson, "We All Can be Directed of the Lord!" *Voice*, April 1962, 1; and "Capital Commentary," *Voice*, April 1963, 16.

54. Sara Diamond, *Roads to Dominion: Right-wing Movements and Political Power in the United States* (New York: Guilford Press, 1995), 233; Paul Gifford, *The Religious Right in Southern Africa* (Bedminster NJ: Baobab Books, 1988); and David Stoll, *Is Latin America Turning Protestant? The Politics of Evangelical Growth* (Berkeley, CA: University of California Press, 1990). See especially chapter eight in Stoll's book for a review of the influence of Demos Shakarian and the FGBMFI in Nicaragua.

55. Tommy Hicks, "Argentina is Opened to the Full Gospel!" *Voice*, May 1954, 4–5.

56. Demos Shakarian, *The Happiest People* (1975), 151–160.

57. Ibid, 175–177.

58. Richard Shakarian and Ron Weinbender, interview by Matthew Tallman, Costa Mesa, CA, January 10, 2005.

59. Demos Shakarian, *The Happiest People* (1975), 152.

60. Donald W. Dayton, *Theological Roots of Pentecostalism* (Peabody, MA: Hendrickson Publishers, 1996).

61. Allan Anderson, *An Introduction to Pentecostalism: Global Charismatic Christianity* (Cambridge, UK: Cambridge University Press, 2004): 10–11.

62. Vinson Synan, *The Holiness-Pentecostal Tradition* (Grand Rapids, MI: William B. Eerdman's Publishers, 1997).

63. Fletcher, *Soviet Charismatics* (1985).

64. Richard Riss, *Latter Rain: The Latter Rain Movement of 1948 and the Mid Twentieth Century Evangelical Awakening* (Mississague, ON: Honeycomb Visual Productions, 1987).

65. William Faupel, *The Everlasting Gospel: The Significance of Eschatology in Pentecostal Thought* (Sheffield, England: Sheffield Academic Press, 1996).

66. Harrell, *All Things are Possible* (1975), 20.

67. Peter Prosser, *Dispensationalist Eschatology and its Influence on American and British Religious Movements* (Lewiston, NY: E. Mellen Publishers, 1999); and Ernest Sandeen, *The Roots of Fundamentalism: British and American Millenarianism, 1800–1930* (Chicago: University of Chicago Press, 1970).

68. Douglas G. Jacobsen, *Thinking in the Spirit: Theologies of the Early Pentecostal Movement* (Bloomington, IN: Indiana University Press, 2003); and Grant Wacker, *Heaven*

Below: Early Pentecostals and American Culture (Cambridge, MA: Harvard University Press, 2001).

69. Anderson, *Vision of the Disinherited* (1992).

70. Wacker, *Heaven Below* (2001).

71. Margaret Poloma, The Assemblies of God at the Crossroads: Charisma and Institutional Dilemmas (Knoxville, TN: University of Tennessee Press, 1989); The Charismatic Movement: Is There a New Pentecost? (Boston: Twayne Publishers, 1982); and Main Street Mystics: The Toronto Blessing and Reviving Pentecostalism (Walnut Creek, CA: Alta Mira Press, 2003).

72. Cecil Bradfield, *Neo-Pentecostalism: A Sociological Assessment* (Washington, DC: University Press of America, 1979).

73. See Kwabena Asamoah-Gyadu, "Missionaries without Robes," (Fall 1997): 167–188.

74. See Hollenweger, *Pentecostalism: Origins and Development* (1997), 211.

75. Synan, *Under His Banner* (1992), 83.

76. Harrell, *Oral Roberts* (1985), 153.

77. Russell Chandler, "Corporations Increase Ties to Christianity," *Los Angeles Times* October 20, 1974, 23.

78. See Mark I. Pinsky, "A Baptism by Fire for Ministry's Upbeat Heir; Richard Shakarian is Rebuilding the Gospel Group for Businessmen," *Orlando Sentinel* August 8, 2001, A1.

79. Asamoah-Gyadu, "Missionaries without Robes," (Fall 1997): 176.

80. See Synan, *Under His Banner* (1992), 121.

81. Bellinger, *Demos: The Man of Fellowship* (1992).

82. Mark I. Pinsky, "A Baptism by Fire," *Orlando Sentinel*, August 8, 2001, A1.

83. See Myrna Oliver, "Obituaries: Demos Shakarian; Founded Religious Group," *Los Angeles Times*, July 30, 1993; and Rose Hills Memorial Park and Mortuary, Whittier, CA.

84. Demos Shakarian, interview by Vinson Synan, Downey, CA, October 5, 1987; Vinson Synan, Downey, CA, February 2, 1988; and also Vinson Synan, Downey, CA, February 15, 1992.

85. Pinsky, "A Baptism by Fire," August 8, 2001, A1.

86. Val Fotherby, *The Awakening Giant* (2000).

87. Richard Shakarian, "Reports of all Nations," annual presentation given at Full Gospel Business Men's Fellowship World Convention, Fort Lauderdale, FL, July 7, 2006; and "Reports of all Nations," annual presentation given at the Full Gospel Business Men's World Convention, Fort Lauderdale, FL, July 4, 2008.

Bibliography

Primary sources

Aglow International. "History." Women's Aglow International. http://www.aglow.org (accessed January 19, 2008).

Armstrong, Bob. *Celebrate the 50th Year Jubilee Anniversary*. Lake Forest, CA: Full Gospel Business Men's Fellowship International, 2002.

_____, editor. *Voice*. 2000– .

Associated Press. "Nixon Speaks to Gospel Fellowship." *The Washington Post and Times Herald*, June 25, 1954, 29.

Associated Telephone Company. *Downey, Bellflower, Norwalk, Artesia, and a Part of Bell Gardens Telephone Directory: March 1947*. Downey, CA: Associated Telephone Company, 1947.

Bartleman, Frank. *How Pentecost Came to Los Angeles*. 2nd ed. Los Angeles: Frank Bartleman, 1925.

_____. *Two Years Mission Work in Europe*. 2nd ed. Los Angeles: Frank Bartleman, 1926.

Becker, Raymond. *FGBMFI Chapter Manual*. Costa Mesa, CA: FGBMFI, 1983.

_____, editor. *Voice*. 1969 – 1985.

Bennett, Dennis. *Nine O'Clock in the Morning*. Plainfield, NJ: Logos International, 1970.

Berokoff, John K., editor. *Selections from the Book of Spirit and Life Including the Book of Prayers and Songs by Maxin G. Rudametkin*. Translated by John K. Berokoff. Whittier, CA: Stockton Trade Press, 1966.

Branham, William. *The Autobiography of William Marrion Branham*. Jeffersonville, IN: Spoken Word Publications, 1975.

Business Men's Fellowship. "Business Men's Fellowship Chapters and Meetings." Business Men's Fellowship-USA. http://www.bmfusa.com/chapter.html (accessed February 15, 2008).

Carrette, John. "Fire Team Outreach in Los Angeles." Full Gospel Business Men's Fellowship International. http://www.fgbmfi.org/events (accessed January 10, 2008).

Corum, Fred T. *Like as of Fire*. A Reprint of *The Apostolic Faith* from September 1906 to May 1908. Wilmington, MA: Fred T. Corum, 1981.

Dart, John. "Full Gospel Fellowship Will Dedicate Building." *Los Angeles Times*, January 26, 1980, B2.

DeCatanzaro, C.J., editor. Symeon *the New Theologian: The Discourses*. New York: Paulist Press, 1980.

Downey Home Telephone and Telegraph Company. *Telephone Directory: Downey,*

Norwalk, Artesia, Bellflower. Downey, CA: Downey Home Telephone and Telegraph Company, 1937.

DuPlessis, David. "A Report on the Full Gospel Business Men's Fellowship International," *Christianity Today*. November 24, 1967, 39.

_____. *A Man Called Mr. Pentecost*. Plainfield, NJ: Logos International, 1977.

First Armenian Pentecostal Church. *Armenian Songbook*. La Habra Heights, CA: First Armenian Pentecostal Church, n.d.

_____. "Credo." La Habra Heights, CA: First Armenian Pentecostal Church, n.d.

Franklin, V. P. *Downey City Directory: 1914–1915*. Watts, CA: V. P. Franklin, 1915.

Full Gospel Businessmen's Fellowship in America. "Minutes of the Organizational Meeting National Council of Directors." Full Gospel Businessmen's Fellowship in America. http://www.fgbmfamerica.org (accessed February 15, 2008).

Full Gospel Business Men's Fellowship International. "Constitution and By-Laws: Articles of the Full Gospel Business Men's Fellowship International Revised to March, 1977. Costa Mesa, CA, 1977.

Full Gospel Business Men's Fellowship International-UK. "Welcome to Women's Support." Full Gospel Business Men's Fellowship International. http://www.fgbmfi.org.uk/fgbmfi/ladies/asp (accessed February 20, 2008).

"Full Gospel Business Men of America Start New National Association." *Healing Waters* (January, 1952): 12.

Herman, Harold. *From Ashes to Gold*. Springfield, MO: Gospel Publishing House, 1995.

International Fellowship of Christian Business Men. "Christ's Ambassadors in the World's Marketplace." IFCB. www.ifcb.org/index.php (accessed February 29, 2008).

Janoian, Jeff and Mark Perumean. *God at Our Side: 100 Years*, DVD. La Habra Heights, CA: Hillside Pentecostal Church, 2005.

Jensen, Jerry, editor. *Voice*, November 1962 – 1968; April 1985 – August 1999.

_____. *Methodists and the Baptism in the Holy Spirit*. Los Angeles: Full Gospel Business Men's Fellowship International, 1963.

_____. *Presbyterians and the Baptism in the Holy Spirit*. Los Angeles: Full Gospel Business Men's Fellowship International, 1963.

_____. *Baptists and the Baptism in the Holy Spirit*. Los Angeles: Full Gospel Business Men's Fellowship International, 1964.

_____. *Episcopalians and the Baptism in the Holy Spirit*. Los Angeles: Full Gospel Business Men's Fellowship International, 1964.

_____. *Lutherans and the Baptism in the Holy Spirit*. Los Angeles: Full Gospel Business Men's Fellowship International, 1966.

_____. *1967 Chapter Directory*. Los Angeles: Full Gospel Business Men's Fellowship International, 1967.

_____. *The Acts of the Holy Spirit among the Disciples of Christ Today*. Los Angeles: Full Gospel Business Men's Fellowship International, 1974.

_____. *Catholics and the Baptism in the Holy Spirit*. Los Angeles: Full Gospel Business Men's Fellowship International, 1976.

_____. *FGBMFI 1988–89 World Chapter Directory*. Costa Mesa, CA: Full Gospel Business Men's Fellowship International, 1989.

Klibanov, A.I. *Religioznoe sektantstvo i sovremennost'* [Religious sectarianism and contemporaneity]. Moscow: Nauka Press, 1962.

_____, editor. *Kritika religioznogo sektantsva* [A critique of religious sectarianism]. Moscow: Mysl' Press, 1974.

Linamen, Karen Scalf. *I'm not Suffering from Insanity...I'm Enjoying Every Minute of It!* Grand Rapids, MI: Fleming H. Revell, 2002.

Lindsey, Hal. *The Late Great Planet Earth.* 2nd edition. Grand Rapids, MI: Zondervan, 1977.

———. *Planet Earth – 2000 A.D.: Will Mankind Survive?* Palos Verdes, CA: Western Front, Ltd., 1994.

Los Angeles County Bureau of Records. Birth Certificate for Demos Shakarian. Los Angeles County. Filed July 22, 1913.

Los Angles County Bureau of Records. Marriage Certificate for Demos Shakarian. Los Angeles County. Filed August 11, 1933.

Los Angeles County Bureau of Records. Death Certificate for Demos Shakarian. Los Angeles County. Filed July 28, 1993.

Los Angeles County Office of the Assessor. "Mapping and Assessment". Los Angeles County. http://maps.assessor.lacounty.gov/mapping/viewer.asp (accessed August 12, 2009).

Los Angeles Directory Company. *Downey City Directory 1948.* Los Angeles, CA: Los Angeles Directory Company, 1948.

Los Angeles Times, April 18, 1906–October 9, 1906; September, 1949 – December 1953; December 10 1966; June 27, 1970; November 28,1970; July 5, 1975; and January 26, 1980.

Luskey Brothers. *Luskey's 1961 Official Downey Blue Book: Criss Cross City Directory.* Anaheim, CA: Luskey Brothers and Company, 1961.

Mardirossian, Moushegh. *The Armenian Church: Celebrating Seventeen Hundred Years.* Los Angeles: Western Prelacy of the Armenian Apostolic Church of America, 2000.

Melvin, Nelson, editor. *FGBMFI Chapter Manual.* Costa Mesa, CA: FGBMFI, 1983.

———, editor. *Voice,* 1969–1984.

Nickel, Thomas R., editor. *Voice,* February 1953 – October 1962.

Oliver, Myrna. "Obituaries: Demos Shakarian; Founded Religious Group." *Los Angeles Times,* July 30, 1993, A28.

Ormanian, Malachia. *The Church of Armenia.* 2nd edition. London: A.B. Mowbray, 1955.

Price, Charles S. *And Signs Followed: The Life Story of Charles S. Price.* Revised edition. Plainfield, NJ: Logos International, 1972.

Price, Charles S. *The Real Faith.* 6th edition. Plainfield, NJ: Logos International, 1972.

Promise Keepers. "Promise Keeper's 2007 Conference Schedule." Promise Keepers. http://www.promisekeepers.org (accessed January 19, 2008).

Ranaghan, Kevin. *Logos Journal* 39:10 (November–December, 1971), 22.

Roberts, Oral. *A Daily Guide to Miracles, and Successful Living through Seed Faith.* Old Tappan, NJ: F.H. Revell, 1975.

———. *Expect a Miracle: My Life and Ministry; An Autobiography.* Nashville: Thomas Nelson Publishers, 1995.

Rogers, Jimmy. *Victory over Shattered Dreams: From Sharecropper to Successful Businessman.* Atlanta: Jimmy Rogers, 2001.

Sarov, Seraphim. "The Life and Spiritual Instructions of Saint Seraphim of Sarov." Edited by A.F. Dobbie-Bateman. Pages 55–76 in *The Spiritual Instructions of Saint Seraphim of Sarov: A Spirit-Baptizer in the Eastern Christian Tradition.* Edited by Da Avabhasa. Clearlake, CA: The Dawn Horse Press, 1991.

Shakarian, Brenda. Personality profile. Submitted to Management By Strengths, Incorporated. Olathe, KS, August 17, 2006.

———. "Welcome to Excellence International." Excellence International. http://www.excellenceint.com (accessed February 13, 2008).

Shakarian, Demos. "God's Dairyman." In *God's Formula for Success and Prosperity.* Edited by Oral Roberts and G.H. Montgomery, 39–53. Tulsa, OK: Oral Roberts, 1956.

_____. *Life Lifters*. 3 vols. Costa Mesa, CA: Gift Publications, 1984.

_____. *An Unexpected Miracle*. Nashville: Thomas Nelson Publishers, 1987.

_____. *Behold the Glory of God!* Costa Mesa, CA: Full Gospel Business Men's Fellowship International, 1988.

_____. *The Ultimate Dimension*. Costa Mesa, CA: Full Gospel Business Men's Fellowship International, 1988.

_____. Personality profile. Submitted to Management By Strengths, Incorporated. Olathe, KS, September 20, 1989.

_____. *Divine Life*. Costa Mesa, CA: Full Gospel Business Men's Fellowship International, 1991.

_____. Excerpts and reflections included in *The Spirit Filled Life Bible: New King James Version*. Nashville, TN: Thomas Nelson Publishers, 1991.

_____. *Come Let Us Exalt Him*. Costa Mesa, CA: Full Gospel Business Men's Fellowship International, 1992.

_____. *A New Wave of Revival: In Your Finances*. Costa Mesa, CA: Full Gospel Business Men's Fellowship International, 1992.

_____. *A New Wave of Revival: The Vision Intensifies!* Costa Mesa, CA: Full Gospel Business Men's Fellowship International, 1992.

_____. "Foreword to the First Edition." In *Grief Relief: Practical Prescriptions to Erase Pain and Hurt After Any Significant Loss*, by Dr. Stan E. DeKoven, 6. Ramona, CA: Vision Publishing, 1993.

_____. *The Shakarian Story*. Revised edition. 1999.

_____. *God's Answer to Twenty Tough Questions*. Costa Mesa, CA: Full Gospel Business Men's Fellowship International, n.d.

_____. *The Vision*, DVD. Costa Mesa, CA: FGBMFI, n.d.

Shakarian, Demos, Elizabeth Sherrill, and John Sherrill. *The Happiest People on Earth*. Chappaqua, NY: Steward Press, 1975.

Shakarian, Richard. Personality profile. Submitted to Management By Strengths, Incorporated. Olathe, KS, December 23, 1986.

_____. "An Introduction to the Full Gospel Business Men's Fellowship International." Full Gospel Business Men's Fellowship International. http://www.fgbmfi.org/who.html (accessed June 8, 2004).

_____. *The Art of Multiplication: Explosive Growth!* Irvine, CA: WWM, Inc., 2005.

_____. "Report of all Nations." Annual presentation given at Full Gospel Business Men's Fellowship World Convention. Fort Lauderdale, FL, July 7, 2006.

_____. "Directors Meeting and Training." Presentation given at the Washington, D.C. Full Gospel Business Men's International Regional Winter Conference. Arlington, VA, February 23, 2008.

_____. "Report of all Nations." Annual presentation given at Full Gospel Business Men's Fellowship World Convention. Orlando, FL, July 4, 2008.

Shubin, Daniel H., ed. *Spirit and Life – Book of the Sun: Divine Discourses of the Preceptors and the Martyrs for the Word of God, the Faith of Jesus, and the Holy Spirit, of the Religion of the Spiritual Christian Molokan-Jumpers*. Translated by John Volkov from the 1928 2nd Russian edition. Privately printed, 1983.

Svenhard, Ronnie. Personality profile. Submitted to Management By Strengths, Incorporated. Olathe, KS, March 30, 1990.

Thomson, Robert W., editor. *The Teaching of Saint Gregory: An Early Armenian Catechism*. Translation and commentary by Robert W. Thomson. Cambridge, MA: Harvard University Press, 1970.

United States Patent Office. "Method of Milking Cows." For Demos Shakarian. Patent number 3,301,215. Patented January, 31, 1967.

Whisenant, Edgar. *The Rapture: Rosh Hash Ana, 1988, and 88 Reasons Why*. Little Rock, AR: Whisenant, 1988.

World Council of Churches. "World Council of Churches History." World Council of Churches.   http://www.oikoumene.org/en/who-are-we/background/history.html (accessed January 2, 2008).

Zedwick, Andy. *Godmobile Ministry Manual of Operations*. Costa Mesa, CA: Full Gospel Businessmen's Fellowship International, 1998.

Secondary sources

Anderson, Allan. *An Introduction to Pentecostalism: Global Charismatic Christianity*. Cambridge, UK: Cambridge University Press, 2004.

Anderson, Robert Mapes. *Vision of the Disinherited: The Making of American Pentecostalism*. Reprint. Peabody, MA: Henrickson Publishers, 1992.

Asamoah-Gyadu, J. Kwabena. "'Missionaries without Robes': Lay Charismatic Fellowships and the Evangelization of Ghana." *Pneuma* 19:2 (Fall 1997): 167–188.

_____. *African Charismatics: Current Developments within Independent Indigenous Pentecostalism in Ghana*. Boston: Brill, 2005.

Aune, David E. *Prophecy in Early Christianity and the Ancient Mediterranean World*. Grand Rapids, MI: William B. Eerdmans Publishing Company, 1983.

Balakian, Peter. *The Burning Tigris: The Armenian Genocide and America's Response*. New York: Harper Collins, 2003.

Barrett, David, George Kurian, and Todd Johnson, editors. *World Christian Encyclopedia: A Comparative Survey of Churches and Religions in the Modern World*. 2 vols. New York: Oxford University Press, 2001.

Barrett, David and Todd Johnson. *World Christian Trends AD 30 – AD 2200: Interpreting the Annual Christian Megacensus*. Pasadena, CA: William Carey Library, 2001.

Barsamian, Khajag. "The Oriental Orthodox Churches." *Ecumenism* (March, 1985): 26–29.

Bellinger, Mark. *Demos: The Man of Fellowship*. Long Beach, CA: Upright Enterprises, 1992.

Berokoff, John. *Molokans in America*. 2nd Reprint. Buena Park, CA: Stockton Trade Press, Inc., 1987.

Bivin, Joyce Keosababian. "The Armenians of Karakala and Their Relationship with Russian Molokans: 1870–1920." Unpublished article. n.d.

Bradfield, Cecil. "An Investigation of Neo-Pentecostalism." Ph.D. diss., American University, 1975.

_____. *Neo-Pentecostalism: A Sociological Assessment*. Washington, DC: University Press of America, 1979.

Brandenburg, Hans. *The Meek and the Mighty: The Emergence of the Evangelical Movement in Russia*. London: Mowbrays, 1974.

Breyfogle, Nicholas. "Heretics and Colonizers: Religious Dissent and Russian Colonization of Transcaucasia." Ph.D. diss., The University of Pennsylvania, 1998.

Briggs, Kenneth A. "Religion is Now an Important Part of Business." *The New York Times*, May 11, 1975, E10.

Burgess, Stanley M. *The Holy Spirit: Ancient Christian Traditions*. Peabody, MA: Hendrickson Publishers, 1984.

_____. *The Holy Spirit: Eastern Christian Traditions*. Peabody, MA: Hendrickson Publishers, 1989.

_____. *The Holy Spirit: Medieval Roman Catholic and Reformation Traditions*. Peabody, MA: Hendrickson Publishers, 1997.

_____. "The Implications of Eastern Christian Pneumatology," in Jan A.B. Jongeneel, editor *Experiences of the Spirit: Conference on Pentecostal and Charismatic Research in Europe at Untrecht University, 1989*, Studien zur interkultureen Geschichte des Christentums. Peter Lang: Frankfurt am Main, 1991, 23–34.

Burgess, Stanley M. and Eduard M.Van Der Mass, editors. *The New International Dictionary of Pentecostal and Charismatic Movements*. Revised edition. Grand Rapids, MI: Zondervan, 2002.

Calian, Carnegie Samuel. "The Armenian Church and Ecumenism." *Christian Century* (August 1964): 1007–1008.

Cantalamessa, Raneiro. *Come Creator Spirit: Meditations on the Veni Creator*. Translated by Dennis and Marlene Barrett; Collegeville, MN: Liturgical Press, 2003.

Caughey, John W. *California: A Remarkable State's Life History*. Englewood Cliffs, NJ: Prentice-Hall, Incorporated, 1970.

Cavarnos, Constantine and Mary-Barbara Zeldin. *St. Seraphim of Sarov*. Vol. 5 of *Modern Orthodox Saints*. Belmont, MA: The Institute for Byzantine and Modern Greek Studies, Inc., 1980.

Chandler, Russell. "Corporations Increase Ties to Christianity." *Los Angeles Times*, October 20, 1974, 23.

_____. "Gospel Fellowship Draws Charismatics." *Los Angeles Times*, July 5, 1975, A27.

Conn, Charles. *Like a Mighty Army: A History of the Church of God*. Revised edition. Cleveland, TN: Pathway Press, 1977.

Conwell, Russell H. *Acres of Diamonds*. New York: Harper & Brothers, 1915.

Culpepper, Robert H. *Evaluating the Charismatic Movement*. Valley Forge, PA: Judson Press, 1977.

Dabney, D. Lyle. "Starting with the Spirit," an essay in Stephen Pickard and Gordon Preece, editors, *Starting with the Spirit: The Task of Theology Today II*. Hindmarsh, Australia: Australian Theological Forum Press, 2002.

Dadrian, Vahakn. *The History of the Armenian Genocide*. Providence, RI: Berghahn Books, 1997.

Dayton, Donald W. *Theological Roots of Pentecostalism*. Peabody, MA: Hendrickson Publishers, 1996.

Denzin, Norman K. *Interpretative Biography*. Newbury Park, CA: Sage Publications, 1989.

Diamond, Sara. *Roads to Dominion: Right-wing Movements and Political Power in the United States*. New York: Guilford Press, 1995.

_____. *Not by Politics Alone: The Enduring Influence of the Christian Right*. New York: Guilford Press, 1998.

Donaldson, Hal. "1951–Present: Full Gospel Businessmen's Fellowship International." *Pentecostal Evangel*, May 31, 1998, 25.

Durasoff, Steve. *Bright Wind of the Spirit: Pentecostalism Today*. Englewood Cliffs, NJ: Prentice-Hall, 1972.

Fletcher, William C. *Soviet Charismatics: The Pentecostals in the USSR*. American University Studies. Series VII: Theology and Religion; vol. 9. New York: Peter Lang, 1985.

Fotherby, Val. *Catching the Vision*. Eastbourne, UK: Kingsway, 1989.

_____. *The Awakening Giant*. UK: Marshall Pickering, 2000.

Frazee, Charles A. "Christian Church in Cilician Armenia: Its Relations with Rome and Constantinople to 1198." *Church History* (June 1976): 166–184.

Friedman, Milton and Anna Jacobson Schwatz. *Monetary History of the United States, 1867–1960*. Princeton, NJ: Princeton University Press, 1963.

Gadamer, Hans. *Truth and Method*. Translated by Joel Weinsheimer and Donald G. Marshall; 2nd revised edition. New York: Continuum, 2004.

Gaines, John and Andrew F. Rolle. *The Golden State: A History of California*. Northbrook, IL: AHM Publishing Corporation, 1965.

Gifford, Paul. *The Religious Right in Southern Africa*. Bedminster NJ: Baobab Books, 1988.

_____. *The New Crusaders: Christianity and the New Right in Southern Africa*. Revised edition. Concord, MA: Pluto Press, 1991.

Glock, Charles Y. "On the Role of Deprivation in the Origin and Evolution of Religious Groups. Pages 200–221 in R*eligion in Sociological Perspective*. Edited by Charles Y. Glock; Belmont CA: Wadsworth Publishing Company, 1973.

Goh, Stephen. "The Full Gospel Business Men's Fellowship & Ministry in Malaysia: Advancing God's Kingdom in the Marketplace (1978–2006)." Unpublished article, 2006.

Guzanov, Vitalii Grigor'evich. *Izuvery* [Fanatics]. Moscow: Znanie Press, 1962.

Haidostian, Paul Ara. "Armenian Evangelical Youth and Political Identity." PhD diss., Princeton Theological Seminary, 1994.

Harrell, David Edwin, Jr. *All Things are Possible: The Healing and Charismatic Revivals in Modern America*. Bloomington, IN: Indiana University Press, 1975.

_____. *Oral Roberts: An American Life*. Bloomington, IN: Indiana University Press, 1985.

_____. *Pat Robertson: A Personal, Religious, and Political Portrait*. San Francisco: Harper & Row, 1987.

Heath, Robert "Persuasive Patterns and Strategies in the Neo-Pentecostal Movement." Ph.D. diss., University of Oklahoma, 1973.

Hill, Napoleon. *Think and Grow Rich*. New York: Fawcett Crest, 1960.

Hollenweger, Walter. *The Pentecostals: The Charismatic Movement in the Churches*. Minneapolis, MN: Augsberg Publishing House, 1972.

_____. "Charismatic Renewal in the Third World: Implications for Missions." *Occasional Bulletin of Missionary Research* 4 (April 1980): 69.

_____. *Pentecostalism: Origins and Developments Worldwide*. Peabody, MA: Hendrickson Publishers, 1997.

Jackson, Sydney. "The Molokans: A Study of a Religious Minority." Thesis, George Fox University, 1962.

Jacobsen, Douglas G. *Thinking in the Spirit: Theologies of the Early Pentecostal Movement*. Bloomington, IN: Indiana University Press, 2003.

Jones, Charles E. *The Charismatic Movement: a Guide to the Study of Neo-Pentecostalism*. Metuchen, NJ: Scarecrow Press, 1995.

Kobzeff, Manya Rudometkin. "Flight from Russian" *Besednyik* 4.4 (December 1991): 6.

Kol'tsov, Nikolai Vasil'evich. *Kto takie piatidesiatniki* [Who are the Pentecostals]. Moscow: Znanie Press, 1965.

Land, Steven. *Pentecostal Spirituality: A Passion for the Kingdom*. Sheffield, England: Sheffield Academic Press, 1993.

Lavendar, David. *California: A Bicentennial History*. New York: Norton and Company, Incorporated, 1976.

Lomask, Milton. *The Biographer's Craft*. New York: Harper & Row, 1986.

Lunkin, Roman and Anton Prokof'yev. "Molokans and Dukhobors: Living Sources of Russian Protestantism." *Religion, State & Society* 28 (2000): 85–92.

Macchia, Frank. "From Azusa to Memphis: Evaluating the Racial Reconciliation Dialogue Among Pentecostals." *Pneuma* 17:2 (Fall 1995): 203–218.

Maciel, Mark and J. Jacquart. *The Seeker: Jeff Johnson's Search for the Clear Light*. Costa Mesa, CA: Calvary Chapel Publishing, 2005.

Makhina, Irina. "Perkoba a pethra a parcho pochni: hotorpathrechia odoxa" [Church and religion in Imperial Russia: A review of recent historiography] *Marburg Journal of Religion* (December 2004): 1–34.

Meier, John P. *A Marginal Jew: Rethinking the Historical Jesus*. New York: Doubleday, 1991.

Menzies, William W. *Anointed to Serve: The Story of the Assemblies of God*. Springfield, MO: Gospel Publishing House, 1971.

Montgomery, Paul L. "Businessmen's Religious Group Strives for Speaking in Tongues." *New York Times*, July 5, 1964, 45.

Moore, Archimandrite Lazarus. *St. Seraphim of Sarov: A Spiritual Biography*. Blanco, TX: New Sarov Press, 1994.

Moore, David S. *The Shepherding Movement: Controversy and Charismatic Ecclesiology*. New York: T&T Clark International, 2003.

Nickel, Thomas R. "The Amazing Shakarian Story." *Voice*, October 1953 – April, 1954.

Niebuhr, Richard. "The Churches of the Disinherited." Pages 198–215 in *The Social Sources of Denominationalism*. Edited by Richard Niebuhr; New York: Henry Holt and Company, 1929.

Pinsky, Mark I. "A Baptism by Fire for Ministry's Upbeat Heir; Richard Shakarian is Rebuilding the Gospel Group for Businessmen." *Orlando Sentinel*, August 8, 2001, A1.

Plekon, Michael. *Living Icons: Persons of Faith in the Eastern Church*. Notre Dame, IN: University of Notre Dame Press, 2002.

Poloma, Margaret. *The Charismatic Movement: Is There a New Pentecost?* Boston: Twayne Publishers, 1982.

_____. *The Assemblies of God at the Crossroads: Charisma and Institutional Dilemmas*. Knoxville, TN: University of Tennessee Press, 1989.

_____. *Main Street Mystics: The Toronto Blessing and Reviving Pentecostalism*. Walnut Creek, CA: Alta Mira Press, 2003.

Pomeroy, Earl. *The Pacific Slope: A History of California, Oregon, Washington, Idaho, Utah, and Nevada*. Las Vegas: University of Nevada Press, 2003.

Priklonsky, Fr. Alexander. *Blessed Athanasia: Disciple of St. Seraphim*. Platina, CA: St. Herman of Alaska Brotherhood, 1980.

"Promise Keepers to Lay Off Paid Staff." *Christian Century* 115:8 (March 11, 1998): 254–255.

Prosser, Peter. *Dispensationalist Eschatology and its Influence on American and British Religious Movements*. Lewiston, NY: E. Mellen Publishers, 1999.

Quebedeaux, Richard. *The New Charismatics: The Origins, Development, and Significance of Neo-Pentecostalism*. Garden City, NY: Doubleday, 1976.

Quinn, Charles Russell. *History of Downey*. Downey, CA: Elena Quinn, 1973.

_____. *The New Charismatics II: How a Christian Renewal Movement Became Part of the American Religious Mainstream*. San Francisco: Harper & Row, Publishers, 1983.

Redgate, A.E. *The Armenians*. Malden, MA: Blackwell Publishers, 1998.

Ricoeur, Paul. *Time and Narrative*. 3 vols. Translated by Kathleen McLaughlin and David Pellauer. Chicago: University of Chicago Press, 1984.

Riss, Richard. *Latter Rain: The Latter Rain Movement of 1948 and the Mid Twentieth Century Evangelical Awakening*. Mississague, ON: Honeycomb Visual Productions, 1987.

_____. *A Survey of 20ᵗʰ-Century Revival Movements in North America*. Peabody, MA: Hendrickson Publishers, 1988.

Robeck, Cecil M. *Prophecy in Carthage: Perpetua, Tertullian, and Cyprian*. Cleveland, OH: Pilgrim Press, 1992.

_____. *The Azusa Street Mission and Revival*. Nashville, TN: Thomas Nelson Publishers, 2006.

Russell, Jeffrey Burton. *A History of Medieval Christianity: Prophecy and Order*. Arlington Heigths, IL: AHM Publishing Company, 1968.

Rybarczyk, Edmund. *Beyond Salvation: Eastern Orthodoxy and Classical Pentecostalism on Becoming Like Christ*. Carlisle, UK: Paternoster Press, 2004.

St. Herman of Alaska Brotherhood. *Saint Seraphim of Sarov*. Vol.1 of *Little Russian Philokalia*. New Valaam Monastery, AK: St. Herman Press, 1991.

Samarin, Paul I. "The Teachings of the Molokan Religion." *The Molokan Review*. 1:2 (1941).

Sandeen, Ernest. *The Roots of Fundamentalism: British and American Millenarianism, 1800–1930*. Chicago: University of Chicago Press, 1970.

Sandweiss, Lee Ann. "The 40-hour Work Week – Dead or Alive?" Indiana University. http://www.homepages.indiana.edu/040904/text/workweek.shtml. April 9, 2004 (accessed November 21, 2008).

Sarkissian, Shahan. "Ecumenism in the Armenian Catholicosate of Cilicia." *Ministerial Formation* (October 2000): 7–9.

Slesinski, Robert F. "Reflections on a Millennium and the Christian vocation of Rus'." *Communio* 15 (1988): 4–18.

Solokoff, Lillian. "The Russians in Los Angeles." *Studies in Sociology* (March 1918): 1–16.

Spidlik, Tomás. "The Theological Renewal of the Russian Startsi." *Communio* 15 (1998): 61–76.

Stoll, David. *Is Latin America Turning Protestant? The Politics of Evangelical Growth*. Berkeley, CA: University of California Press, 1990.

Strickland, John. "Orthodox Patriotism and the Church in Russia, 1888–1914." Ph.D. diss., The University of California Davis, 1999.

Syméon, Igumen. "The Search for God in the Hesychast Tradition." *Russian Patriarchal Diocese of Sourozh* 73 (Translated by Sister Seraphina, 1998): 30–35.

Synan, Vinson. *Under His Banner*. Costa Mesa, CA: Gift Publications, 1992.

_____. *The Holiness-Pentecostal Tradition*. Grand Rapids, MI: William B. Eerdman's Publishers, 1997.

_____. *Old Time Power: A Centennial History of the International Pentecostal Holiness Church*. Franklin Springs, GA: Life Springs Resources, 1998.

_____. *The Century of the Holy Spirit*. Nashville: Thomas Nelson Publishers, 2001.

Toossi, Mitra. "A Century of Change: The U.S. Labor Force, 1950–2050." *Monthly Labor Review* (May, 2002): 15–28.

Vartanian, Nicole. "A Fruitful Legacy." Armeniapedia. http://www.armeniapedia.org/index/diaspora/usa (accessed December 29, 2007).

Vorontsova, Lyudmila and Sergei Filatov. "Paradoxes of the Old Believer Movement." *Religion, State & Society* 28 (2000): 53–62.

Wacker, Grant. *Heaven Below: Early Pentecostals and American Culture.* Cambridge, MA: Harvard University Press, 2001.

Wagner, C. Peter. *The Third Wave of the Holy Spirit: Encountering the Power of Signs and Wonders Today.* Ann Arbor, MI: Vine Books, 1988.

Wardin, Albert W. "Pentecostal Beginnings among the Russians in Finland and Northern Russia (1911–1921)." *Fides et Historia: Journal of the Conference on Faith and History* 26:2 (1994): 50–61.

Weaver, Douglas. *The Healer-Prophet, William Marrion Branham: A Study of the Prophetic in American Pentecostalism.* Macon, GA: Mercer University Press, 1987.

Weber, Max. *The Sociology of Religion.* Translated by Ephraim Fischoff. Boston: Beacon Press, 1963.

Webley, Donald Stanford. "An Introduction to Saint Seraphim of Sarov and the Great Process of Spiritual Transmission, in the Light of the Wisdom-Teaching of Da Avabhasa (The 'Bright')." Pages 28–52 in *The Spiritual Instructions of Saint Seraphim of Sarov: A Spirit-Baptizer in the Eastern Christian Tradition.* Edited by Da Avabhasa. Clearlake, CA: The Dawn Horse Press, 1991.

Weinberg, Steve. *Telling the Untold Story: How Investigative Reporters are Changing the Craft of Biography.* Columbia, MO: University of Missouri Press, 1992.

Yong, Amos. *Spirit — Word — Community: Theological Hermeneutics in Trinitarian Perspective.* Eugene, OR: Wipf & Stock, 2002.

Young, Pauline V. *The Pilgrims of Russian-Town: The Community of Spiritual Christian Jumpers in America.* Chicago: University of Chicago Press, 1932.

Zander, Valentine. *St. Seraphim of Sarov.* Translated by Sister Gabriel Anne. Crestwood, NY: St. Vladimir's Seminary Press, 1975.

Name Index

A

Adams, Billy 109–110
Agalstaff, Aleksy 51
Aguilar, Humberto 247, 260, 281, 298
Anderson, Robert Mapes 114–115, 122, 301, 304, 308, 310, 315
Athanasius 27
Alexander I 26, 31
Alexander II 38
Alger, Horatio 184
Allen, A. A. 112, 120
Anderson, Allan 303, 309
Aquinas, Thomas 27
Aram I 23, 42
Arganbright, Miner 104, 141, 143, 145, 147, 151, 175, 226, 273
Armstrong, Bob, 257, 262, 279–80, 298, 311
Arnold, Gene 245, 259, 283
Ashcraft, Tom 151, 236, 242–244, 258
Ashcroft, J. Robert 211
Augustine 285
Aune, David 315

B

Badir, Kamal 216
Bakker, Jim 239, 256
Barcelo, Carlos Romero 214
Barrett, David 17, 43, 182, 196 97, 230, 233–234, 277–80, 284, 315–16
Bellinger, Mark 245–46, 254–60, 282, 284, 296, 310, 315
Bennett, Dennis 173, 183, 193, 311
Berokoff, John 37, 45–46, 60–69, 79, 300, 307, 311, 315
Berge, Renee 279
Bignold, Bob 261, 273, 298
Birgitta of Sweden 27
Bivin, Joyce 19, 41, 43, 51, 64, 66
Blankenship, Virginia 180
Boddy, Alexander 113
Boldt, Abraham 240
Bonhomne, Arthur 175
Bonnke, Reinhard 247

Subject Index

CPSIA information can be obtained
at www.ICGtesting.com
Printed in the USA
FFOW03n1126100417
34353FF

9 781609 470029